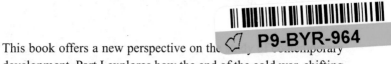

This book offers a new perspective on the study of contemporary development. Part I explores how the end of the cold war, shifting relations among capitalist powers, globalization of trade and production, changing patterns of finance, and new ideological currents have altered the development context in four major third world regions. Part II suggests how different regions responded and development options were molded by the dominant international power in each region: the United States in Latin America, Japan in East Asia and Southeast Asia, and Europe with the international financial institutions in Africa. Part III provides a conceptual framework for analyzing regional performance: variation in economic capacity, trade opportunities, and access to finance shaped the development chances of each region, producing dynamism in Asia, slow growth in Latin America, and economic contraction in Sub-Saharan Africa during the 1980s and early 1990s. It also speculates about future trends based on various development models and international relationships.

Global change, regional response

The proceedings on which this book is based were cosponsored by the Joint Committee on Latin American Studies of the Social Science Research Council and the American Council of Learned Societies, and by the Global Studies Research Program of the University of Wisconsin-Madison.

Global change, regional response

The new international context of development

Edited by

BARBARA STALLINGS

CAMBRIDGE
UNIVERSITY PRESS

Published by the Press Syndicate of the University of Cambridge
The Pitt Building, Trumpington Street, Cambridge CB2 1RP
40 West 20th Street, New York, NY 10011-4211, USA
10 Stamford Road, Oakleigh, Melbourne 3166, Australia

First published 1995

Printed in the United States of America

Library of Congress Cataloging-in-Publication Data
Global change, regional response : the new international context of
development / edited by Barbara Stallings.
p.   cm.
Includes index.
ISBN 0-521-47227-X. – ISBN 0-521-47806-5 (pbk.)
1. Developing countries – Foreign economic relations.
2. Developing countries – Economic conditions – Regional disparities.
3. Post-communism.   I. Stallings, Barbara.
HF 1413.G58   1995
337'.09172'4 – dc20   95-1254
                                                                  CIP

A catalog record for this book is available from the British Library.

ISBN 0-521-47227-X Hardback
ISBN 0-521-47806-5 Paperback

Contents

Part II   Regional responses

Part III   Conclusions

List of tables and figures

Figures

Contributors

THOMAS J. BIERSTEKER is Henry Luce Professor of Transnational Organization and Director of the Watson Institute of International Studies at Brown University. He has a Ph.D. in political science from MIT and is the author of several books and numerous articles on international relations theory, multinational corporations, and economic policy in developing countries. His latest book is *Dealing with Debt* (Westview).

MICHAEL CHEGE is currently a visiting scholar at the Center for International Affairs at Harvard and served previously as a program officer in the Ford Foundation office in Harare, Zimbabwe, and as Director of the Institute of International Studies at the University of Nairobi. He is a political scientist with a Ph.D. from the University of California, Berkeley, and has written extensively on governance and development in Africa.

YUN-HAN CHU is Professor of Political Science at National Taiwan University and Program Director of the Institute for National Policy Research in Taipei. He holds a Ph.D. from the University of Minnesota and specializes in the political economy of the East Asian NICs. He has written and edited a number of books on this topic, including *The Asian Regional Economy* (Institute for National Policy Research).

GARY GEREFFI is Professor of Sociology at Duke University with a Ph.D. from Yale. He is an expert on Latin American and East Asian development strategies and a coeditor of *Manufacturing Miracles: Paths of Industrialization in Latin America and East Asia* (Princeton University Press). Recently he has been working on the global commodity chain framework as an approach to international political economy and has edited *Commodity Chains and Global Capitalism* (Praeger).

STEPHANY GRIFFITH-JONES is a Research Fellow at the Institute for Development Studies at the University of Sussex. She has a Ph.D. in economics from Cambridge University and works mainly in the area of international finance for developing countries. Among her recent books are *Cross-Conditionality, Banking Regulation, and Third World Debt* (Macmillan) and *Coping with Capital Surges: Latin America in the 1990s* (Lynne Rienner).

FRED HALLIDAY is Professor of International Relations at the London School of Economics, where he also received his Ph.D. He is an expert on the Middle East and, more broadly, on international relations. His recent books include *From Kabul to Managua: Soviet–American Relations in the 1980s* (Pantheon) and *Rethinking International Relations* (University of British Columbia).

LINDA Y. C. LIM, a Singaporean economist, is Director of the Southeast Asia Business Program and Associate Professor of Business Administration at the University of Michigan. She also has a Ph.D. in economics from the University of Michigan. She is a coauthor of three books and many articles on trade and investment in developing countries and is the founder and a coeditor of the *Journal of Asian Business*.

BARBARA STALLINGS is Director of the Economic Development Division of the UN Economic Commission for Latin America and the Caribbean in Santiago, Chile. She is on leave from the University of Wisconsin-Madison, where she was Director of the Global Studies Research Program. She has Ph.D.'s in economics from Cambridge University and political science from Stanford. She has written or edited six books and many articles on development issues and international political economy. Her most recent book is *Japan, the United States, and Latin America: Toward a Trilateral Relationship in the Western Hemisphere* (Macmillan and Johns Hopkins University Press).

WOLFGANG STREECK is Director of the Max Planck Institute for Research on Societies, Cologne. Formerly, he was Professor of Sociology and Industrial Relations at the University of Wisconsin-Madison. His fields of expertise include interest groups, industrial change, and European integration. Among his recent books are *Governing Capitalist Economies* (Oxford University Press) and *Public Interest and Market Pressures: Problems Posed by Europe 1992* (Macmillan). He is currently working on a project involving models of capitalism in Europe, Asia, and the United States.

AUGUSTO VARAS is a Senior Researcher at the Latin American Faculty of Social Science (FLACSO) in Santiago, Chile, and is currently serving as a program officer for the Ford Foundation. He has a Ph.D. in sociology from Washington University, St. Louis, and has written or edited many volumes on democratic governance, sociopolitical actors and institutions, and external influences on political processes in Latin America.

Acknowledgments

I have accumulated a large number of debts in the lengthy process of completing this book, and I would like to acknowledge them here. First and most important, I want to thank the Joint Committee on Latin American Studies of the Social Science Research Council and the American Council of Learned Societies, whose program director is Eric Hershberg, and the Global Studies Research Program of the University of Wisconsin-Madison under the leadership of Dean David Trubek. These two organizations jointly financed the conference that took place at the University of Wisconsin in May 1992 to discuss early drafts of the chapters. Much more important, Hershberg and Trubek provided intellectual guidance, practical help, and unwavering support for the project. Also at the University of Wisconsin, I benefited greatly from the multifaceted assistance of Mary Clark, Phil Ruder, and Carol Torgeson. Jennifer Raskin and Alexandra Cordero of the SSRC also went beyond the call of duty in responding to various requests. At the UN Economic Commission for Latin America and the Caribbean, where I am currently working, Alejandra Tagle and María Angélica Van der Schraft helped with many of the final details of putting the manuscript together. María Angélica Monardes provided efficient last-minute help with proofreading. Without these people, this book would not exist.

With the support of a seed grant from the SSRC president's fund for comparative and transnational research, a meeting was held at the SSRC in June 1991 to discuss the central issues that might be addressed in an eventual project. That meeting was sponsored by SSRC's Latin America committee, which provided ongoing input into the project, in collaboration with the committees on Japan and Korea. In addition to those who participated in the conference that resulted in this volume, the planning phase of the project benefited from the advice of Christopher Chase-Dunn, Ellen Comisso, Thomas Ferguson, and Susan Pharr.

Earlier versions of the first and last chapters were presented at the Mac-Arthur Programs on International Peace and Security at the University of Wisconsin and the University of Chicago; the Seminar on International Political Economy at Columbia University; the Watson Institute at Brown University; the North–South Center at the University of Miami; the New School for Social Research; and the biennial conference of the Latin American Council for Social Science Research (CLACSO). The comments of the participants improved both the ideas and their presentation. The University of Wisconsin conference was especially important for the development of the book. In addition to the chapter authors, many other scholars attended as discussants and provided valuable input to individual authors. They included Stephen Anderson, Bradford Barham, Peter Bloch, Suthiphand Chirathivat, Ian Coxhead, Bruce Cumings, Joseph Elder, Donald Emmerson, Peter Evans, Richard Feinberg, Edward Friedman, Ashok Guha, Eric Hershberg, Shafiq Islam, Atul Kohli, Joan Nelson, Joel Rogers, Gay Seidman, Peter Smith, David Trubek, Cynthia Truelove, Robert Wade, Laurence Whitehead, and M. Crawford Young.

Finally, I would like to thank Scott Parris of Cambridge University Press. Despite many delays in the completion of the manuscript, Parris maintained his enthusiasm for the book. Mary Racine ably managed the production editing and improved the final product.

Abbreviations

ADR	American depository receipts
AFTA	ASEAN Free Trade Area
APEC	Asia-Pacific Economic Cooperation (forum)
ASEAN	Association of Southeast Asian Nations
BIS	Bank for International Settlements
CAP	Common Agricultural Policy
COMECON	Council for Mutual Economic Assistance
DFI	direct foreign investment
EAEG	East Asian Economic Group
EAI	Enterprise for the Americas Initiative
EANIC	East Asian newly industrialized country
EBRD	European Bank for Reconstruction and Development
EC	European Community (now European Union)
EFTA	European Free Trade Area
EIU	Economist Intelligence Unit
EOI	export-oriented industrialization
EPZ	export-processing zone
ESAF	Enhanced Structural Adjustment Facility
EU	European Union
FTA	free-trade area
GATT	General Agreement on Tariffs and Trade
GCC	global commodity chain
GDR	global depository receipts
GSP	Generalized System of Preferences
IBRD	International Bank for Reconstruction and Development
IDA	International Development Association
IFIs	international financial institutions

IMF	International Monetary Fund
ISI	import-substitution industrialization
LDC	less developed country
MFA	Multifiber Arrangement
MITI	Ministry of International Trade and Industry (Japan)
NAFTA	North American Free Trade Agreement
NATO	North Atlantic Treaty Organization
NBER	National Bureau of Economic Research
NIC	newly industrialized country
NIEO	New International Economic Order
OAS	Organization of American States
OAU	Organization of African Unity
OBM	original brand-name manufacturing
ODA	official development assistance
ODM	original design manufacturing
OECD	Organisation for Economic Cooperation and Development
OECF	Overseas Economic Cooperation Fund (Japan)
OEM	original equipment manufacturing
OMA	orderly marketing arrangement
OPEC	Organization of Petroleum Exporting Countries
SAF	Structural Adjustment Facility
SAL	structural adjustment loans
SII	Structural Impediments Initiative
TNC	transnational corporation
UN	United Nations
UNCTAD	United Nations Conference on Trade and Development
UNCTC	United Nations Centre on Transnational Corporations (now part of UNCTAD)
UNDP	United Nations Development Program
UNECA	United Nations Economic Commission for Africa
UNECLAC	United Nations Economic Commission for Latin America and the Caribbean
UNICEF	United Nations Children's Fund
UNIDO	United Nations Industrial Development Organization
USAID	United States Agency for International Development
VER	voluntary export restraints

CHAPTER 1

Introduction: global change, regional response

BARBARA STALLINGS

The 1980s and early 1990s witnessed historic changes in the patterns of economic development that had prevailed since the end of World War II. New winners and losers emerged within what had traditionally been called the "third world." Thus, as the new century approaches, East Asia's newly industrialized countries (NICs) are on the verge of joining the developed world. At the other extreme, a large part of the African continent has experienced an absolute decline in living standards, and its future prospects appear dim. In between, other countries in Asia, Latin America, and the Middle East are trying – with various degrees of success – to reposition themselves to take advantage of new global dynamics. Finally, a new group of third world nations has appeared as a consequence of the collapse of communism. Eastern Europe and the former Soviet republics are now facing many of the same problems as other developing countries and competing with them for available resources.

There has been a great deal of debate about the reasons for the differential success in achieving economic development.[1] In this book, the authors stress the importance of two sets of variables: international and regional. While not denying the role of domestic economic, political, and cultural factors, we believe that recent analysis has seriously underestimated the relevance of international variables and overlooked the importance of geographic location. Moreover, there has been an interaction between interna-

---

[1] For an analysis of the relative importance of international and domestic factors in economic policy making, see Joan M. Nelson (ed.), *Economic Crisis and Policy Choice: The Politics of Adjustment in the Third World* (Princeton, N.J.: Princeton University Press, 1990), and Stephan Haggard and Robert Kaufman (eds.), *The Politics of Economic Adjustment* (Princeton, N.J.: Princeton University Press, 1992).

tional and regional factors in ways that skew an individual nation's chances of achieving rapid growth with a measure of equity.

Dramatic international changes have rearranged the world that developing countries must face in the 1990s. The end of the cold war, new relations among advanced capitalist powers, increased globalization of trade and production, shifting patterns of international finance, and new ideological currents are the five key elements of what we call the new international context of development. In the 1980s, it appeared that the combined impact of these international changes was to place severe restrictions on the kinds of policies that third world countries could follow. "Acceptable" policies stressed the role of the private sector and an open economy. They also tended to equate development with growth, postponing the issue of more equitable distribution. The elimination of the Soviet Union as a source of support and an alternative development model, the emergence of the United States as "the only remaining superpower," the increased importance of multilateral conditionality in obtaining finance, and a new ideological consensus all appeared to push in the same direction.

As we moved into the 1990s, however, it became clear that the situation was more complicated than the previous analysis implied. Despite the general acceptance of market orientation and international openness, some subtle but significant differences remained. The latter were closely linked to other aspects of the new international context. Of particular importance was differentiation within the capitalist world, which became more apparent once the cold war ended. Japanese and European models of capitalism have many distinct characteristics in comparison with that of the United States (and perhaps Britain). Trade, production, and financial networks are tied into the differing models. In addition, cracks have begun to appear in the ideological consensus, and they also seem to be linked to capitalist variation.

The new international trends of the 1980s and 1990s were superimposed onto a regional grid, which led to a differential impact and response across areas of the third world. In the Western Hemisphere, where U.S. influence is strongest, one government after another announced the adoption of programs that drastically scaled back the role of state activity, slashed tariff and other trade barriers, and welcomed any type of foreign capital. In the Japanese sphere of influence in East Asia, by contrast, some privatization took place, but governments continued to collaborate closely with private-sector firms to deal with new international challenges. Likewise, liberalization was relatively selective. In the areas most closely associated with one or another European power, a more mixed picture has emerged. In North Africa and especially Eastern Europe, the European Union assumed an important role in promoting development, while in Sub-Saharan Africa, the European Union took a more hands-off attitude, offering substantial amounts of foreign aid but relying on the international financial institutions (IFIs) to provide policy guidance. The combination has not succeeded in preventing the growing marginalization of Sub-Saharan Africa from the international economy. Important parts of South Asia and the Middle East, other areas where Europe has historically been a leading actor, also seem to be experiencing increased marginalization from international trade and investment flows.

This book explores the proposition that changes in the developing-country hierarchy in the 1980s were closely associated with these international and regional trends. It also argues that they will play a crucial role in shaping development possibilities in the 1990s. Both propositions are based on the premise that the Japanese model of development is more conducive than its U.S./IFI counterpart to producing rapid growth with equity. The reasons, which will be systematically discussed in the final chapter of the volume, include the priority the Japanese model puts on high investment and the development of human capital. But they also relate to the greater access to finance for Asian developing countries, the integration of these countries into trade and production networks, and the rapid regional growth with positive spillover effects. The U.S./IFI model has yet to prove it can produce high growth rates on a long-term basis, and some evidence indicates it generates increasing concentration of income and wealth. For Latin American countries, these are serious problems; for Africa, they verge on disaster.

To understand these new trends and their implications, three tasks must be carried out. First, we need to identify and examine the key international changes that have occurred in the past decade. Second, we must analyze the impact and response in various third world regions. Finally, we have to construct or reconstruct a theoretical framework adequate for explaining the international role in the 1990s. The rest of this chapter and Chapters 2–10 center on the first two tasks; Chapter 11 returns to the third.

In this volume, certain definitions and emphases are adopted. By "development," we mean primarily economic development: growth and equity of distribution. Political development is considered only insofar as it affects economic chances. Moreover, we are not trying to identify and evaluate all the reasons why development has or has not occurred, will or will not take place; this would be a much larger task. We want to focus specifically on the international and regional impact in policy choice and development outcomes. This is a broad and ambitious agenda, but it does have limits.

International changes in the 1980s and 1990s

Probably everyone would agree that the world in the mid-1990s looks different than it did a decade before. Nonetheless, some hark back to earlier eras and find similarities – especially in the interwar years before the cold war set in – while others concentrate on more recent periods and find much that is new.[2] Likewise, there are differences of opinion about which trends are worthy of note, even among those who emphasize change. We have chosen to focus on the five processes mentioned earlier, although admitting that others could be added. For example, the new wave of democratization will make some development strategies easier and others more difficult. The spread of ethnic and religious conflicts will bring to the fore goals that subordinate economic concerns to cultural ones. And attention to environmental problems may have a significant impact on how development is defined and pursued. Nonetheless, we believe that our five factors together constitute the core of the new international context of development.

End of the cold war

The cold war had multiple facets, but the most basic was the bipolar division between the United States and the Soviet Union. The U.S.–Soviet rivalry, in turn, divided the rest of the world into two hostile camps, defended by the nuclear prowess of the two superpowers. The security dimension was exacerbated by economic, political, and ideological battles as "capitalism" and "socialism" struggled to expand their respective turf. For the purposes of this analysis, two consequences of the cold war are central. First, the cold war promoted U.S. hegemony among its capitalist allies because of the premium on military power; the importance of this point will be elaborated

---

[2] The idea of continuity is especially common among world-systems theorists. See, e.g., Christopher Chase-Dunn, *Global Formation: Structures of the World-Economy* (Oxford: Basil Blackwell, 1989).

in the next section. Second, as Fred Halliday explains in Chapter 2, the U.S.–Soviet rivalry spilled over into the third world, opening the way for governments to gain access to economic and military resources. In the process, a set of "client states" was formed around each country, using political loyalty as a means to tap resources. A few nations, especially those in strategic geopolitical locations, were able to play the two off against each other and maintain more independence.

With the ascension of Mikhail Gorbachev to power in the Soviet Union, and the Gorbachev–Shevardnadze foreign policy of cooperation with the West, many third world countries that had relied on the Soviets for assistance began to witness a shrinkage of support. Seeing the handwriting on the wall, some moved to change their policies and seek reconciliation with the West. Indeed, even before the arrival of Gorbachev on the scene, the Soviet government had made clear that it was unwilling (or unable) to provide extensive support for additional countries. Thus, for example, Angola and Mozambique began to shift alliances during the 1980s, and the Sandinista government was advised both by the Soviets and the Cubans to maintain Western ties.[3]

Later, with the collapse of the Soviet economy and eventually the state itself, the trend toward reconciliation with the West was accelerated. With the exceptions of Cuba and North Korea, all of the ex-Soviet allies have embraced capitalism in some form; even these two are making concessions. Beyond governments allied with the Soviet Union, the latter's collapse has also had a negative impact on parties and movements in the third world, which looked to the Soviets for material assistance and a model of socialism (or at least growth with greater equity than a capitalist model seemed to provide). These groups have also tended to moderate their positions and shift their alliances within their own domestic contexts.

Within the U.S. sphere of influence, the implications of the end of the cold war are less clear. The dominant view seems to be that it will lead to a lessened U.S. involvement in the third world insofar as much of the previous interest was purportedly based on checking Soviet activities. Although an alternative opinion suggests that the lack of a Soviet counterweight will allow the United States to intervene as it wishes, especially in Latin America, this view is based heavily on the Panama invasion of

[3] Fred Halliday, *From Kabul to Managua: Soviet–American Relations in the 1980s* (New York: Pantheon Books, 1989).

December 1989 and drug-related activities in the Andean region. This second interpretation is at odds with other trends, especially the decline in U.S. resources and demands that available resources be used at home. The quasi-isolationist tendencies of some key members of the new Republican majority in the U.S. Congress increases the likelihood of what Michael Chege (in Chapter 10) calls an "exit response" with respect to the problems of the third world.[4]

Competition among capitalist powers

While the postwar world was dominated by the U.S.–Soviet rivalry, the United States in turn dominated its capitalist allies. In particular, the two rising capitalist countries – West Germany and Japan – were constrained by postwar agreements to rely on U.S. nuclear deterrence for their defense. Beyond the military issue, however, the United States was also unrivaled economically for nearly two decades after World War II. U.S. corporations dominated Europe as well as the third world; U.S. aid bought influence in many parts of the world; and U.S. exports, backed by sophisticated U.S. technology, could outperform those of any rivals.

When to date the shift and how to interpret the current situation are both controversial, as Barbara Stallings and Wolfgang Streeck discuss in Chapter 3. The changes began to emerge in the 1970s, when Japan and Europe had recovered from the war, but they were distorted by the oil price hikes since Japan and most of Europe are reliant on petroleum imports. The Reagan era, supposedly devoted to the restoration of U.S. power, in reality undermined it further by creating huge budget deficits that were quickly mirrored in trade deficits. At the same time, the Reagan administration convinced U.S. citizens that they were overtaxed and overburdened by government, thus placing major political obstacles both to eliminating the so-called twin deficits and to generating the financial resources to back up the U.S. "victory" in the cold war.

The waning of the cold war also called attention to growing differences

---

[4] For different interpretations of the impact on Latin America of the end of the cold war, see Abraham Lowenthal, "Rediscovering Latin America," *Foreign Affairs* 69, 4 (Fall 1990), 27–41, and Mark Falcoff, "A Look at Latin America," in Nicholas X. Rizopoulos (ed.), *Sea-Changes: American Foreign Policy in a World Transformed* (New York: Council on Foreign Relations Books, 1990), pp. 71–83.

between the United States and its European and Japanese rivals.[5] On the one hand, it seemed clear that the latter were more dynamic in terms of growth and productivity. On the other hand, with socialism eliminated from the picture, the different types of capitalism came into focus. U.S. and Japanese variants seemed particularly different. Savings and investment propensities, time horizons, the relationship between public and private sectors as well as between capital and labor, views about equality and national security – all highlighted the fact that capitalism is not the same around the world. Trying to extend this analysis to a European style of capitalism is hindered by variations across countries. By some measures, for example, the differences between Germany and Britain are nearly as great as those between the United States and Japan. Nonetheless, various characteristics of European economic systems further emphasized the variation within what once appeared to be a monolithic capitalism.

The importance of differences among models of capitalism was magnified as the three parts of the capitalist world – Europe, North America, and Asia – appeared to move toward the formation of regional blocs. The trend began with the European decision to move rapidly ahead with economic integration. It was furthered by the long stalemate in the General Agreement on Tariffs and Trade (GATT) deliberations, the initiation of North American Free Trade Agreement negotiations, and various proposals for an Asian grouping (even though the latter continues to be opposed by Japan).[6]

The consequences of de facto, even if not de jure, economic spheres of influence can be quite profound for the third world – especially when combined with the growth and productivity trends already mentioned. Those third world areas associated with the most dynamic growth poles in the advanced countries stand to gain at the expense of those associated with less dynamic countries. For example, East and Southeast Asia are benefiting from Japanese investment and finance, as well as capital flows from the East Asian countries themselves; even South Asia may be incorporated into this pattern. Mexico expects to prosper from closer ties to the U.S. market,

---

[5] Lester Thurow, *Head to Head: The Coming Economic Battle among Japan, Europe, and America* (New York: Morrow, 1992); Jeffrey Garten, *A Cold Peace: America, Japan, Germany, and the Struggle for Supremacy* (New York: Times Books, 1992); and Jeffrey Hart, *Rival Capitalists: International Competitiveness in the United States, Japan, and Western Europe* (Ithaca, N.Y.: Cornell University Press, 1992).

[6] On trade blocs and regionalism, see Charles Oman, *Globalisation and Regionalisation: The Challenges for Developing Countries* (Paris: OECD, 1994).

and other Latin American countries are eager to jump on the bandwagon too. While the United States has a very large market to offer, it is not clear that U.S. investors will direct enough resources toward Latin America to stimulate a vigorous hemispheric economy.

In addition to the differentiation that may emerge among third world countries associated with one of the three blocs, a distinction will also result between all of these countries and those left on the sidelines. Most African countries, probably some of South Asia, and perhaps substantial parts of Latin America and the Middle East may be further marginalized in a region-alization process. The future of the marginalized group is made bleaker by the fact that some of these countries had managed to benefit in the past by tying themselves into the cold war rivalry. With that over, their "special positions," whether vis-à-vis the United States or the Soviet Union, have also ended.[7]

Globalization of production and trade

The decade of the 1980s brought important changes in technology, the organization of production, and trading networks. Rapid innovations in microelectronics, materials science, and biotechnology jointly led to what some have called a new technological revolution. Research and develop-ment in these fields involved complex and expensive laboratory facilities and, in some cases, increased use of proprietary research. The latter, of course, increased barriers to entry as did the speed of technological ad-vance. At the same time, microelectronics made possible the transition from mass production to flexible specialization, producing smaller batches of differentiated goods.[8]

These developments have made it increasingly advantageous for multina-tional corporations to spread production around the globe. In Chapter 4, Gary Gereffi argues that the resulting processes have been organized in two main forms: producer-driven networks and buyer-driven networks.

[7] Michael Chege, "Remembering Africa," *Foreign Affairs* 71, 1 (1991–92), 146–63.
[8] Perhaps the most influential analysis of changing production patterns remains Michael J. Piore and Charles F. Sabel, *The Second Industrial Divide* (New York: Basic, 1984). A more recent statement within this approach is Paul Hirst and Jonathan Zeitlin, "Flexible Specializ-ation versus Post-Fordism: Theory, Evidence and Policy Implications," *Economy and So-ciety* 20 (February 1991), 1–55. Implications for developing countries are discussed in Raphael Kaplinsky, "From Mass Production to Flexible Specialization: A Case Study of Microeconomic Change in a Semi-industrial Economy," *World Development* 22, 3 (1994), 337–53.

Producer-driven networks are centralized, vertically integrated production chains, found in capital-intensive sectors such as autos, computers, and aircraft. Subcontracting involves production of parts in various countries around the world for later assembly in appropriate locations. Buyer-driven networks are decentralized, design-intensive industries such as clothing and footwear. Subcontractors produce finished goods according to specifications for retail outlets in advanced countries.

These trends in production and trade offer both obstacles and opportunities for third world countries, many of which have decided to put more emphasis on exports, especially of manufactured goods.[9] Insofar as they succeed, the questions then become what to produce and how to ensure access to markets. The new premium on technological development has made it much more difficult for third world nations to break into high-value-added production, but the costs of not doing so have risen. While there are certainly niches for specialization in low-value-added goods, countries that rely exclusively on these products run the risk of falling ever further behind. Not only do they face the traditional problems of low income elasticities of demand for basic food items, textiles, low-grade steel, and so on, but the spillover in terms of training and technology are lost. Of course, those countries that continue to concentrate their exports on raw materials are at an even greater disadvantage because the new technologies minimize the use of such inputs.

The other question concerns market access. One way of gaining entry into world markets has been through incorporation into international production/trade networks. Asian countries have gone farthest along this path, although some Latin American countries have also made some attempts. As Gereffi makes clear, the particular way countries are incorporated is important in determining their future ability to rise in the production hierarchy. Other third world nations have preferred to maintain independent production and trade status. This has been relatively easy in the case of primary exports with established markets, but more difficult with manufactured exports. Brazil is an example in its steel and footwear industries, as well as more sophisticated goods like aircraft and weapons. Its problems with U.S. protectionism in addition to keeping up with technological ad-

---

[9] On manufactured exports in the third world, see UNCTAD, *Trade and Development Report, 1993* (New York: United Nations), chap. 2, and World Bank, *Global Economic Prospects and the Developing Countries, 1992* (Washington, D.C.: World Bank, 1992).

vances show many of the difficulties with the independent approach.[10] Some large Korean conglomerates have been more successful in electronics and even autos. While an independent strategy may have the highest payoffs, chances of success are low.[11]

As a result of differing approaches to trade and production, huge gaps have opened up within the third world in terms of productive capacity and international marketing sophistication. Some third world firms have themselves become significant foreign investors (the East Asian NICs), while the majority cannot even sell in their domestic markets without high levels of protection (Africa, South Asia, and much of Latin America). As these levels of protection decline, the situation of the latter group of countries becomes ever more precarious.

New patterns of development finance

Closely related to the problems of production and trade are the issues of international capital flows. The latter shifted in significant ways during the 1980s in comparison with the earlier postwar period. The overall volume of capital flows doubled during the 1980s, partly due to the increase in trade volume. At the same time, there were also important shifts in both suppliers and recipients of capital. Since capital flows are the counterpart to trade, it is not surprising that successful exporters, especially Japan and Germany, became the principal suppliers of capital. Simultaneously, the United States and some other industrial countries became major capital importers to cover their trade (and budget) deficits. As Griffith-Jones and Stallings show in Chapter 5, the share of capital flows circulating among industrial countries increased from 58 percent in the early 1980s to 86 percent at the end of the decade.

The other side of this reorientation was the lesser availability of capital for the third world and the "flight to quality" after the debt crisis broke out. Thus, East and Southeast Asia retained their access to capital, while Latin America became a capital exporter from the point of view of net transfers (new flows minus debt service and profits). Africa maintained small posi-

---

[10] Jeffrey Cason, "Development Strategy in Brazil: The Political Economy of Industrial Export Promotion, 1964–1990," Ph.D. dissertation, University of Wisconsin-Madison, 1993.

[11] Naeyoung Lee, "The Politics of Industrial Restructuring: A Comparison of the Mexican and South Korean Automobile Industries," Ph.D. dissertation, University of Wisconsin-Madison, 1993.

tive net transfers but was unable to take advantage of the flows. Types of capital flows going to third world countries also changed during the 1980s. While private bank loans had dominated in the 1970s, they were substituted by public-sector credits and direct investment in the 1980s.[12]

In the early 1990s, total capital flows again increased by over 50 percent, and although the share going to industrial countries remained high, the pattern among third world recipients changed. Asia continued to receive the highest proportion, but Latin America suddenly regained its access to international finance; the counterpart was a sharp fall in the share of flows to Africa and the Middle East.

Focusing on patterns in the early 1990s, important differences are apparent in the composition of capital going to different regions: in Asia the main type was direct foreign investment (DFI), in Latin America it was portfolio investment, while African capital inflows mainly consisted of grants and concessional loans. These differences have important implications for development potential. DFI has various advantages in comparison with portfolio flows. It is less volatile, brings access to technology and markets, and has a less negative impact on exchange rates. The volatility problem became particularly obvious in the problems following the Mexican devaluation in late 1994. Grants and concessional loans are, in principle, the most advantageous types of finance because they either do not have to be repaid or have low interest rates and long maturities. But they are only made available to very poor countries, which often lack the capacity to use them efficiently.

International finance may also influence development policies and outcomes, via conditionality. During the binge of private bank finance in the 1970s, governments outside Africa had little need to seek loans from agencies (especially the World Bank and IMF) that put high levels of conditionality on their loans. A decade later, the situation changed dramatically. Creditors and borrowers alike turned to the IFIs for help in dealing with the debt crisis. The rising share of capital inflow accounted for by the IFIs, together with their increased role as coordinator of finance, gave them an enhanced influence in determining economic policies and strategies. The result was a greatly increased force in favor of the market-oriented policy consensus to be discussed in the next section.[13] More recently, the IFIs and

---

[12] World Bank, *World Debt Tables,* various issues.
[13] For different opinions on the policy influence of external lenders, see Barbara Stallings,

bilateral donors have added political and environmental conditions to the more traditional economic requirements.

With the greater availability of private finance in the 1990s came changes in conditionality. The share of capital flows coming from the IFIs was cut in half, so their ability to impose conditions declined accordingly. To some extent, however, the explicit conditionality of the IFIs was replaced by the implicit conditions of private investors. That is, in analyzing the credit-worthiness of potential recipients, investors were concerned about appropriate economic policies – especially in light of the debt crisis of the 1980s – but the definition of "appropriate" varied by investor. In line with the differences in models of capitalism, U.S. and Japanese investors differed in their evaluation of what policies should be followed. U.S. investors often tended to prefer policies similar to those advocated by the IFIs, while Japanese investors were open to more active governments and some trade restrictions.

New ideological currents

As both cause and effect of the political and economic changes already described, an ideological consensus had emerged worldwide by the mid-1980s. Although not completely new – elements had been present among certain groups throughout the postwar period – it differed substantially from the dominant developmentalism of the 1950s and 1960s and the more radical approaches of the 1970s.[14] Going under names ranging from neoliberalism to neoconservatism to neo-orthodoxy, the consensus featured three main elements: macroeconomic stability (especially smaller fiscal deficits), a reduced government role in the economy (deregulation and privatization), and greater openness to the outside (reduced barriers to trade and a more hospitable approach to foreign capital).[15] In Chapter 6, Thomas

"International Influence on Economic Policy: Debt, Stabilization, and Structural Reform," pp. 41–88, and Miles Kahler, "External Influence, Conditionality, and the Politics of Adjustment," pp. 89–136, both in Haggard and Kaufman (eds.), *The Politics of Economic Adjustment*.

[14] Miles Kahler, "Orthodoxy and Its Alternatives: Explaining Approaches to Stabilization and Adjustment," in Nelson (ed.), *Economic Crisis and Policy Choice*, pp. 33–61.

[15] The most influential statements of this model are John Williamson, *Latin American Adjustment: How Much Has Happened?* (Washington, D.C.: Institute for International Economics, 1990), and World Bank, *World Development Report, 1991*. An updated version of the former is John Williamson, "Democracy and the 'Washington Consensus,'" *World Development 21*, 8 (August 1993), 1329–36.

Biersteker analyzes the role that ideas played in bringing about changes toward these kinds of economic policies.

The ideological consensus embraced previously disparate groups, whose own views had been shaped by intellectual arguments and "real world" events during the 1980s. One of the latter was the emergence of more conservative forces in the advanced industrial countries, epitomized by Reagan, Thatcher, and Kohl. Even Mitterrand moved in this direction after a brief flirtation with expansionary policies, and the Japanese also liberalized substantial parts of their economy. The growing evidence of problems in Eastern Europe and eventually the Soviet Union, culminating in the fall of the communist governments, was the most dramatic of the recent world changes and had ideological as well as practical reverberations. Finally, the marked success of the East Asian countries – high growth with relative equality – in contrast to the dismal performance of Latin America and Africa on both of these dimensions, added further weight to the consensus, despite (or because of) some distortions in the interpretation of the former's success.[16]

Intellectual arguments drew on some of these currents, especially the comparisons of economic performance in different parts of the world. The renewed financial power of the IMF and the World Bank, which espoused the ideology in a particularly forceful way, enabled them to influence borrowing governments. The latter were themselves observing international trends, sometimes arriving at similar conclusions, sometimes bowing to the realities of power. One of the most fascinating aspects of the late 1980s was the list of third world governments that became outspoken advocates of privatization, free trade, and fiscal austerity, even though they or their political parties had long followed a different path.

By the early 1990s, some cracks were beginning to appear in the consensus. In part, the proponents themselves (especially in the IFIs) were beginning to have some doubts about the efficacy of their recommendations. At the same time, the Japanese were beginning to put voice behind their votes in the IFIs. Their own successful development model was based on a much more active state and greater protection than would be consistent

---

[16] For comparisons between Latin America and East Asia, see Stephan Haggard, *Pathways from the Periphery: The Politics of Growth in the Newly Industrializing Countries* (Ithaca, N.Y.: Cornell University Press, 1990); Gary Gereffi and Donald Wyman (eds.), *Manufacturing Miracles: Paths of Industrialization in Latin America and East Asia* (Princeton, N.J.: Princeton University Press, 1990).

with the laissez-faire policies being advocated for the third world in the 1990s. Gradually, the Japanese have begun to express doubts about key elements of the consensus and are demanding recognition of their own achievements and those of their protégés in East Asia.[17] Partly as a result of the new Japanese initiatives, the World Bank recently completed a large-scale study of the "East Asian Miracle."[18] It has already increased the debate on the most appropriate development policies.

Responses across third world regions

Many references have been made in the preceding discussion to disparate regional responses to the international changes. In this section, we will collect those observations and illustrate the extent of the differences in both policy choice and performance. The tables at the end of the chapter provide a systematic picture of cross-regional variations. The principal focus of the book is on four regions: East Asia, Southeast Asia, Latin America, and Sub-Saharan Africa. The tables, however, also provide comparative data on South Asia, the Middle East, and Eastern Europe to put our four regions into perspective. We will return to these other regions in the final chapter.

The emphasis on *inter*regional variation should not be taken to mean that *intra*regional differences do not exist. Indeed, substantial variation occurs in each of our four regions. Examples of "outliers" include the Philippines in Southeast Asia, Chile in Latin America, and Mauritius in Africa. Even within a more seemingly homogeneous region as East Asia, differences between South Korea and Taiwan, to say nothing of the city-states of Hong Kong and Singapore, are significant. Nonetheless, there are also commonalities that unite the regions, and that is where we put our focus.

One way of summarizing the distinctions among the four regions is to view them on a spectrum from an aggressive and successful response to the international trends just reviewed at one end to a defensive setback at the other. The two extreme cases are East Asia and Sub-Saharan Africa: East Asia has managed to take advantage of the new international conditions to surge ahead, becoming increasingly part of the advanced industrial world, while Sub-Saharan Africa has found few new opportunities and many new

---

[17] An early document introducing the Japanese critique was OECF, "Issues Related to the World Bank's Approach to Structural Adjustment: Proposal from a Major Partner," OECF Occasional Paper No. 1, October 1991.
[18] World Bank, *The East Asian Miracle: Economic Growth and Public Policy* (New York: Oxford University Press, 1993).

problems. In between are Southeast Asia and Latin America. Pushed by international as well as domestic forces, the latter regions have begun to experiment with new development strategies, but the outcomes are far from certain.

East Asia

The "four tigers" of East Asia (South Korea and Taiwan plus the city-states of Hong Kong and Singapore) are the examples behind the development model currently in vogue. Ironically, with the exception of Hong Kong, these countries themselves followed only a few parts of the model, principally the promotion of industrial exports. Imports were generally not allowed free access, nor was foreign capital always welcomed. Moreover, the state played a major role in the East Asian economies although there is substantial debate over the nature of that role and why a strong state was more successful there than in other regions.

Until the early 1960s, the East Asian countries followed a typical import-substitution industrialization (ISI) strategy with much of the capital coming from U.S. foreign aid. Only when the United States announced that its aid would be terminated did import substitution give way to labor-intensive export promotion as the most feasible alternative for obtaining foreign exchange. The advantage of moving to this type of export promotion, as opposed to "deepening" import substitution as occurred in Latin America, was that much less capital was required. Thus, domestic firms could satisfy these requirements without seeking large amounts of foreign resources. During the 1960s and 1970s, the East Asian economies became extremely successful. Per capita income rose from only $110 (South Korea) and $170 (Taiwan) in 1962 to $1,620 and $2,250, respectively, in 1980, while the productive structure diversified into much more sophisticated products, and East Asian industrial exports became competitive in the advanced industrial countries. At the same time, observers were impressed because the East Asian countries were characterized by greater equality than their Western counterparts.[19]

The key point for purposes of this discussion, however, and the focus of Chapter 7 by Yun-han Chu, is the past 15 years. Far from being a "lost

---

[19] Peter Evans, "Class, State, and Dependence in East Asia: Lessons for Latin Americanists," in Frederic C. Deyo (ed.), *The Political Economy of the New Asian Industrialism* (Ithaca, N.Y.: Cornell University Press, 1987), pp. 203–26.

decade" in East Asia, the 1980s were a very successful period. The region was able to escape a potential debt crisis because its export-oriented strategy provided the resources to service the debt accumulated during the 1970s. In the case of South Korea, for example, the debt/GNP ratio was as high as Latin America's in the early 1980s, but the debt service/export ratio was much lower.[20] In addition, East Asia's strong growth performance (see Table 1.1) meant that it continued to have abundant access to private sources of external finance (Table 1.2). Together with high domestic savings rates, East Asia could therefore benefit from investment ratios in the 1980s and early 1990s that were far higher than any other region (Table 1.3). But the most dramatic success came in export growth (Table 1.4). East Asian manufactured goods – including Korean automobiles – broke into the U.S., European, and even Japanese markets in an unprecedented way for the third world; much of this was via international subcontracting channels. Social indicators also suggest that East Asia gave high priority to education and health expenditures (Table 1.5).

The success of the 1980s and 1990s can be seen as a highly positive response to the new international context of development. East Asian countries profited by their association with a rising capitalist power (Japan) and privileged access to finance. Despite the appreciation of their currencies and greater protectionism in the United States, they were able to take advantage of new production and export opportunities to upgrade and market their products, and they eventually became substantial foreign investors themselves. Their very success led them to implement many aspects of the new ideological consensus, but they did so under continuing government supervision. Of the five trends discussed earlier, only the end of the cold war, which has yet to occur in Asia, might have negative consequences. Much of East Asia's access to U.S. aid in the early postwar period, and the U.S. market later on, was attributable to cold war conditions. But new regional opportunities in Asia may more than compensate for any increased U.S. protectionism.

Southeast Asia

Throughout the cold war, Southeast Asia was a region divided: the ASEAN countries with strong Western influence, and Indochina with links to the Soviet Union and China. During the Vietnam War in particular, these coun-

---

[20] Barbara Stallings, "The Role of Foreign Capital in Economic Development," in Gereffi and Wyman (eds.), *Manufacturing Miracles*, pp. 55–89.

tries had very different experiences, but their diverging paths have continued until recently. The results are evident in current GNP statistics: nearly a thousand dollars per capita for ASEAN versus a few hundred dollars for Indochina (Tables 1.1 and 8.2).

Both parts of the region have been dramatically changed by international forces. Abandoned by its former Soviet benefactors, Vietnam was forced not only to withdraw from Cambodia, but also to reorient its own economy toward capitalism. It is still too early to tell how successful the outcome will be. In the ASEAN countries, as portrayed by Linda Lim in Chapter 8, the positive results of the international changes are already evident. With the help of Japan and the East Asian tigers, they have begun to follow in the footsteps of their mentors, joining the so-called flying geese formation. (This metaphor refers to the process of a lead nation spinning off less technologically advanced industries to other nations following its path.) Moreover, there are indications that ASEAN, in turn, may extend the chain into Indochina. In the meantime, the Western presence in Southeast Asia has declined substantially.

Building on strong growth in the 1970s and early 1980s, the ASEAN countries experienced an important turning point with the Plaza Accords of 1985. With the increase in the value of the yen vis-à-vis the dollar, Japanese companies began shifting production offshore; Southeast Asia was the primary beneficiary. As seen in Table 1.2, foreign investment in the ASEAN countries nearly quadrupled between 1985 and 1990, with special emphasis on manufactured exports (Table 1.4). Japanese official development assistance (ODA) has also been in generous supply, which helped to improve social indicators (Table 1.5). As a secondary trend, South Korea and Taiwan became major investors and have now surpassed Japan in some sectors. These trends mean that Southeast Asia has become tightly bound into the Asian production/trade networks.[21] Malaysia's prime minister, Mohamad Mahathir, has proposed a more formal version of these relationships through an Asian trade bloc, but neither Japan nor other Asian countries are enthusiastic about such a prospect.[22]

Although Southeast Asia seems similar in many ways to its East Asian

---

[21] Linda Y. C. Lim and Pang Eng-Fong, *Foreign Direct Investment and Industrialisation in Malaysia, Singapore, Taiwan and Thailand* (Paris: OECD, 1991).

[22] Lee Poh-ping, "Japan and the Asia–Pacific Region: A Southeast Asian Perspective," in Craig C. Garby and Mary Brown Bullock (eds.), *Japan: A New Kind of Superpower?* (Washington, D.C.: Johns Hopkins University Press for the Woodrow Wilson Center, 1994), pp. 121–39.

neighbors, there are at least two differences that should be noted. First, like Latin America and Africa, and unlike the four tigers, Southeast Asia has abundant natural resources. This makes the latter highly complementary to resource-poor East Asia (including Japan) and the overall area potentially self-sufficient. Another point that distinguishes Southeast from East Asia is the role of foreign capital. With the exception of Hong Kong, the East Asian countries relied relatively little on DFI, while Japanese (and recently Korean and Taiwanese) investment has been extremely important for Southeast Asia. Much more than in the East Asian cases, Southeast Asian development has depended on outside help.[23]

Latin America

Like Southeast Asia, Latin America has been heavily buffeted by international changes. The end of the cold war brought Soviet withdrawal from Cuba and Nicaragua, and the end of support for the Salvadoran guerrillas. Simultaneously, the newly independent countries of Eastern Europe and the former Soviet Union have come to absorb most of the attention and resources of Western Europe. The combination has returned the United States to a position of hegemony it has not enjoyed since the early postwar years. The debt crisis and a decade of capital outflow have left the region extremely vulnerable and searching for ways to restructure its economies. In this context, U.S. and other pressures for a new economic strategy have encountered a positive reaction.[24]

In the earlier postwar period, Latin America diverged from its East Asian counterparts in perpetuating an ISI strategy much longer. While East Asia moved toward export promotion in the 1960s, Latin America deepened its import-substitution path. This was possible because its rich natural resource endowment provided a source of export revenues. But it also meant that DFI increased in importance because of the need for large amounts of capital and advanced technology to create industries such as steel, petrochemicals, and automobiles. Most of this investment was from the United States.

Before the 1980s, this combination led to substantial success in savings, investment, growth, and even industrial exports (Tables 1.1, 1.3, and 1.4).

[23] For an explicit comparison of the political economy of East and Southeast Asia, see Andrew MacIntyre (ed.), *Business and Government in Industrializing Asia* (Ithaca, N.Y.: Cornell University Press, 1994).

[24] Abraham Lowenthal and Gregory Treverton (eds.), *Latin America in a New World* (Boulder, Colo.: Westview, 1994).

Indeed, countries such as Brazil were extremely successful, often compared to the East Asian NICs, although growth in Latin America had greater costs in terms of equity.[25] Problems were created in the 1970s, however, when the region tried to escape from its dependence on direct investment by borrowing large amounts from private banks. The lack of an adequate export base to support the resulting debt service, once it could not be paid by new loan inflows, led to the debt crisis and the disastrous decade of the 1980s. As Table 1.2 shows, the contrast with other regions is striking, especially with Africa, which by some indicators has a heavier debt burden than Latin America but positive net transfers. Only in the early 1990s did the Latin American region regain its access to international finance. The other troublesome indicator is investment; the decline in investment during the 1980s and early 1990s will have long-term negative effects even if the rates are now restored. Social indicators were maintained for the region as a whole, but some individual countries suffered reverses (Tables 1.5 and 9.2).

By the mid-1980s, several Latin American governments had adopted a fairly radical version of the model sponsored by the World Bank and the IMF. Mexico, Bolivia, and Costa Rica joined Chile – which had been an adherent since the mid-1970s and whose success was an important reason for other countries' enthusiasm. By the early 1990s, Argentina, Venezuela, Colombia, Peru, Jamaica, and others had joined the bandwagon. A partial holdout was Brazil, and in 1994 Venezuela's new government backtracked on its previous policies. In all cases, the policies have been directed toward macroeconomic stability, trade liberalization, and extensive deregulation and privatization. As a result of these changes and the situation in the international financial markets, Latin America suddenly regained its access to foreign capital in 1990. The new money, in turn, helped stimulate growth, but that growth remains anemic in comparison with Asian growth rates and subject to serious problems of volatility, as seen in 1994–95.[26]

Because of continuing low growth as well as increases in inequality, there is more opposition in Latin America than in Asia to the policies being implemented, and some subregional distinctions are also important, as Au-

---

[25] Comparisons of the performance of Latin American and the East Asian NICs can be found in Colin I. Bradford, "Policy Interventions and Markets: Development Strategy Typologies and Policy Options," in Gereffi and Wyman (eds.), *Manufacturing Miracles*, pp. 32–51.

[26] World Bank, *Latin America and the Caribbean: A Decade after the Debt Crisis* (Washington, D.C.: World Bank, 1993); UNECLAC, *Latin America and the Caribbean: Policies to Improve Linkages with the Global Economy* (Santiago: UNECLAC, 1994).

gusto Varas shows in Chapter 9. Mexico, of course, has now joined the United States and Canada as a member of NAFTA. As a result of NAFTA and its own more open economy, Mexico expects to attract new capital to enable it to modernize its production facilities and become competitive in international markets. The problems following the peso devaluation, however, will postpone these benefits. A second group consists of the generally small and poor nations in Central America and the Caribbean, which have traditionally been closely tied to the United States for economic and security reasons. It was undoubtedly the closeness of these ties that led several countries in this group to try to escape their dependency via approaches to the Soviet Union, but now this alternative is gone. (Even in Cuba, changes are now occurring in economic policies.) It is likely that these countries will, de facto if not de jure, also become part of a North American economic zone. Finally, there is South America. For geographic and historical reasons, it has had much looser ties with the United States. Now it is simultaneously trying to strengthen those ties and to increase intraregional links. Thus, regional integration, which had been a dead issue since the 1970s, has reemerged, but it is now an "open regionalism," aimed at constituting a building block for closer international integration if this proves possible.[27]

Sub-Saharan Africa

Africa has by far the most serious problems of the four regions under consideration. The 1980s and early 1990s provided extreme examples of these problems. As shown in Tables 1.1–1.5, per capita income in Sub-Saharan Africa declined by 1.2 percent per year during the 1980s, gross investment fell sharply, and exports contracted. The impact on social conditions has been quite negative. These trends occurred despite the fact that Africa had the largest net foreign resource transfers of any third world region during the 1980s. The situation has deteriorated further in the early 1990s.

As Michael Chege discusses in Chapter 10, Africa's economic trajectory since independence has been generally downward, both in relative and absolute terms. Some of the problems have been due to adverse international conditions, but much has been based on domestic political and economic factors. The state in most African countries is both very pervasive

---

[27] UNECLAC, *Open Regionalism in Latin America and the Caribbean* (Santiago: UN-ECLAC, 1994).

and extremely inefficient. It has not fostered a competitive private sector, nor has the public sector itself provided services conducive to economic growth. Africa's rich natural resource endowment has meant that the region could rely on raw materials exports without having to develop alternatives. The costs of this strategy were wildly fluctuating terms of trade and a tendency to rely on external forces for rescue from economic problems. The import-substitution policies, together with large state bureaucracies, also caused increased inequality as resources were concentrated among a relatively small and privileged group of urban residents. Civil wars and the decay of many of the authoritarian or one-party political systems formed after independence have added to the unfavorable environment.

Given these characteristics, Africa has been unable to exploit possible opportunities presented by the new international context of development. The end of the cold war meant the elimination of economic support for a number of African countries, especially Angola, Mozambique, and Ethiopia. It has also meant the cessation of long-time military conflicts, but the benefits have yet to be reaped. There is great fear that the end of U.S.– Soviet hostilities, together with the move toward regional blocs, will simply leave Africa forgotten and abandoned. Particular concern has centered on possible declines in foreign aid flows to Africa, even though objectively the opposite has occurred.[28] New production and export opportunities have had little meaning in the African context because of an incapacity to produce internationally competitive goods. And, while a number of African countries have tried to follow policies in line with the new consensus, few successes have resulted.[29]

This is not to imply that the situation is totally hopeless on the African continent, and perhaps the democratic transitions underway there will bring to the fore a new generation of leaders with fresh ideas for promoting

[28] On this topic, see "Aid at the End of the Cold War," in World Bank, *Global Economic Prospects and the Developing Countries, 1993* (Washington, D.C.: World Bank, 1993), pp. 45–51.

[29] On African marginalization from the world economy, see Michael Barratt Brown and Pauline Tiffin, *Short Changed: Africa and World Trade* (London: Pluto Press, 1992), and Thomas Callaghy and John Ravenhill (eds.), *Hemmed In: Responses to Africa's Economic Decline* (New York: Columbia University Press, 1993). Two approaches for the future have been recently proposed by two international organizations. For the UNICEF recommendations, see Giovanni Andrea Cornia, Ralph van der Hoeven, and Thandika Mkandawire (eds.), *Africa's Recovery in the 1990s: From Stagnation and Adjustment to Human Development* (New York: St. Martins, 1992). The World Bank's most recent statement on Africa is *Adjustment in Africa: Reforms, Results, and the Road Ahead* (New York: Oxford University Press, 1994).

development. Along these lines, the current trend toward political conditionality on international loans may be helpful to Africa over the long run.
Even during the 1980s, there were some countries that made progress.
Ghana, for example, is frequently cited as an "African success story." In
comparison with its own postwar history and that of many of its neighbors,
Ghana made important strides in the 1980s. After deciding to abandon its
previous socialist development strategy, the current government has cut
back its deficits, taken some steps toward liberalization and privatization,
and resumed economic growth after years of contraction. After several
years of this strategy, international resources finally began to flow into the
country to support the new policies.[30]

Summary and a look ahead

The preceding sections have provided a brief overview of the five processes
constituting the new international context of development. Since these
changes were global in scope, it might be assumed they would have a
similar impact throughout the third world. Such a homogeneous effect was
prevented, however, by the regional prism that refracted international
changes so as to produce substantially different regional environments.

On the one hand, development models vary across regions. While an
analysis of the 1980s concluded that a major impact of the international
changes was to force third world countries to "open" their economies and to
follow "market-oriented" policies, it became clear by the early 1990s that
this similarity in language was masking important differences. Having an
open economy in Asia means being export-oriented, not necessarily open to
imports. In Latin America and Africa, it has primarily meant the latter.
Likewise, market-oriented economies in Asia were not stripped of state
capacity to provide infrastructure, training, and other incentives. In Latin
America and Africa, market orientation (plus the debt crisis) meant that
states were so weakened that they often could not perform basic functions.
In other words, the Asian countries were following the highly successful
Japanese model of capitalism, while Latin America and Africa were follow-
ing the less successful Anglo-American variant.

[30] Thomas Callaghy, "Lost between State and Market: The Politics of Economic Adjustment
in Ghana, Zambia, and Nigeria," in Nelson (ed.), *Economic Crisis and Policy Choice*, pp.
257–319.

Moreover, the East and Southeast Asian countries were incorporated into the economic networks of Japan; later East Asia itself assumed a leading role. This gave the developing Asian nations access to markets, technology, and finance, which promoted their rapid growth and increased the symbiosis between their economic policies and those of their neighbors. Latin America, by contrast, as a result of the debt crisis, became more dependent on the United States and the IFIs during the 1980s. Its access to financial resources was sharply curtailed as well as heavily conditioned on adoption of market-oriented policies. In the 1990s, access to private financial markets suddenly resumed, in the typical boom–bust fashion that has characterized the region, but exports have not grown much. Sub-Saharan Africa, where the IFIs were sometimes directly in charge of economic decision making, saw attempts to introduce a market model, but the decaying political systems were generally unable to implement any kind of coherent policies. The debt crisis, which still continues in Africa, further exacerbates these problems.

As a result, the dynamism of the various regions is quite different. The East/Southeast Asian area is growing very rapidly. Growth rates range from China (at near 10 percent) to Korea and Taiwan (at a mere 6 percent). Japan is currently bringing up the rear, as its economy recovers from recession. In the Western Hemisphere, despite the fact that the United States leads the recovery among advanced industrial countries, growth is likely to average only 2–3 percent over the coming years. Positive growth rates have returned to Latin America after the "lost decade," although they seem to have reached a plateau in the 3 percent range. Only in Sub-Saharan Africa does economic contraction continue, meaning that the poorest countries are becoming poorer still.

The book is organized around the three tasks discussed at the beginning of the chapter. Part I describes five main global trends: the end of the cold war, shifting relations among capitalist powers, globalization of trade and production, changing patterns of development finance, and new ideological currents. Part II looks at the responses across four third world regions: East Asia, Southeast Asia, Latin America, and Sub-Saharan Africa. Part III provides a conceptual framework for analyzing the regions' differential performance and the relation between performance, policy choice, international links, and geographic location. It also speculates about future trends and the chances for increased polarization, based on different development models and relations with the international economy. The results are not very optimistic for some regions.

Table 1.1. *GDP and GDP growth in seven third world regions, 1970–92*

Region	1992 GDP (billions of dollars)	1992 population (millions)	1992 GDP per capita (dollars)	Average annual GDP growth[a]		
				1970–80 (percent)	1980–90 (percent)	1990–92 (percent)
East Asia[b]	631	74	8,527	9.1 (7.0)	8.3 (6.9)	6.5 (5.4)
Southeast Asia[c]	347	325	1,068	6.9 (4.4)	5.8 (3.5)	6.3 (4.2)
Latin America[d]	1,219	453	2,691	6.2 (3.6)	1.3 (−0.9)	3.1 (1.3)
Sub-Saharan Africa[e]	166	503	330	3.5 (0.7)	1.9 (−1.2)	1.7 (−1.4)
South Asia[f]	297	1,178	252	3.0 (0.6)	5.5 (3.2)	3.3 (1.1)
Middle East[g]	366	211	1,735	5.5 (2.7)	3.6 (0.5)	3.6 (0.5)
Eastern Europe[h]	187	96	1,948	na	0.9 (0.4)	−7.2 (−7.9)

[a]Figures in parentheses are per capita GDP growth.

[b]East Asia: Hong Kong, Singapore, South Korea, Taiwan.

[c]Southeast Asia: Indonesia, Malaysia, Philippines, Thailand.

[d]Latin America: Antigua and Barbuda, Argentina, Barbados, Belize, Bolivia, Brazil, Chile, Colombia, Costa Rica, Dominican Republic, Ecuador, El Salvador, Guatemala, Guyana, Haiti, Honduras, Jamaica, Mexico, Nicaragua, Panama, Paraguay, Peru, St. Lucia, Suriname, Trinidad and Tobago, Uruguay, Venezuela.

[e]Sub-Saharan Africa: Benin, Botswana, Bourkina Faso, Burundi, Cameroon, Cape Verde, Central African Republic, Chad, Comoros, Congo, Côte d'Ivoire, Equatorial Guinea, Ethiopia, Gabon, Gambia, Ghana, Guinea, Guinea-Bissau, Kenya, Lesotho, Madagascar, Malawi, Mali, Mauritania, Mauritius, Mozambique, Namibia, Niger, Nigeria, Rwanda, Senegal, Seychelles, Sierra Leone, Somalia, Tanzania, Togo, Uganda, Zaire, Zambia, Zimbabwe.

[f]South Asia: Bangladesh, Bhutan, India, Nepal, Pakistan, Sri Lanka.

[g]Middle East: Algeria, Egypt, Iran, Jordan, Morocco, Oman, Saudi Arabia, Syria, Tunisia.

[h]Eastern Europe: Bulgaria, former Czechoslovakia, Hungary, Poland, Romania.

Sources: World Bank, *World Development Report, 1994,* and Republic of China, *Taiwan Statistical Data Book, 1994* (for GDP, population, and per capita GDP); World Bank, *World Tables, 1992* (for 1970–90 growth rates); World Bank, *World Tables, 1994,* and Asian Development Bank, *Asian Development Outlook, 1994* (for 1990–92 growth rates).

Table 1.2. *Net long-term resource flows and transfers in seven third world regions, 1970–92 (millions of dollars)*

Region	1970	1980	1985	1990	1992
East Asia[a]					
Net resource flows[b]	455	2,440	2,979	1,296	5,899
Long-term loans	271	2,426	2,649	59	2,923
Grants	119	8	2	6	6
DFI[c]	66	6	328	1,461	2,970
Interest and profits	−81	−1,701	−2,894	−2,001	−2,226
Net transfers[d]	374	740	85	2,979	3,673
Southeast Asia					
Net resource flows	1,069	7,307	5,733	14,915	20,249
Long-term loans	765	5,859	4,148	6,586	10,227
Grants	110	249	404	878	945
DFI	195	1,198	1,180	7,454	9,077
Interest and profits	−485	−7,193	−8,868	−11,872	−13,244
Net transfers	584	114	−3,135	3,044	7,004
Latin America					
Net resource flows	4,163	29,353	13,239	19,272	20,796
Long-term loans	2,945	22,878	7,691	8,012	5,317
Grants	130	360	1,258	2,492	3,089
DFI	1,087	6,115	4,290	9,111	22,389
Interest and profits	−3,381	−22,127	−32,917	−25,270	−25,363
Net transfers	782	7,226	−19,678	−5,998	5,443
Sub-Saharan Africa					
Net resource flows	1,277	11,008	9,364	16,503	17,260
Long-term loans	821	7,899	3,765	3,801	2,089
Grants	363	3,089	4,559	11,846	13,413
DFI	92	20	1,040	856	1,757
Interest payments	−180	−2,172	−3,427	−10,148	−10,181
Net transfers	373	5,946	4,417	6,355	7,079
South Asia					
Net resource flows	1,320	5,465	5,748	9,434	10,126
Long-term loans	1,007	3,217	4,010	6,135	5,360
Grants	284	2,441	1,581	2,725	3,949
DFI	29	106	157	574	818
Interest and profits	−299	−929	−2,047	−4,230	−4,009
Net transfers	1,021	4,836	3,701	5,204	6,116
Middle East					
Net resource flows	929	11,605	9,757	8,130	11,450
Long-term loans	484	6,414	6,721	−1,000	4,239
Grants	334	3,805	1,540	7,534	5,647
DFI	111	1,387	1,495	1,596	1.564
Interest and profits	−1,110	−4,923	−4,688	−7,107	−6,732
Net transfers	−180	6,683	5,068	1,023	4,718

(*continued*)

26

Table 1.2. (*continued*)

Region	1970	1980	1985	1990	1992
Eastern Europe					
Net resource flows	na	na	2,383	1,361	4,573
Long-term loans			2,368	911	1,129
Grants			0	0	0
DFI			0	450	3,444
Interest and profits			−3,357	−2,526	−3,223
Net transfers			−974	−1,165	1,352

*a*For a basic list of countries included in the regional categories, see Table 1.1; East Asia here includes only South Korea and there are some additions/exclusions among small countries in all regions except Southeast Asia.
*b*Net resource flows consist of inflows minus repayments.
*c*Direct investment includes portfolio equity flows in the 1990s.
*d*Net transfers consist of net flows minus interest payments and profits.
Source: World Bank, *World Debt Tables, 1991–92, 1993–94.*

Table 1.3. *Investment and savings in seven third world regions, 1970–92 (percent of GDP)*

Region	1970	1975	1980	1985	1990	1992
*East Asia*ᵃ						
Gross domestic investment	24.9	28.0	34.1	26.0	31.3	31.5
Gross domestic savings	20.8	28.1	28.2	31.1	35.0	32.7
Southeast Asia						
Gross domestic investment	18.3	25.3	25.4	24.4	31.5	34.4
Gross domestic savings	17.2	24.4	29.2	24.3	28.2	33.2
Latin America and Caribbean						
Gross domestic investment	21.4	25.7	24.7	18.9	19.6	19.5
Gross domestic savings	20.7	23.1	23.3	23.6	21.9	18.4
Sub-Saharan Africa						
Gross domestic investment	16.7	23.3	21.9	13.1	16.1	16.7
Gross domestic savings	15.5	16.6	19.7	13.1	15.5	12.0
South Asia						
Gross domestic investment	16.3	18.3	20.5	22.6	24.7	22.0
Gross domestic savings	14.3	16.1	15.2	17.8	20.9	19.1
Middle East						
Gross domestic investment	na	24.9	25.5	23.9	23.2	23.7
Gross domestic savings	na	37.9	34.1	19.3	22.9	22.2
Eastern Europe						
Gross domestic investment	na	na	33.2	28.8	29.0	25.5
Gross domestic savings	na	na	29.2	30.8	29.3	24.6

*a*For a basic list of countries included in the regional categories, see Table 1.1.
Sources: World Bank, *World Tables, 1992* and *1994;* Republic of China, *Taiwan Statistical Data Book, 1994.*

Table 1.4. Growth of export value in seven third world regions, 1972–92

Region	Exports (billions of dollars)				Real growth rate[a] (percent per year)		
	1972	1980	1990	1992	1972–80	1980–90	1990–92
East Asia[b]	9.5	69.8	213.7	251.5	16.8	9.4	7.4
Primary goods	1.7	11.2	20.3	21.5	3.9	9.5	7.5
Manufactures	7.8	58.6	193.4	230.0	19.6	9.5	7.4
Southeast Asia	5.6	47.0	86.1	116.8	10.6	8.0	17.4
Primary goods	5.1	40.1	40.7	47.1	8.0	3.0	11.9
Manufactures	0.5	6.9	45.4	69.7	29.5	17.3	22.0
Latin America	17.4	91.5	122.2	125.3	4.4	4.4	3.1
Primary goods	14.6	75.0	81.5	77.3	1.9	3.7	1.4
Manufactures	2.8	16.5	40.7	48.0	16.1	6.3	7.0
Sub-Saharan Africa	7.7	45.3	34.6	34.3	2.7	0.3	3.8
Primary goods	7.1	43.4	31.3	30.9	2.4	0.1	4.0
Manufactures	0.6	1.9	3.2	3.5	7.9	2.2	3.1

South Asia	3.7	12.0	26.8	31.8	5.3	7.2	8.4
Primary goods	1.8	5.6	7.3	8.4	1.5	4.3	10.1
Manufactures	1.9	6.4	19.5	23.4	8.1	8.6	7.8
Middle East	12.2	152.0	90.7	92.7	3.7	-0.7	7.0
Primary goods	11.5	148.6	81.6	83.2	3.3	-1.2	7.8
Manufactures	0.7	3.4	9.1	9.5	13.4	7.4	0.5
Eastern Europe	11.9	36.9	29.1	28.3	2.9	-3.7	-1.0
Primary goods	3.7	12.7	9.7	10.7	-4.2	-0.3	9.2
Manufactures	8.2	24.2	19.4	17.6	6.4	-5.0	-6.3

[a]The following deflators were used: IMF, indexes of nonfuel primary products and oil prices (for primary goods); UNCTAD, index of unit values for manufactured goods from developed countries (for manufactures).

[b]For a basic list of countries included in the regional categories, see Table 1.1; exclusions with respect to Table 1.1 are some small countries in Sub-Saharan Africa, Bhutan in South Asia, and the former Czechoslovakia in Eastern Europe.

Sources: World Bank, *World Tables, 1994*; Republic of China, *Taiwan Statistical Data Book, 1994.*

Table 1.5. *Selected social indicators in seven third world regions,*
1965–92

| Region | 1965 | 1980 | 1992 | Average annual growth (percent) | |
				1965–80	1980–92
Infant mortality per 1,000 live births					
East Asia[a]	56	29	12	−4.3	−7.0
Southeast Asia	107	82	51	−1.8	−3.9
Latin America	91	64	44	−2.3	−3.0
Sub-Saharan Africa	155	122	99	−1.6	−1.8
South Asia	148	122	85	−1.3	−3.0
Middle East	146	104	58	−2.3	−4.8
Eastern Europe	na	na	15	na	na
Primary school enrollment rate (percentage of eligible age)					
East Asia	100	105	105[b]	0.3	0.0
Southeast Asia	82	100	113	1.3	1.1
Latin America	98	105	106	0.5	0.1
Sub-Saharan Africa	42	80	66	4.4	−1.8
South Asia	68	74	89	0.5	2.2
Middle East	67	87	98	1.8	1.1
Eastern Europe	na	na	94	na	na
Secondary school enrollment rate (percentage of eligible age)					
East Asia	34	77	86[b]	5.5	1.0
Southeast Asia	19	36	49	4.5	2.9
Latin America	19	38	47	4.8	2.0
Sub-Saharan Africa	4	15	18	8.8	1.7
South Asia	24	26	39	0.4	3.8
Middle East	18	41	56	5.6	2.9
Eastern Europe	na	na	81	na	na

[a]For a basic list of countries in the regional categories, see Table 1.1; there are some exclusions among small countries in Latin America and Sub-Saharan Africa.
[b]Data are for 1991.
Sources: World Bank, *World Development Report, 1983, 1992,* and *1994;* Republic of China, *Taiwan Statistical Data Book, 1994;* World Bank, *Social Indicators of Development, 1993–94.*

PART I

Global changes

CHAPTER 2

The third world and the end of the cold war

FRED HALLIDAY

The earthquake that hit the international system at the end of the 1980s is conventionally summarized in one phrase: "the end of the cold war." In reality, however, it involved at least four distinct elements: the end of the East–West conflict; the breakup of the Soviet Union and its alliance system; the collapse of communism as a global challenge to the West; and the triumph, in ideology if not in practice, of a political and economic model of liberal capitalism. The first three are historical processes that have important implications for the third world. The fourth is more a postulate than a reality, posing as many questions for the future of the third world as it provides answers about the end of the cold war.

The end of the East–West conflict has removed the bipolar contest that fueled most third world conflicts, when it did not generate them, and served as the framework for many North–South financial and military flows. While the end of the cold war has made great power military conflict seem less likely than at anytime in the past century,[1] new strategic issues have emerged, born of the breakup of the USSR, with regard to the regional impact of postcommunist rivalries and to nuclear proliferation. One very important concomitant of the end of communist hegemony has been the breakup of multinational states, ending the understanding in place since 1945 whereby the existing map of the world, unjust and arbitrary as it was, should prevail. The fragmentation of the USSR, Czechoslovakia, Yu-

I am grateful to Bruce Cumings, Eric Hershberg, Barbara Stallings, Maxine Molyneux, Michael Donelan, and Saul Landau for their helpful comments on an earlier draft of this chapter.
[1] The classic argument on this is Michael Doyle, "Liberalism and World Politics," *American Political Science Review* 80, 4 (December 1986), 1151–68. Doyle is theoretically right, but historically too trusting. His listings of which countries attained democracy, and when, is precipitate and gives a misleading overall picture. Fukuyama's argument on the same subject is equally jejune; see note 30 below.

33

goslavia, and Ethiopia could have incalculable demonstration effects on the third world – on Africa, India, Pakistan, and potentially even parts of Latin America. The breakdown of the post-1945 regime has also led to the erosion of state boundaries by fusion – first in Yemen and Germany and, almost inevitably, in Korea and eventually China.

Politically, the end of the cold war has removed the source of support for many states and movements, which either received backing from one bloc or the other or which sought to play one off against the other. At the same time, it has removed the model of an alternative path of development that provided inspiration and aid to radical forces in the third world. In the economic field, it has raised the prospect of a significant redirection of financial and trade flows away from the third world toward the postcommunist countries. This process is likely to occur both because of the strategic threat that crisis in these countries may pose to the West and because these states now reemerge as what they were prior to the establishment of communism, namely, semiperipheral states competing with their counterparts for trade and investment.

Before assessing these changes in more detail, a number of cautionary notes must be struck. First, the end of communism, if by this is meant the end of Communist Party rule, is still far from complete and has so far been confined to the European arena. Of the 1.7 billion people ruled by Communist parties at the end of 1988, 1.3 billion remained so at the end of 1994: in China, Korea, Vietnam, and Cuba. Their economic systems may be adjusting, most obviously in the Chinese case, and their political systems and ideologies may in the long run be doomed, but so far the "end of communism" has been a European affair, as has the "triumph of democracy." Second, it would be mistaken to see this as a unilinear process. In the strategic field, the end of the cold war has been accompanied by an attempt to resolve a dozen regional conflicts. Yet initial impressions suggest that the end of the cold war may foster greater conflicts between and within states, while arms manufacturers will be even more eager to send arms to the third world.

Third, and most important, while this is undoubtedly a time of major change for the third world, not all the changes are the result of the end of the cold war. The most significant process affecting the third world began two decades ago, with the industrialization of a small group of East Asian countries, followed by a number in Latin America and elsewhere in Asia. In other respects too, the new international context of development long predates the collapse of Soviet communism in 1989. The third world itself had over several decades become more and more disaggregated, as a result of the uneven spread of capitalist industrialization. Interstate and interethnic rivalries, separate from any East–West dimension, were growing in many areas. There was a rising dissatisfaction with the project of the postcolonial modernizing state, especially in the Islamic world. "Development" itself was in crisis, both as a theoretical concept and as a policy. It did not take 1989 to cast doubt on prospects for a noncapitalist, "autocentric," "self-reliant," or "delinked" project of economic development. In these, as in other regards, the end of the cold war compounded and added to a set of changes already underway, which themselves contributed to the crisis of the communist project.

If the overall significance of these processes will take years to work themselves out, they have already confounded some of the expectations held before the events of 1989–91. One is the belief that with the end of the cold war, there would be a comprehensive reduction in international tension. While the overarching threat of great power war has receded, the threat of localized interstate and interethnic war has, if anything, increased. Another belief apparently confounded is the hope that with the end of an authoritarian and sanguinary socialism in the East, it would be easier for a democratic socialism to develop in the West and South. The trend in most of the third world remains away from all traditional forms of state ownership and social intervention. Also refuted is the expectation that the development of the South, long inhibited by the diversion of resources to the arms race, could be promoted by greater resources. Arms expenditures in the developed states will fall, but the resources saved are not generally going to be spent on development aid. In 1991, for example, as military budgets fell, total OECD aid to the third world rose by only 1 percent in real terms.[2]

---

[2] *OECD Letter* 2, 8 (October 1993), 7. The figures for the United States tell their own story: expenditures on national defense (i.e., Defense Department plus other related agencies) went from $299 billion in 1990 to $282 billion in 1992 (current dollar figures). See International Institute for Strategic Studies, *The Military Balance 1994–1995* (London: IISS, 1995), p. 22. U.S. development aid expenditures for 1991 and 1992 were $11.4 and $11.3 billion, respectively. See World Bank, *World Development Report 1994*, p. 198. For one calculation of the fall in NATO defense expenditures over the period 1985–95, see Simon Lunn, "A Reassessment of European Security," in Manfred Wörner et al., *What Is European Security after the Cold War?* (Brussels: Philip Morris Institute for Public Policy Research, December 1993), p. 53. Calculated in 1985 prices (and rounded off to nearest billion) U.S. expenditure fell from $258 billion in 1985 to $203 billion in 1995. U.K. expenditure fell from $24 to $18 billion, French from $21 to $18 billion, and German from $20 to $15 billion.

So mistaken have these assumptions turned out to be, at least in the medium term, that it is not necessary to discuss them further, but only to register that what had been expected to be three positive consequences for the international system, and for the third world in particular, have not come about. Likewise, the expectations for a global triumph of liberal capitalism may also turn out to be another illusion that is a casualty of the post–cold war reality.

The cold war and the third world

Analysis of how the end of the cold war has affected the third world requires some preliminary examination of the impact of the cold war itself on Asia, Africa, and Latin America, not least because the term "third world" was coined in the late 1950s to denote a group of countries that, for all their other differences, were distinct from the "first" and "second" worlds.

The term "cold war" has been used in two senses, to denote periods of particularly intense East–West conflict, as in the first cold war of 1947–55 and the second cold war of 1979–86, or the much longer, enduring conflict between capitalist and communist states that began in 1917 and ended in 1989.[3] In this chapter, where the issue is the impact on the third world, it is being used in the broader sense, to identify a period of several decades in which the hegemony of the advanced capitalist world was challenged by a rival that seemed for some time to pose a serious alternative. The rivalry took a number of forms: military competition, maximization of alliance systems, diplomatic confrontation, and competition between social and political systems. While the major focus of the cold war was the competition between the cores of the two blocs, focusing on the strategic arms race and the division of Europe, the third world was drawn into this conflict in a variety of ways, and its history over those four decades was substantially shaped by it. The impact of the cold war on the third world can be summarized in the following four points.

---

[3] For further discussion of the meaning of "cold war," see Fred Halliday, *The Making of the Second Cold War* (London: Verso, 1983), chaps. 1 and 2. On the Soviet defeat, see Fred Halliday, "A Singular Collapse: The Soviet Union, Market Pressure and Inter-State Competition," *Contention* 1, 2 (1992), 121–41.

End of colonialism

The collapse of the European empires after 1945 had several causes, including the exhaustion of the colonial states in World War II and changes in patterns of hegemony that made formal control less important. But a major contributing factor was the challenge of the Soviet Union. The denunciation of colonialism by Moscow, its aid to third world nationalist and radical movements, and the spread of communist revolution to China and elsewhere encouraged the Western powers to bring colonialism to an end. The United States also fostered this process, in part to contain communism. The result was that by the mid-1980s colonialism as a major phenomenon had ceased to exist, even if some 30 million people worldwide still lived under formal colonial rule. Whatever kinds of war may now break out in the third world, anticolonial wars, in the sense of revolt against white domination, are largely over. Even the most intractable of all colonial legacies – South Africa and the Palestine question – have been transformed, if not resolved, by recent changes.

Strategic rivalry

If before 1945 the USSR had been on its own, with only Mongolia as an ally, after World War II it came to play a major strategic role in the third world, as an ally of radical movements and states. This process took place in three phases: the immediate post-1945 period, which saw the Chinese revolution and the establishment of communist regimes in Korea and Vietnam; the late 1950s and early 1960s, which saw the radicalization of Arab nationalism, the Cuban revolution, and the emergence of several radical African governments; and the years from 1974 to 1980, when revolutionary movements came to power in 14 countries. They included Vietnam, Cambodia, and Laos in Southeast Asia; Iran and Afghanistan in Central Asia; Ethiopia, Zimbabwe, Angola, Mozambique, Guinea-Bissau, São Tomé, and Cape Verde in Africa; and Nicaragua and Grenada in the Caribbean. At its zenith in the early 1980s, the Soviet alliance comprised around 20 countries, ranging from core communist allies, through the more advanced states of socialist orientation, to less clearly defined radical allies (Table 2.1).

Both the East and the West saw this process in strategic, zero-sum terms and sought to counter the advances of the other. The result was a competitive arms race and the use of economic aid for strategic purposes. The third

Table 2.1. *The third world in Soviet perspective, 1982*

Core Communist Party–ruled states
Afghanistan
Cambodia
Cuba
Laos
Mongolia
Vietnam

Leading states of socialist orientation
Angola
Ethiopia
Mozambique
Nicaragua
South Yemen

Independent Communist Party–ruled states
China
North Korea

Less advanced states of socialist orientation
Algeria
Benin
Burma
Cape Verde
Congo-Brazzaville
Guinea
Guinea Bissau
Iraq
Libya
Madagascar
São Tomé
Syria
Tanzania
Zimbabwe

Marginal states of socialist orientation
Upper Volta (later Burkina Faso)
Ghana
Seychelles
Surinam

Source: Fred Halliday, *From Kabul to Managua* (New York: Pantheon, 1990), p. 99.

world also became the arena for the most overt East–West confrontations. With the European core frozen, it was in the third world where the major crises broke out – from Azerbaijan in 1946 and Korea in 1950 to Cuba in 1962, Vietnam in the late 1960s, the Middle East in 1973, Afghanistan in 1979, and Nicaragua and El Salvador in the early 1980s. This was reflected in the strategic doctrines evolved by both sides to justify their actions: the Soviet vision of a "correlation of forces" shifting in the direction of the socialist camp as against a succession of U.S. doctrines bearing the names of their presidents – from Truman, through Eisenhower, Kennedy, and Nixon, to Carter and Reagan.[4]

Alternative development project

The Bolshevik revolution presented itself not just as a challenge to capitalist hegemony in the developed world, where it was quite unsuccessful, but also in the third world, where it offered a rival model of development, based upon planning, radical redistribution, the mobilization of labor, and a break-ing of exploitative economic relations with the outside world. The rival model came in two forms. One was the presentation of the Soviet economic experience as an example for the third world, given that before 1917 Russia had been a semiperipheral state.[5] The other was the singling out of the development achievements allegedly found in the USSR's periphery (i.e., Central Asia and Transcaucasia). As the number of communist or allied states increased, the policy of an alternative international trading bloc emerged, delinked from the world market and based on a "socialist division of labor."

The realities were always far less than the aspirations and claims, but for decades this model served as an inspiration to third world nationalist and revolutionary regimes seeking to break the ties of dependency they saw as oppressing them. If the inspiration of the Chinese revolution lay in the agrarian model it supposedly offered, that of the USSR lay in the appeal of

---

[4] For the Soviet theory of "correlation of forces," see Margot Light, *The Soviet Theory of International Relations* (London: Harvester/Wheatsheaf, 1987). Although based on a mis-taken view of historical teleology, this concept nonetheless captured more accurately than the Western category of "balance of power" the way in which a variety of factors – cultural and political, as well as military – affected interbloc relations and how in the end one side was to prevail over the other. On changes in Soviet and U.S. thinking on the third world, and the evolution of the "Reagan Doctrine," see Fred Halliday, *From Kabul to Managua, Soviet–American Relations in the Third World in the 1980s* (New York: Pantheon, 1990).
[5] See Teodor Shanin, *Russia as a Developing Country*, 2 vols. (London: Macmillan, 1986).

heavy industry and planning, plus the prestige of military linkage to the USSR. Indeed it can be argued that the appeal of the Soviet economic model had as much to do with the military success of the USSR as it did with its economic success as such.

The practical impact of Soviet and other communist bloc aid on the third world was more limited, but in some respects significant.[6] Despite the appearance of strategic military parity, the Soviet bloc countries were always far weaker economically than the capitalist West, and the quantity and quality of their aid was often lower. A comparison of developed capitalist and Soviet bloc aid to the third world in the 1980s shows the latter as representing about 10 percent of the total (Table 2.2). Nevertheless, a selective transfer of resources did occur, and in some cases it involved forms of aid that were more generous than those provided by the West: long-term interest-free or low-interest loans for specific development projects, commodity aid such as foodstuffs and oil, five-year fixed-price commodity agreements.[7] In the 1950s and 1960s, Soviet aid took the form of help with certain prestige projects in the third world, designed to symbolize Soviet influence and enhance the development of the countries concerned: the Aswan Dam in Egypt, for example, or the Bhilai steel project in India.

By the 1980s Soviet aid was focused almost entirely on a group of six countries where strategic and other considerations were paramount, and which were deemed to be "socialist countries": Vietnam, Cambodia, Laos, Mongolia, Afghanistan, and Cuba. In 1983, for example, $2.6 billion out of a total $2.9 billion in Soviet aid went to these states (Table 2.3). Here the economies were heavily dependent on Soviet aid and trade. Mongolia and Cuba both conducted around 80 percent of their trade with the USSR, and the Cuban economy was to a considerable degree kept afloat by a transfer of resources from the USSR, estimated by one source at $26 billion for the period 1970–83 alone.[8] Elsewhere, in the separate category of "states of socialist orientation," Soviet aid was welcomed and significant, but from

---

6 On Soviet aid to the third world, see Elizabeth Valkenier, *The Soviet Union and the Third World* (New York: Praeger, 1983), and Elizabeth Valkenier, "Revolutionary Change in the Third World: Recent Soviet Reassessments," *World Politics* (April 1986), 415–34. See also Quentin Bach, *Soviet Economic Assistance to the Less Developed Countries: A Statistical Analysis* (Oxford: Clarendon Press, 1987).

7 Robert Cassen (ed.), *Soviet Interests in the Third World* (London: Royal Institute of International Affairs, 1985).

8 Bach, *Soviet Economic Assistance to the Less Developed Countries*, p. xv. This total is made up as follows: sugar price subsidies, $16.2 billion; oil price subsidies, $6.3 billion; nickel price subsidies, $273 million; and project aid, $3 billion.

Table 2.2. *Sources of total net ODA receipts of developing countries,*
1980–87 (percent)

Source	1980–81	1982–84	1985	1986	1987
Bilateral ODA	79	78	77	79	80
OECD	49	56	59	59	62
OPEC	21	12	8	9	6
COMECON	8	9	9	11	11
Other	1	1	1	1	1
Multilateral ODA	21	22	23	21	20
Total ODA					
Percent	100	100	100	100	100
$ Billions	37	34	37	44	49

Source: Organisation for Economic Cooperation and Development, *Financing and External Debt of Developing Countries, 1987* (Paris: OECD, 1988).

Table 2.3. *Soviet economic aid to the third world, 1983*

Country	Amount (millions of dollars)	Percent
Vietnam	1,025	35.1
Mongolia	620	21.3
Cuba	500	17.1
Afghanistan	312	10.7
Cambodia	110	3.8
Laos	38	1.3
Total nations ruled by Communist parties	2,605	89.3
Others	312	10.7
Total	2,917	100.0

Source: Soviet, East European and Development Aid, 1976–83, Foreign Policy Document No. 108, Policy Planning Dept., Foreign and Commonwealth Office, n.d. Given the obscurities of Soviet figures and the difficulties of independent calculation, these amounts should be treated more as indications as to gross orders of magnitude than as precise foreign exchange equivalents.

the early 1980s at the latest, most notably in a speech by Andropov in 1983, these countries were warned that the USSR could not meet their major financial and trade needs, and they should turn instead to the West and to multilateral and regional alternatives.[9]

Contradictions of bloc formation

The appearance of a world divided into two rival camps, with a third world separate from both, provided the leitmotif of international politics for four decades but concealed a more complex picture that became clearer once the cold war came to an end. First, there was a distinction between the strategic situation, one of loose bipolarity, and the economic one, in which there was really only one pole, the developed capitalist world. At the height of the second cold war in the early 1980s, the combined GNP of the Soviet bloc was probably a quarter that of the U.S. bloc.

Aid and trade figures showed the same picture. This asymmetry was reflected in the policies of the Group of 77, which emerged from the 1964 United Nations Conference on Trade and Development, and in the program for a New International Economic Order (NIEO) propounded in 1973 at the Algiers summit of the Non-Aligned Movement. While putting the Moscow and Washington camps on a parallel footing as far as strategic rivalry was concerned, the third world states knew all too well that for economic development purposes their best bet lay in closer integration with the West. Hence, the strategies of either collective negotiation, a global Keynesianism represented by the campaign for the NIEO, or the more successful strategy of individual export-led industrialization pursued by the newly industrialized countries (NICs). The Soviet Union gave verbal backing to the NIEO campaign but had nothing to contribute to it and was unable to prevent the West from blocking the whole process. The end of the cold war therefore involved no fundamental shift in the economic trends that had been in train for decades.

Even in political terms, the impact of cold war was uneven. If it had its major impact in Asia (China, Vietnam, and Korea) and some relevance for

---

[9] Thus, the Soviet Union's main ally in the Arab world, South Yemen (the PDRY), obtained about a third of its total aid of $2 billion in the period 1967–85 from the Soviet bloc, the rest coming from Arab sources, the United Nations, and Western governments. Ethiopia, the main ally in Africa, acquired an even smaller percentage of its economic aid from the bloc. This limited economic assistance contrasted with the almost total reliance on Moscow for military assistance.

interstate relations in the Middle East, it was of much less importance for Africa or Latin America. Moreover, even within the political and strategic fields, the degree of control exercised by the two hegemons was less than they or their rivals implied. This was true in three significant respects. First, it was often not possible for the bloc leaders to maintain control of the international behavior of third world allies. On occasion this led third world states to engage in initiatives that ran counter to those of the hegemon: for the USSR, most notably China from the early 1960s onwards, but also North Korea, Vietnam, and Cuba; for the West, Egypt in the 1950s, Brazil in 1964, the OPEC states in the early 1970s. The idea that third world states simply acted on the orders of great powers failed to describe accurately governments whose actions were always more autonomous than conceptions of imperialism (on the Left) or Soviet proxy (on the Right) would have implied.

Second, the internal conduct of third world states, in regard to both economic and political issues, was often more autonomous than appeared at the time. Among revolutionary states, there was considerable variation in the transformations carried out after the overthrow of the old regimes, a tendency that in several instances (Chinese communes from 1958, Cuban pursuit of unorthodox "Guevarist" development up to 1970) caused friction with the USSR.[10] Similarly on the Western side, the United States and its allies did not look favorably on the growing assertion of control over foreign investment by third world capitalist states.

Third, despite the division of major states into blocs, a measure of intra-bloc rivalry continued in the third world, at both the economic and political levels. As discussed in Chapter 3, rivalry between major capitalist states had been the dominant theme of international relations in the nineteenth century, leading to World War I. It remained dominant up to the end of World War II, when the conflict with communism became the main concern. Even during the cold war, however, these rivalries continued over trade, investment, and arms sales. Political divisions were also considerable, as is evident in different policies between the United States and its European allies toward the revolutions in China and Cuba, and over the Suez crisis of 1956.

---

[10] Gordon White, Robin Murray, and Christine White (eds.), *Revolutionary Socialist Development in the Third World* (London: Harvester/Wheatsheaf, 1983); "Socialism and Development," *World Development* (special issue) 9, 9–10 (1981), 803–1037; and Richard Fagen, Carmen Diana Deere, and José Luis Coraggio (eds.), *Transition and Development: Problems of Third World Socialism* (New York: Monthly Review Press, 1986).

In both political-economic and strategic terms, the bipolarity of the cold war period was a loose one, allowing considerable leeway for individual deviation and involving only a partial overlap between the bloc competition of the cold war and the mainly intracapitalist North–South relationship.

The end of the cold war, 1985–91

The cold war rivalry between the Bolshevik revolution and the capitalist world was concluded in the period 1985–91, largely as a result of the policies of the Soviet leadership under Gorbachev. One of the key factors in precipitating the change was the secular fall in Soviet and East European growth rates. The ending of the cold war, more rapid and less bloody than almost anyone could have imagined, took place in three phases. First, between 1985 and 1988, the Soviet leadership sought to reform their economic system, while at the same time trying to reduce conflict with the United States in both the arms race and the third world. This was the process known as *perestroika;* it was accompanied by political opening, or *glasnost.*[11] A second phase took place between 1988 and 1990. The internal process of change in the USSR and the Soviet bloc accelerated very rapidly as the idea that the economic system could be changed was abandoned, and Communist Party rule was overthrown throughout Eastern Europe. For the third world, this was a period when the USSR, increasingly working with the United States, sought to resolve a range of regional problems through cooperative diplomacy. It gave rise to the term "New World Order," implying a partnership of the two major powers. The third phase, 1990–91, saw the collapse of the USSR itself, its fragmentation into fifteen republics, the outlawing of the Communist Party of the Soviet Union, and the end of the Soviet Union as a credible rival or partner for the United States.[12]

Third world role in Soviet decline

The third world played a significant role in this process of disintegration, but not the major one. Myth would have it otherwise. On the Soviet side, official policy from the 1950s onward looked to national liberation move-

---

[11] For a representative view of the possibilities of reform, see Abel Aganbegyan, *The Economics of Perestroika* (London: Hutchinson, 1987).

[12] Among many accounts, see Gabriel Partos, *The World That Came in from the Cold* (London: BBC/Royal Institute of International Affairs, 1993), and Michael Hogan (ed.), *The End of the Cold War* (Cambridge University Press, 1992).

ments in the third world as allies in the consolidation of socialism worldwide. At the same time, however, a vocal current could be found in the
Soviet specialist literature that questioned the capabilities and claims of
these socialist-oriented states. In fact, long before the prospects of socialism
began to be questioned in the USSR, Soviet writers had begun to be critical
of the record of the noncapitalist or national democratic road in the third
world.[13]

Moreover, as critics began to point out after 1985, the Soviet commitment
to the third world had been a costly one. The main issue that was seized on
within the USSR, namely, the economic cost of subsidizing inefficient third
world allies, was probably much less than was alleged; the problems of the
Soviet economy had little to do with these comparatively minor outlays.
More important was the political cost, in terms of relations with the West, of
the commitment to revolutionary forces in the third world, culminating in
the intervention in Afghanistan in late 1979.

On the Western side, alternative myths could be found. In the pre-1985
period, it was believed that the USSR was somehow stronger because of its
third world alliance system; in retrospect this was false. An opposing view
began to develop within the Reagan administration: a belief that the USSR
was most vulnerable in the third world and that by challenging the Soviet
empire at the margins, through backing anticommunist guerrilla movements, it would be possible to weaken the system as a whole. This was the
strategic consideration that underlay support for the guerrillas in Cambodia,
Afghanistan, Angola, and Nicaragua and the sanctions maintained against
Cuba.[14] Economic overextension and a possible demonstration effect of
overthrowing pro-Soviet regimes in the third world would weaken the system at the center.

In the end, however, it worked the other way around. Although the
Reagan doctrine led to immense havoc in third world countries, it was not in
Kabul, Aden, Luanda, or Managua that the setbacks first came, but rather in
the core communist states of Europe. Even there the real weakness came in
the Soviet Union itself, not the Eastern European client states. Indeed it was
striking how strong the third world regimes proved to be, especially as
compared with their Eastern European counterparts. Vietnam, Korea, and

---

[13] Jerry Hough, *The Struggle for the Third World* (Washington, D.C.: Brookings Institution, 1985).
[14] See Halliday, *From Kabul to Managua,* chap. 3; for an alternative account, downplaying its impact, see Martin Walker, *The Cold War* (London: Fourth Estate, 1993), pp. 287–88.

Cuba may have been heavily reliant on the USSR, but they were not simply clients as East Germany, Bulgaria, Czechoslovakia, and Poland proved to be. Even the war in Afghanistan had a rather different impact than that conventionally ascribed to it in Western and most Russian analysis. The cost was diplomatic more than economic or human, and the strategic goal of the Brezhnev intervention was attained – namely, the protection of the Kabul regime, with the ironic outcome that a communist regime, now renamed the Hizb-i Vatan or Fatherland Party, survived in power in Kabul for three years after the Soviet withdrawal and even after the Communist Party had been removed from most of the Central Asian republics to the north. It was the comparison of the overall economic and social performance between the core states of the two blocs, one increasingly unfavorable to the East, which did more than anything to convince the Soviet leadership under Gorbachev that things had to change.

If there was a third world input into the crisis of the Soviet system, then it was arguably the challenge of third world capitalist states and the implications for the Soviet model of development and international relations. A cornerstone of Soviet theory had held that the third world could not develop, and above all industrialize, because of imperialist domination. Yet from the 1960s onward, there was increasing evidence of at least selective industrialization in the third world. This was something that Moscow and other Eastern European states could not ignore since the exports of these countries came increasingly to compete with Soviet bloc exports on Western markets. It also became shockingly evident to Soviet observers that, in some respects (e.g., infant mortality and life expectancy), the USSR lagged behind the more developed third world nations.

The conclusions articulated after 1985 by a range of Soviet writers, and by some third world authors, were twofold. First, the model of development espoused by the USSR and exported to the third world, involving reliance on the state sector, had serious weaknesses and was often inferior to that of capitalist development. Second, far from retarding economic development, interaction with the West, with "imperialism," might well enhance it by releasing initiative, promoting technological innovation, and reducing parasitic state intervention.[15] Coming together with changes in the strategic field, whereby the Western military was seen as less menacing and arms control agreements were being reached, this revision of the economic per-

---

[15] See ibid., pp. 123–27, for this revision of the view on imperialism.

ception of the West and of capitalist development in the South was an important part of rethinking international relations and the model of socio-economic development as a whole.[16] The ironic conclusion was that the USSR was undermined less by the crisis of socialism in its third world allies than by the success of capitalism in Seoul, Taipei, Singapore, São Paulo, and Monterrey.

New Soviet policies toward the third world

At the same time that third world developments had this limited role in bringing about change in Soviet policy and undermining the belief in an inevitable transition to socialism, the Soviet leadership sought to develop a set of policies for the third world consonant with its own reform efforts. In this context there arose "new thinking" and international glasnost.[17] The central theme in the new thinking was that the previously dominant view of international relations as determined by class conflict, between and within states, should now give way to a pursuit of policies designed to advance and realize the universal, supraclass and supranational, interests of humankind. By 1988, when this approach was fully elaborated with regard to the third world, it comprised several interrelated concepts: the delinking of third world conflicts from East–West relations; the demilitarization of Soviet relations with the third world; the deideologization of Soviet relations with third world states, so Moscow's policy would henceforth be determined by "national interest" not "internationalist solidarity"; and the search for com-promise, under the rubric of "national reconciliation," in third world con-flicts. These constituted the main themes enunciated by Gorbachev and his advisers in regard to a new Soviet approach to the third world.

There were, however, two additional elements that came to play a signifi-cant role in the course of Soviet policy. The first was what came to be called international glasnost, by which was meant openness about international issues, in terms of both the enunciation in public of divergent views within the USSR and a more critical attitude to former allies and friends, especially on the Left. The second element was the Soviet view that the members of

---

[16] A similar perception seems to have played a role in the rethinking by the Chinese leader-ship, with Hong Kong, Taiwan, and South Korea on their doorstep. During a visit to Singapore in 1978, Teng Hsiau-ping is reported to have said to Lee Kuan Yew: "If I had only Shanghai, I could do as well as you. My problem is I have the whole of China."

[17] On new thinking in this regard, see Margot Light, "Soviet Policy in the Third World," *International Affairs* 67, 2 (April 1991), and Halliday, *From Kabul to Managua*, chap. 4.

the bloc, in Eastern Europe and in the third world, should learn from the experiences of perestroika. This entailed a contradictory message, since it simultaneously enjoined Soviet allies to pursue their own independent paths of domestic and foreign policy and encouraged them (very much in the manner of the old centralist discipline of the communist movement) to follow the reforms being introduced in the USSR. That this ambiguous message was being sent to Havana, Hanoi, and points in between at a time when Soviet support and influence were waning, made its reception all the more contradictory. Indeed, after 1989, and even more so after the complete collapse of the Soviet system in August 1991, the lesson third world leaders might have drawn from perestroika was that they should avoid it as much as possible.

This new thinking on third world issues was characteristic of the period 1988–90, which was earlier called the second phase of the collapse of communism. In that short period alone, it led to a number of diplomatic successes or at least to the initiation of processes designed to reduce third world tension: the withdrawal from Afghanistan in 1989; the independence of Namibia; the negotiations toward national reconciliation in Cambodia, Angola, Mozambique, and South Africa; the increasing isolation of North Korea. In the case of Cuba, the situation was more complicated. While the withdrawal of Soviet economic assistance and Moscow's refusal to honor existing trade agreements hit Cuba hard, Cuba's economic relations with Western European and some Latin American countries were not affected. In other cases the waning or removal of Soviet support was accompanied by more dramatic changes: the decision by the leadership of the People's Democratic Republic of Yemen to merge with North Yemen in May 1990, the electoral defeat of the Sandinistas in Nicaragua in February 1990, and the overthrow of the Mengistu regime in Ethiopia by an ex-Maoist guerrilla movement from Tigre Province in May 1991.

As the situation within the USSR changed in 1990 and thereafter, these planned diplomatic initiatives were compounded by other processes – the economic dislocation that made agreements on aid and trade increasingly meaningless and, from August 1991 onward, the determined turning away by the new Russian leadership from all of what were seen as internationalist commitments. What had begun as an attempt by Gorbachev to negotiate a new relationship with third world nations and with the United States on third world matters, ended up in a precipitate, though not disorderly, withdrawal.

The Western response

The reaction to this process on the part of the United States and its allies was itself phased, responding to perceived changes in the USSR. At first, Soviet new thinking was seen as a ploy, akin to dramatic offers on arms control, and it was only in 1987 and 1988 that serious U.S.–Soviet negotiations on third world issues got underway. Hitherto, in regard to the Arab–Israeli peace process, or Naval Arms Limitation Talks in the Indian Ocean and Persian Gulf, U.S. policy had been to keep the Soviet Union at a distance. Even as these negotiations got underway, however, it was evident that the two sides had different agendas, the United States seeing this as a situation in which it could push the USSR backward and, where necessary, renege on agreements it did not like. An example was the April 1988 agreement on Afghanistan, which explicitly called for an end to U.S. and Pakistani arms supplies to the Afghan mujahidin; without a murmur of complaint from Moscow, however, Washington ignored the agreement. Similarly, in the Arab–Israeli process, Moscow secured Palestine Liberation Organization (PLO) willingness to recognize the right of an Israeli state to exist, while pushing to get the Palestinians to drop their demand, long supported by Moscow, for the immediate establishment of an independent Palestinian state.

As events in the USSR unfolded, and as Western perceptions of Soviet policy changed, pushing Moscow backward was replaced by attempts to work with Russia to resolve problems. But by 1990, having lost Eastern Europe and beset by economic and political problems internally, the Soviet Union had ceased to be an equal partner in these processes and was reduced to taking a minor role, hoping that cooperation with the United States would yield benefits in some way. It appeared relieved to be divested of its third world commitments and saw itself increasingly as a passive partner in Western policy.

Few in Moscow seemed to regret the change of policy with regard to their former third world allies. The defeat of the Sandinistas was welcomed as one less headache; the fall of Mengistu was likewise seen as the departure of another dictatorial encumbrance. Few worried about the disappearance of South Yemen; Cuba and North Korea became symbolic whipping boys for the sins of the communist internationalist past. At the same time, a flourishing capitalist South Korea and the exile community in Miami received favorable coverage in the press. International glasnost came more and more to involve critical, at times scandalous, coverage of former friends and uncritical accounts of former foes.

The culmination of this retreat came with the Gulf crisis of 1990–91. Despite domestic criticism of his pro-Western policy and a few frustrated attempts by elements in the Soviet military to help Iraq, Gorbachev supported U.S. initiatives in the UN Security Council and did not oppose the plan to use force to drive Saddam Hussein from Kuwait, once a negotiated settlement appeared to have failed.[18] The impact of the victory of U.S. military strategy and might against Saddam only served, in Russia and also in China, to reinforce admiration for Western technological superiority. Insofar as Saddam Hussein was perceived by pro-Western elements inside the USSR as embodying all that was worst about the communist past, opposition to him was a product of the new orientation. Once the Arab–Israeli peace talks got started in November 1991 in Madrid, the marginalization of the former USSR was even clearer, since the agenda, organization, and work were all in the hands of the United States. Moscow had but a symbolic role in regard to a crisis where it had once been a major actor. When the third round of talks was held in Moscow in January 1992, the Russians sided with the Americans against Arab and European Community representatives on the issue of Palestinian representation.

In strategic and military terms, the Soviet superpower had become another middle-ranking power, like Britain, France, or Germany, and not necessarily the most influential. In economic terms, it had become even less important. Its former links to the third world, never on a par with its political and military ties, broke down, partly due to revised policies, partly due to the disruption of production and trade within the former Soviet Union itself. If Russia had a role in the new world economy, it was very much on the terms set by others and not as the focus for an alternative path of development or of a rival bloc, military or economic.

Consequences for the third world

Provisional as any assessment of the import of these changes must be, it is possible to identify a number of respects in which the end of the cold war and the collapse of the USSR have had and/or may have consequences for

---

[18] On the Soviet role in the Gulf War, see Lawrence Freedman and Ephraim Karsh, *The Gulf War, 1990–1991* (London: Faber & Faber, 1993), and Evgeni Primakov, *Missions à Baghdad* (Paris: Sevil, 1991).

the third world. The following discussion is designed to indicate some general areas, with the evident proviso that they overlap in reinforcing or contradictory ways.

Changes in great power competition

The cold war, in the sense of East–West rivalry, ended in 1989–90 in the third world as it did in Europe. Moscow ceased to be a strategic and ideological rival to Washington and abandoned its former internationalist commitments, along with the idea that it could be strengthened by consolidating a rival bloc. The effect is evident in both diplomatic and strategic terms. Former allies of the USSR were forced to search for compromises with their cold war adversaries – be this Vietnam against China, the PDRY against North Yemen, Syria and the PLO against Israel, Nicaragua against the United States. In many cases, local governments objected strongly to changing priorities in Moscow and tried to forestall the process; examples include Damascus, Pyongyang, Kabul, Tripoli, and Havana. But the reality was that the USSR, and then the successor Russian government, was not prepared to provide the kind of support it once did and actively tried, within the resources of its waning international influence, to cooperate with the United States in resolving a range of intractable third world conflicts.

At the same time, as discussed in Chapter 3, the falling away of the cold war discipline may mean that competition between advanced capitalist countries will increase, first at the economic and perhaps later at the political and strategic levels. The trade disputes between the United States and the European Union, and the enduring U.S.–Japanese economic competition, indicate how future rivalries may evolve to include influence in the third world. A century ago this rivalry took the form of competition for areas of formal, colonial control; today such control is not acceptable or necessary, having been replaced by trading blocs, investment, access to raw materials and labor, and ideological influence. Thus, great power competition in the third world may be seen as having passed through three historic phases: the quest for areas of formal colonial control (1870s–1945); cold war rivalry between the Soviet and U.S. blocs (1945–90); and a phase of informal, predominantly economic, competition (1990 onward). Economic competition was always present – evident, for example, in the oil industry – but it has now become the predominant form, with the falling away of the Soviet challenge. What form it will take is unclear. One, currently remote, possibility is a division of the world into three major trading blocs – North America, Europe, and Asia. But whatever the institutional context that economic competition assumes, the third world will inevitably be pulled into the disputes. This theme will be elaborated in Chapter 11.

Regional conflicts and their resolution

The desire to extricate the Soviet Union from third world conflicts that were diplomatically and economically costly was an important part of Gorbachev's new thinking. He was largely successful in this aim; no significant and contentious third world commitments remained by 1990, except in former republics of the USSR (Georgia and Tajikistan). Among other things, the USSR abandoned its previous policy of providing arms in return for political and strategic benefits, an approach that had dominated its arms-supply policy to the third world for the preceding four decades. In common with the United States and other permanent members of the Security Council, Moscow committed itself to an international register of arms transfers, effective from January 1993, and to restraint in situations of interstate conflict.

Achieving political solutions was more difficult. The end of the cold war had an impact on these conflicts but did not automatically resolve them. In some, success was evident. The independence of Namibia in March 1989 reflected a positive combination of diplomatic and strategic concerns. The evolving situation in South Africa owed something to the end of the cold war, even if the decisive factors – Soviet military backing for the African National Congress (ANC) and U.S. congressional pressure for tougher sanctions – were more products of the cold war itself. Nevertheless, the Pretoria regime felt a little more able to open dialogue with the ANC because the broader strategic threat of communism had receded. On the ANC side, the shift in Soviet policy, and the attenuation of Moscow's military commitment, may also have made dialogue easier, although it has to be said that Nelson Mandela himself and those close to him had envisaged such a solution long before anyone in Moscow began to think of national reconciliation. Elsewhere in southern Africa, Mozambique and Angola, deprived of Soviet military backing and exhausted by a decade and a half of war, were forced to enter into negotiations with their opponents,

RENAMO and UNITA, respectively. The Soviet Union and the United States both encouraged such an outcome.

In South Yemen, the USSR's longest-standing Arab ally, exhausted by internecine conflict and sensing a waning of Soviet military and economic support, entered into negotiations with the larger North Yemen that culminated in the unification of May 1990. Here the ebbing of the cold war operated on both sides: both Yemeni states had long proclaimed their commitment to unity, but had been restrained by the fears of their cold war patrons – North Yemen by Saudi Arabia, Egypt, and the United States; South Yemen by the USSR. With the cold war over, both sides agreed that Yemeni unity was not a real threat, leaving the Saudis to oppose it for regional reasons. A similar process of mutual adjustment could be observed in Cambodia, where the willingness of both sides to find common ground was encouraged by the end of cold war: China was less fearful of an independent, Vietnam-dominated Cambodia, and Vietnam was more willing to allow a coalition government to come into place. The Western powers, which had implicitly backed China's support for the Khmer Rouge, were also less committed to this strategy as the Soviet Union's influence waned.

This was far from meaning that all regional issues had been resolved. Some, with little or no cold war dimension, continued to defy resolution: Cyprus, Western Sahara, Ireland, Burma, Kashmir, Punjab, Sudan, and Somalia to name but some. Even where international negotiating procedures had been set up, as in Afghanistan and the Arab–Israeli process, local animosities continued to rage. Moreover, regional conflicts were continuing to command international attention for two other reasons, which appeared likely to offset whatever gains might have been achieved by the end of the cold war. On the one hand, from the 1970s onward, there had been a growth of interethnic and communal conflicts in the third world, be this in Sri Lanka or various provinces of India, Burma, Pakistan, Lebanon, Somalia, Ethiopia, and Yugoslavia. In other words, the trend was for greater ethnic conflict, irrespective of the cold war, with the result that increasing areas of the third world had become ungovernable and subject to forms of banditry and tribal violence.[19]

On the other hand, the end of the cold war itself, by releasing previously

---

[19] Mighael Ignatieff, *Blood and Belonging* (London: BBC, 1993).

established forms of hegemony and coercive control, introduced new elements of interethnic and interstate rivalry. In Yugoslavia, Czechoslovakia,
Georgia, Nagarno-Karabakh, Chechnya, Ingushera, Tajikistan, and elsewhere, the collapse of communist authority meant not democracy but
greater fragmentation and violence. Interstate conflict and rivalry were also
fomented by the collapse of Soviet rule. This was most obviously the case
between former components of single multiethnic states – the USSR, Ethiopia, Yugoslavia – but it was also true of the opening up of new interstate
competitions for influence in formerly communist areas. In Central Asia,
the new rivalry between Iran and Turkey, with participating roles from
Israel, Saudi Arabia, Pakistan, and China, threatened to become a major
focus of international concern. In the Balkans, old alliances evident before
World War I were revived, with Germany and Turkey backing Croatia,
while the countries of Orthodox Christianity, especially Greece and Russia,
were sympathetic to Serbia.

It is in this context that the complex issue of the Gulf War can be seen.
Exactly how the end of the cold war contributed to the Iraqi invasion of
Kuwait is debatable. Many observers, especially in the Arab world, believed it was because Saddam did not realize how far Soviet policy had
changed that he invaded his neighbor. What seems more plausible is that the
increased U.S. commitment to "democratic values," albeit selectively
defined, combined with the evidence of Soviet willingness to allow its allies
to be overthrown, alarmed Saddam and led him to decide to act first, to
boost his economic resources before external pressure accelerated. While it
is too simple to say that, had the cold war continued, Saddam would not
have invaded Kuwait (since Soviet allies in the past have committed rash
acts that provoked international crises), a partial connection is hard to deny.
And the concerted international counterattack would have been unimaginable in earlier times.

Changes in Eastern Bloc trade and aid

The Soviet bloc as a whole sought to organize international trade and
provide economic aid on a basis substantially different from that of the
West. To some extent it succeeded, but in the end it failed to provide a
sufficient basis to boost economic growth in the countries concerned. The
main element in Soviet bloc exports was Soviet oil sold in the West, and no
Soviet third world ally was a major participant in international trade. At the

same time, the Soviet Union did have among its significant third world commercial partners states that were not aligned with it politically but that, for a combination of strategic and economic reasons, developed substantial trade with the USSR. Turkey, Iran, and India were key examples.

The end of the cold war and the collapse of the USSR has had serious implications for these trade and aid flows. As a first step, the Russians tried to put their trade with other countries, including members of Council for Mutual Economic Assistance (COMECON), on a market basis. Thus, from January 1991, all intra-COMECON trade was to be based on world prices and demarcated in hard currency, and well before that date the terms of agreements between members had started to change. But this reorganization of intrabloc trade was overtaken by the collapse of the bloc itself, including the dissolution of COMECON.

Information is still fragmentary, but it would seem that most trade of the former USSR has been curtailed as a result of the crisis.[20] Eastern European countries now have to acquire most of their energy from the world market and find other outlets for their manufactured goods. A country such as Finland lost one-third of its trade and, in part because of this, ended up with a 20 percent unemployment rate. In the third world, Cuba has seen its trade with the USSR fall by up to 80 percent for a combination of political and technical reasons. India, which conducted around 20 percent of its trade with the USSR, has suffered substantially from the breakdown. What this all will mean in the longer run is still unclear. Some former trading partners of the USSR have tried to maintain links with Moscow on a modified basis and at the same time to negotiate new agreements with the republics. Thus, Cuba has signed agreements on petroleum with Azerbaijan, while Iran has signed a deal to provide energy to Ukraine. Pakistan, Turkey, and Israel are all interested in finding partners in the former Soviet republics. The least that can be said is that because of the triple disruption – renegotiated trading terms, disruption of production within the former USSR, fragmentation of the Union itself – trade with the outside world has been severely curtailed. It will take years to establish new patterns.

Soviet aid was a significant factor in the development of some third world nations, notably Mongolia, Vietnam, Afghanistan, and Cuba. In all four

[20] Figures for 1991 show a 32 percent fall in overall trade between the former Soviet Union and developing countries, thus comprising a fall of 29 percent in exports and 36 percent in imports. See G. W. Kolodko, "Stabilisation, Recession and Growth in a Postsocialist Economy," *Moct-Most* 1 (1993), 156.

cases, the years 1985–89 saw a gradual reduction in the volume of aid, and increased criticism within the USSR of the way in which these states handled their affairs. In 1990–92 the cutoff became more serious. In part this was because of disorder within the former Soviet Union itself,[21] but the political dimension, both domestic and international, cannot be overlooked. Throughout the former Soviet bloc, aid to the third world has become very unpopular and is blamed, inaccurately, for many of the economic problems of these countries. This change also has an international dimension, in that the Yeltsin government wanted to make it demonstrably clear that it was not backing states regarded as dangerous by the United States – hence, the disparagement of Castro, Gaddafi, and others by Russian journalists and officials, many of whom were mouthing the platitudes of socialist fraternity only a short time before.

The consequences within these states were substantial. In Cuba the reduction and virtual cessation of economic links with the USSR led to the introduction of an austerity program, known as the "Special Period in a Time of Peace," in which production was cut back, energy sparingly used, transport reduced, and the population prepared for a long phase of restricted goods and services. In Nicaragua, the economic and social situation had already begun to deteriorate after the mid-1980s, under the pressure of the contra war, but worsened substantially with the change of government in 1990. Peace, far from bringing a return to prosperity, was associated with a decline in state provision and a minimal increase in external assistance.

In Mongolia the virtual cessation of Soviet economic aid has led to dramatic disruptions in economic output and a search for alternative sources of support, notably Japan. In Vietnam, where Soviet assistance was proportionately less significant, but still the main source of external aid, there has been a gradual liberalization of the economy, to allow domestic capitalists to flourish, while at the same time international business has been invited to come in and share in the development of the country's oil resources. Prostitution is now rife in Vietnam again, as it is in Cuba. In Afghanistan, the cessation of Soviet aid after the August 1991 coup has led to great hardship, inflation, and misery in the government-held areas and contributed to the

---

[21] According to OECD figures, Soviet aid disbursements fell from $3 billion in 1989 to $1.1 billion in 1991; they can be assumed to have stopped thereafter.

willingness of the Najibullah regime to find a compromise with the muh-jahidin opposition, one that the latter, internally fragmented, proved unable to honor.

The qualitative impact of the cutoff in Soviet aid is significant too. In certain respects, and for all its delays and inefficiencies, Soviet economic policy toward the third world did meet the needs of some third world nations. Trade agreements, for five years and at fixed prices, enabled countries to manage their economic policy with greater certainty. For some third world capitalist nations, such as India and Egypt, access to Soviet markets enabled them to export goods they would have found difficult to sell in the more advanced countries. For others, such as Turkey, Soviet help with industrialization of some sectors provided more appropriate assistance, and on better terms, than that provided from the West. In the case of Nicaragua, where Soviet bloc aid rose to account for over half of the total by the end of the Sandinista regime (including the oil subsidy), the ending of Soviet support was a further blow to the economy.

Nonetheless, the impact of the end of the cold war on third world economies has not been wholly negative. First, while this charge has been exaggerated, much of the Soviet aid was inefficient, distorting of the local economies, and inferior in quality and quantity to that available from Western or multilateral sources. As such, it contributed to the slow economic development in these countries. Second, positive changes in international trade resulting from the collapse of communism may be considerable. Newly independent republics of the USSR are keen to develop export agreements with third world nations. The latter may find new export opportunities, especially in Eastern Europe: in oil, since Soviet supplies are likely to remain scarce and unreliable, and then in selected areas, such as textiles and tropical fruits. ("We want kiwis and nectarines" was one slogan of East Germans who came to the West when the wall came down.)[22] Insofar as the postcommunist countries will be in competition with industrializing third world nations for the markets of the developed world, the consequences will

---

[22] Compared with those of Eastern Europe, Western Europe's 1989 per capita import levels of tropical products in 1989 were 2 times as high for tea, 4 times for coffee, 5 times for bananas, and 370 times for tinned pineapple. (See "Eastern Europe and the Developing Countries," Overseas Development Institute, Briefing Paper, London, June 1991.) In early 1992, the situation was in some ways reversed: East German levels of consumption were almost 2 times as high as those of West Germany for bananas, oranges, and tangerines (*International Herald Tribune*, March 26, 1992).

be negative, but this must be countered by the longer-run possibilities, provided economic collapse is avoided.

An area of particularly contradictory consequences is migration. In the 1970s and 1980s, there developed considerable labor migration from poorer to richer COMECON states, notably that of Vietnamese, but also Mozambiqueans, Cubans, and others, to Soviet bloc states, especially the USSR and East Germany. The collapse of communism has been very hard for these people, who have seen their jobs disappear, their remittances blocked, and increasing racist abuse from the local inhabitants. For Vietnam, in particular, this has been a serious blow. The broader migratory consequences concern out-migration, which communism had prevented.[23] The result of the breakdown of these controls is likely to be substantial migration to more developed countries. Here immigrants from the East are likely to be direct competitors for the jobs of third world migrants, especially in Western Europe, where anxiety about ethnic and religious diversity will make the supply of white, more or less Christian, migrants from the East more attractive. In the case of Israel, and treating this issue in its purely economic dimension, the flow of Soviet Jews has reduced the need for a Palestinian labor force and may have made it easier to envisage withdrawal from territories occupied in 1967.

A model discredited

Beyond the flow of Soviet aid and arms, and the organization of trade, the existence of the USSR acted as a model for third world regimes, sustaining as it did the belief that some alternative to market-based development was possible. Not all the responsibility for the widespread incidence of this model needs to be ascribed to communism, since the imperatives for planning, import substitution, protection, resources distribution, nationalization and so forth were as much from within any country as they were externally inspired. The example of Kemalist Turkey in the 1920s and 1930s, which, without communist influence, pursued a neo-Bismarckian path of what

---

[23] For some discussion of the implications of the end of communism for migration, see Sara Collinson, *Europe and International Migration*, 2d ed. (London: Royal Institute of International Affairs and Frances Pinter, 1994); Gil Loescher, *Refugee Movements and International Security* (London: International Institute for Strategic Studies, Adelphi Paper No. 268, 1992); "The Journey: Movements of Migrants and Refugees," special issue of *Oxford International Review*, 3, 1 (1991).

would later be called national democratic development, shows how this was possible. Likewise, the policies pursued by India, Egypt, Peru, and a range of other states in the 1960s were not simply a result of Moscow's influence. Nonetheless, the existence of the USSR and the inspiration provided by its apparent successes, including industrialization of the 1930s, the defeat of Nazi Germany, and the launching of the first person into space, gave the USSR a prestige that affected relations with third world states. Often these states tried to differentiate themselves from the communist model by particularist invocations – the "Arab socialism" of Nasser and the Ba'th "African socialism" of Nyrere, Kaunda, and Nkrumah – or by proclaiming even more radical and revolutionary forms – as in China, Korea, and Cuba. But all were variants that claimed legitimacy from the central tenet of the Bolshevik revolution, that some alternative to capitalism was possible and, in some longer-run scheme of things, inevitable.

The collapse of the USSR obviously discredited this model, not only at the level of economic management, but also as a political project – one of revolutionary action designed to accelerate change and avoid the constraints of a system dominated by the West.[24] It therefore weakened confidence in "anti-imperialism" in general, as well as in state-run economic policy. After 1991, it was much harder to claim that some alternative path of development was possible. All seemed to be condemned to accepting the dictates of the market, be this through the influence of private firms or multilateral agencies. Acceptance of free-market policies became, along with political conditions such as respect for human rights and political pluralism, a condition not just for international economic support, but even for membership of international political bodies such as the Conference on Security and Cooperation in Europe, and the new extension of NATO, the North Atlantic Council. The definition of what constituted acceptable politics and economics was unambiguously the prerogative of the United States and its closest allies. While these conditions were defined in the West, they were nowhere more spiritedly defended than in the former capitals of the communist East: here the market acquired the status of a new fetish, and all that contradicted it was seen as representative of the now-outmoded communist approach. Even such issues as women's rights or the welfare of the poor

---

[24] For the rethinking occasioned in Latin America, see Jorge Castañeda, *Utopia Unarmed: The Latin American Left after the Cold War* (New York: Knopf, 1993).

were regarded by much of the postcommunist elite, and by significant sections of the population, as somehow part of the communist legacy.

Yet this process was more complex than it appeared. First, the discrediting of the orthodox state-centered approach to economic development had begun well before 1989, going back to the first crises of the system in the 1960s. It was then that the first Soviet attempts at reform were made under Khrushchev. In the 1970s, a number of third world states began to move away from their versions of socialism. Egypt was a prime example, but the most important was China, with the launching of the "four modernizations" in 1978. Cuba initiated a set of liberalizing economic reforms in 1981, and throughout the 1980s third world states, for reasons both domestic and international, had moderated their previous commitment to heavy industry, planning, and state control of prices. Indeed the orthodox model of socialist development was being modified in the third world before it began in the Soviet bloc countries. The difficulty with this modification process was not so much with the internal changes themselves as in the inadequate response from the international system, especially at a time of falling commodity prices, and the political risks involved in economic liberalization. For example, political risk was the factor that led to Cuba's catastrophic reverse into so-called rectification in 1985 and to the Tienanmen crisis in China in 1989, as well as to the factional explosions that fragmented the regimes in both Grenada and South Yemen. This contradiction between economic change and political stasis was to prove the undoing of perestroika.

Second, while the international trend throughout the 1980s was toward a Western definition of market economics, there were two strong, if divergent, countertrends: in some countries a combative socialist backlash against the cautious liberalization of the 1980s, and in others a populist revolt against the whole project of state-led modernization, which was seen as some kind of Western imposition. The collapse of perestroika only reinforced the socialist backlash, since it was seen to demonstrate the folly of Gorbachev's attempts to liberalize both economy and politics. In Cuba, for example, until 1993, when some economic changes were implemented, Castro resolutely set himself against international trends and sought to defy the example of perestroika. In China, there was a widespread sense after the collapse of the USSR and the attendant economic crisis, even among those who had supported the reforms of premier Zhao Ziyang in 1989 and the Tienanmen demonstrators, that economic reform had to precede political reform. In other countries revolutionary parties drew the lesson that they had to be even more orthodox and militant than before. Sendero Luminoso in Peru, the Kurdish Workers' Party in Turkey, and for a time the Ethiopian People's Revolutionary Democratic Front were examples of this left backlash, a tendency also present, if not dominant, within the African National Congress in South Africa and among some Middle Eastern Communist parties.

The alternative backlash was that of Islamic fundamentalism, a movement strong in several Islamic countries. It attacked what it saw as capitalism, represented by corruption and the dictates of the market, but it also consciously presented itself as an alternative to communism, both as a radical anti-imperialist movement and as a project for recasting state and society. Its rise in the 1970s was in part a result of the failures of the secular Left, both as opposition forces (e.g., in Iran) and as secular modernizing states (e.g., Egypt and Algeria). The fundamentalists claimed to have a distinctive economic policy based on Islam: what it amounted to was a radical social project (tied to the law, family policy, gender relations, education) linked to a revived 1960s developmentalist project (state intervention, income redistribution, protection of infant industry, consumer austerity). Fundamentalism represented above all a new form of anti-imperialism, one that mistakenly believed it could resist international pressures.[25]

The difficulty with both these oppositions to the orthodoxy of the late 1980s was that, while they drew on a range of forces from nationalism to religious populism to dislike of the Western model, they offered no solution to the problem of living standards, which had long underlain third world upheaval and also served to discredit the Soviet model.[26] The ability of revolutionary socialism to deliver on this front had appeared plausible in the 1950s and 1960s, but had disappeared by the 1980s. On the one hand, capitalist states clearly outperformed communist states in terms of growth. On the other hand, the terms of the competition itself had changed, from

[25] Fundamentalisms of all kinds – Islamic, Hindu, Judaic, Christian – are above all movements for the acquisition or maintenance of political power, not theological or conversion trends. See Juan Cole and Nikki Keddie (eds.), *Shi'ism and Social Protest* (New Haven, Conn.: Yale University Press, 1986); Sami Zubeida, *Islam, the People and the State* (London: Routledge, 1989); and Fred Halliday and Hamza Alavi (eds.), *State and Ideology in the Middle East and Pakistan* (London: Macmillan, 1988).

[26] On Islamism, see Olivier Roy, *L'écher de l'islam politique* (Paris: Sevil, 1992).

rivalry in "old" terms – heavy industry and gross output – to competition in "new" terms, born of the consumerist revolution and the changes of the third industrial revolution. As I have argued elsewhere, the main reason for the collapse of the Soviet model was not so much military pressure from without, or political pressure from below, but the perceived failure to sustain competition in the economic domains valued both by the new elites and by the increasingly informed populations.[27] This was true for the USSR, where the key changes and decisions were taken, but it applied equally to a range of third world countries – China, South Yemen, and Vietnam among them.

Redirection of economic resources

The greatest single anxiety expressed about the impact of the end of the cold war on the third world is that it will lead to a displacement of the developing world in terms of aid and trade. In the first place, it is feared that aid to the third world will be diverted to Eastern Europe and that private-sector and multilateral agency funding will also be so reallocated. The very fact of increased lending to ex-communist states, and their substantial debt repayment problems (Soviet debt in 1991 at $70 billion was comparable to that of some Latin American countries, e.g., Brazil's at $112 billion), may put strains on world interest rates and on financial resources. It is also feared that with the decline in cold war rivalries, the political motive behind third world aid will decrease, most obviously in the United States, where the foreign aid budget is the object of attack from both Right and Left. On the trade front it is feared that improvements in quality and volume of industrial output in former communist states will make it more difficult for third world states to market goods in developed countries.

There must be some validity in these fears. The sums of money involved in revitalizing the East are enormous and will continue to be so for years to come. The strain put on the German economy by reunification is eloquent enough in this respect. Economic considerations apart, the West has a political interest in ensuring stability and growth in the former communist world, to contain the dangers of war, refugee flows, nuclear proliferation, fundamentalist resurgence, and the like. The European Bank for Reconstruction and Development (EBRD), set up in April 1991 in London, had an initial capital of $13 billion, compared with a total of multilateral official lending

---

[27] Halliday, "A Singular Collapse."

to the third world of $12 billion in 1989. The West committed itself to $8.9 billion worth of food aid to the former Soviet Union by the end of 1991, $2.8 billion of which came from the European Community.[28] The successor states to the USSR have joined the IMF and the World Bank and can be expected to make claims on resources there as well. Arab states, notably Saudi Arabia and Kuwait, have also begun to loan to the former Soviet republics. Assuming the difficulties of these countries continue for years if not decades, then competition for markets and funds will continue.

There are, however, some reasons for qualifying this picture. In the first place, the sum of finance available for lending and investment is not static, but depends on macroeconomic trends irrespective of what happens in the postcommunist world. The amounts of money diverted or not diverted are small compared with other outlays – an $11.4 billion U.S. development aid budget for 1991 compared with a military budget for the same year of $290 billion or a savings and loan loss of at least $500 billion. The turnaround in Japanese policy in 1991, when the economy went from an average surplus of $165 billion in outward capital flows between 1984 and 1989 to a net inflow of around $50 billion in 1992, is of much greater significance than strains on the IMF or EU aid budgets. Changes in the world economy are, overall, of far more importance than the fluctuations in the amounts of money made available by aid donors.

In the aid field, most donor states and agencies have so far been careful to keep their financial operations vis-à-vis the postcommunist world separate from their programs for the third world: separate lines, such as the United Kingdom's Know How Fund, a program designed to transfer market skills, have been established. The same thinking lies behind the EBRD. This does not, however, apply to the United States, and as time passes the distinction between the traditional third world and the postcommunist countries may well be dropped. A problem is already evident in the area of scholarships. Postcommunist countries themselves have cut training programs for third world students, while Turkey for one has shifted its educational assistance program from the third world to the Turkic peoples of Central Asia. Inside multilateral and bilateral aid agencies, the main strain is not on funds but on personnel, those able to administer programs and carry out missions in the relevant countries: here the East is diverting resources that might otherwise

[28] Figures from *Western Assistance to the Former Soviet Union,* Background Brief, Foreign and Commonwealth Office, London, February 1992.

Table 2.4. *Direct foreign investment: selected countries,*
1990–92 (millions of dollars)

Country	1990	1991	1992
Third World			
Argentina	2,036	2,439	4,179
Chile	595	576	737
Indonesia	964	1,482	1,774
Malaysia	2,902	4,073	4,469
Nigeria	588	712	897
Pakistan	249	257	349
Philippines	530	544	228
Singapore	4,808	3,584	5,637
Thailand	2,376	2,014	2,116
Communist/ex-communist			
Bulgaria	na	4	42
China	3,489	4,366	11,156
Czechoslovakia	207	600	na
Hungary	na	1,462	1,479
Poland	89	291	678
High income			
Australia	7,086	4,833	4,968
France	12,733	15,235	21,843
Italy	6,413	2,403	3,072
Japan	1,760	1,370	2,720
Spain	13,841	10,502	28,058
United Kingdom	33,392	21,537	18,053
United States	37,190	11,500	2,370

Source: World Bank, *Global Prospects and the Developing Countries*
(Washington, D.C.: World Bank), various years.

have been allocated to the South. Likewise, there is likely to be competition
in regard to middle-income third world states, not so much with regard to
aid for which they are generally not eligible, but private-sector lending and
investment. Most direct foreign investment in the third world goes to
middle-income countries, economies broadly similar to those in the
postcommunist world, but available evidence suggests that Eastern European countries are much less attractive to investors than the Asian/Pacific

areas or even Latin America (see Table 2.4). In 1994, for example, total direct foreign investment in the ex-Soviet region (i.e., the former USSR and Eastern Europe, excluding Germany) was around $6 billion, equal to investment in Mexico alone, and significantly less than that invested in China, estimated at $28 billion. In addition to political uncertainties and lack of infrastructure, both physical and legal, the overall levels of demand in these countries remained comparatively low: based on official figures, themselves reflecting undervalued exchange rates, the total output of the former Soviet economies was equal to only twice that of Spain.[29]

What emerges, on the basis of current speculation, is a contradictory picture. On the one hand, there will be competition for resources and in some areas, such as textiles and footwear, for markets. On the other hand, the apparent end to global recession can benefit everyone by stimulating trade and financial flows, and there are new opportunities for third world nations. In the markets of Eastern Europe, oil will now be sold by third world producers, replacing the USSR, and the demands for tropical fruits in particular will rise. Matters will be more protracted and uncertain within the former Soviet Union, but there are evidently great commercial possibilities here for a range of third world states, notably Turkey, Iran, and Pakistan. South Korea is also looking to a major role in this area.

Conclusion: the uncertainties of capitalist development

A longer-run answer to the question of how the end of the cold war will affect the third world rests upon assessing a set of underlying issues in the international system. At the political-strategic level, the question is how far a system of peaceful and cooperative relations between states can be maintained without hegemonic controls. If some hegemonic controls are necessary, the question is whether the developed capitalist countries, in particular the United States, are willing or able to exercise them in a way that meets the interests of the system as a whole. A world of interstate and intrastate conflict will benefit no one and hurt the weaker states most.

Moreover, there is the question of whether the evident universalizing trends in the world political and economic system will be able to diffuse prosperity and reduce the gap between richer and poorer states. This is an argument that has been much debated within liberal economic and Marxist

[29] "East Europe's Failure to 'Emerge': Speculative Foreign Money Has Moved Elsewhere," *International Herald Tribune*, February 4–5, 1995.

camps for the past four decades, recently receiving a notable reassertion in the interesting, if flawed, work of Francis Fukuyama.[30] The least one can say is that the jury is still out: incomes in most states are rising, but the gap between rich and poor is widening, and new problems – ecological, demographic, interethnic – threaten many states. As Giovanni Arrighi has pointed out, there appear to be very strong rigidities in the international hierarchy. Despite considerable alteration of position within the group of high-income states, over a century and a half none has left this group and only one, Japan, has joined.[31]

In broad terms, this was precisely the question that communism sought to address, in its seven decades of existence. It was a crude, for a time quite successful but very costly, attempt at an alternative development project: the creation of semiperipheral states. Now it has foundered in the face of more successful developmental projects, and the communist states have been returned like escaped laborers, chastened and resubjugated, to their place in the international capitalist hierarchy. Communism failed to come up with an answer that was either politically acceptable or economically competitive. Whether capitalism can do so for the majority of the world's population remains to be seen. The irony is that Karl Marx was one person who believed that developed capitalism could transform the whole world in its image and that, grosso modo, it was doing a good job at it.[32] In this respect, the new international context of development looks very much like the old, not least because it has now been stripped of two diversions: the artificial cover of colonialism (1870–1960) and the chimera of a revolutionary alternative (1917–91). In the fundamental issues it raises – peace, democracy, and economic growth – this international context turns out to have varied remarkably little over the past century and a half.

---

[30] Francis Fukuyama, *The End of History and the Last Man* (London: Hamish Hamilton, 1991). For critical discussion, see Fred Halliday, "An Encounter with Fukuyama," *New Left Review* 192 (May–June 1992), 89–95, and Perry Anderson, *A Zone of Engagement* (London: Verso, 1992).

[31] Giovanni Arrighi, "World Income Inequalities and the Future of Socialism," *New Left Review* 189 (September–October 1991).

[32] For a critique of dependency theory and the Leninist underconsumptionist tradition, as well as a spirited defense of the classical Marxist position on capitalism's ability to transform the world, see Bill Warren, *Imperialism, Pioneer of Capitalism* (London: Verso, 1980).

CHAPTER 3

Capitalisms in conflict? The United States, Europe, and Japan in the post–cold war world

BARBARA STALLINGS AND WOLFGANG STREECK

The end of the cold war and the disappearance of socialism as a major political-economic force opened the way for important changes in the capitalist world. These changes were of at least two types. On the one hand, the cessation of cold war hostilities between the United States and the Soviet Union downgraded the role of military in favor of economic power. This shift, in turn, increased the international standing of Europe and Japan at the expense of the United States, since the former are much stronger economically than militarily. On the other hand, the disappearance of socialism as an economic system focused attention on the differences among models of capitalism. In the 1990s, much more heed is being paid to variations in the ways of doing business in the United States, Europe, and Japan. While neither of these trends is totally new, the changed international panorama since the fall of the Berlin Wall greatly increased their salience.

For theorists and practitioners alike, a major question concerns the characteristics of the post–cold war international political economy. At the macrostructural level, debate centers on whether the emerging system will be a multilateral, interdependent one, with close cooperation among capitalist powers, or a regionalized one consisting of trade and investment "blocs" in North America, Europe, and Asia. Our argument is that both of these processes are happening and will continue to do so. This simultaneity, which we call "nonhegemonic interdependence," results in an unstable situation. The participants respond by trying to improve their own positions in the global economy, by convincing their competitors to degrade theirs, or by creating new rules and institutions to contain conflict.

This chapter analyzes these emerging relationships among major capital-

The authors thank Phil Ruder and Akira Suzuki for research assistance.

ist powers. It presents the two main positions in the structural debate and then moves to "test" the two arguments by looking at some quantitative and qualitative data on relations among the three centers of capitalism. Quantitative analysis focuses on trade and investment flows, while qualitative analysis examines behavior within international organizations, especially the General Agreement on Tariffs and Trade (GATT) and the World Bank. Next we briefly sketch out what we think are the main differences among the three versions of modern capitalism and place them in the context of global economic conflict and cooperation. Finally, in line with the overall goals of the volume, the chapter concludes with some hypotheses on the implications for the third world of changing relations among capitalist powers.

Debates on the structure of capitalism

Debate on the structure of capitalism has arisen repeatedly when major political and economic changes have occurred in the world. Thus, the antecedents of the current controversy can be traced back at least to the early years of the twentieth century, when they arose out of the "scramble for colonies" among European nations and the hypothesized causes of World War I. The primary protagonists at that time were Marxists, especially Lenin and Kautsky. Lenin argued that strong rivalry (ultimately resulting in war) was the natural relationship among nations, while Kautsky suggested that a form of "ultraimperialism" was a possible alternative.

As the war began, Kautsky, the leading figure in the German Social Democratic Party, published an article in which he suggested that the exhausting effects of the war might lead to a "holy alliance of the imperialists."[1] His reasoning was that the capitalist economy was seriously threatened from two quarters: opposition was growing among the more developed colonial nations, and the working class in the industrial nations was also protesting against increased taxes to support wars. A possible solution, according to Kautsky, was an alliance of industrial nations to jointly exploit the rest of the world.

Lenin wrote shortly afterward to attack Kautsky's position, arguing that the real tendency was for cartels to be formed within countries, but for

---

[1] Karl Kautsky, "Ultra-Imperialism," *New Left Review* 59 (January–February 1970 [1914]), 3–18, at 46.

competition to take place between them.[2] Subsequently, the cartels would divide the world among themselves. While agreeing that alliances might be formed, Lenin believed they would be only temporary since strength, which forms the basis of the division of territory, changes unevenly among the participants. Those who grow more rapidly will pull out of the alliance and go to war to increase their share.

Fifty years later, as U.S. hegemony began to decline just as that of Britain did in the years leading up to World War I, conflicts among advanced capitalist countries began to reemerge, and a similar debate arose with respect to the United States and Western Europe. In this second round, many of the same questions and arguments were heard. Was the basic character of relations among advanced capitalist nations unity or rivalry? Who was the primary enemy – other capitalist nations or "outsiders" (i.e., socialist countries and socialist groups in peripheral nations)?

There was an additional dimension, however, in terms of the role of the United States. While there were a few analysts who spoke of a Kautskian type of alliance, where nations voluntarily cooperated, the dominant version of the unity hypothesis in the 1960s was represented by those believing that U.S. hegemony would not only continue but perhaps become even stronger in the future. Based on their alleged superiority, deriving from their greater size and access to technology, U.S. firms were expected to subordinate European capital. U.S. military superiority would also be an asset, creating a unified capitalist world under the hegemony of the United States; contradictions between nations would become increasingly insignificant.[3]

Arguing that the previous position greatly exaggerated U.S. power was a group of European analysts.[4] They pointed out that the size advantage of

---

[2] V. I. Lenin, *Imperialism: The Highest Stage of Capitalism* (New York: International Publishers, 1939 [1917]).

[3] This type of argument was put forward in the 1960s by both the Marxist Left and more mainstream economists and policy makers on both sides of the Atlantic. See, e.g., Harry Magdoff and Paul Sweezy, "Notes on the MNC," Parts 1 and 2, *Monthly Review* 21, 5 (October 1969), 1–13, and 21, 6 (November 1969), 1–13; Gaston Defferre, "De Gaulle and After," *Foreign Affairs* 44, 3 (April 1966), 436–45; Anthony Eden, "The Burden of Leadership," *Foreign Affairs* 44, 2 (January 1966), 229–38.

[4] The case for an independent Europe was also put forward by advocates of many political positions, although their conclusions varied. Some saw more conflictual relations developing as a result of a united Europe. See, e.g., Ernest Mandel, *Europe versus America?* (London: New Left Books, 1970), and Bob Rowthorn, "Imperialism in the 1970s: Unity or Rivalry?" *New Left Review* 69 (September–October 1971), 31–54. Others saw a unified Europe as necessary for the EC to participate in an interdependent Atlantic Alliance. See, e.g., Michael Stewart, "Britain, Europe and the Alliance," *Foreign Affairs* 48, 4 (July 1970),

U.S. firms was being rapidly eliminated by mergers in Europe, and that Europe's lower wages could provide an advantage in export competition. In addition, they predicted that European governments would come to the defense of their firms, leading to increased contradictions within the capitalist world. The emergence of a supranational European state would put Europe on an equal footing with the United States.

As the old bipolar system broke down in the 1990s, the same debates surfaced once again. International political economists have put forward two main answers to the question of how the new system will work. One group of analysts argues that the new world order is best characterized as a single global system superimposed upon individual nation-states, which are themselves losing importance. Other analysts find the world breaking up into three blocs centered on the United States, Japan, and Europe (or perhaps Germany). The resulting political-economic zones are said to be further differentiated as to the models or "styles" of capitalism prevailing there.

In a provocative recent analysis, whose sponsors describe it as "explod[ing] the myth that the world is moving inexorably into regions and exclusive trading blocs," Albert Fishlow and Stephan Haggard argue that globalism is the more likely outcome.[5] Echoing the debates of the 1960s, they give particular weight to the role of the United States as a global actor – a member of several regions simultaneously – which is projected to militate against regionalism. The authors provide data to show that interregional trade between the United States and Asia, and Asia and Europe, is growing as fast as intraregional trade. Turning to investment, they argue that even more than with trade, interregional flows dominate those within regions. "There is thus reason to expect that capital mobility can provide an escape valve from the trend toward 'degenerate regionalism.'"[6]

On the political side, they are dubious that regional integration can be successfully constructed without strong economic underpinnings. Preferences and barriers alone, if the "natural" economic links do not exist, are probably doomed to failure. As examples, they point to failed attempts to

---

643–59; Walter Scheel, "Europe on the Move," *Foreign Policy* 4 (Fall 1971), 62–76; Zbigniew Brzezinski, "America and Europe," *Foreign Affairs* 49, 1 (October 1970), 11–30.
[5] Albert Fishlow and Stephan Haggard, *The United States and the Regionalisation of the World Economy* (Paris: OECD Development Centre, 1992). The quotation is from the back cover of the publication.
[6] Ibid., p. 19.

construct regional or subregional groups in Africa and Latin America. Moreover, there may also be barriers to increasing political types of integration. Historically based tensions in the Asian area have thus far impeded attempts to institutionalize the increased economic interactions. Such tensions seem to have been submerged for the moment in the Western Hemisphere as Latin American governments express great interest in the American Free Trade Area that has been proposed as a successor to the North American Free Trade Agreement (NAFTA), but they may well reappear.

Coming from a different theoretical position as a world-systems analyst and using historical data to make his case, Bruce Cumings also argues that a "trilateral regime of cooperation and free trade" is likely to develop "with the three great markets of each region underpinning and stabilizing inter-capitalist rivalry in the world system."[7] Comparing the post–cold war period with the hundred-year peace (1815–1914) described by Polanyi, Cumings says that "today, as in the 19th century, we find several great powers of roughly equivalent weight with a stronger interest in creating wealth than in accumulating power."[8] Germany and Japan, he argues, have left their militarist pasts behind them and have "had their democratic revolutions, even if it took World War II to get them."[9] Under these structural circumstances, trilateral cooperation, such as that put forward under the Carter administration, would unite Washington, Tokyo, and Berlin to preside over a boom period for the advanced industrial world. The boom would be fueled by new technologies and new markets in Central Europe and East Asia.

Lester Thurow is perhaps the best known of the analysts who foresee the world turning toward regional blocs. The basis of Thurow's argument is that "the GATT–Bretton Woods trading system is dead."[10] The postwar multilateral system died, he says, as the normal result of its great success. While the logical next step would be another Bretton Woods conference to write new rules for the world economy, this is politically impossible without a hegemonic power. Consequently, the new rules will be written by those who control the largest market: in this case, Europe. The type of rules to emerge

---

[7] Bruce Cumings, "Trilateralism and the New World Order," *World Policy Journal* 7, 2 (Spring 1991), 195–222, at 211–12.

[8] Ibid., p. 203.

[9] Ibid., p. 204.

[10] Lester Thurow, *Head to Head: The Coming Economic Battle among Japan, Europe, and America* (New York: Morrow, 1992), p. 65.

will be "managed trade" and "quasi trading blocs"; the blocs will be centered on the European Union (led by Germany), Japan, and the United States. Countries within blocs will get special privileges not offered to others.

Relations among these quasi-blocs, according to Thurow, will center on a new kind of competition. While competition in the second half of the twentieth century involved "niche competition," where different countries or groups of countries specialized in different activities, the twenty-first century will witness "head-to-head competition." In the latter, all want the same industries – for example, microelectronics, biotechnology, telecommunications, computers, robotics – because these are the leading sectors that produce high-wage, high-skill jobs. With niche competition, all players can win; head-to-head competition produces many losers.

Among the reasons that losers will emerge in the new system are the differences among types of capitalism practiced in the blocs. Thurow identifies two basic types: Anglo-Saxon and German-Japanese; more subtle differences are found between the latter two:

America and Britain trumpet individualistic values: the brilliant entrepreneur, Nobel Prize winners, large wage differentials, individual responsibility for skills, easy to fire and easy to quit, profit maximization, and hostile mergers and takeovers – their hero is the Lone Ranger. In contrast, Germany and Japan trumpet communitarian values: business groups, social responsibility for skills, teamwork, firm loyalty, industry strategies, and active industrial policies that promote growth. Anglo-Saxon firms are profit maximizers; Japanese business firms play a game that might better be known as "strategic conquest." Americans believe in "consumer economics;" Japanese believe in "producer economics."[11]

Thurow clearly believes that the German-Japanese style of capitalism is superior in the context of the late twentieth and early twenty-first centuries. Without changes in U.S. policy – similar in kind if not in degree to those proposed by the Clinton administration – the prognosis is clearly for the United States to fall further and further behind.

Quantitative tests: trade and investment flows

The economic underpinnings of the most recent debate on capitalist unity or rivalry are trade and investment flows. Higher densities of economic trans-

---

[11] Ibid., p. 32. A similar argument is presented in Jeffrey Garten, *A Cold Peace: America, Japan, Germany, and the Struggle for Supremacy* (New York: Times Books, 1992).

actions across regions would support the former argument, while greater flows within regions would provide evidence for the latter. Both absolute values and recent trends are important indicators of emerging political-economic patterns.

In earlier periods, international trade was by far the most important economic link among countries and regions. Now it is rivaled by investment and financial flows, which can sometimes obscure the meaning of trade figures, but it is still useful to start with trade. Table 3.1 displays data on trade flows among the countries that many observers have come to call the "triad" (the United States, the European Union, and Japan) and within the three regions centered in North America, Europe, and Asia.[12] At the beginning of the 1980s, exports to and from members of the triad represented 9 percent of total world exports; a decade later the share had risen to 12 percent. All three pairs within the triad also increased their trade links.

Trade within the European, Asian, and North American regions, however, overshadowed trade among triad members. It both started from a much higher base and grew more rapidly. Exports within the three regions rose from 31 percent of total world exports in 1980 to 43 percent in 1992. Again, all three subgroups contributed to the increase, but European and Asian trade outpaced that in North America. To facilitate comparison of these shifts, the last column in Table 3.1 shows the average annual growth rates of exports in nominal dollar terms over the period. Triad trade increased by 8 percent, while intraregional trade rose by 9 percent. Among the regions, the fastest growing was Asia where intraregional trade grew by 13 percent. Trade within the European Union increased by 7 percent, while North America contributed with 8.5 percent growth.

Since all of these sets of trading partners increased their interactions faster than the growth of world trade as a whole, other countries and regions were clearly losing out. As Table 3.1 shows, one clear loser was the Middle East, which is a proxy here for third world oil exporters. (About two-thirds of OPEC exports came from Middle East members in the early 1980s.) Oil price declines meant that Middle Eastern exports to the rest of the world fell from 12 percent of world trade to less than 4 percent. Other linkages that declined in absolute terms were those of the former Soviet Union and Eastern Europe with the rest of the world, but trade between less developed

---

[12] Note that the European Union plays a double role: it is both a member of the triad and a region. Defining the "European Area" as the region would be a more symmetrical alternative.

Table 3.1. *International trade patterns, 1980–92 (billions of dollars)*

Territory	1980	1992	Annual average growth, 1980–92 (percent)
Triad	175	427	7.7
	(9.2)	(11.6)	
U.S.–Japan	53	145	8.7
	(2.8)	(3.9)	
U.S.–EU[a]	97	198	6.1
	(5.1)	(5.4)	
Japan–EU[a]	25	84	10.7
	(1.3)	(2.3)	
Intraregional	583	1,577	8.7
	(30.6)	(42.9)	
Intra-EU[b]	385	895	7.3
	(20.2)	(24.3)	
Intra-Asia[c]	96	411	13.0
	(5.0)	(11.2)	
North America[d]	102	271	8.5
	(5.4)	(7.4)	
Other	1,145	1,674	3.2
	(60.2)	(45.5)	
Middle East[e]	234	144	−4.0
	(12.3)	(3.9)	
Other Ind–Ind	201	445	6.8
	(10.6)	(12.1)	
Other LDC–LDC	79	117	3.3
	(4.2)	(3.2)	
Other Ind–LDC	476	859	5.0
	(25.0)	(23.4)	
USSR/Eastern Europe[e]	155	109	−2.9
	(8.1)	(3.0)	
World total	1,906	3,678	5.6
	(100.0)	(100.0)	

Note: Data are exports; figures in parentheses are percentages.
[a]Excludes intra-EU trade.
[b]EU in 1980 excludes Spain and Portugal.
[c]Japan, East Asia, Sotheast Asia, South Asia.
[d]United States, Canada, Mexico.
[e]To rest of world.
Sources: IMF, *Direction of Trade Statistics Yearbook, 1987, 1993;* UN, *World Economics Survey, 1994* (for USSR/Eastern Europe in 1980).

Table 3.2. *U.S., Japanese, and EU trade flows, 1980–92 (billions of dollars)*

To	From the United States		From Japan		From the EU	
	1980	1992	1980	1992	1980	1992
U.S.	—	—	31.9	96.7	38.4	92.3
			(25.7)	(28.4)	(5.6)	(6.4)
Japan	20.8	47.8	—	—	6.7	26.5
	(9.7)	(10.7)			(1.0)	(1.8)
EU	58.9	102.9	18.2	62.9	385.2	895.3
	(27.4)	(23.0)	(14.7)	(18.5)	(56.6)	(61.8)
Other industrial	45.7	111.1	9.0	23.8	72.6	161.8
nations	(21.2)	(24.8)	(7.3)	(7.0)	(10.7)	(11.2)
Asia	23.3	74.1	31.5	117.6	21.0	71.8
	(10.8)	(16.6)	(25.4)	(34.6)	(3.1)	(5.0)
Latin America	38.7	75.7	8.3	15.1	21.5	32.4
	(18.0)	(16.9)	(6.7)	(4.4)	(3.2)	(2.2)
Other LDCs	23.3	30.0	20.6	21.8	104.0	112.9
	(10.8)	(6.7)	(16.6)	(6.4)	(15.3)	(7.8)
USSR/Eastern	4.6	5.5	4.4	2.1	30.7	54.8
Europe	(2.1)	(1.1)	(3.6)	(0.6)	(4.5)	(3.8)
Total	215.3	447.1	123.9	340.0	680.1	1,447.8
	(100.0)	(100.0)	(100.0)	(100.0)	(100.0)	(100.0)

Note: Data are exports; figures in parentheses are percentages.
Source: IMF, *Direction of Trade Statistics Yearbook, 1987, 1993.*

countries (LDCs) and between LDCs and industrial nations fell in percentage terms.

Another way of looking at trade patterns is provided by Table 3.2, which shows the changing distribution of triad exports in their own terms rather than as a share of world trade. This table also permits us to examine possible links between triad countries and other regions, as well as among members of the triad and within their "own" regions. For the United States, the biggest increase came in trade with developing Asia; U.S. trade with other areas stagnated or fell during the decade. For Japan, trade rose with the United States, the European Union, and especially with developing Asia. The largest growth in EU trade was intraregional.

These trends in international commerce over the past decade provide some evidence with which to evaluate the contending hypotheses about the emerging international political economy. In general, Table 3.1 appears to support the regionalist hypothesis, especially for Asia. Trade in North America also began to pick up in anticipation of NAFTA, but when all of the Western Hemisphere was included and measured as a percentage of U.S. trade (Table 3.2), the share actually fell between 1980 and 1992. This was partly due to the debt crisis in Latin America, but also to a modified version of the Fishlow–Haggard hypothesis about the global role of the United States. While there was no increase in the share of U.S. trade with Europe, the United States did step up its trade with Asia, both Japan and developing Asia, and with non-EU industrial nations.

Although we can draw some tentative conclusions based on trade data, they are becoming increasingly difficult to interpret with the globalization of the international economy. Especially since the mid-1980s, with the exchange rate shifts coming out of the Plaza Accords and the announced acceleration of the Single European Market, foreign investment has undermined our ability to distinguish a North American product from one "made in Europe" from one originating in Asia. (For more discussion of globalization, see Chapter 4, this volume.)

This intermingling of products can come about in several ways. The most familiar is through direct foreign investment (DFI), whereby companies based in one country set up subsidiaries elsewhere to produce parts and/or finished goods. In the more traditional form of DFI, finished goods were sold in the host-country market or exported back to the home country. In addition, of course, they could be sold in third-country markets. In the earlier part of the postwar period, most DFI went from industrial to third world countries, but the pattern has shifted dramatically since the 1980s. Japanese and European firms have invested heavily in the United States, while U.S. and Japanese firms have increased their assets in Europe. The threat of protection was an important motive for these new trends, but the weakened dollar also played a role.

Table 3.3 displays data on direct foreign investment. It should be noted that such data are far less reliable and complete than trade data (which themselves have problems of coverage). Only the United States, Britain, and Germany provide good information on investment flows to and from their countries. Recently, however, the United Nations Conference on Trade and Development (UNCTAD) has begun publishing an annual *World In-*

Table 3.3. *International investment stocks, 1980–92 (billions of dollars)*

	1980	1988	1992	Average growth (percent) 1980–88	Average growth (percent) 1988–92
Triad	142	411	597	14.2	9.5
	(27.0)	(39.7)			
U.S. to Japan	6	18	27	14.1	10.6
	(1.2)	(1.7)			
Japan to U.S.	5	53	98	35.5	16.7
	(0.9)	(5.1)			
U.S. to EU	81	131	207	6.3	12.2
	(15.4)	(12.7)			
EU to U.S.	47	194	221	19.3	3.4
	(9.0)	(18.8)			
Japan to EU	3	13	35	22.3	28.1
	(0.5)	(1.3)			
EU to Japan	*a*	2	9	19.6	45.6
	(0.1)	(0.2)			
Intraregional	125	285	472	10.9	13.5
	(24.3)	(27.6)			
Intra-EU	50	160	273	15.6	14.3
	(9.7)	(15.5)			
Intra-Asia[b]	12	35	75	14.3	21.0
	(2.3)	(3.4)			
North America[c]	63	90	124	4.6	8.4
	(12.3)	(8.7)			
Other	257	338	na	3.5	na
	(49.0)	(32.7)			
Other inv. in triad	88	168	na	8.4	na
	(16.8)	(15.4)			
LDCs/EFTA/Oceania/etc.	169	170	na	0.0	na
	(32.2)	(17.3)			
World	524	1,034	na	8.9	na
	(100.0)	(100.0)			

Note: Data are exports; figures in parentheses are percentages.
*a*Less than $500,000.
*b*Japan, East Asia, Southeast Asia.
*c*United States, Canada, Mexico.
Sources: For 1980 and 1988: UNCTC, *World Investment Report, 1991* (for triad, intra-EU, and world total investment); UNCTC, *World Investment Directory, 1992: Asia and the Pacific* (for intra-Asia); Commerce Dept., *Survey of Current Business,* and Statistics Canada, *Canada's International Investment Position: Historical Statistics, 1926 to 1992* (for North America). For 1992: *Survey of Current Business* and author's estimates based on OECD, *International Direct Investment Statistics Yearbook, 1994.*

vestment Report; this report is an important step toward the broader collection of investment data and their standardization.[13]

Drawing on UNCTAD data, Table 3.3 indicates that 40 percent ($411 billion) of total DFI *stock* was located within the triad in 1988, up from 27 percent ($142 billion) in 1980. This represented an annual growth rate during the eight years of over 14 percent. Of that 40 percent, 24 percent was located in the United States, 14 percent in the European Union (excluding intra-EU investment), but only 2 percent in Japan. The largest absolute increases were EU investments in the United States, U.S. investments in the EU countries, and Japanese investments in the United States.

More disaggregated data in Table 3.4 enable us to examine the investment portfolios of triad members with respect to recipient regions. Concentrating on investment *flows* in the most recent period (1990–92), it can be seen that, for the United States, investment in the European Union dominates, with Latin America in a distant second position. The fastest-growing investment site, however, is the developing Asian region. The Japanese profile shows the United States as the preferred investment site, followed by the European Union; Asia ranks in third place. Finally, EU investment (represented here by Germany and the United Kingdom, the two largest EU foreign investors that together accounted for well over half of the EU total)[14] has been heavily concentrated in other EU countries.

If we compare the investment data with those on trade, it is clear that the latter underestimate the degree of economic linkage among the triad countries. Tables 3.3 and 3.4 provide strong support for the globalist hypothesis about the international political economy. Such a conclusion is further buttressed by processes that do not necessarily show up in DFI figures. One important complementary process involves so-called strategic alliances. Such alliances occur when firms (often from different countries) join forces to share costs for research and development, marketing, and/or production facilities. For example, several U.S. and Japanese auto firms have undertaken joint ventures, either globally or in specific plants. Many such ventures are currently under discussion in the airline and communications industries. Perhaps the most dramatic strategic alliance was that an-

---

[13] The OECD has also begun to publish a yearbook on investment data of member countries. See its *International Direct Investment Statistics Yearbook, 1994.*

[14] Ibid. During the 1981–90 decade, Britain and Germany together accounted for 57 percent of total EU outward investment (including intra-EU investment). The other major investor is France, which accounted for 18 percent of the EU total (calculated from p. 14).

Table 3.4. *Annual average U.S., Japanese, and EU investment flows, 1979–92 (millions of dollars)*

To	From the United States 1979–81	1990–92	From Japan[a] 1979–81	1990–92	From the EU[b] 1979–81	1990–92
U.S.	—	—	1,728	19,324	7,113	4,263
			(27.8)	(46.9)	(32.9)	(12.2)
Japan	435	652	—	—	202	376
	(2.5)	(2.4)			(0.9)	(1.1)
EU	8,090	9,825	548	9,579	5,109	19,428
	(46.5)	(35.8)	(8.8)	(23.3)	(23.7)	(55.4)
Asia	1,492	5,073	1,823	6,471	880	1,381
	(8.6)	(18.5)	(29.4)	(15.7)	(4.1)	(3.9)
Latin	3,035	5,177	607	776	1,295	2,007
America[c]	(17.5)	(18.8)	(9.8)	(1.9)	(6.0)	(5.7)
Africa[d]	306	−482	58	22	671	989
	(1.8)	(−1.8)	(0.9)	(0.1)	(3.1)	(2.8)
Other	4,032	7,223	1,443	5,011	6,330	6,594
	(23.2)	(26.3)	(23.3)	(12.2)	(29.3)	(18.8)
Total	17,391	27,468	6,206	41,183	21,601	35,037
	(100.0)	(100.0)	(100.0)	(100.0)	(100.0)	(100.0)

Note: Figures in parentheses are percentages.
[a]Intentions to invest as reported to Ministry of Finance.
[b]Germany and United Kingdom only.
[c]Excluding Caribbean financial centers (and Japanese shipping investment in Panama).
[d]Excluding Japanese shipping investment in Liberia.
Sources: For 1979–81: Commerce Dept., *Survey of Current Business,* various issues (for United States); Finance Ministry, *Annual Report, International Finance Bureau,* various issues (for Japan); Government Statistical Service, *Overseas Transactions,* various issues (for United Kingdom); Deutsche Bundesbank, *Statistische Beihefte zu den Monatsberichten der Deutschen Bundesbank. Reihe 3, Zahlungsbilanzstatistik,* various issues (for Germany). For 1990–92: OECD, *International Direct Investment Statistics Yearbook, 1994.*

nounced – but apparently never consummated – between Mitsubishi and Daimler Benz.[15]

Despite the dynamism portrayed in the data on direct investment among triad members, regionalism also continues unabated. Indeed, regional activity seems to have equalled or outpaced triad investment in two of the regional groupings discussed earlier. According to Table 3.3, total intraregional investment stock grew from $125 billion in 1980 to $285 billion in 1988, an average increase of 11 percent; it grew a further 13.5 percent in average rate to reach $472 billion in 1992. The largest increase was within the European Union (nearly 16 percent growth per year in 1980–88), but intra-Asian investment proceeded at only a slightly slower pace (average growth of more than 14 percent). In the more recent period, the latter overtook the former. Intra–North American investment did not keep up with its counterparts in the 1980–88 period, but it also began to increase more rapidly at the end of the decade.

The most advanced of the three regions is clearly Europe, where a movement toward integration has been underway – in fits and starts – since the 1950s. Trade flows grew as tariff and other barriers were lowered. In addition, intra-EU investment stock more than quintupled between 1980 and 1992, rising from $50 to $273 billion. Firms invested in neighboring countries to position themselves for the single market; investors from France, the Netherlands, and the United Kingdom were particularly active in the 1980s.[16] At the same time, U.S. and especially Japanese investment in Europe also rose, as firms from those countries tried to avoid being shut out of the huge European market.

Europe's integration history is not only longer than that of any other region, but it is also deeper. Accompanied by supranational institution building and enforced by an independent bureaucracy, European integration extended to political and social questions as well as economic relations. For example, political agreement was reached on preferential treatment for former European colonies in trade and aid under the Lomé Conventions.[17]

---

[15] The literature on "strategic alliances" is a growing one. Christopher Freeman, "Networks of Innovators," *Research Policy* 20, 5 (1991), 499–514, includes a useful bibliography.

[16] OECD, *International Direct Investment Statistics Yearbook, 1994*, various tables.

[17] On the Lomé Conventions, see John Ravenhill, *Collective Clientelism: The Lomé Conventions and North–South Relations* (New York: Columbia University Press, 1985). A brief update can be found in John Ravenhill, "Africa and Europe: The Dilution of a 'Special Relationship,'" in John W. Harbeson and Donald Rothchild (eds.), *Africa in World Politics* (Boulder, Colo.: Westview, 1991), pp. 179–201.

Of much greater import, however, are agreements on a so-called European Economic Area, which are being negotiated with other European nations, West and East, that want to join the European Union.[18] The situation in the Asian region is different. While Japan was investing rapidly in Europe and the United States, very little investment was flowing into Japan itself. Moreover, Western investment (both U.S. and European) grew very slowly in East and Southeast Asia during the 1980s. Thus, most of the rapidly rising Asian investment came from within the region. Japanese investment stock in Asia grew by 21 percent annually between 1980 and 1988, from $7 to $20 billion.[19] For some of Asia's developing countries, however, investments from the Asian newly industrialized countries (NICs) (South Korea, Taiwan, Hong Kong, and Singapore) were at least as important. For the four NICs themselves, plus the four major ASEAN countries (Indonesia, Malaysia, the Philippines, and Thailand), direct investment stock from developing Asia rose from $5 billion in 1980 to $15 billion in 1988, an annual increase of 25 percent.[20]

Throughout Asia in the 1980s, and especially after the currency realignments in 1985, de facto economic integration was occurring without any institutional framework. While painful memories of the Japanese occupation of East Asia during World War II made its neighbors reluctant to see Japan reestablish a prominent political role in the region, they generally welcomed its money. Japanese firms, and later those from the NICs, moved whole industries to other locations in Asia to get access to cheaper labor and resources such as energy. Many of the products were imported back into the home countries, but they were also sold in Asia's burgeoning domestic markets. The process came to be known as the "flying geese formation," with Japan as lead goose. Most recently the process has expanded into Indochina. (See Chapters 7 and 8, this volume, for more detailed discussion.)

As regional economies flourished in Europe and Asia, some proposals were also floated in the Western Hemisphere. The U.S.–Canada Free Trade

---

[18] See Steve Weber, "EC Conditionality," in Laurence Whitehead (ed.), *Economic and Political Liberalization in Latin America and Eastern Europe* (Oxford University Press, forthcoming).

[19] These data are based on information from Asian recipient nations as reported in United Nations Centre on Transnational Corporations, *World Investment Directory, 1992: Asia and the Pacific.* Japanese data, which are declarations of intention to invest, show much higher figures.

[20] Ibid. The increase has continued, but no systematic data are available.

Agreement went into effect in 1989, and the Mexican government asked to join and expand the integration scheme into a North American agreement. Following a contentious approval process, NAFTA came into being on January 1, 1994. Great enthusiasm about joining NAFTA has also been shown by other Latin American countries, in contrast to their previously ambivalent attitude toward the United States. This reaction reflects not only the new economic policies underway in Latin America, but also the increased trade dependence on the United States that had developed during the 1980s.[21]

U.S. trade and investment patterns, however, were more mixed. While Latin America languished during the "lost decade" of the 1980s, U.S. trade (and later investment) flowed increasingly toward Asia. Political logic mixed with economic, as the Asians tried to keep the United States involved as a counterpoint to Japan. For their part, U.S. firms clearly did not want to be shut out of the world's fastest growing economic zone. Thus, as Latin America became *more* reliant on trade with the United States, the United States traded *less* with Latin America (and more with Asia).[22] The same was true with investment during the 1980s. It is only in the most recent period that U.S. investment has begun to surge into Latin America again. Much of it is to Mexico; U.S. DFI in Mexico increased by nearly 25 percent per year in the 1988–92 period.[23] As discussed in Chapter 5, however, most of the new investment is volatile short-term flows, including billions of dollars going into Latin American stock markets.

Qualitative tests: relations in international organizations

The preceding section contains a mixed message on the relative strength of globalist versus regionalist tendencies. The rapid increase of investment within the triad, despite the apparently thin trade linkages, implies that the economies are becoming increasingly intermingled. At the same time, investment and trade are growing even more quickly within the three regions.

---

[21] Useful analyses of Latin American views on a possible Western Hemisphere Free Trade Area are contained in Sylvia Saborio (ed.), *The Premise and the Promise: Free Trade in the Americas* (Washington, D.C.: Overseas Development Council, 1992).

[22] Roberto Bouzas, "U.S.–Latin American Trade Relations: Issues in the 1980s and Prospects for the 1990s," in Jonathan Hartlyn et al. (eds.), *The United States and Latin America in the 1990s* (Chapel Hill: University of North Carolina Press, 1993), pp. 152–80.

[23] These data are from Department of Commerce, *Survey of Current Business,* August issues (on U.S. foreign investment). Mexican investment in the United States is also growing.

The data are fairly clear for Europe and Asia; the upsurge of U.S. investment in the Western Hemisphere is too recent to be captured fully by
available statistics. This section tries to push the analysis a bit further by
examining political relationships in two multilateral fora – GATT and the
World Bank. In this way, it should be possible to reach a better understanding of conflicts and possibilities for their resolution among triad countries.

The Uruguay Round of GATT, which began in September 1986, was
supposed to have been completed in December 1990. The aims of the round
were very ambitious: to go beyond the traditional focus on lowering barriers
to trade in manufactures and move into the more politically sensitive areas
of agriculture, services, and intellectual property. The chief protagonists
among the industrial countries were the United States and the European
Community (now the European Union). Despite its overwhelming interest
in the international trading system, Japan generally adopted a low profile.[24]
The main bone of contention was agricultural price supports, an issue that
had been sidestepped since it was first introduced in the GATT negotiations
at the start of the Kennedy Round in 1963.

The European Community, via its Common Agricultural Policy (CAP),
heavily subsidizes its small farm population. These subsidies, in turn, have
produced large agricultural surpluses and made it possible for Europeans to
undersell their competitors. Although the United States also provides farm
subsidies, U.S. farmers believe they have lost markets to the Europeans. In
fact, EC food exports rose from 8.3 to 18.3 percent of the world total
between 1976 and 1981, when the new GATT round began to be considered; the U.S. share remained fairly constant at about 18 percent.[25] Other
agricultural exporters, who joined forces as the "Cairns Group" in preparation for the round, have an even stronger case since they generally do not
provide subsidies.

The United States and the Cairns Group won a victory as the round
began, when an ambitious agricultural liberalization goal was adopted.
Despite progress on many other issues, however, the midterm review meeting in Montreal in 1988 broke down over agriculture. The radical U.S.
position – a timetable for abolishing all farm subsidies, later trimmed back
to 75 percent of internal supports and 90 percent of export subsidies – was

---

[24] The United States and Japan, of course, also had extensive disagreements over trade, but the
normal approach was to engage in bilateral negotiations rather than use GATT procedures.
[25] Thomas R. Graham, "Global Trade: War and Peace," *Foreign Policy* 50 (Spring 1983),
124–30, at 130.

unacceptable to Europe. The 15 percent cut in supports offered by the European Community at the Houston Summit in July 1990 was not enough to bring the round to the scheduled conclusion by the end of the year. Negotiations eventually resumed, but another three years of contentious debate were required to reach an agreement.

For our purposes, it is important to analyze the reasons why the Uruguay Round was especially difficult.[26] One obvious factor is that the end of the cold war eliminated the previously perceived necessity to maintain unity among the major capitalist powers. Not only was the Soviet "menace" eliminated during the course of the negotiations, but Russia is actually petitioning to become a member of GATT. Moreover, the cessation of cold war hostilities undermined U.S. leadership, making decision making more difficult than in earlier rounds.

A closely related reason is that both the European Community and, increasingly, the United States saw an alternative to multilateralism in the form of regionalization. The initiation of the Uruguay Round came shortly after the European Community announced the accelerated drive toward the Single European Market for January 1, 1993. And, indeed, the European stand on price supports was primarily due to the effort to maintain unity among the principal EC members. While Britain and Germany did not want to jeopardize the round over the price support issue, they felt obliged to support France since giving in to U.S. demands threatened the CAP, a basic element of the European Community itself.

Once it became clear that its EC partners were going to support France, the United States – either by coincidence or design – began to look to its own neighbors as a partial alternative to pushing for completion of the GATT round. As discussed earlier, the U.S.–Canada Free Trade Agreement went into effect in 1989; negotiations to expand the agreement to include Mexico began in 1990; and gestures about joining were made soon after to the rest of Latin America. The surprisingly enthusiastic response of the Latins can be attributed to many factors, but one was probably the new GATT-based alliance between the United States and the Cairns Group. The latter included a number of key Latin American agricultural exporters: Argentina, Brazil, Chile, Colombia, and Uruguay. Whereas previous GATT

---

[26] This is not to imply that other negotiations have been easy. The Tokyo Round, for example, began in 1973 and was to last two years; it was finally completed in 1979. See *Economist,* December 8, 1990.

negotiations had set the third world against the industrial countries, the Uruguay Round saw third world unity disintegrate and new alliances form. If GATT focused attention on differences between the United States and Europe, recent events in the international financial institutions (IFIs) have begun to pit Japan against the United States – insofar as World Bank and IMF policies can accurately be characterized as reflecting the preferences of the United States as the chief shareholder. The main issue is differences of opinion on appropriate development strategies for third world countries.[27] Until recently, such disagreements have been hard to discern since the Japanese have been very reluctant to criticize the United States. Indeed, one found the ironic situation of Japan underwriting policies in developing countries that were at odds with those that had proved so successful in Japan itself. This happened, in large part, because Japan has tried to coordinate its activities closely with the IFIs, and much of its lending has been carried out through cofinancing with them.

Recently, however, the Japanese have become more critical of IFI conditionality. One of the first public manifestations was an October 1991 document prepared by the Overseas Economic Cooperation Fund (OECF), Japan's principal aid agency,[28] and its main ideas were backed up by statements to the press by high-level Japanese officials. As one said: "I think Japan has traditionally borne financial burdens in various forms and was in a position only to supply funds. . . . We are [now] saying, 'We should contribute intellectually too.'"[29]

Japan's initiatives have juxtaposed its own model of capitalism to that of the United States and the IFIs. The latter was characterized in the World Bank's *World Development Report, 1991,* which advocated a "market-friendly approach" to development. Recommendations included: a stable macroeconomic foundation (prudent fiscal and monetary policy); a climate favoring private enterprise (deregulation, protection of property rights, competition, "getting the prices right"); integration with the global econ-

---

[27] While the Japanese have chosen to take a stand on development strategy issues within the World Bank, the European Union has taken a different path. It has concentrated its efforts on a new organization, the European Bank for Reconstruction and Development (EBRD), established to aid the former Soviet and East European countries. Insofar as the Europeans have a distinctive development philosophy, it is most likely to be seen in this context. See Weber, "EC Conditionality."

[28] OECF, "Issues Related to the World Bank's Approach to Structural Adjustment: Proposal from a Major Partner," OECF Occasional Paper No. 1, October 1991.

[29] *Washington Post,* April 27, 1992.

omy (openness to trade and foreign investment); and investing in people (population control, concentration of public-sector spending on education and health, partnership with the private sector in providing social services). The Japanese critique does not deny the usefulness of markets or an open economy. It does, however, suggest that the speed of marketization and liberalization could cause major problems. The OECF document made four main criticisms of the World Bank approach to structural adjustment. First, it argued that simply introducing market mechanisms and eliminating restrictions on the private sector would not necessarily lead to increased investment. Additional measures, such as preferential tax treatment and lending by public-sector development banks, might be necessary. Second, the OECF said that "excessive reliance" on trade liberalization is risky, and overly hasty liberalization could have heavy costs. Third, with respect to the financial sector, the OECF document cautioned about assuming that underdeveloped financial institutions would necessarily allocate resources efficiently. When the market does not function properly, the Japanese have advocated the use of "two-step loans" (low-cost loans from a foreign source to the government of a developing country, which on-lends to its own firms, passing on some or all of the subsidy). Fourth, the query is raised as to whether privatization "is always the solution for improving efficiency of the public sector."

The World Bank's April 1992 response to the OECF document was largely negative. Claiming that the common element behind all of the Japanese criticisms was the question, "To what extent should the government provide a guiding hand to industrial development?" it went on to provide the following answer: "For most developing countries, relying on imperfect markets – rather than imperfect governments – has the greater chance for promoting growth."[30]

In what is potentially a more far-reaching initiative, the Japanese government urged on the World Bank, and jointly financed, a massive study on the "East Asian Miracle." The multivolume project undertook to study the particular characteristics that have defined the successful development strategy followed by Japan and seven other Asian countries during the postwar period. The World Bank study is somewhat more favorable to the Asian model than the previously cited comments. It agrees that the eight

---

[30] Memo from Lawrence Summers, Chief Economist, World Bank, to Kiyoshi Kodera, Alternate Executive Director, April 1992.

Asian countries examined have had substantially higher growth over an extensive period than virtually any other countries, but there has been disagreement on the reasons. The World Bank argued for the primary role of "fundamental" policies (macroeconomic stability, investment in human capital, secure financial systems, and openness to foreign technology), while the Japanese have continued to put more emphasis on the role of government and industrial policy.[31]

Our analysis of trade and investment flows and our two case studies concerning GATT and the World Bank confirm that the post–cold war international system has opened space for conflict, as well as intensified the links between the leading capitalist nations. There are simultaneous tendencies toward regionalism and unity, and there is increased rivalry and linkage at the same time. Struggles among the United States, Europe, and Japan over trade policy, as well as between the United States and Japan over development policy, highlight a new willingness of Japan and Europe to challenge the United States. Recent years have witnessed disagreement in the military-security realm as well, especially in the former Yugoslavia. One may add to this the high potential for conflict in Central and Eastern Europe, which may be about to develop into a German zone of influence, and Russia, where the Japanese have refused to commit major resources because of the Kurile Island dispute. Still, internationalist groups within triad countries have held their ground, and continuing efforts are being made to patch up quarrels and find ways to compromise when difficulties arise. In the following section, we try to relate this complex picture to the differences among the internal characteristics of the three conflicting, as well as cooperating, models of capitalist political economy.

Models of capitalism: between conflict and cooperation

The analytical challenge, we suggest, is to understand the dynamics of nonhegemonic interdependence among three capitalist centers with their own heterogeneous socioeconomic characteristics. Nonhegemonic interdependence entails simultaneous conflict as well as cooperation in global economic relations, and probably steady oscillation between the two.

---

[31] World Bank, *The East Asian Miracle: Economic Growth and Public Policy* (Washington, D.C.: World Bank, 1993). Perhaps the most important example of the alternative Japanese view is Eisuke Sakakibara, *Beyond Capitalism: The Japanese Model of Market Economics* (Latham, Md.: University Press of America, 1993). See also Toru Yanagihara, "Anything New in the 'Miracle' Report? Yes and No," *World Development* 22, 4 (April 1994), 663–70.

Differences in internal structures constitute sources of competitive advantage and disadvantage in the international economy. These structural differences can also be used as instruments of political protection from the social dislocations caused by international and domestic markets, in effect turning domestic characteristics into a subject of international politics and, potentially, conflict.

As has been said, with the end of the cold war, advanced capitalism is increasingly viewed, not as one economic system, but as a family of sub-systems of considerable diversity.[32] Three types of capitalism are commonly distinguished, represented by the three leading centers of economic activity: the (Anglo-)American, the continental-Western European, and the Japanese versions. To the extent that the United States, the European Union, and Japan are regarded as potential hegemons of regional blocs, it is assumed that the domestic structures of other, geographically proximate bloc members will be more or less similar to those of the respective hegemonic powers. Still, each bloc is itself internally heterogeneous – although arguably less so than the global system – and thus replicates internally some of the problems of the "management of diversity" that exist between blocs. This applies in particular to Western Europe, but there are also important differences among the United States, Canada, and Mexico, which contributed to the tensions over NAFTA, and among the countries regarded as following an East Asian extension of the Japanese model.

The growing interest in capitalist diversity is a response to differences in national economic performance in the 1970s and 1980s, which appeared hard to explain in strictly economic terms. Since Britain and the United States lagged in performance, most of the growing literature on the subject is aimed at identifying features of the socioeconomic systems of their main competitors, Germany and Japan, which could account for their economic ascendancy and the relative decline of Anglo-American capitalism.[33] Theo-

---

[32] In addition to authors referred to earlier in this chapter (Thurow and Garten), see Michel Albert, *Capitalisme contre capitalisme* (Paris: Seuil, 1991); Ronald Dore, "Japanese Capitalism, Anglo-Saxon Capitalism: How Will the Darwinian Contest Turn Out?" Occasional Paper No. 4, Centre for Economic Performance, London School of Economics, 1992; and Jeffrey Hart, *Rival Capitalisms: International Competitiveness in the United States, Japan, and Western Europe* (Ithaca, N.Y.: Cornell University Press, 1992).

[33] On declining U.S. competitiveness, see, e.g., Michael L. Dertouzos, R. K. Lester, and R. M. Solow, *Made in America: Regaining the Protective Edge* (Cambridge, Mass.: MIT Press, 1989); Michael E. Porter, *The Competitive Advantage of Nations* (New York: Free Press, 1990); and Stephen Cohen and John Zysman, *Manufacturing Matters: The Myth of the Post-Industrial Economy* (New York: Basic, 1987).

ries of capitalist diversity focus on differences among leading market economies in both institutional structures and cultural orientations – from government industrial policies to "work ethic" and "trust" – which may explain why some countries fared better than others in the increasingly dynamic and competitive technological and economic environment of the period. We will briefly summarize the three models as they are typically portrayed and then explore how the differences among them may interact with the external relations among the three interdependent capitalist blocs.

Japanese capitalism has been described as significantly different from received Anglo-American models of capitalist economy, especially with respect to the way markets – for labor, capital, and final products – are embedded in social and political institutions and relations. In one version of the model, the state bureaucracy plays the central role in the governance of Japanese capitalism, suspending or deploying competitive markets in the service of national economic and political objectives.[34] In other accounts, it is a highly cohesive and disciplined civil society, structured by strong premodern institutions and orientations, which is easy to mobilize for collective action and protects Japanese capitalism from the dysfunctions of possessive individualism, excessive competition, and noncooperative, particularistic rationality.[35]

Either way, the result is described as a capitalist economy functioning on the basis of robust long-term commitments of resources and loyalties and supported by densely integrated primary social structures, which provide large firms with lasting commitments to work, as well as high legitimacy for authority and hierarchy. Moreover, it appears that the Japanese state or Japanese society, or both, have a capacity to contain inequality, thereby protecting social cohesion, as well as effectively suppress disobedience and discontent – a puzzling combination that leads Western observers alternatively to describe the Japanese system as based on both coercion and consensus.

The Anglo-American model, by comparison, expects high economic performance from socially and politically unregulated market transactions and

---

[34] Chalmers Johnson, *MITI and the Japanese Miracle: The Growth of Japanese Industrial Policy, 1925–1975* (Stanford, Calif.: Stanford University Press, 1982).

[35] See Ronald Dore, *Taking Japan Seriously: A Confuscian Perspective on Leading Economic Issues* (Stanford, Calif.: Stanford University Press, 1987), and David Friedman, *The Misunderstood Miracle: Industrial Development and Political Change in Japan* (Ithaca, N.Y.: Cornell University Press, 1988).

from unconstrained choices of rational, self-seeking individuals unencumbered by preeconomic social ties. Its basic operating principles are those of nineteenth-century laissez-faire liberalism and neoclassical economics, with their emphasis on individual liberty and the formal rationality of monadic actors pursuing exogenous preferences.[36]

The key to productivity and competitiveness in the Anglo-American model is "flexibility": the capacity of private economic actors to change their commitments rapidly as external conditions shift, to invest and divest as they see fit, and to enter and exit at their discretion. Economic institutions must be designed to facilitate this; for example, market access must be easy, labor markets must be open, and capital markets must be efficient. Also, for private individuals to be able to pursue their perceived interests independently, and for markets to be allocatively efficient, state intervention must be limited to guaranteeing the essential conditions of free markets; commitments of resources must be reversible in the short term; and organizational or social loyalties must not interfere with individuals' pursuit of market advantage. While in the Japanese model the emphasis is on commitment, the Anglo-American system prefers flexibility.[37]

It is more difficult to sketch out a Western European type of capitalism. In part, this is because Europe is internally much more heterogeneous than the United States or Japan. Note that the European Union includes Britain, which is in many respects more similar to the United States than to continental Europe. It also includes Greece and Portugal, which are, for all practical purposes, developing countries. Even France and Germany, the two major EU powers, are very different political economies. Internal diversity, for example, in the regulation of labor markets or in national institutions of monetary policy making, is at the root of the present frictions holding up the further integration of the European Union. In fact, those who refer to a Western European model of capitalism often mean the largest and

---

[36] Neoclassical theorists are often accused of having generalized the defining properties of one type of capitalist economy, turning them into universally applicable prescriptions. In particular, markets are conceived in this model not as expedient sociopolitical constructs, but as a state of nature preceding all other social institutions, as the natural right of individuals inherently disposed to "truck and barter." The *locus classicus* for a critical review is Karl Polanyi, "The Economy as Instituted Process," in G. Dalton (ed.), *Primitive, Archaic, and Modern Economies: Essays of Karl Polanyi* (Boston: Beacon, 1968), pp. 139–74.

[37] This is the conceptual core of Ronald Dore and Wolfgang Streeck's ongoing project, "Varieties of Capitalism: Economic Institutions in the United States, United Kingdom, Japan, and Germany."

most powerful European country, Germany, somehow making the problematic assumption that its socioeconomic institutions will eventually spread to all of Western Europe through the European Union or other channels.

Like Japan, the "European" model is typically described as sustained by strong social controls and commitments that favor long-term orientations and suppress preferences for short-term liquidity.[38] But in Europe, such "rigidity" is sustained, not primarily by cultural norms of discipline and obedience, but in large part by politically constructed and democratically legitimated public institutions, which serve as substitutes for traditional loyalties and inherited primary group integration. To this extent, the European model is not halfway between the United States and Japan, but represents a separate "social democratic" type of advanced capitalism in its own right.

In particular, "trust," long-term cooperation, and acceptance of collective objectives in the European model are based on social, industrial, and political citizenship rights. Together, these constitute a highly developed welfare state securing a high floor of provision for each citizen, as well as institutionalized rights of individuals and organized groups to participation and voice in the polity and at the workplace, making exit less necessary for expressing discontent. The traditional acceptance of authority and cultural identification of large corporate organizations with village or family-like communities, as prevail in Japan, are replaced with politically negotiated social compacts in a "bargained economy." Institutional arrangements that impose and enforce a high floor of social standards on the economy both require and, ideally, give rise to a high-wage economy that relies on developed human capital and professional, participatory work motivations for a production pattern geared toward quality-competitive markets for diversified goods and services.[39]

The belief that there may be inherent performance differences among the Anglo-American free-market, Japanese socially integrated, and European politically bargained models of capitalism reflects the catching up of Germany and Japan with the United States in the 1970s and 1980s, the associ-

---

[38] Many authors, including Thurow and Albert, find similarities between the Japanese and the European, or German, models of advanced capitalism, contrasting both Japan and continental Western Europe (Albert's "Rhenish" version of capitalism) with the United States and, to some extent, Britain.

[39] See Peter J. Katzenstein (ed.), *Industry and Politics in West Germany: Towards the Third Republic* (Ithaca, N.Y.: Cornell University Press, 1989).

ated long-term decline in the value of the dollar, persistent trade imbalances, and the failure of the U.S. manufacturing sector to upgrade its products and restructure its production to take advantage of new flexible technologies and more differentiated global markets. While it is difficult to relate divergent performance to specific institutional features of the three models, at the center of the debate is the observation that both the Japanese and the continental-Western European economies display various kinds of social and institutional rigidities, that is, arrangements that, in one way or other, contain, condition, or control the operation of free markets.

While in the received wisdom of neoclassical economic theory and Anglo-American capitalist practice these rigidities should obstruct competitive performance, declining U.S. competitiveness gave rise to the suspicion that they may in fact be essential for it. Correspondingly, attention began to focus on the possible price in economic efficiency of what was increasingly seen as excessive flexibility, mobility, and individual rationality in Anglo-American free-market capitalism. Indeed, as close investigation of both Japanese and German production systems found them to be highly flexible on a wide range of crucial dimensions (such as product turnover or worker redeployment), discussions of the economic consequences of the institutional differences among the three models of capitalism increasingly centered on the question of which society provides its economy with the most productive combination of rigidities and flexibilities.[40] Exactly which institutions are needed to defend economic efficiency against the detrimental effects of excessive market flexibility is not entirely clear; candidates include the Asian family, the MITI bureaucracy in Japan, workplace training, German codetermination, and many others.[41]

The claim that socially supported "flexible rigidities" are essential for good economic performance is not uncontested. Defenders of the Anglo-American model argue that institutional rigidities give rise to competitive advantage only insofar as they grant unfair privileges to some market participants at the expense of others and of overall allocative efficiency.[42] Examples include Japanese capital markets and corporate governance,

[40] Ronald Dore, *Flexible Rigidities: Industrial Policy and Structural Adjustment in the Japanese Economy, 1970–80* (Stanford, Calif.: Stanford University Press, 1986).
[41] Lowell Turner, *Democracy at Work: Changing World Markets and the Future of Labor Unions* (Ithaca, N.Y.: Cornell University Press, 1991).
[42] See, e.g., Dennis J. Encarnation, *Rivals beyond Trade: America versus Japan in Global Competition* (Ithaca, N.Y.: Cornell University Press, 1992).

which make it almost impossible for outside investors to acquire control over a Japanese company, or the European Charter of Fundamental Social Rights for Workers, which is suspected by U.S. observers as laying the foundation for protectionist trade policies to defend high European labor standards. It is at this point that the debate over the comparative advantage of different institutional variants of capitalism intersects with the discussion of the maintenance of cooperative external relations among capitalist systems.

As yet, the nature of nonhegemonic interdependence among different models of capitalism, and the questions it poses for global economic coordination and governance, are not well understood. To the extent that differences in internal characteristics give rise to divergent economic performance, trade and monetary imbalances among the three models can be assumed to be endemic, resulting among other things in periodic monetary crises and recurrent pressures for realignment of currencies. As exchange rate adjustments redistribute competitive advantage, they are often difficult to accomplish cooperatively and may be undertaken unilaterally with national or bloc "sovereignty" over monetary matters deployed as a weapon in international economic rivalry.

In particular, regional trading blocs representing different versions of advanced capitalism will seek refuge in coordination within blocs if coordination between blocs is not possible, or is possible only on terms that are deemed, nationally or internationally, unacceptable. In this sense, blocs that are relatively homogeneous internally represent partial solutions to global coordination problems, internalizing some of the externalities that are created by an internationalized economy, while leaving others to be negotiated among a reduced number of larger and more powerful entities.[43]

Just as they are moving between conflict and cooperation, heterogeneous societies under global interdependence are exposed to simultaneous pressures for divergence and convergence.[44] For example, international free trade places a variety of pressures on interdependent domestic regimes to

---

[43] An example is the European Monetary System, which was devised by France and West Germany in the late 1970s as a protection against the vagaries of the dollar and the use by the U.S. government of the dollar exchange rate in the service of U.S. domestic and international policy objectives.

[44] J. Rogers Hollingsworth and Wolfgang Streeck, "Countries and Sectors: Concluding Remarks on Performance, Convergence and Competitiveness," in J. Rogers Hollingsworth, Philippe C. Schmitter, and Wolfgang Streeck (eds.), *Governing Capitalist Economies* (New York: Oxford University Press, 1993), pp. 270–300.

become more similar to each other, while it also mobilizes powerful domestic constituencies in defense of national institutions as sources of competitive advantage or political protection. Less successful systems that cannot escape from free trade find themselves searching for ways to improve their competitiveness, above all by the assimilation of international "best practice." Today, this mode of adjustment is facilitated by the rapid global diffusion of information and DFI in "transplants," which makes superior production systems easily observable in lagging recipient countries.

Still, there seem to be narrow limits to convergence as a response to declining competitive position. To the extent that superior economic practices are rooted in their home country's social institutions and cultural values, recipient countries may be unable to adapt them in other than a marginal way. For example, even if MITI-style industrial policy was undeniably a source of international competitive advantage, it is hard to see how the U.S. Department of Commerce could ever become a U.S. MITI. Similarly, while German vocational training may have enabled German manufacturing to master successfully the restructuring of the past two decades, it cannot easily be grafted onto U.S. social structure and culture. And, even where international best practice is not incompatible with a declining country's social fabric or cultural identity, its introduction may be opposed by strong interest groups that would be negatively affected by it. If their resistance cannot be broken, convergence will not occur, regardless of the resulting competitive disadvantage.

A country that is unable to converge toward a superior model may try to employ political or military power to make the latter converge on itself, eliminating international imbalances in performance by imposing its own – less competitive – practices on its competitor. An example of this would be the Structural Impediments Initiative, initiated by the Bush administration in an attempt to make possible continued free trade with Japan. Threatening loss of access to its domestic market, the United States tried to convince Japan to help reduce the U.S. trade deficit by making major changes in its domestic economic institutions, including an expansion of consumer credit to lower the national savings rate, a greater role for stock markets, and more reliance in industrial procurement on spot markets as opposed to long-term contracting among related firms. Refusing to give up what they, and many others, regarded as sources of competitive advantage, the Japanese suggested seeking convergence on best rather than second-best practice, urging the United States to increase its savings and investment rate, improve its educational system, and train its workers better. Little came of the initiative, and it is hard to see how it could. Disagreement among the parties is fundamental: what from the perspective of one model is superior economic practice, an exclusively domestic concern, is restraint of trade and protectionism for the other, in breach of international codes of good conduct.

Just as little, if not less, is to be expected from a third possible mode of convergence: the construction of an international regime in which system competition would be embedded and partially suspended, prohibiting participants in free trade from seeking advantage by undercutting a set of common social standards. Such a regime existed by and large in the postwar world of globally organized capitalism, in which central aspects of domestic labor regimes were taken out of international competition, and labor-inclusive industrial relations systems, with extensive social policies, free collective bargaining, and political responsibility for the maintenance of full employment were de facto conditions of admission to international free trade.[45]

Today such restraints on regime competition at the expense of social protection of workers have mostly disappeared. Defection from the joint standards of the postwar period began with the nonadversarial reorganization of the Japanese industrial relations system in the early 1960s, and continued with the deunionization of the U.S. economy in the 1970s and 1980s and the final abandonment of the New Deal in the past decade, when income inequality rose dramatically and real incomes of about half of the workforce declined. Being the last holdout of postwar labor-inclusive industrial pluralism and adversarialism, Western Europe now is faced with the question of how it can sustain its social democratic domestic arrangements and still compete with Japan and the United States, where social expenditures are low and working time is longer. This question was behind the "Eurosclerosis" debate in the early 1980s. It is also in the background of present, not very successful, attempts in the European Union to attach a labor-inclusive "social dimension" to the internal market – an effort that, as

---

[45] It is important to remember that the social democratic labor–capital settlement, which lasted for the first two decades after the war, was enforced by the United States as the hegemonic power of the capitalist world, not least to ensure that the burdens the New Deal had imposed on its domestic economy would have to be carried by its competitors as well. Another intention was to stabilize parliamentary democracy throughout the Western world against both communist and fascist alternatives and as a condition of political and military cohesion under U.S. leadership.

has been mentioned, U.S. observers see as a first step toward trade protectionism.[46]

The obstacles to convergence being what they are, continued diversity and conflict among the three variants of capitalism are highly likely. At the same time, each system's stake in continuing exchange and cooperation will probably remain high, ensuring that conflict will be accompanied by and embedded in efforts at cooperation. In special cases, competitive pressures may elicit constructive domestic responses that upgrade competitiveness without upsetting domestic balances and provide social protection through superior productive performance – as in Germany and, to some extent, in Japan during the 1970s and 1980s. But inevitably this will lead to calls from less lucky competitors for changes either in the internal structures of successful systems, or in the international arrangements under which they were successful. Pacts between systems to manage competition cooperatively will be tried at times, but given profound institutional divergence and widely different views of what is a legitimate subject of international politics and what belongs to a sovereign country's domestic affairs, there will always be strong temptations to defect in the pursuit of unilateral advantage. Rather than pursuing this subject further here, we will now turn to an exploration of how the specific mix of conflict and cooperation that results from the differences among the three leading models of capitalism reflects on the developing world.

Implications for third world development

Three initial questions arise with respect to the relevance of the differences among the three central capitalist models for economic development on the periphery: (1) To what extent can the several models of capitalism be exported to other countries? (2) Do the triad members, in their struggle for influence in the developing world, want or have to export their versions of capitalism to "client countries" in order to ensure access and control for themselves? (3) Do the models differ in their capacity to help countries develop economically?

On the surface, the Anglo-American model would appear easy to export, given that all it seems to require is the destruction of institutions and

---

[46] Wolfgang Streeck, "National Diversity, Regime Competition and Institutional Deadlock: Problems in a European Industrial Relations System," *Journal of Public Policy* 12, 4 (1993), 301–30.

traditions that prevent the emergence of "free" markets. As the Central and Eastern European experience is beginning to show, however, even free markets are not a "state of nature," as assumed in economic theory, but depend on complicated legal and social conditions. Market creation requires institution building of an extent that comes unexpected to free-market enthusiasts informed by standard economics. For example, the development of an efficient administrative infrastructure, the establishment of private property rights and of institutions for trading such rights, and the building of effective hierarchical management control in private firms are all necessary prerequisites.

This does not mean that the more visible institutionalized Japanese or continental-Western European models are easier to export. Quite the contrary, it would appear that the Japanese path depends on a combination between a strong or even authoritarian state with high, normatively based cohesion in civil society. European-style capitalism requires a developed system of citizenship combined with and blending into a residual supply of economic and social traditionalism. Both sets of conditions are even more difficult to create intentionally than a free market, unless there are favorable circumstances that supply them, as it were, by accident. An interesting point for our analysis is the degree to which past geographic (and therefore historical-cultural) links within regimes provide these prerequisites.

Concerning the second question, it is far from clear to what extent and under what conditions hegemony of one country over another requires that the domestic institutions of the weaker country mirror those of the stronger one. This is an important question for future research. It would appear that a free-market and free-trade economy like that of the United States would depend comparatively strongly on other countries adopting the same principles. This might explain the Structural Impediments Initiative and other pressures for convergence placed by the United States on Japan.

The Japanese, by contrast, might be quite comfortable with free-market conditions in countries to which they want access. At the same time, they may also prefer such countries to be more like themselves if this means that they will be more difficult for rivals to penetrate. The European Union, of course, must be strongly interested in exporting its labor and environmental standards to Eastern Europe. But, apart from this, given the Union's lack of a common foreign policy capacity – the main countries, especially Britain and France, insisting on maintaining their traditional national zones of influence – it is hard to see where the question of a common European

hegemony and its domestic preconditions in developing countries might arise in the first place.

As to the relative performance of the three models with respect to economic development, we have seen that rival claims have been put forward about the superiority of a "Japanese" or "Asian" path to development over the type of free-market policies advocated by the United States and the IFIs. No claims, as far as we are aware, have been made for the superiority of a "European" model, perhaps above all because it is not quite clear what this model is.[47] If we look at some empirical evidence on the question of performance in developing countries, it seems clear that the dominant trend over recent decades, accentuated by the 1980s, is growing differentiation. The question concerns the relationship between such differentiation and a particular region's insertion in the international political economy.

The differentiation is captured at the most general level by the notion that the 1980s were a "lost decade" – a decline in per capita income to levels not seen since the early 1970s or even the 1960s – for Africa and Latin America, while the Asian countries grew very rapidly. Indeed, the superior performance of the Asian countries over a long period has been most notable. The star performer was Japan itself, but the World Bank study referred to earlier demonstrates that all eight of the Asian countries it studied have performed well above their counterparts in other regions. The 1980s exacerbated this trend: per capita income in East Asian developing countries grew by an average of 7 percent per year, while per capita income shrank in Africa and Latin America (see Table 1.1).

Over this same period, developing countries as a whole saw their share of world resources fall, but Asian countries have generally been the exception. Take market access, for example. Developing Asia's share of world exports rose in the 1980s from 8 to 13 percent, while those of Latin America and Africa fell from 9 to 6 percent.[48] At least some of this difference can be attributed to Japanese firms, especially the trading companies, incorporating Asian labor and raw materials into their exports. Also, while their worldwide share of financial flows fell, Asia was the only developing

---

[47] European unions certainly claim that high labor standards are in the long run beneficial to developing countries, and this message is also heard from the International Labour Organisation. There are doubts, however, whether this is accepted even by an EU country like Spain, which is led by a Socialist government. In any case, the German "social market economy" is only rarely offered as an export article, and it has recently been found difficult to export even from West to East Germany.

[48] IMF, *Balance of Payments Yearbook*, Part 2, *1987* and *1993*.

region that maintained access to the private capital markets (see Chapter 5). At the opposite extreme, Sub-Saharan Africa has been marginalized almost completely from private capital flows and has to rely on shrinking amounts of foreign aid. Again, Japanese capital, both public and private, was crucial in providing the Asian advantage.

Two important questions, then, come out of this chapter in terms of economic development. Does association with a particular part of the triad skew the development chances of third world countries or regions? And, if so, what are the processes behind any positive or negative effects? Three basic hypotheses seem worthy of investigation. First, differential access to investment and other financial resources might influence possibilities for development in the third world. Second, incorporation into trade/investment networks or lack thereof might skew changes for success. Third, the influence of models of capitalism might be among the most important aspects of regional location. These hypotheses will be examined further in Chapter 11.

CHAPTER 4

Global production systems and third world development

GARY GEREFFI

Over the past several decades, the world economy has undergone a fundamental shift toward an integrated and coordinated global division of labor in
production and trade. In the 1950s and 1960s, production tended to be
organized within national boundaries. International trade consisted, to a
large degree, of raw materials flowing from the periphery to the industrialized core of the world economy, while manufactured exports were sent
by U.S., European, and Japanese firms from their home bases to all corners
of the globe. Direct foreign investment in manufacturing emerged as a
response to the protectionist policies implemented by core and peripheral
nations alike that wished to diminish the foreign exchange drain of an
excessive reliance on imports and augment the employment benefits from
locally based production.

Today the most dynamic industries are transnational in scope. Modern
industrialization is the result of an integrated system of global trade and
production. Open international trade has encouraged nations to specialize in
different branches of manufacturing and even in different stages of production within a specific industry. This process, fueled by the explosion of new
products and technologies since World War II, has led to the emergence of a
global manufacturing system in which production capacity is dispersed to
an unprecedented number of developing as well as industrialized countries.

New patterns of specialization between countries entail the fragmentation

The research for this chapter was partially funded by grants from Taiwan's Chiang Ching-Kuo
Foundation for International Scholarly Exchange (United States), the Social Science Research
Council's Korea Program, and the Arts and Sciences Research Council at Duke University. I
gratefully acknowledge these sources of support. I also thank Barbara Stallings, Bradford
Barham, Cynthia Truelove, and Robert Wade for their valuable comments on earlier drafts of
this chapter, as well as Lu-Lin Cheng, Stephanie Fonda, and Abdul Latif Haji-Salleh at Duke
for their research assistance.

and geographic relocation of manufacturing processes on a global scale in ways that slice through national boundaries. As almost every factor of production – money, technology, information, and goods – moves effortlessly across borders, the very idea of distinct U.S., German, or Japanese economies is virtually meaningless. In an era where products consisting of many components are made in a wide variety of countries, what is a "U.S." computer, a "German" car, a "Japanese" camera, a "Korean" microwave oven, or a "Taiwanese" bicycle? Corporations are becoming increasingly disconnected from their home nations as manufacturers, traders, bankers, and buyers simultaneously scour the globe for profitable opportunities.

This chapter focuses on the main features of economic globalization, as well as its consequences for third world development. Given the emphasis on export-oriented development since the 1970s, it is especially important to understand the nature of the global production systems that shape the insertion of third world regions into the international economy. Most developing nations have been rather unsuccessful in exploiting the backward and forward linkages inherent in these export-oriented strategies of growth, which has exacerbated the uneven impact of globalization between as well as within regions. The development options for third world countries thus depend to a significant degree on the kinds of export roles they assume in the global economy and their ability to proceed to more sophisticated, high-value industrial niches. For newly industrialized countries (NICs) to continue to prosper, they will need to devise strategies that emphasize the creation of a local institutional environment conducive to technological upgrading and the integration of industrial production with modern services.

The chapter begins by describing the current era of economic globalization, with reference to the predominant institutions of modern capitalism. It then analyzes the recent production and trade trends in five third world regions, confirming that a global manufacturing system exists. To conceptualize the linkages between firms, industries, and countries, a perspective on global commodity chains is introduced. A distinction is drawn between producer-driven and buyer-driven commodity chains, which represent alternative modes of organizing international industries. Next, five export roles are identified that tie third world regions to the world economy. Developing nations have evolved through particular sequences and combinations of these roles, which vary in their preconditions for success and their consequences for national development. Finally, several strategies for "moving up" in the global economy are identified: government policies to increase productivity, new relations with foreign and domestic capital, and linkages with regional economic blocs. These options are evaluated in terms of their implications for integrated development and improved welfare in the third world.

The contemporary era of economic globalization

The contemporary era of global capitalism has five central characteristics: intensified global competition and the emergence of new centers of production; an exceptionally innovative technological environment; the proliferation, spread, and restructuring of transnational corporations (TNCs); a diversified global financial system; and important changes in the state's role in domestic and global economic affairs.[1] A closer look at these features of globalization provides a glimpse into its dynamic and contradictory nature.

First, intensified global competition has led to the emergence of new centers of production. This is best exemplified by the NICs of East Asia and Latin America, which in the 1970s and 1980s significantly expanded their world share in the production and export of manufactured goods. The NICs, in turn, are now being challenged by the labor-intensive manufactured exports of their neighbors in China, Southeast and South Asia, Central America, and the Caribbean. Low labor costs and the improved skill levels and productivity of workers in the third world make the global sourcing of production a virtual necessity for every corporation that seeks to enhance its international competitive position. Companies are engaged in a frantic scramble to find low-wage export platforms in various parts of the world. The result has been the emergence of new regional divisions of labor that exploit the diverse resources of core, semiperipheral, and peripheral nations.

Second, modern technology has facilitated economic globalization. Innovative transportation and communication technologies have shrunk both space and time, thus permitting managers to run complex global organizations in an integrated fashion. Dramatic improvements in transport systems, including commercial jet aircraft, vastly larger ocean-going vessels, and the

[1] See Nigel Harris, *The End of the Third World* (New York: Penguin, 1987); Peter Dicken, *Global Shift: The Internationalization of Economic Activity,* 2nd ed. (New York: Guilford, 1992); and Peter Dicken, "Globalization Processes and Local Economies," paper presented at the conference Globalization and the North American Free Trade Agreement: Impact on Rural Communities, Aspen Institute, October 1993.

shift to containerization, together with global communications systems utilizing satellites, facsimile machines, and teleconferencing, radically reduce the time as well as the cost required to send goods, messages, and people from one part of the world to another. State-of-the-art information technologies based primarily on microelectronics, such as computer-aided design and computerized numerically controlled machinery, give "flexible" automation the potential to manufacture high-quality, diversified goods inexpensively and efficiently in small batches as well as large volumes.[2] The microelectronics-based information technologies that permit systems of flexible production and quick response to consumer demand, however, may allow high-cost countries to retain manufacturing activities that otherwise would go to lower-cost parts of the world. In other words, modern technology can strengthen the forces of localization as well as globalization in the production process.

Third, TNCs are the chief economic organizing agent in global capitalism. Previous theoretical paradigms foundered because they did not have a good way to tie the activities of TNCs into the structure of the world economy (e.g., dependency theory), or conversely because they did not embed transnational capital into the peculiarities and dynamism associated with local economies (e.g., world-systems theory).[3] A new framework called the global commodity chain (GCC) perspective tries to move beyond the limitations of both types of theorizing. The GCC framework identifies several novel features of global capitalism: it distinguishes between producer-driven and buyer-driven commodity chains, and thus highlights the central roles played by industrial and commercial capital, respectively; it tries to bridge the macro–micro gap in development research by focusing on the local context of global production and showing how globalization actually reinforces localization processes in the world economy; and the framework directs our attention to the multiple export roles that link countries to the world economy, although with varied consequences for national development.

[2] See Kurt Hoffman (ed.), "Microelectronics, International Competition and Development Strategies: The Unavoidable Issues," special issue of *World Development* 13, 3 (1985), 263–463; and Kurt Hoffman and Raphael Kaplinsky, *Driving Force: The Global Restructuring of Technology, Labor, and Investment in the Automobile and Components Industries* (Boulder, Colo.: Westview, 1988).

[3] For a review of these debates, see Gary Gereffi, "Rethinking Development Theory: Insights from East Asia and Latin America," *Sociological Forum* 4, 4 (Fall 1989), 505–33.

Fourth, international production and trade are buttressed by a global financial system. Large commercial banks followed TNC manufacturers in the 1960s and 1970s into their most significant overseas markets in Europe, Latin America, and Asia. By the late 1970s and early 1980s, however, there was great alarm over the debt crisis caused by the massive bank lending that had been fueled by a glut of petrodollars during the oil export boom, overly ambitious investment and spending programs by key third world borrowers, and sharp hikes in real interest rates when these loans were refinanced. The debt crisis was particularly severe in Latin America and helped to usher in a set of neoclassical economic reforms that spelled the demise of import-substitution industrialization (ISI) as a development strategy. International financial institutions, such as the World Bank and the IMF, were particularly influential in using their leverage to force developing nations to adopt orthodox economic stabilization policies. In the 1990s, the global financial system may once again be perceived as an opportunity rather than a constraint in many regions of the third world. International financial institutions and new private-sector investors (e.g., mutual funds and pension funds) appear to have ample money to lend, and attention in the 1990s has shifted from the debt crisis to how to deploy fresh resources to restore international competitiveness and generate nontraditional exports.

Fifth, state policies have played a major role in fostering the globalization of economic activity. A favorable international trading and investment regime was indispensable to the globalization of production in the postwar era. The relatively liberal international trading environment embodied in the provisions of the General Agreement on Tariffs and Trade (GATT) since World War II has permitted many third world exporters to have extensive, albeit regulated, access to developed-country markets, especially the United States. Throughout the history of the GATT regime, however, a variety of exceptions have been made to the nondiscrimination norm. Tariffs, import quotas, and other restrictive measures were used by the European Community, the United States, and Canada for over 30 years to regulate trade in industries such as textiles and apparel, footwear, automobiles, color televisions, and appliances. Although the clear intent of these policies was to protect developed-country firms from a flood of low-cost imports that threatened to disrupt major domestic industries, the result was exactly the opposite: protectionism led to heightened competitive capabilities of the major third world manufacturers.

Industrial upgrading in the NICs was one of the major consequences of import quotas since it permitted successful Asian exporters to maximize the foreign exchange earnings and profitability of quantitative restrictions on trade. Japan followed a similar strategy in the automobile industry. It complied with U.S. voluntary export restraints by sending high-priced luxury cars instead of low-priced compact models to the U.S. market, which further eroded the domestic sales of U.S. auto manufacturers. Protectionism by core countries had a second consequence as well: the diversification of foreign competition. The imposition of quotas on an ever-widening circle of third world exporters led producers in Japan and the East Asian NICs (EANICs) who had to contend with escalating labor costs and U.S.-mandated currency appreciations, to open up new satellite factories in low-wage countries that offer either quota or labor advantages.

These broad determinants of economic globalization have forged a complex interdependence of nations at all levels of development. Three specific trends in the international economy serve to illustrate the nature of the contemporary global manufacturing system in greater detail: the spread of diversified industrialization to large segments of the third world; the shift toward export-oriented development strategies in peripheral nations, with an emphasis on manufactures; and high levels of product specialization in the export profiles of most third world countries, along with continual industrial upgrading by established exporters among the NICs. The impact of these processes of change in the third world is highly uneven, with some nations improving their position in the global economy and others becoming marginalized from it.

Worldwide industrialization

A new global division of labor has changed the pattern of geographic specialization between countries. The classic core–periphery relationship in which the developing nations supplied primary commodities to the industrialized countries in exchange for manufactured goods is outdated. Since the 1950s, the gap between developed and developing countries has been narrowing in terms of industrialization. By the late 1970s, the NICs as a whole not only caught up with but overtook the core countries in their degree of industrialization.[4] As developed economies shift predominantly

---

[4] Giovanni Arrighi and Jessica Drangel, "The Stratification of the World-Economy: An Exploration of the Semiperipheral Zone," *Review* 10, 1 (1986), 9–74, at 54–55.

toward services, vigorous industrialization has become the hallmark of the periphery. This can be seen by taking a closer look at production and trade patterns within the third world.

Industry outstripped agriculture as a source of economic growth in all regions of the third world. From 1965 to 1990, industry's share of GDP grew by 13 percentage points in East and Southeast Asia, by 10 percent in Sub-Saharan Africa, 5 percent in South Asia, and 3 percent in Latin America. Agriculture's share of regional GDP, on the other hand, fell by 16 percent in East and Southeast Asia, 11 percent in South Asia, 8 percent in Sub-Saharan Africa, and 6 percent in Latin America.[5]

Manufacturing has been the cornerstone of development in East and Southeast Asia. In 1990, 34 percent of the GDP of East and Southeast Asia was in the manufacturing sector, compared with 26 percent for Latin America, 17 percent for South Asia, and only 11 percent for Sub-Saharan Africa. The manufacturing sector's share of GDP in some developing nations, such as China (38 percent), Taiwan (34 percent), and South Korea (31 percent), was even higher than Japan's manufacturing/GDP ratio of 29 percent. These differences in performance are corroborated over time as well.

Diversified, export-oriented industrialization

World trade expanded nearly 30-fold in the three decades since 1960. Manufactured goods as a percentage of total world exports increased from 55 percent in 1980 to 75 percent in 1990. Furthermore, the share of the NICs' manufactured exports that can be classified as "high tech" soared from 2 percent in 1964 to 25 percent in 1985, and those embodying "medium" levels of technological sophistication rose from 16 percent to 22 percent during this same period.[6] China topped the list of individual exporters in 1992 with $85 billion in overseas sales, followed by Taiwan ($81 billion), South Korea ($76 billion), and Singapore ($63 billion). In the next tier, Brazil, Mexico, Hong Kong, and several of the Southeast Asian nations (Malaysia, Indonesia, and Thailand) all generated substantial exports, ranging from $41 to $27 billion. Exports accounted for 22 percent of GDP in

---

[5] The percentages used in this section come from World Bank, *World Development Report, 1992* (New York: Oxford University Press, 1992), pp. 222–23.

[6] Organisation for Economic Co-operation and Development, *The Newly Industrializing Countries: Challenge and Opportunity for OECD Industries* (Paris: OECD, 1988), p. 24.

East and Southeast Asia, compared with an export/GDP ratio of 23 percent for Sub-Saharan Africa, 15 percent for the advanced industrial countries, 11 percent for South Asia, and 10 percent for Latin America and the Caribbean (Table 4.1).

In exports as in production, manufactures are the chief source of the third world's dynamism. In 1992, manufactured items constituted well over 90 percent of total exports in three of the four EANICs, and they were approximately three-quarters of all exports in China, Singapore, and South Asia. For Brazil and Mexico, the share of manufactures in total exports is over one-half, while in Sub-Saharan Africa the manufacturing figure is around 25 percent (Table 4.1). In every region of the world, the relative importance of primary commodities in exports as well as GDP has decreased, usually quite sharply, since 1970. Asian nations have moved fastest and furthest toward manufactured exports during this period. Sub-Saharan Africa and Latin America are still mostly primary commodity exporters, although to a lesser degree than in the past and with substantial subregional variation.

The maturity or sophistication of a country's industrial structure can be measured by the complexity of the products it exports. Here again, the EANICs are the most advanced. In Singapore and South Korea, overseas sales of machinery and transport equipment, which utilize capital- and skill-intensive technology, grew as a share of total merchandise exports by 41 and 33 percent, respectively, from 1970 to 1992. Taiwan's exports in this category increased by 23 percent and Hong Kong's by 12 percent. In Southeast Asia, Malaysia (a 36 percent increase) and Thailand (22 percent) have been strong performers in this sector, while in Latin America, Mexico (20 percent) and Brazil (17 percent) also made machinery and transport equipment a dynamic export base (Table 4.2).

Textiles and clothing, the preeminent export sector in the EANICs in the 1960s and 1970s, actually shrank as a proportion of total exports in these nations between 1970 and 1992. This fact highlights the workings of the product life cycle and industrial upgrading in the Asian region. While the EANICs were shifting into higher-value-added production in the 1980s and 1990s, clothing exports became a growth pole for countries at lower levels of development such as Bangladesh, Pakistan, Sri Lanka, Indonesia, and Thailand. Furthermore, a more detailed look at this sector indicates that Taiwan, South Korea, and Hong Kong have increased their exports of textile fibers, yarn, and fabrics to the same Asian nations that now are displacing

Table 4.1. Growth of exports in major world regions, 1980–92

Region/country	Exports ($ billions)		Exports/GDP (percent)		Manufactured exports/total exports (percent)	
	1980	1992	1980	1992	1980	1992
Advanced industrial countries	na	2,811.9	na	15	na	82
Germany	192.9	429.8	24	24	82	89
United States	216.7	420.8	8	7	66	80
Japan	129.2	339.5	12	9	92	98
East and Southeast Asia	na	282.4	na	22	na	74
Taiwan	19.8	81.3	48	43[a]	91	93
South Korea	17.5	76.4	30	26	58	93
Singapore	19.4[b]	63.4[b]	185[b]	138[b]	46	78
Hong Kong	19.7[b]	30.3	97[b]	39	54	95
Malaysia	13.8	40.7	58	71	16	61
Indonesia	21.9	33.8	31	27	2	47
Thailand	6.5	32.5	19	29	15	66
Philippines	6.0	9.8	17	19	29	73
China	18.3	84.9	8	17	25	79

South Asia	na	31.9	na	11	na	73
India	6.7	19.8	5	9	41	71
Pakistan	2.6	7.3	12	17	16	79
Bangladesh	0.8	1.9	7	8	17	82
Latin America and the Caribbean	na	127.6	na	10^c	na	38
Brazil	20.1	36.0	10	9^c	34	58
Mexico	15.3	27.2	9	8	36	53
Argentina	8.0	12.2	6	5	21	26
Sub-Saharan Africa	na	63.2	na	23	na	24
South Africa	26.1	23.9	35	23	53	47
Nigeria	26.0	11.9	29	40	1	1
Kenya	1.3	1.3	22	19	13	29
Tanzania	0.5	0.4	12	17	9	15

^{a}1990.
^{b}Includes substantial reexports.
^{c}1991.

Sources: World Bank, *World Development Report, 1982, 1994;* Republic of China, *Taiwan Statistical Data Book, 1991.*

Table 4.2. *Structure of merchandise exports by type of industry, 1970–92 (percent share)*

	Primary commodities		Textiles and clothing		Machinery and transport equipment		Other manufactures	
	1992	Δ1970–92	1992	Δ1970–92	1992	Δ1970–92	1992	Δ1970–92
Advanced industrial countries	18	−9	5	−1	43	+8	34	+2
Germany	11	0	5	−1	50	+3	35	−2
United States	20	−10	2	0	48	+6	30	+4
Japan	2	−5	2	−9	67	+26	28	−14
East and Southeast Asia	26	−41	20	+7	25	+19	30	+16
Taiwan	7	−17	14	−15	40	+23	39	+9
South Korea	7	−17	20	−16	40	+33	33	0
Singapore	22	−48	5	0	52	+41	21	+6
Hong Kong	5	+1	40	−4	24	+12	31	−9
Malaysia	39	−54	6	+5	38	+36	17	+12
Indonesia	53	−45	18	+18	4	+4	26	+25
Thailand	34	−58	17	+16	22	+22	28	+21
Philippines	27	−66	10	+9	17	+17	46	+39
China	21	−9	30	+1	15	0	34	+8

		Δ1970–92		Δ1970–92		Δ1970–92		Δ1970–92
South Asia	27	−26	41	+13	5	+2	28	+11
India	29	−19	25	0	7	+2	39	+17
Pakistan	21	−22	69	+22	0	0	10	0
Bangladesh	18	−16	72	+23	0	−1	9	−6
Latin America and the Caribbean	62	−26	3	+2	14	+12	21	+13
Brazil	42	−44	4	+3	21	+17	33	+23
Mexico	47	−21	2	−1	31	+20	19	0
Argentina	74	−12	1	0	8	+4	18	+9
Sub-Saharan Africa	76	−7	2	+1	3	+1	19	+5
South Africa	53	0	1	0	5	0	41	0
Nigeria	99	+1	0	0	0	0	1	0
Kenya	71	−16	3	+2	10	+10	16	+5
Tanzania	85	−2	7	+5	1	+1	8	−3

Note: Δ1970–92 refers to the increase or decrease in percent share of total exports between 1970 and 1992.

Source: World Bank, *World Development Report, 1994.*

the EANICs as apparel exporters.[7] The textiles and apparel complex, despite its status as a declining sector in developed countries, represents the leading edge of economic globalization for many third world nations.

Geographic specialization and export niches

While the diversification of the NICs' exports toward nontraditional manufactured items is a clear trend, less well recognized is the tendency of the NICs to develop sharply focused export niches. In the footwear industry, for example, South Korea has specialized in athletic footwear, Taiwan in vinyl and plastic shoes, Brazil in low-priced women's leather shoes, Spain in medium-priced women's leather shoes, and Italy in high-priced fashion shoes. Mainland China traditionally was a major player in the low-priced end of the world footwear market, especially in canvas and rubber shoes. Because of its low wages and vast production capacity, however, China now has displaced Taiwan and South Korea from many of their mid-level niches, and it is challenging Brazil, Spain, and even Italy in the fashionable leather footwear market.[8] Today China is the world's foremost volume exporter of inexpensive consumer goods, such as clothing, footwear, toys, and bicycles.

Similar trends are apparent for many consumer items and even intermediate goods, such as semiconductors. South Korea, for instance, has focused on the mass production of powerful memory chips; Taiwan, by contrast, makes high-value designer chips that carry out special functions in toys, video games, and electronic equipment. Singapore has upgraded its activities from the assembly and testing of semiconductors to the design and fabrication of silicon wafers, while Singapore and Malaysia produce the majority of hard disk drives for the world's booming personal computer market. Although the location of hard disk drive production in Singapore and Malaysia reflects efforts by TNCs to reduce manufacturing costs, these nations were chosen as export sites primarily because of their skilled labor forces, well-developed transportation and communication infrastructures, and appropriate supporting industries (such as precision tooling).

---

[7] For a vivid illustration of this transition in Taiwan, see Gary Gereffi and Mei-Lin Pan, "The Globalization of Taiwan's Garment Industry," in Edna Bonacich et al. (eds.), *Global Production: The Apparel Industry in the Pacific Rim* (Philadelphia, Pa.: Temple University Press, 1994), pp. 126–46.

[8] See Gary Gereffi and Miguel Korzeniewicz, "Commodity Chains and Footwear Exports in the Semiperiphery," in William Martin (ed.), *Semiperipheral States in the World-Economy* (Westport, Conn.: Greenwood, 1990), pp. 45–68.

The global production systems discussed in this chapter raise a host of questions for third world development. How can countries ensure that they enter the most attractive export niches in which they have the greatest relative advantages? To what extent is a country's position in the global manufacturing system structurally determined by the availability of local capital, domestic infrastructure, and a skilled work force? What is the range of development options available to third world countries? While these queries cannot be answered fully here, several implications of current global changes for third world development will be suggested.

Global commodity chains

GCCs are rooted in transnational production systems, which link the economic activities of firms to technological, organizational, and institutional networks that are utilized to develop, manufacture, and market specific commodities.[9] In global capitalism, economic activity is not only international in scope, but also global in organization. Although "internationalization" refers simply to the geographic spread of economic activities across national boundaries, "globalization" implies a degree of functional integration among these internationally dispersed activities. What is novel about GCCs is not the spread of economic activities across national boundaries per se, but rather the fact that international production and trade are increasingly organized by industrial and commercial firms involved in strategic decision making and economic networks at the global level.

GCCs have four main dimensions: a value-added chain of products, services, and resources linked together across a range of relevant industries; a geographic dispersion of production and marketing networks at the national, regional, and global levels, comprised of enterprises of different sizes and types; a governance structure of authority and power relationships between firms that determines how financial, material, and human resources are allocated and flow within a chain; and an institutional framework that identifies how local, national, and international conditions and policies shape the globalization process at each stage in the chain. The

---

[9] This section adapts and extends an earlier discussion of this topic in Gary Gereffi, "The Organization of Buyer-Driven Global Commodity Chains: How U.S. Retailers Shape Overseas Production Networks," in Gary Gereffi and Miguel Korzeniewicz (eds.), *Commodity Chains and Global Capitalism* (Westport, Conn.: Praeger, 1994), pp. 95–122.

Producer-driven commodity chains

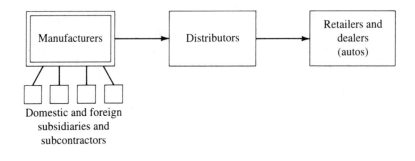

Buyer-driven commodity chains

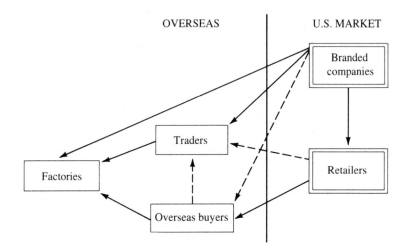

Figure 4.1. The organization of producer-driven and buyer-driven global commodity chains. Solid arrows are primary relationships; dashed arrows are secondary relationships.

governance structure of GCCs is essential to the coordination of transnational production systems. Two distinct types of governance structures have emerged in the past two decades, which for the sake of simplicity can be called "producer-driven" and "buyer-driven" commodity chains (Figure 4.1).

Producer-driven commodity chains refer to those industries in which TNCs or other large integrated industrial enterprises play the central role in controlling the production system (including its backward and forward linkages). This is most characteristic of capital- and technology-intensive industries like automobiles, computers, aircraft, and heavy machinery. The geographic spread of these industries is transnational, but the number of countries in the commodity chain and their levels of development are varied. International subcontracting of components is common, especially for the most labor-intensive production processes, as are strategic alliances between international rivals. What distinguishes producer-driven systems is the control exercised by the administrative headquarters of TNC manufacturers.

The automobile industry offers a classic illustration of a producer-driven commodity chain. In his comparative study of Japanese and U.S. car companies, Hill shows how both sets of enterprises organize manufacturing in multilayered production systems that involve thousands of firms (including parents, subsidiaries, and subcontractors). The average Japanese automaker's production system, for example, comprises 171 first-tier, 4,700 second-tier, and 31,600 third-tier subcontractors.[10] Florida and Kenney have found that Japanese automobile manufacturers actually reconstituted many aspects of their home-country supplier networks in North America.[11] Doner extends this framework to highlight the complex forces that drive Japanese automakers to create regional production schemes for the supply of auto parts in a half-dozen nations in East and Southeast Asia.[12] Henderson also supports the notion that producer-driven commodity chains have

---

[10] Richard Child Hill, "Comparing Transnational Production Systems: The Automobile Industry in the USA and Japan," *International Journal of Urban and Regional Research* 13, 3 (September 1989), 462–80, at 466.
[11] Richard Florida and Martin Kenney, "Transplanted Organizations: The Transfer of Japanese Industrial Organization to the United States," *American Sociological Review* 56, 3 (June 1991), 381–98.
[12] Richard F. Doner, *Driving a Bargain: Automobile Industrialization and Japanese Firms in Southeast Asia* (Berkeley: University of California Press, 1991).

established an East Asian division of labor in his study of the internationalization of the U.S. semiconductor industry.[13]

Buyer-driven commodity chains are found in those industries where large
retailers, branded marketers, and trading companies play the pivotal role in
setting up decentralized production networks in a variety of exporting countries, typically located in the third world. This pattern of trade-led industrialization has become common in labor-intensive consumer goods industries such as garments, footwear, toys, housewares, consumer electronics,
and a variety of hand-crafted items (e.g., furniture, ornaments). Production
is generally carried out by locally owned third world factories that make
finished goods (rather than components or parts) for foreign buyers. The
specifications are supplied by the branded companies or large retailers that
design and order the goods.

One of the main characteristics of the branded firms that fit the buyer-
driven model, such as athletic footwear companies like Nike, Reebok, and
L.A. Gear, and branded apparel companies like The Limited, The Gap, and
Liz Claiborne, is that they usually do not own any production facilities.
These companies are marketers that design, but do not make, the branded
products they order. They rely on complex tiered networks of overseas
production contractors to perform most of their specialized tasks. Branded
marketers farm out part or all of their product development activities, manufacturing, packaging, shipping, and even accounts receivable to different
agents around the world.

The crucial job of the core company in buyer-driven commodity chains is
to manage these production and trade networks and to make sure all the
pieces of the business come together as an integrated whole. Profits in
buyer-driven chains derive not from scale, volume, and technological advances as in producer-driven chains, but rather from unique combinations of
high-value research, design, sales, marketing, and financial services that
allow the retailers and branded marketers to act as strategic brokers in
linking overseas factories and traders with evolving product niches in their
main consumer markets.[14]

---

[13] Jeffrey Henderson, *The Globalisation of High Technology Production: Society, Space and
Semiconductors in the Restructuring of the Modern World* (New York: Routledge, 1989).
[14] The complex role of strategic brokers and other contemporary symbolic analysts is explored in Robert B. Reich, *The Work of Nations: Preparing Ourselves for 21st-Century
Capitalism* (New York: Knopf, 1991).

Producer-driven and buyer-driven commodity chains arise from the barriers to entry that allow core industrial and commercial firms, respectively, to control the backward and forward linkages in the production process. Industrial organization economics argues that profitability is greatest in the relatively concentrated segments of an industry characterized by high barriers to the entry of new firms. Producer-driven commodity chains are capital- and technology-intensive. Thus, manufacturers making advanced products like aircraft, automobiles, and computers are the key economic agents in these producer-driven chains not only in terms of their earnings, but also in their ability to exert control over backward linkages with raw material and component suppliers, as well as forward linkages into distribution and retailing. Buyer-driven commodity chains, by contrast, tend to be labor-intensive at the manufacturing stage. This leads to very competitive and globally decentralized factory systems. These same industries are also design- and marketing-intensive, however, which means that there are high barriers to entry in product development, advertising, and electronic data interchange linkages between stores and their suppliers for inventory control and automatic reorders. Therefore, whereas producer-driven commodity chains are controlled by industrial firms at the point of production, the main leverage in buyer-driven industries is exercised by retailers and branded merchandisers at the marketing and retail end of the chain.

The distinction between producer-driven and buyer-driven commodity chains overlaps with the difference between mass production and flexible specialization forms of industrial organization.[15] Mass production is a producer-driven model in which vertically integrated manufacturers lower the costs of making standardized goods by using dedicated (special-purpose) machinery, interchangeable parts, and narrowly trained workers in factories organized around continuous assembly lines. Flexible production, by contrast, is based on flexible (multiuse) equipment, customized parts, and relatively skilled workers in factories or workshops frequently located in industrial districts where cooperative networks form to facilitate innovation and adaptation. It has been spawned in large part by the growing importance of segmented demand and more discriminating buyers in developed-country markets.

[15] Michael J. Piore and Charles F. Sabel, *The Second Industrial Divide* (New York: Basic, 1984).

While the flexible specialization perspective deals primarily with the organization of production in domestic economies and local industrial districts, the notion of producer-driven and buyer-driven commodity chains focuses on the organizational properties of global industries. Furthermore, the emergence of flexible production in a buyer-driven commodity chain is explained at least partially by changes in the structure of consumption and retailing in major export markets, which in turn reflect demographic shifts and new organizational imperatives. Finally, while some discussions of flexible specialization imply that it is a superior manufacturing system that could eventually displace or subordinate mass production, buyer-driven and producer-driven commodity chains are viewed as divergent (but not mutually exclusive) poles in a spectrum of industrial organization possibilities.

Triangle manufacturing

How do countries in buyer-driven commodity chains deal with the competition from lower-cost suppliers? What tactics are utilized to ensure a smooth transition from declining sectors to higher-value-added activities? One of the most important adjustment mechanisms for maturing export industries in East Asia has been the process of "triangle manufacturing." The essence of triangle manufacturing, which emerged in the 1970s and 1980s, is that U.S. (or other overseas) buyers place their orders with the NIC manufacturers from whom they have sourced in the past (e.g., Hong Kong, Taiwanese, or Korean apparel firms), who in turn shift some or all of the requested production to affiliated offshore factories in low-wage countries (e.g., China, Indonesia, or Guatemala). These offshore factories may or may not have equity investments by the EANIC manufacturers; they can be wholly owned subsidiaries, joint-venture partners, or independent overseas contractors. The triangle is completed when the finished goods are shipped directly to the overseas buyer under the U.S. import quotas issued to the exporting nation.

Triangle manufacturing thus changes the status of NIC manufacturers from suppliers for U.S. retailers and branded marketers to "middlemen" in buyer-driven commodity chains. The key asset possessed by the EANIC manufacturers is their close relationship with foreign clients, which is based on the trust developed through numerous successful export transactions. Since the buyers have no direct production experience, they prefer to rely on the EANIC manufacturers they have done business with in the past to ensure that the buyers' standards in terms of price, quality, and delivery schedules will be met by untested contractors in other third world locales. As the volume of orders expands in new production sites, however, the pressure grows for the large U.S. buyers to bypass their EANIC intermediaries and deal directly with the factories that fill their orders.

The process of third party production began in the late 1960s when Japan relocated numerous plants and foreign orders to the EANICs (often through Japanese trading companies, or *sogo shosha*) for both economic and environmental reasons. When U.S. import quotas were imposed on Hong Kong, Taiwan, South Korea, and Singapore in the 1970s, this led to the search for new quota-free production sites elsewhere in Asia.[16] European and U.S. import quotas were calculated in terms of the quantity of goods shipped, rather than their value. This arrangement, chosen in part because it was easier to enforce by the importing countries, had an unforeseen effect. In the words of Kenneth Fang, one of Hong Kong's leading apparel exporters, "It encouraged the Hong Kong manufacturers to move from textiles to clothing and then from simple to fancy clothing, in order to generate more income and employment per square yard."[17] This process of quota-induced industrial upgrading was repeated throughout East Asia. At the same time, NIC manufacturers were busily locating cheap overseas production sites for their lower-priced orders from foreign buyers. In the 1980s, the shift toward triangle manufacturing accelerated because of a series of changes in the EANICs: escalating wages, labor shortages, and currency appreciations. Today the EANICs are extending their factory networks to far-flung production frontiers in Asia, Latin America, and Africa.

Triangle manufacturing has important implications for third world development. As industries have become globalized and producers in different parts of the world are more tightly linked, the pace of change has quickened and exporters have shorter periods in which to exploit their competitive advantages. In footwear, for example, while an export industry took more than 20 years to develop in Japan and about 15 years in Taiwan and South Korea, experts estimate that China's footwear sector will peak in

---

[16] In 1992, nearly 50 countries had bilateral agreements with the United States for textile and apparel import quotas, as permitted under the provisions of the 1973 Multifiber Arrangement (MFA). But the new GATT treaty, which took effect on January 1, 1995, will phase out the MFA and its system of import quotas over a 10-year period.

[17] James Lardner, "Annals of Business: The Sweater Trade," Part 1, *New Yorker,* January 11, 1988, pp. 39–73, at 46.

world markets in 8 to 10 years. When export windows for third world manufacturers narrow this fast, countries face the problems of "boom-and-bust" phases of economic growth tied to fluctuating external demand and intense regional competition. The shortening of product life cycles for countries pursuing export-oriented industrialization (EOI) has multiple causes: rapid technological innovation; the growing number of buying seasons for fashion goods; the proliferation of new models of popular consumer products; the spread of third world manufacturing capabilities; and the speed with which the United States and other developed countries have imposed tariffs, quotas, and other import restrictions on successful exporting countries.

Triangle manufacturing is socially and culturally embedded, which helps to explain the evolution of transnational production and trade networks. Each of the EANICs, for example, has a different set of preferred countries where it sets up its new factories. Hong Kong and Taiwan have been the main investors in China (Hong Kong has taken a leading role in Chinese production of quota items such as cotton and synthetic apparel, while Taiwan is a leader for nonquota goods like footwear, as well as leather and silk apparel); South Korea has been especially prominent in Indonesia, Guatemala, the Dominican Republic, and North Korea; and Singapore is a major player in Southeast Asian sites, such as Malaysia and Indonesia. These production networks are explained in part by social and cultural factors (e.g., ethnic or familial ties, common language), as well as unique features of a country's historical legacy (e.g., Hong Kong's British colonial ties gave it an inside track on investments in Jamaica and Mauritius).

Export roles and national development

Economic globalization has heightened the role of trade, especially of manufactures, in the world economy. In absolute terms, most countries now are significant exporters. In 1992, two-thirds of the nations for which data were available (78 out of 117) had exports of $1 billion or more.[18] Furthermore, there has been a tendency for dynamic world regions to upgrade their exports with higher levels of local value added, thereby amplifying the domestic multiplier effects of trade. In relative terms, exports in 1992 accounted for two-fifths of GDP in East Asia (excluding China), nearly one-

[18] World Bank, *World Development Report, 1994* (New York: Oxford University Press, 1994), pp. 186–87.

fourth in Southeast Asia and Sub-Saharan Africa, one-sixth in the advanced industrial countries, and one-tenth in Latin America and South Asia (see Table 4.1).

Countries are connected to GCCs through the goods and services they supply in the world economy. These trade linkages can be conceptualized as a set of five major export roles: (1) primary commodity exports, (2) export-processing (or in-bond) assembly operations, (3) component-supply subcontracting, (4) original equipment manufacturing (OEM); and (5) original brand-name manufacturing (OBM). Each type of manufactured exporting (roles 2–5) is progressively more difficult to establish because it implies a higher degree of domestic integration and local entrepreneurship. Therefore, industrial development is enhanced as countries move from the second to the fifth options.

These export roles are not mutually exclusive. In fact, most nations are tied to the world economy in multiple ways. The EANICs employed all five export roles from the 1960s to the mid-1990s, although they currently are focusing almost exclusively on component-supply subcontracting, OEM, and OBM. Most of the countries in Southeast Asia and Latin America are involved in the first three roles. The bulk of exports in South Asia and Sub-Saharan Africa fit the first two roles, with many African nations limited only to primary commodity exports (Table 4.3). An overview of the principal export roles in the third world is provided next, emphasizing their institutional foundations and development tradeoffs.

Primary commodity exports

Primary commodity exports have been an important feature in the economic growth of every third world region, but all substantially reduced their reliance on this type of export between 1970 and 1992 (see Table 4.2). In general, this reduction has been a conscious decision because raw materials have well-known disadvantages as an export base. The disadvantages multiply when, as is frequently the case, a country relies heavily on a single primary commodity.

Commodity exporters confront several problems. First, the prices of primary goods are highly volatile. This volatility arises in part from the concentrated pattern of production, where a few countries control a relatively high percentage of world output. A fall in production in a single location – because of labor problems, weather, or natural disaster – can cause sharp

Table 4.3. *Export roles in the global economy occupied by major third world regions, 1965–95*

	Primary commodity exports	Export-processing assembly	Component-supply subcontracting	Original equipment manufacturing	Original brand-name manufacturing
East Asia	X	X	X	X	X
Southeast Asia	X	X	X		
Latin America and the Caribbean	X	X	X		
South Asia	X	X			
Sub-Saharan Africa	X	X			

price changes around the world. Oversupply or international recession may have similar effects. A second problem is the alleged tendency for the terms of trade for primary products to deteriorate. Despite evidence against the claim of a long-term decline, such problems can wreak havoc on primary product exporters over shorter periods. Thus, nonfuel primary producers' terms of trade have fallen substantially over the past 20 years.[19] Other problems relate to particular products. For example, agricultural productivity in most parts of the third world is very low, while mineral extraction has high productivity but often little spillover to the rest of the economy.

Various solutions to these problems have been tried. In the 1970s, following the success of the OPEC cartel in raising oil prices, attempts were made to form other producer groups to regulate output and thus control prices. These have not proved successful and, in any case, go against the market-oriented policies that many third world governments have adopted in the past decade. The use of futures and options has gained some adherents, but the requirements for participating in these markets are so stringent that most third world countries have shied away from them. Perhaps the most successful strategy has been to upgrade primary production, either by shifting to "nontraditional" products (e.g., the exports of exotic fruits and vegetables to developed-country markets) or processing raw materials more before selling them. Indeed, the most dynamic Latin American exports in the 1990s have been "industrial commodities," such as paper, petrochemicals, and steel. Nonetheless, most third world regions continue to rely heavily on traditional primary exports. Sub-Saharan Africa still earns three-quarters of its export revenues this way, while Latin America and Southeast Asia mix primary commodity and industrial exports.

Export-processing assembly

The export-processing role emphasizes the labor-intensive assembly of simple manufactured goods from imported components, typically in foreign-owned plants. Often special zones are created with incentives for foreign capital to locate in a designated set of industries, such as apparel, electronics, and other light manufacturing sectors. The main advantages of

---

[19] An improvement in prices is expected for the rest of the decade, with a resumption of the downward trend thereafter. For the latest quantitative data and analysis of primary commodity exports, see World Bank, *Global Economic Prospects and the Developing Countries, 1994* (Washington, D.C.: World Bank, 1994).

export-processing zones (EPZs) for the host country are jobs and foreign exchange earnings. Since they rely on cheap labor with minimal skills, EPZs represent the first stage of EOI for most third world countries. Although every region of the third world has some experience with EPZs, these zones tend to migrate from the more advanced to the least developed nations.

The first EPZs were set up in the 1960s in Asia and Mexico, where they were part of a border industrialization program based on export-oriented *maquiladora* factories.[20] In the EANICs, however, EPZs have been declining since the mid-1970s in response to spiraling labor costs and the systematic efforts of these nations to upgrade their mix of export activities by moving toward skill- and technology-intensive products. As the EANICs abandoned the export-processing role, it was occupied by neighboring low-wage areas such as China, Southeast Asia, and South Asia. Many countries, including Mexico, which has the world's largest export-processing sector with 550,000 employees, have extended the benefits of EPZs to all export-oriented firms without requiring them to be located in special zones.

The steep hierarchy among world regions in terms of their labor costs has influenced the location of export-processing activities. The EANICs are by far the most expensive production sites in the third world. Labor costs decrease sharply as one moves from East Asia to Latin America, Southeast Asia, South Asia, and China. In 1991, India, China, Pakistan, the Philippines, Indonesia, and Honduras had apparel labor costs of under $0.50 per hour. Indonesia's labor cost of $0.18 per hour was less than one-twentieth Taiwan's cost ($3.74) and nearly one-fortieth that of the United States ($6.77).[21] This explains the appeal of particular third world export sites in global sourcing arrangements. From the vantage point of developing nations, however, low wages provide only a transient competitive edge because they can fluctuate rapidly and are relatively easy to duplicate elsewhere.

Most third world export industries are characterized by a pronounced gender division of labor. The majority of workers in low-wage industries like apparel, electronics, toys, and footwear are young unmarried women, who constitute a "part-time proletariat" that frequently combines home-

---

[20] See Leslie Sklair, *Assembling for Development: The Maquila Industry in Mexico and the United States* (Boston: Unwin Hyman, 1989).
[21] Mary T. O'Rourke, "Labor Costs – From Pakistan to Portugal," *Bobbin* 34, 1 (September 1992), 116–22, at 116–18.

based work with jobs in formal and informal factories. The prevailing patriarchal order in these societies reinforces the traditional roles of wives and mothers, and militates against organized resistance by women to improve their working conditions.[22] As industrial labor in the NICs has become costly and relatively scarce, however, male and older female factory workers have become more prevalent. Today at least 25 percent of the labor force in Hong Kong's apparel industry are men, and nearly one-third of the managers and one-quarter of the assembly workers are over 40 years of age.[23] This changing composition of the workforce is likely to alter the social dynamics in some export-oriented industries, especially if male workers galvanize the sporadic efforts to unionize export sectors. So far, the unionization of export-oriented factories has progressed the furthest in South Korea, where the class consciousness of workers has been sharpened by harsh employer practices and low wages in large-scale factories in the auto, steel, and textile industries.[24]

Sub-Saharan Africa lags behind the other third world regions in terms of its limited number of EPZs, largely because of the inadequate transportation and communication infrastructure in many parts of the African region, its shortage of concentrated pools of low-wage labor, and a difficult political and cultural environment for foreign investors. Nonetheless, there are a few successful EPZs in Africa that have flourished due to special external conditions. One such case is Mauritius, an island of 1.1 million people located off the southern coast of Africa. The EPZ sector in Mauritius, which is dominated by textiles and clothing, has been the focal point of the country's development strategy in the 1980s and 1990s. Between 1982 and 1990, the number of EPZ firms increased nearly fivefold from 120 to 570, and employment in these companies quadrupled from 20,000 to 80,000. About 70 percent of the island's EPZ exports, which totaled over $770 million in 1990, went to the European Community where Mauritius has privileged access. The disadvantages of the Mauritius location in cost terms have been

---

22 See June Nash and María Patricia Fernández-Kelly (eds.), *Women, Men, and the International Division of Labor* (Albany: State University of New York Press, 1983), and Kathryn Ward (ed.), *Women Workers and Global Restructuring* (Ithaca, N.Y.: ILR Press, School of Industrial Relations, Cornell University, 1990).

23 Hong Kong Government Industry Department, *Techno-Economic and Market Research Study of Hong Kong's Textile and Clothing Industries, 1991–1992* (Hong Kong: Government Printing Office, 1992), p. A17.

24 See Frederic C. Deyo, *Beneath the Miracle: Labor Subordination in the New Asian Industrialism* (Berkeley: University of California Press, 1989).

offset by a concentration on high-unit-value products, such as "Scottish" knitwear (mainly jerseys and pullovers). Labor productivity in Mauritius, where most workers are immigrants from India, is regarded as significantly higher than in the Caribbean. The largest source of foreign capital in the EPZs is Hong Kong entrepreneurs, who came to the island in response to political uncertainties about the future of Hong Kong, but the political stability and favorable tax treatment offered by Mauritius also make it an attractive site for Indian and now South African investors.[25]

Component-supply subcontracting

Component-supply subcontracting refers to the manufacture and export of component parts in technologically advanced industries in the NICs, with final assembly usually carried out in the developed countries. The primary advantage of this export role is that it can facilitate industrial upgrading and technology transfer in the NICs, and it may generate significant backward linkages to local suppliers. A potential liability is that these economic networks often are controlled by TNCs, which subordinate national development criteria to their own objectives of global profitability and flexibility.

The component-supplier role has been a major niche for the Latin American NICs' manufactured exports during the past two decades. Brazil and Mexico have been important production sites since the late 1960s for vertically integrated exports by TNCs to developed-country markets, especially the United States. This is most notable in the motor vehicle, computer, and pharmaceutical industries.[26] U.S. and Japanese automotive TNCs, for example, have advanced manufacturing plants in Mexico and Brazil for the production of engines, auto parts, and completed vehicles destined for the U.S., European, and Latin American markets. By the 1970s, component-supply exporting had become an integral part of the regional division of labor in East Asia's electronics industry. In the 1980s, Japanese automotive

---

[25] See Narud Fowdar, "Textiles and Clothing in Mauritius," *Textile Outlook International* (November 1991), 68–86, and A. Werberloff, *Textiles in Africa: A Trade and Investment Guide* (London: Alain Charles, 1987).

[26] See Richard Newfarmer (ed.), *Profits, Progress and Poverty: Case Studies of International Industries in Latin America* (Notre Dame, Ind.: University of Notre Dame Press, 1985), and Harley Shaiken, *Mexico in the Global Economy: High Technology and Work Organization in Export Industries* (La Jolla: Center for U.S.–Mexican Studies, University of California, San Diego, 1990).

firms took the lead in creating an elaborate parts supply arrangement with foreign and local capital in Southeast Asia.[27] The regional integration scheme for autos, which stretches from Japan across East and Southeast Asia, entails strategic export-oriented investments similar to those in the North American auto complex that link component suppliers in Canada and Mexico with a variety of car assemblers in the U.S. market.

An interesting variation on the component-supplier arrangement are the subregional cooperation zones in East and Southeast Asia, known as "growth triangles."[28] These subregional divisions of labor typically involve neighboring countries at different levels of development that cooperate in the outsourcing and assembly of various kinds of products, ranging from cars to computers to clothes. The participants each have specific roles. In the Greater South China Economic Region, for example, Hong Kong is the service and finance center, Taiwan typically provides investment capital and technological expertise, and Fujian and Guangdong Provinces in South China offer land and labor. There are several such triangles operating or planned in Southeast Asia, the best known of which links Singapore, Johor State in Malaysia, and Riau Province in Indonesia. What these subregional integration pacts have in common is a well-defined division of labor in which TNCs farm out the production and assembly of parts to individual nations, eventually to be sent to an overseas destination. While the private sector decides where its investments should go, this arrangement often is facilitated by trade incentives offered by national governments.

Original equipment manufacturing

OEM refers to the production of finished consumer goods by contract manufacturers, which frequently are locally owned factories in the third world. The sourcing of inputs and the making of the final product are responsibilities assumed by the contractor, and the output is distributed and marketed abroad by large trading companies, foreign retail chains, or branded marketers. Also known as specification contracting, OEM has been the major export niche filled by the EANICs in the world economy since the

---

[27] See Henderson, *The Globalisation of High Technology Production,* and Doner, *Driving a Bargain.*

[28] For various illustrations of how these subregional growth triangles work in Asia, see Xiangming Chen, "The New Spatial Division of Labor and Commodity Chains in the Greater South China Economic Region," in Gereffi and Korzeniewicz (eds.), *Commodity Chains and Global Capitalism,* pp. 165–86. See also Chapters 7 and 8 (this volume).

1960s. In 1980, for example, Hong Kong, Taiwan, and South Korea accounted for 72 percent of all finished consumer goods exported by the third world to the advanced industrial countries, other Asian nations supplied another 19 percent, while just 7 percent came from Latin America and the Caribbean. The United States was the leading market for these consumer products, absorbing 46 percent of the export total.[29] Recently third world exporters have begun to decrease their reliance on their traditional overseas markets, however, especially the United States. By 1989, the four EANICs had cut their dependence on the U.S. market to the point where it represented only 25 to 40 percent of their total exports.[30]

The OEM role is a potentially profitable, but demanding and unstable, export niche. Unlike the prior two export roles, which are both forms of "subcontracting" because they involve a linkage with foreign firms that take full responsibility for supplying (in export-processing assembly) or buying (in component-supply subcontracting) all component parts for their factory affiliates, OEM producers make finished products that will be sold under another company's brand name. The contract manufacturer must have the capability to interpret designs, source the needed inputs, monitor product quality, meet the buyer's price, and guarantee on-time delivery. The fee charged by the contractor covers all material and production costs, plus a usually modest profit. Buyers reap the biggest gains in the chain.

The EANICs have excelled at OEM production, which has been the key to their export growth during the past several decades. There are various reasons for this success. In part, it has to do with East Asia's classic "pull" rather than "push" approach to exporting. In the push approach, typical among raw material or standardized product exporters, the manufacturer's philosophy is, "I will sell what I make." In the pull approach, the manufacturer's attitude is more market-oriented: "I will make what you need." This consumer-driven export mentality has allowed East Asian entrepreneurs to become full-range "package suppliers" for foreign buyers. Learning how to piece together all the material and service inputs required to make a wide range of finished consumer goods has given OEM producers a unique organizational capability for creating and managing elaborate, horizontal

---

[29] Donald B. Keesing, "Linking Up to Distant Markets: South to North Exports of Manufactured Consumer Goods," *American Economic Review* 73 (1983), 338–42, at 338–39.

[30] The U.S. market was most important for Taiwan (39 percent of total exports), followed by South Korea (35 percent), Singapore (30 percent), and Hong Kong (27 percent) (Dicken, *Global Shift*, p. 37).

networks of suppliers and buyers. Expertise in OEM production increases over time and it can lead to important forms of organizational innovation.

In addition, the pressures exerted by foreign buyers for new products have made industrial upgrading and backward linkages an intrinsic part of the OEM process. The EANICs are the only third world nations that have been able to create the diverse array of efficient supporting industries required by a dynamic model of specification contracting. While their governments have been supportive of this process, the key factor probably lies with an abundant supply of local entrepreneurs. East Asian factories tend to be locally owned and vary greatly in size. Large vertically integrated companies, such as South Korea's *chaebol,* have significant advantages in supplying world markets because of their scale economies and substantial financial support from the state. Established exporters in small-firm-dominated economies like Taiwan and Hong Kong also have been successful in their efforts to develop the technology and manufacturing expertise needed for high-quality global production, and to adjust their output flexibly to more sophisticated export items.[31]

The main advantage of the OEM export role is that it enhances the scope for local entrepreneurs not only to learn how to make internationally competitive finished consumer goods, but also to generate substantial backward linkages to the domestic economy. East Asian producers confront intense competition from lower-cost production sites in various parts of the third world. Furthermore, they have discovered that it is very difficult to establish forward linkages to their developed-country markets, where the biggest profits are made in buyer-driven commodity chains. East Asian manufacturers have tried to maintain close ties with foreign buyers, which has permitted the former to become middlemen in the triangle manufacturing networks that shift production of consumer goods to cheaper export sites. But foreign buyers frequently are driven by cost considerations to set up direct contacts with their main third world suppliers. Thus, a number of the firms in the EANICs that pioneered OEM are now pushing beyond it to

---

[31] Two excellent detailed monographs that deal with the role of local firms in South Korea and Taiwan, respectively, are Alice H. Amsden, *Asia's Next Giant: South Korea and Late Industrialization* (New York: Oxford University Press, 1989), and Robert Wade, *Governing the Market: Economic Theory and the Role of Government in East Asian Industrialization* (Princeton, N.J.: Princeton University Press, 1990). For comparisons with Hong Kong and Singapore, see Lu-Lin Cheng and Gary Gereffi, "The Informal Economy in East Asian Development," *International Journal of Urban and Regional Research* 18, 2 (June 1994), 194–219.

OBM by integrating their manufacturing expertise with the design and sale of their own brands of merchandise.

Original brand-name manufacturing

A final stage in the development of an export economy is to move beyond production for foreign buyers to the establishment of proprietary brand names that give third world exporters a more visible presence in both local and developed-country retail networks. South Korea is the most advanced of the East Asian countries in this regard, with Korean brands of automobiles (Hyundai), computers (Leading Edge), and household appliances (Samsung and Goldstar), among other items, being sold in North America, Europe, and Japan. Taiwan also sells its own brands of Acer and Mitac computers, Giant bicycles, Pro-Kennex tennis rackets, and Travel Fox shoes in overseas markets. Mexican beer has been one of the only branded products in Latin America that has developed a solid retail niche in the U.S. market.

Hyundai is the most prominent example of a third world manufacturer that decided to integrate forward to the marketing end of a producer-driven commodity chain. Hyundai entered the North American market for cars in the late 1980s by building an independent marketing network. By contrast, Daewoo and Kia, South Korea's other two major auto companies, relied on their OEM networks with General Motors (GM) and Ford, respectively, to market and sell GM and Ford car models that were made in Korea. Hyundai's strategy was risky because it only had 183 dealers in the U.S. market in 1987, compared with 3,000 dealers in GM's Pontiac Division and 5,700 dealers for Ford. But the strategy was also profitable. Hyundai obtained a 3.7 percent profit margin from production and a 7 percent margin from its marketing subsidiary, Hyundai Motor America. Daewoo earned a 3.6 percent profit margin, while GM appropriated an 8–9 percent yield from the marketing process. In response to competitive pressures, however, Hyundai changed its marketing system from single-point (or exclusive) dealerships to dual-point dealerships (i.e., dealers could sell other brands), and it launched an export diversification strategy by entering European markets.[32]

---

[32] For a more complete discussion of Hyundai's efforts to build its own retail network to sell cars in the United States, see Hyung Kook Kim and Su-Hoon Lee, "Commodity Chains and the Korean Automobile Industry," pp. 281–96, and Naeyoung Lee and Jeffrey Cason, "Automobile Commodity Chains in the NICs: A Comparison of South Korea, Mexico, and

Many Hong Kong apparel manufacturers have embarked on ambitious programs of forward integration into retailing, using their own brand names and retail chains for the clothing they make. These retail outlets started out selling in the Hong Kong market, but now there are Hong Kong–owned stores throughout East Asia (including China), North America, and Europe. A good example is the Fang Brothers, one of the principal Hong Kong suppliers for Liz Claiborne, who have several private-label retail chains (Episode, Excursion, Jessica, and Jean Pierre) in a variety of countries, including the United States.[33]

In the personal computer industry, Taiwanese companies were more in-clined to export their own brands of computers than their South Korean counterparts. In 1986, exports of personal computers by each country to-taled about $400 million. "Own-brand" computers comprised 28 percent of Taiwan's overseas sales, but only 16 percent of the Korean total. Con-versely, OEM sales of personal computers accounted for 44 percent of the Korean exports, but only 22 percent for the Taiwanese. The remainder were personal computer exports by subsidiaries of TNCs. This contrast in OBM versus OEM orientation reflects the two countries' distinct industrial capabilities: whereas Korea's much larger companies have sought a com-petitive edge based on price and standardized, mature products, Taiwan's smaller firms have emphasized flexibility, innovation, and market niches for nonstandardized products.[34]

The difficulties of OBM should not be underestimated, however, and some East Asian companies are shifting back to OEM work. In 1990 Mitac Corporation, the main competitor to Acer in Taiwan's personal computer market, made 70 percent of its computers under its own brand name and 30 percent for OEM clients. By 1993 the OEM ratio was back up to 60 percent. The reason, according to Mitac's president C. S. Ho, is that the firm was more profitable when it concentrated on its core competencies. "We asked ourselves: What functions are we best at? Our strengths are in R&D, design and manufacturing," says Ho. "We are now focusing on designing and supplying products and key components for major OEM customers, whose

Brazil," pp. 223–43, in Gereffi and Korzeniewicz (eds.), *Commodity Chains and Global Capitalism.*

[33] See Lardner, "The Sweater Trade," p. 46; Dianne M. Pogoda, "Two Foreign Retailers Find Niche in U.S.," *Women's Wear Daily,* July 7, 1992; and Zelda Cawthorne, "Paris Chapter for Episode," *South China Morning Post,* July 24, 1993.

[34] Brian Levy, "Korean and Taiwanese Firms as International Competitors: The Challenges Ahead," *Columbia Journal of World Business* (Spring 1988), 43–51.

brands are better-known but which have withdrawn from fully integrated manufacture."[35] The OBM option, while still remote for relatively advanced third world regions like Latin America and Southeast Asia, establishes a benchmark against which the most ambitious export firms will be measured.

Sequences of export roles

There are typical sequences of export roles. Virtually all countries begin exporting primary commodities (or raw materials), and then turn to staple consumer items such as garments and footwear. At this juncture, countries can go in either of two directions: they can increase the sophistication and local content of their finished-goods production by filling the OEM orders of foreign buyers, or they can make components or parts that will be exported for more complex finished goods assembled abroad (component-supply subcontracting). Either of these two intermediate export roles can lead to the export of local brands of finished goods (OBM production), such as Hong Kong clothes, Taiwanese tennis rackets, or Korean cars.[36]

The prominence and sequencing of these export roles varies markedly across third world regions. This reflects differences in the timing and impact of outward- and inward-oriented development strategies.[37] The East Asian approach was to combine EOI with selective forms of state intervention (export subsidies, import licenses, nontariff trade barriers, preferential credit, privileged access to quotas, and the like), and then to roll back these policies under internal and external pressure after successful export industries had been established. In Latin America and other third world regions, however, state intervention was used to promote ISI, not EOI. When the liberalizing reforms of the 1980s took hold, many nations opened their economies before the majority of their firms were internationally competitive. As discussed in Chapter 9, the resulting import surge has led to widespread plant closures (especially among small and medium-sized firms), job loss, and a worsening of income distribution. At the same time, some of the largest firms have raised their productivity and are increasing exports.

---

[35] Michael Selwyn, "Radical Departures," *Asian Business* (August 1993), 22–5, at 24.

[36] Another phase in the industrial development cycle is original design manufacturing, a key ingredient in product innovation. A number of firms in the EANICs already are at this stage.

[37] For a historical and comparative analysis of ISI and EOI development strategies, see Gary Gereffi and Donald L. Wyman (eds.), *Manufacturing Miracles: Paths of Industrialization in Latin America and East Asia* (Princeton, N.J.: Princeton University Press, 1990).

In contrast to those who would argue that EOI by itself can lead to sustained economic growth, the experience of the EANICs actually shows that a diversified array of backward linkages is essential in moving toward the more complex component-supply, OEM, and OBM export roles. The EANICs have been successful in upgrading their export industries in large measure because of their highly efficient networks of suppliers for intermediate goods (e.g., plastics, textiles) and components (e.g., semiconductors, computer chips, auto parts). These supporting industries allow East Asia's exporters to receive high-quality inputs at world-market prices. In addition, the EANICs have developed a full range of local design, financial, transportation, and communication services that give them major advantages over other third world production sites. The directions the East Asian economies can move in terms of industrial upgrading, however, are constrained by the availability of the natural resources on which these suppliers depend. The importance of raw material supply networks for successful export industries creates opportunities for resource-rich regions of the third world. East Asian nations have been forced to adjust to their escalating production costs and labor shortages by gravitating to higher-order forms of competitive advantage that are durable, add more value, and lead to constant improvement and industrial upgrading.[38]

Third world strategies for "moving up" in the global economy

National development implies technological advance and organizational learning, which are needed to climb a ladder of industrial complexity. Progress requires a dynamic enterprise base, supportive state policies, and improving skills and higher wages in the workforce. For most nations in the third world, joining the ranks of developed countries is an ever-receding frontier, complicated by a growing technology gap and a constantly changing international environment. Third world nations have utilized several strategies in recent decades to try to improve their global positions. These include government policies and organizational initiatives to increase productivity, new relations with foreign and local capital, and participation in regional economic blocs.

[38] See Michael Porter, *The Competitive Advantage of Nations* (New York: Free Press, 1990).

Narrowing the productivity gap

Third world regions confront a significant productivity gap with regard to the developed nations. The productivity gap, which is a rough indicator of the effect of disembodied technological progress on long-term economic growth, is about 2.5 to 1 between Latin America and the OECD countries, and it has grown wider over time. East Asia, by contrast, appears to have made major strides in closing this gap, while less advanced regions like Sub-Saharan Africa and South Asia presumably lag the furthest behind the global pacesetters. In the period 1950–89, Latin America's increase in total factor productivity was one-seventh that of the EANICs and one-fifth that of the developed nations.[39] A major problem is that most third world countries fail to use internationally available "hard" and "soft" technologies. This is apparent in outdated equipment, obsolete production methods, a deficient organization of labor, rigidly vertical industrial relations, inadequate quality, and poor after-sales service.

In their efforts to narrow the productivity gap, third world governments have pursued a variety of policy and institutional reforms. A coherent, stable macroeconomic policy that focuses on issues like exchange rates, inflation, and interest rates is widely assumed to be the necessary starting point for improved economic performance. This frequently is coupled with related mesoeconomic changes that affect the institutional environment within which firms operate (e.g., infrastructure, linkages with the scientific and technological system, training, finance, and the promotion of exports or new overseas markets). There is much less agreement, however, on the role to be played by microeconomic policies that directly affect the operations of firms in specific industrial sectors. In addition, serious questions have been raised about the contributions made by low-wage export industries to broader development objectives in the third world, such as upgraded skills, technology transfer, backward linkages to local suppliers, and improved living conditions. The experience of Mexico typifies these dilemmas.

Until the past decade, Mexico's *maquiladora* plants were relegated to a low-wage, export-processing role in the world economy. A major concern for Mexico was how to push beyond the enclave model of EOI represented by its traditional, labor-intensive *maquiladora* plants in order to adopt a

---

[39] UNECLAC, *Latin America and the Caribbean: Policies to Improve Linkages with the Global Economy* (Santiago: UNECLAC, 1994), p. 141.

more dynamic, industrially upgraded development strategy. This would generate higher incomes and better skills for Mexico's workers, and at the same time allow Mexican exports to be internationally competitive in technologically advanced sectors. In the 1980s, a new wave of *maquiladora* plants began to push toward a more sophisticated type of component-supplier production, making parts for capital- and technology-intensive consumer durable items like automobiles and computers.[40]

To successfully carry out this shift from the "old" to the "new" *maquiladoras,* however, Mexico must move from its wage-depressing export strategy to more productivity-enhancing strategies. So far, it has taken the "easy road" to export expansion, since the sharp devaluations of the Mexican peso in the 1980s and most recently in 1994–95 have significantly eroded real wages in the manufacturing sector. The EANICs, meanwhile, are moving in the opposite direction. They have diversified their exports in the face of a substantial appreciation (rather than devaluation) of their currencies, rising (not declining) real wages, and labor scarcity (rather than labor surpluses).

Although policy reforms have been central concerns of the political economy literature on third world development, scant attention has been given to the role of local innovations in stimulating economic growth and productivity increases in developing nations. There are several kinds of innovation that should be distinguished in the process of economic development. First, there are breakthrough innovations: the discovery of new products and processes that allow leading firms to fundamentally redefine the cost structure of modern industries so that old products and technologies become obsolete. Examples include the restructuring of the telecommunications industry around fiber optics and satellite systems (instead of copper cables), and the informatics revolution that replaced the mechanical and electrical business machines of several decades ago with a dazzling array of handheld and desktop computers that can be plugged into global information networks. Path-breaking innovations of this sort tend to be introduced in the most advanced nations, which helps them to retain their competitive edge in the world economy by ushering in new product cycles.

A second form of progress stems from less dramatic adaptive innovations, which are increasingly found in the NICs, especially in East Asia.

---

[40] See Gary Gereffi, "Mexico's Maquiladora Industries and North American Integration," in Stephen J. Randall (ed.), *North America without Borders?* (Calgary: University of Calgary Press, 1992), pp. 135–51.

These innovations involve the use of modern technologies by small and medium-sized firms in traditional as well as advanced industries. In the export-oriented garment sectors of South Korea, Taiwan, and Hong Kong, for example, new synthetic materials, laser cutting machines, and computer-aided designs are routinely employed to enhance the upgrading of garment exports destined for developed-country markets. Adaptive innovations are commonplace in the NICs' other major export industries as well, such as footwear, toys, semiconductors, and computers.

A third form of productivity-enhancing innovation that is often overlooked in developing nations is organizational in nature. There are numerous organizational innovations that have been critical to East Asia's economic superiority in recent decades. Japan is widely attributed with pioneering "lean production" as an alternative to "mass production" in the automobile industry,[41] a form of manufacturing organization that is now being widely emulated in other industries and by TNCs of all nationalities. East Asian production and export networks in producer-driven and buyer-driven commodity chains also rely on a wide range of regionally based vertical and horizontal organizational forms (e.g., trading companies, dense subcontracting networks, specification contracting, and triangle manufacturing), sustained by social ties involving ethnicity, kinship, and local communities. Finally, the evolution of the OEM and OBM export roles contains many innovative elements that constitute dynamic sources of competitive advantage in the world economy. Improvement in the organization of production is one of the social foundations of East Asia's export success, and it is an area where there is considerable scope for local innovations.

New relations with foreign and local capital

Economic liberalization has forced third world states to renegotiate their relationships with private capital, both foreign and local. In the past decade, direct foreign investment (DFI) has grown dramatically in most of the third world regions. By 1992, the global stock of DFI had reached approximately $2 trillion, with worldwide outflows of DFI recording steady gains from 1982 until 1991, when there was a decline. Whereas developing countries account for only 5 percent of the global stock of DFI, they received about 25

---

[41] See James P. Womack, Daniel T. Jones, and Daniel Roos, *The Machine That Changed the World* (New York: Macmillan, 1991).

percent of all inflows in 1991.[42] This leap can be traced to various factors, including privatization programs, debt-for-equity swaps, the growth of developing-country markets, and the rise of DFI by East Asian and other third world investors.

Liberalization trends alone are not sufficient to attract increased DFI. Foreign investment policy is just one element in a coherent and well-balanced development strategy that typically includes both macroeconomic and political stability, as well as a clear sense of the ground rules by which enterprises must operate. Frequently, countries such as those in Latin America and South Asia, which had adopted highly regulated environments and policies of assertive industrialization in the 1970s, have reopened sectors like mining and agriculture that previously were off limits to foreign capital, and lowered joint-venture requirements and other entry barriers in many manufacturing and service sectors. Among the most important lessons learned during the 1970s and 1980s, however, is that DFI policy should involve explicit commitments with respect to key national priorities such as export promotion and technological innovation, and that successful local firms are an important element in national development strategies.

The process of integrated international production is carried furthest by TNCs. This is promoted by a variety of new conditions, such as advances in information technology, a convergence in national patterns of consumer demand, intense global competition, and a less restrictive environment for trade and investment. Regional and global strategies by TNCs are replacing those geared to maximizing profits in individual countries; the latter were reinforced by the third world's ISI development strategies in the 1960s and 1970s. The challenge is for third world governments to harness the productive potential of TNCs, while at the same time learning how to capitalize on the multiple ways of linking up with the global economy. Buyer-driven commodity chains, in particular, involve non-DFI relations with foreign capital (i.e., buyers rather than manufacturers), and they also create more opportunities for learning by local firms.

In most of the EANICs, the state has induced local private capital to take a mercantilistic approach to global markets, where overseas sales are equated with enhanced national security and prestige. Exporting is viewed as a matter of long-term necessity, rather than short-term convenience. East

---

[42] UNCTAD, *World Investment Report, 1993: Transnational Corporations and Integrated International Production* (New York: United Nations, 1993).

Asian governments have used financial controls, export and import licenses, and other bureaucratic devices to exercise leverage over local exporters. Domestic firms in East Asia and other third world regions have a far greater incentive than do foreign companies not only to export, but also to establish more extensive backward linkages to local suppliers.

Shifting patterns of regional integration

A great deal of attention has been given to the growth of regional economic blocs in the past decade. As discussed in Chapter 3, these blocs take two quite different forms. On the one hand, the United States has joined the European countries in promoting formal regional agreements. Both the European Union and the North American Free Trade Agreement (NAFTA) are trade-based regional blocs, created and sustained by government policies. The Asia–Pacific Economic Cooperation forum (APEC), by contrast, is a fledgling agreement that advocates free trade by the year 2020 within a framework of "open regionalism." One of the issues at stake here is whether regional economic blocs are a stepping stone to a strengthening of multilateral institutions like GATT, or whether regional integration is merely a defensive maneuver that is used to exclude certain groups of countries from global markets.[43]

The Asian region is of interest in this regard for another reason as well. De facto regional integration in East Asia has been occurring through the strategies of Japanese, U.S., and European TNCs, largely in the absence of intergovernmental agreements. These regional divisions of labor in East Asia have been fostered by the lowering of trade barriers in the region, the shift of Japanese TNCs toward more offshore sourcing in low-cost production sites after the appreciation of the yen, and the emergence of new manufacturing centers in East and Southeast Asia.[44] Thus, we may refer to East Asia as a market-induced, rather than policy-induced, form of economic integration.

While trade alone tends to promote regional integration, DFI appears to be better at spanning different regional blocs and moving toward global economic integration. Trade-based forms of cross-border linkage, including EPZs, outsourcing, and free-trade areas, are "shallow" forms of economic

[43] UNECLAC, *Open Regionalism in Latin America and the Caribbean* (Santiago: UNECLAC, 1994).
[44] UNCTAD, *World Investment Report, 1993*, p. 129.

integration. "Deep" integration, on the other hand, involves the production of goods and services as a result of complex corporate strategies and network structures. The world economy seems to be evolving toward this more complex form of integrated international production, in which TNCs are key actors.[45] Strategic alliances have expanded, particularly in those industries with short product cycles and high research and development costs, while competitive pressures are forcing firms to seek cost savings from all segments of global commodity chains. In this light, it is interesting to examine the cross-regional impact of DFI from East Asia in Mexico and the Caribbean.

Burgeoning investments from Japan and the EANICs in North America are leading to a deepening of multilateral ties between the two regions. In anticipation of NAFTA, which took effect on January 1, 1994, Asian investors were anxious to set up transplant factories in Mexico and the Caribbean Basin in order to gain preferential access to the U.S. market.

Likewise, many of Mexico's traditional *maquiladora* exports are shifting to Caribbean venues, which are likely to become the favored locale for these low-wage activities. By the early 1990s, EPZs had become a leading source of exports and manufacturing employment in various Caribbean nations. In the Dominican Republic, for example, EPZs employed 142,300 Dominicans in 1992 (primarily in garment assembly) and generated $1 billion in trade, netting $300 million toward the balance of payments. In terms of employment, the Dominican Republic was the fourth largest EPZ economy in the world (the fifth if China's Special Economic Zones are included), and 11 percent of the more than 300 EPZ firms in the Dominican Republic were Asian.[46] Furthermore, East Asian projects were found to contribute more jobs, bigger investments, higher levels of local value added, and a greater utilization of skilled labor than the assembly-oriented sewing operations by other foreign firms.[47]

---

[45] Ibid.

[46] See EIU, *Dominican Republic, Haiti, Puerto Rico: Country Profile* (London: EIU, 1993–94), p. 20; Raphael Kaplinsky, "Export Processing Zones in the Dominican Republic: Transforming Manufactures into Commodities," *World Development* 21, 11 (1993), 1851–65; and Alejandro Portes, José Itzigsohn, and Carlos Dore-Cabral, "Urbanization in the Caribbean Basin: Social Change during the Years of the Crisis," *Latin American Research Review* 29, 2 (1994), 3–37.

[47] United States International Trade Commission (USITC), *Production Sharing: U.S. Imports under Harmonized Tariff Schedule Subheadings 9802.00.60 and 9802.00.80, 1985–1988*, USITC Publication No. 2243 (Washington, D.C.: USITC, 1989), ch. 6, p. 5.

Despite these gains, one should be skeptical of the longer-term role that labor-intensive EOI can play in the development of Caribbean nations. Although export-processing activities such as those that have grown so rapidly in Mexico and the Caribbean Basin in recent years have undeniable benefits in job creation, foreign exchange earnings, and the fostering of industrial experience, they do not by themselves constitute a sufficient basis for a long-term development strategy. Export-processing industries are best seen as a transitional phenomenon: the first stage in a process of moving to a higher level of industrial development, in which domestic inputs and diverse services also are required.

While many Caribbean nations are just now making the basic transition from farm to factory, Mexico is moving further up the industrial export ladder from clothes to complex components to computers. But they both have a long way to go before matching the success of the EANICs. The latter nations are shifting from their role as the principal suppliers of merchandise sold under the foreign buyers' labels in U.S. and European department stores, to making goods for export under their own brand names with a growing emphasis on booming Asian markets. Hong Kong, Taiwanese, and Korean manufacturers thus are closing the commodity chains for consumer items like apparel by moving all the way from raw material supply through retailing within the Asian region, while the North American consumer goods commodity chains still are stymied by their weakest link – production. It is an open question whether Mexican or Caribbean manufacturers, or their U.S. or Asian counterparts, will step forward to fill this regional gap.

Conclusions

Globalization is not inevitable, nor is it an unmixed blessing in terms of development. Its foundations are political as well as economic, and therefore far from stable. Globalization also generates substantial social and cultural resistance because of its uneven and in some cases marginalizing consequences within as well as between countries and regions. The tumultuous changes wrought by economic globalization affect all regions of the world. The East Asian nations, which have consolidated their position as economic front-runners during the past 25 years, are in the midst of a radical transformation in their industrial and export profiles, as low-wage industries are being shed for a technologically sophisticated and more service-oriented image. For other regions of the world, however, problems remain as countries try to escape wage-depressing export strategies, low productivity, and marginal forms of integration into the world economy.

From a neoclassical economics perspective, a global economy in which nations compete according to their resource endowments and factor costs is applauded because it promotes greater efficiency in the world as a whole. It is to be expected that labor-intensive industries will chase cheap labor all over the globe, while countries that invest in technology and capital will reap the benefits of innovation and industrial upgrading. A statist perspective, on the other hand, claims that efficiency needs to be counterbalanced by a regulatory framework that emphasizes national development for the entire society, not just for a few segments. Rampant globalization is criticized because it leaves too many groups in society unprotected. The dilemma facing state actors today is that they want to exercise more control in defending national economic interests, but they are not willing to risk being delinked from the world economy.

Although export performance can be a meaningful measure of international competitiveness for nations and regions alike, it should not be confused with full-fledged national development. Economic globalization has spurred EOI as a development strategy, but EOI investments tend to target specific sectors and geographic areas within a country. In a globalized environment, EOI can generate intense activity in circumscribed locales but leave vast portions of a country untouched. Furthermore, since the basic sources of competitive advantage in export-processing assembly or first-stage EOI (i.e., low wages and political stability) are transitory, many export industries are footloose and highly mobile. This means that the jobs, infrastructure, and other resources attracted to an export site may be left with few or no economic alternatives if foreign buyers or investors suddenly decide to go elsewhere.

Countries can pursue several related goals in an effort to make EOI part of an integrated development strategy: they can diversify into multiple export roles in order to spread the benefits of EOI to various sectors and regions of the country; they can move toward higher-value-added export activities, establishing backward and forward domestic linkages wherever possible; and they can combine EOI with appropriate phases of ISI since the complementarity of these two development paths helps to avoid the inherent limitations of an exclusive reliance on either external or domestic markets. Notwithstanding these caveats, third world nations have much to gain by expanding their participation in global export networks. Autarchy is not a viable option in an interdependent world where for most countries delinking means marginalization. This fate is often considered worse than incorporation under conditions of exploitation or dependency. At least in the latter situation, nations have strong incentives to improve their position in the world economy, mechanisms for technology transfer and organizational learning are available, and absolute improvements in living conditions frequently occur.

The main challenge for third world states in the contemporary era of global restructuring is the need to deal simultaneously with three fundamental issues: productivity, dependency, and equity. Productivity requires significant entrepreneurship to generate nontraditional exports, to increase the efficiency of firms, and to help provide workers with new skills relevant to a modern economy. Productivity-enhancing entrepreneurship has been in short supply in many third world settings, and where it does flourish, as in East Asia, it often relies on social networks and cultural orientations that are beyond the reach of state policies.

Dependency is entailed by the third world's open approach to foreign capital, and by the emphasis on free trade policies that leave national industrial sectors largely unprotected from the cyclical swings of the global economy. Local capital has begun to strengthen its relationship with third world states in the past decade, and it could become an effective counterweight to the influence of TNCs in national development strategies. The most successful countries in industrial upgrading and diversified exporting, such as the EANICs, have given a very prominent role to locally owned firms in their export sectors.

Equity involves fundamental concerns about jobs, workers, and the quality of life. In most third world regions, income distribution seems to have become more inequitable, even when national and sectoral indicators show that economies are growing. Programs aimed at strengthening small and medium enterprises generally lack the financing and training components required to improve the situation. Low levels of agricultural productivity are leading to an exodus of migrants to overcrowded urban centers, and modern export industries do not seem capable of providing enough stable jobs to substantially reduce high levels of unemployment in the least developed areas of the third world. More integrated and innovative national development strategies are needed to cope with these competing development objectives.

CHAPTER 5

New global financial trends: implications for development

STEPHANY GRIFFITH-JONES AND
BARBARA STALLINGS

One of the most dramatic political-economic changes over the past 15 years has been the shift in patterns of international finance. At the beginning of the 1980s, a select group of prosperous third world nations had privileged access to an enormous volume of commercial bank credit. They could also attract fairly important levels of direct investment. For all practical purposes, finance was no longer a binding constraint on the development strategies of this group of countries. Although poorer developing nations could not rely on private credit or investment, many of them had access to substantial amounts of funds via bilateral donors and the international financial institutions (IFIs). The industrial world, to a much greater extent, relied on its own domestic capital markets to meet its financial requirements.

By the latter half of the 1980s, in contrast, third world countries from Latin America and Africa had become largely marginalized from global capital flows, which were increasingly circulating among industrial nations. Insofar as they were still available to developing countries, capital inflows were swamped by amortization and especially by burgeoning interest payments. Indeed, a significant number of developing countries had become capital exporters. The result was a reversal of what development theorists had traditionally argued were the appropriate roles for developed and developing economies. The former were supposed to save more than they spent and export more than they imported, while the latter were supposed to consume more than they were able to save and import more than they exported. As a result, capital flows would go from developed to developing countries.

In the 1990s, a third pattern emerged. Although developed countries

The authors thank Phil Ruder for valuable assistance with the statistical work in this chapter. The chapter was previously published in *Pensamiento Iberoamericano*, September (1995).

continue to absorb the vast majority of funds, an increase in the total amounts in circulation, in the context of reforms in developing countries and lower international interest rates, led to a massive return of private flows to Latin America and some other developing countries. Unlike the 1970s and early 1980s, these inflows are coming mainly via portfolio and direct investment rather than commercial bank lending; more than expected, they are proving to be fragile and subject to investor swings of confidence. The sell-off of stocks and bonds in the so-called emerging markets in 1995, following the Mexican peso devaluation, have forced third world governments to rethink their financing strategies.

This chapter explores these financial trends to document their characteristics, explain their occurrence, and investigate their consequences. It provides data on the shifts in suppliers and recipients of foreign capital. To account for these shifts, it looks at structural changes in the financial markets themselves, the underlying macroeconomic and trade patterns in the industrial countries, the debt crisis of the 1980s, and changes in developing countries' economic policies. Next it focuses in more detail on financing patterns in different parts of the third world, including the return of private capital flows to several developing nations in the early 1990s, and the costs and benefits of the different patterns. The chapter concludes with a discussion of the implications for development strategy and outcomes in different third world regions in the years ahead.

Changing financial structures and patterns

Trends

While there is no doubt that both suppliers and users of foreign capital changed during the 1980s and early 1990s, it is not easy to provide a systematic picture of these changes. Most analysts have been interested either in flows among industrial countries or flows to and from the developing countries; thus, the relevant data are rarely presented in a comparable form for all countries. Moreover, the IMF – which does collect information on all countries – has discovered large discrepancies when trying to aggregate data for the entire world.[1] Keeping these problems in mind, we first

---

[1] To study the growing discrepancies in balance-of-payments statistics, the IMF has commissioned two reports. The first dealt with the current account; see *Report on the World Current*

present data on long-term capital flows by recipient region during the 1980–92 period (Table 5.1) and then turn to data on the composition of capital flows (Table 5.2) and the suppliers of funds (Table 5.3).

Four subperiods can be identified in the period analyzed. The first was 1980–82, the years before the debt crisis erupted, which were largely a continuation of trends present during the 1970s. The second was 1983–86, the period of early adjustment to the debt crisis and the "flight to quality." The latter involved a new preference for low-risk investment in highly creditworthy borrowing nations. The third period was 1987–90, when the overall volume of capital flows increased dramatically following the 1985 Plaza Accords, which raised the value of the yen and led to increased Japanese investment abroad, but the emphasis on quality investment continued. The last period was 1991–92, when total capital flows continued to increase very rapidly, but the share of flows going to developing countries started to grow again, mainly due to a rise in the share of capital going to Latin America.

Table 5.1 presents data during these four periods for average *net long-term capital flows* to industrial and developing countries and for *net transfers*.[2] As can be seen, the industrial countries' share of net capital flows increased from 57 percent in 1980–82, to 73 percent in 1983–86, and to 85 percent in 1987–90.[3] A parallel shift occurred within the developing world. Asian countries, which were perceived as the best credit risks in the third world, increased their share of the diminished financial resources still available to nonindustrial nations, from 22 percent in 1980–82 to 37 percent in

---

Account Discrepancy (Washington, D.C.: IMF, 1987). The second looked at the capital account; see *Report on the Measurement of International Capital Flows* (Washington, D.C.: IMF, 1992).

[2] Net long-term capital flows are defined as loan disbursements minus amortization plus official grants and direct foreign investment. Long-term is more than one year. Net transfers are defined as new resource flows minus interest payments on loans and profit repatriation on DFI. Note that neither category nets out capital provided to other parts of the world, which is captured in Table 5.3 on supply of capital.

[3] During the 1980s, short-term net flows were more biased toward industrial countries than were long-term net flows. Thus, industrial countries received 86.5 percent of short-term inflows in 1980–82, 91.7 percent in 1983–86, and 97.4 percent in 1987–90. Total short-term flows in nominal dollar terms are about the same as long-term flows: an annual average of $272 billion in 1980–82, $252 billion in 1983–86, and $522 billion in 1987–90. When *total* net flows (long- plus short-term flows) are examined, the percentages for industrial countries are the following: 72.3 percent in 1980–82, 82.1 percent in 1983–86, and 91.4 percent in 1987–90. In 1991–92, by contrast, short-term flows to industrial countries were negative because the Japanese banks were liquidating foreign assets to repatriate funds for use at home. (Sources and assumptions are explained in the notes to Table 5.1.)

Table 5.1. *Annual average long-term net inflows and net transfers of foreign capital by recipient, 1980–92 (billions of dollars)*

Recipient	1980–82	1983–86	1987–90	1991–92
Total net inflows[a]	257 (100.0)	288 (100.0)	540 (100.0)	845 (100.0)
Industrial nations[b]	147 (57.2)	210 (72.9)	458 (84.8)	700 (82.8)
Developing nations[b]	110 (42.8)	78 (27.1)	82 (15.2)	145 (17.2)
Africa[b]	16 (14.5)	11 (14.1)	17 (20.7)	19 (11.7)
Asia[b]	24 (21.8)	27 (34.6)	30 (36.6)	55 (37.9)
Western Hemisphere[b]	44 (40.0)	19 (24.4)	20 (24.4)	49 (33.8)
Other[b,c]	26 (23.6)	21 (26.9)	15 (18.3)	22 (15.2)
Total net transfers[d]	69 (100.0)	78 (100.0)	206 (100.0)	530 (100.0)
Industrial nations	33 (47.8)	84 (107.7)	217 (105.3)	488 (92.1)
Developing nations	36 (52.2)	−6 (−7.7)	−11 (−5.3)	42 (7.9)
Africa	7 (19.4)	1 —[e]	3 —[e]	3 (7.1)
Asia	9 (25.0)	8 —[e]	6 —[e]	19 (45.2)
Western Hemisphere	12 (33.3)	−21 —[e]	−19 —[e]	14 (33.3)
Other	8 (22.2)	6 —[e]	−1 —[e]	6 (14.3)

Note: Figures in parentheses are percentages.
[a]Net inflows are the flows into region (of types shown in Table 5.2) minus repayments.
[b]Categories as defined by IMF.
[c]Other is the Middle East and "nonindustrialized" Europe.
[d]Net transfers are the long-term net inflows minus income on long-term investment (authors' estimates based on World Bank figures; see note *b*, Table 5.2).
[e]Percentages not meaningful because of negative total for developing nations.
Source: Calculated from IMF, *Balance of Payments Yearbook*, Vol. 2, *1987, 1991, 1993.*

1987–90. The increased Asian resources during the 1980s came mainly at the expense of Latin America and of the Middle East (included in "other" in the table); Africa's share actually increased a bit during the 1980s, largely as a result of industrial governments' response to the serious crises and emergencies in Africa.

In the early 1990s, the pattern shifted in some significant ways. The share of capital flows going to industrial nations fell slightly from the 1987–90 peak, declining from 85 to 83 percent, but it remained at a very high level. Among developing regions, the Asian share continued its upward trend, but other regions underwent major changes. The absolute value of capital inflows to Latin America more than doubled, while the region's share rose from 24 to 34 percent. The main loser was Sub-Saharan Africa, whose share fell from 21 to 12 percent of total capital inflows; the "other" regions also saw a smaller decline from 18 to 15 percent.

The trend in net transfers was even more dramatic as the industrial nations went from 48 percent of the total in 1980–82 to 105 percent in 1987–90.[4] The latter was possible because developing countries became capital exporters by the last half of the decade. A disaggregation among the developing countries highlights the particularly negative situation of Latin America in the 1980s. That region experienced heavy net outflows on the order of 4 percent of GDP, while the Asian nations continued to receive large net inflows. Net transfers to the African countries fell sharply after 1982 but never became negative. The most important change in the early 1990s was that developing countries as a group again became capital importers, that is, they again had positive net transfers. The change was mainly caused by Latin American countries, whose net transfer position shifted from fairly large negative flows to large positive ones.

Table 5.1 also shows the increase in overall volume of capital flows circulating among countries. The average more than doubled (in nominal dollar terms) from $257 billion in 1980–82 to $540 billion in 1987–90; it again increased very significantly to $845 billion in 1991–92. This represents an annual average rise of nearly 15 percent over the 12-year period. Discounting for inflation, the increase in real terms was around 10 percent per year,[5] well above the GDP growth rate for even the fast-growing Asian region. This would seem to provide evidence that the fears in the late 1980s of a worldwide capital shortage were not valid, even though a large proportion of the capital flows among countries does not involve investment or trade but activities such as foreign exchange speculation. The allocation of

---

[4] Short-term net transfers are much larger than the long-term figures shown in Table 5.1, but the industrial-developing-country ratios are similar with the exception of the earliest period. The industrial countries received 87.3 percent of short-term net transfers in 1980–82, 100.1 percent in 1983–86, and 100.9 percent in 1987–90. For 1991–92, see note 3. (For sources and assumptions, see Table 5.1.)

[5] Data are deflated by the consumer price index for the industrial countries; see IMF, *International Financial Statistics Yearbook, 1993*.

Table 5.2. *Annual average long-term net inflows and net transfers of foreign capital by type of flow, 1980–92* (billions of dollars)

Type of flow	1980–82			1983–86			1987–90			1991–92		
	Ind.	Dev.	Total	Ind.	Dev.	Total	Ind.	Dev.	Total	Ind.	Dev.	Total
Official transfers	23	15	38 (14.8)	26	16	42 (14.6)	51	20	71 (13.1)	97	26	123 (14.6)
Direct investment	37	18	55 (21.4)	43	14	57 (19.8)	138	23	161 (29.8)	109	45	154 (18.2)
Portfolio investment	48	4	52 (20.2)	112	3	115 (39.9)	188	6	194 (35.9)	374	37	411 (48.6)
Other long-term capital	32	56	88 (34.2)	17	12	29 (10.1)	78	−7	71 (13.1)	119	8	127 (15.0)
Exceptional financing	7	17	24 (9.3)	12	33	45 (15.6)	3	40	43 (8.0)	1	29	30 (3.6)
Total net inflows	147	110	257 (100.0)	210	78	288 (100.0)	458	82	540 (100.0)	700	145	845 (100.0)
Investment income[a]	114	74	188	126	84	210	241	93	334	212	103	315
Total net transfers	33	36	69	84	−6	78	217	−11	206	488	42	530

Note: Ind. refers to industrial countries; Dev. to developing countries. Figures in parentheses are percentages of total net inflows.
[a] Long-term investment income for loans is approximated by using the relevant percentages for long- and short-term interest payments provided in *World Debt Tables*.
Source: Calculated from IMF, *Balance of Payments Yearbook*, Vol. 2, 1987, 1991, 1993.

capital between developed and developing countries is a separate issue that may be a cause of greater concern.

Table 5.2 highlights the changing composition of capital flows during the period analyzed. Overall, the most important increase was in portfolio investment, which rose from 20 to 49 percent of the total. Direct investment, which increased from 21 to 30 percent in the 1980s, saw its share decline sharply to only 18 percent in the early 1990s. "Other long-term capital," mostly commercial bank loans but also including official (bilateral and multilateral) loans at commercial rates, fell in absolute as well as relative terms in the 1980s, declining from 34 percent of total capital flows in 1980–82 to 13 percent in 1987–90. The share increased somewhat in the early 1990s.

For industrial nations, virtually all types of capital flow rose substantially during the 1980s, although the most important increases were in direct and portfolio investment. In the early 1990s, there was a fall in direct investment going to industrial countries; at the same time, portfolio flows to industrial nations doubled.

Developing countries experienced a drop in net inflows during the 1980s, most of it accounted for by the decline of commercial bank credit. Only exceptional financing (flows resulting from debt restructuring) showed a large increase. Summing new bank loans and the restructuring components, however, still produced a significant decline in bank credit, which had been the dominant type of international finance for developing countries during the 1970s and early 1980s. Direct investment flows to developing countries increased sharply in the early 1990s, but portfolio flows to these countries increased far more, growing by more than 500 percent between 1987–90 and 1991–92. In this latter respect, flows to developing countries in the early 1990s began to follow trends similar to those in the industrial world during the 1980s. Another significant development was that commercial bank credit to developing countries as a whole again turned positive, signaling the improved outlook for the debt problem. Nonetheless, the fact that there were still substantial amounts of restructuring finance (although less than in the second half of the 1980s) showed that some countries, especially those in Africa, continued to suffer a severe debt crisis.

One particularly surprising trend seen in Table 5.2 is that official transfers (grants and concessional loans) to industrial countries increased dramatically, both in absolute terms and as a proportion of total transfers. While official transfers going to developing nations increased from $15

billion in 1980–82 to $26 billion in 1991–92 (less than twofold), official
transfers to industrial countries increased from $23 billion in 1980–82 to
$97 billion in 1991–92 (increasing fourfold). It should be noted that the
latter figure includes an extraordinary one-time item: the large transfers by
Saudi Arabia and Kuwait to the United States to pay for the Gulf War. If
these are excluded, official transfers to industrial nations reached around
$75 billion in 1991–92, a level that is more than triple the 1980–82 level.
The unexpected fact that official transfers to developed countries grew far
faster than those to developing nations seems to be explained by an important increase in official transfers within the European Community. Indeed,
the decision to establish the Single European Market and the third enlarge-
ment of the Community provided the catalyst for a major increase in the
European Commission's expenditure on the so-called structural funds.
Thus, the resources allocated through those funds almost doubled in real
terms between 1987 and 1993, reaching ECU 62 billion ($77 billion) in
1993.[6]

Finally, Table 5.3 suggests some of the shifts in the major suppliers of
foreign capital. At the beginning of the decade, the United States was the
single largest exporter of capital to the rest of the world. Between 1980 and
1982, it provided 15 percent of all capital. Other large industrial country
suppliers were the United Kingdom (11 percent), Germany (10 percent),
and France and Japan (8 percent each). The Middle East, mainly Saudi
Arabia and Kuwait, was also a major supplier, providing 13 percent of the
total volume of foreign capital in 1980–82.

By the end of the 1980s, the picture had shifted in several ways. The U.S.
share of capital supply had fallen to 8 percent; the UK and French share
declined marginally (to 10 and 7 percent, respectively), and the Middle East
share had nearly disappeared (less than 1 percent). Indeed, in the 1983–86
period, the Middle East was a net capital importer. The other side of this
picture was the increased role of Germany (12 percent of total capital) and
especially Japan (25 percent). Among developing countries, Asia had come
to surpass the Middle East with 1.5 percent of total capital export. The IFIs
(the World Bank and the regional development banks, excluding the IMF)
increased their share of net capital flows between 1980–82 and 1983–86,

---

[6] See Stephany Griffith-Jones and Christopher Stevens, "Regional Trade Liberalization
Schemes: The Experience of the EC," paper presented to IDB-ECLAC Seminar on Hemispheric Trade Liberalization, Washington, D.C., May 1992.

Table 5.3. *Annual average long-term net outflows of foreign capital by supplier, 1980–92 (billions of dollars)*

Supplier	1980–82		1983–86		1987–90		1991–92	
Industrial nations	185	(72.0)	260	(83.3)	528	(86.6)	675	(81.8)
United States	39	(15.2)	37	(11.9)	51	(8.4)	95	(11.5)
United Kingdom	29	(11.3)	38	(12.2)	62	(10.2)	82	(9.9)
Germany	25	(9.7)	32	(10.3)	75	(12.3)	103	(12.5)
France	21	(8.2)	16	(5.1)	44	(7.2)	69	(8.4)
Japan	22	(8.6)	77	(24.7)	153	(25.1)	94	(11.4)
Other	49	(19.1)	60	(19.2)	143	(23.4)	232	(28.1)
Developing nations	39	(15.2)	5	(1.6)	20	(3.3)	45	(5.5)
Africa	1	(0.4)	1	(0.3)	1	(0.2)	1	(0.1)
Asia	1	(0.4)	3	(0.9)	9	(1.5)	16	(1.9)
Western Hemisphere	2	(0.8)	1	(0.3)	4	(0.7)	7	(0.8)
Southern Europe	1	(0.4)	1	(0.3)	1	(0.2)	—	—
Middle East	34	(13.2)	−1	(−0.3)	5	(0.8)	21	(2.5)
International organizations	33	(12.8)	47	(15.1)	62	(10.2)	105	(12.7)
Total net outflows[a]	257	(100.0)	312	(100.0)	610	(100.0)	825	(100.0)

Note: Figures in parentheses are percentages.
[a]In principle, total net outflows for Tables 5.1–5.3 should be identical (except for the inclusion of international organizations in Table 5.3); as has long been observed in practice, however, there are serious statistical problems in reconciling international accounts. See note 1 for a source on this issue.
Source: Calculated from IMF, *Balance of Payments Yearbook,* Vol. 2, *1987, 1991, 1993.*

from 13 to 15 percent, but it fell in the last part of the decade (to 10 percent) since the IFIs' new loans did not keep up with repayments on older credits.[7]

In the early 1990s, the United States increased its share of capital supply to 11.5 percent of the total, but it was only the second largest supplier; the largest was Germany with 12.5 percent. Japan's share fell sharply in the early 1990s to only 11 percent. This decline resulted from a fall in Japan's direct investment in the United States and in Japanese purchases of U.S.

[7] Richard Feinberg, "Overview: An Open Letter to the World Bank's New President," in Richard Feinberg and contributors, *Between Two Worlds: The World Bank's Next Decade* (Washington, D.C.: Overseas Development Council, 1986), pp. 3–31.

Treasury Bonds, as an unprecedented economic crisis in Japan itself caused a strong portfolio shift to shore up domestic businesses.

In summary, then, there were four major changes in international capital flows during the period analyzed. First, the overall volume of flows increased significantly. Second, a major change in recipients shifted money away from the developing countries and toward the industrial nations during the 1980s, a trend that was partially reversed in the early 1990s. Within the developing world, from the mid-1980s Asia replaced Latin America as the largest recipient of foreign finance and investment. Third, direct investment and portfolio investment displaced commercial bank credit as the major types of capital flows. Fourth, the United States was displaced by Japan and Germany as the largest supplier of capital as of the late 1980s. By the early 1990s, the three were at a roughly even level, as U.S. capital exports rose and those of Japan fell.

Explanations

These four changes – increased volume of capital in circulation, increased absorption by industrial countries, increased importance of direct and portfolio investment, and increased role of Japan and Germany as suppliers – are interrelated. Thus, the various explanatory factors to be discussed jointly account for this set of changes in patterns of global financial flows during the 1980s.

One of the most important factors involved changes in the structure of the financial markets. Such changes had actually begun in the 1960s with the emergence of the Euromarkets. These offshore financial markets grew very rapidly, from an estimated $100 billion in 1970 to over $800 billion in 1980. The reasons for this growth are well known: lack of regulation of the Euromarkets in general, including the lack of reserve requirements, supplemented by petrodollar deposits after the 1973–74 and 1979 oil price increases.[8]

Initially, these new international markets were separated from domestic capital markets in the industrial nations. Gradually, however, the wall began

---

[8] Data are from the Bank for International Settlements, *Annual Report,* various issues. On the history and structure of the Euromarkets, see M. S. Mendelsohn, *Money on the Move: The Modern International Capital Market* (New York: McGraw-Hill, 1980), and Geoffrey Bell, *The Eurodollar Market and the International Financial System* (London: Macmillan, 1974).

to fall as industrial governments liberalized access and the major markets became more integrated. Liberalization had several manifestations. First was the dismantling of barriers to cross-border financial flows. This involved the elimination of taxes, exchange controls, and various types of restrictions on access to domestic markets. Second, as a result of the new access, banks began to set up branches or to buy other banks in industrial countries. This trend was especially noteworthy in the United States, where Japanese and European banks became important actors. With the acceleration of European integration, branching in Europe also became popular, but greater obstacles to foreign banking remained in Japan. Once branches were established, they had to justify their existence by increased lending. Third, many new financial instruments were developed, which also speeded up growth of capital markets. In general, securitization became more important at the expense of bank loans, assets were packaged into tradeable securities, and futures and options gained popularity. Swaps were added in the 1980s, and international mutual funds brought individual investors into the market and increased available capital. In the early 1990s, the international bond markets opened again to developing nations, and American and global depository receipts (ADRs/GDRs) provided their companies with access to the industrial countries' stock markets.[9]

During the 1970s, these innovations had led to greatly increased access to international finance for some developing countries via the Eurocurrency market. A subset of middle-income developing countries became favored clients of the international banks. In the 1980s, however, financial innovations, in conjunction with other developments, led to a greater concentration of capital flows to the industrial countries.

One of these developments was the debt crisis that erupted in August 1982.[10] When the Mexican government declared it could not continue to meet its payments on the previously agreed upon schedule, the bubble burst

---

[9] For excellent analyses of the international capital markets, see the IMF's annual publication *International Capital Markets*. This publication provides both statistical data and information on structural changes.

[10] The debt crisis continues to be the subject of analysis. Recent general sources include William Cline, *International Debt Reexamined* (Washington, D.C.: Institute for International Economics, 1994), and Barry Eichengreen and Peter Lindert (eds.), *The International Debt Crisis in Historical Perspective* (Cambridge, Mass.: MIT Press, 1990). On Latin America, see Robert Devlin, *Debt and Crisis in Latin America: The Supply Side of the Story* (Princeton, N.J.: Princeton University Press, 1989). On Africa, see Carol Lancaster and John Williamson (eds.), *African Debt and Financing* (Washington, D.C.: Institute for International Economics, 1986). The major source of statistics is the World Bank's annual publication *World Debt Tables*, which also provides analysis of recent trends.

on third world debt. Thus, bankers as a group decided to stop loans to virtually all nations in Latin America and the few in Africa that had been able to borrow on the private markets. With the exception of the Philippines, however, Asian borrowers were viewed as more creditworthy and continued to have access to commercial bank finance. The loans of the 1970s and early 1980s had been voluntary, since the banks had eagerly sought to make them as a way to increase their profits. It was these voluntary loans that ended for Latin America and Africa.

In their place came "involuntary" loans, but their volume was significantly lower than those they replaced. Involuntary loans were one component of the package deals put together by the international financial institutions and the governments of the industrial countries to deal with the debt crisis. That is, banks were forced to provide new loans, equivalent to a certain percentage of their exposure, in order to obtain help in securing their existing loans. The loans were combined with ongoing negotiations to reschedule amortization payments falling due. Although euphemistically referred to as "new money," the involuntary loans mainly served to enable debtor countries to maintain interest payments on their debts.

The quid pro quo for the rescheduling and new loans in Latin America and Africa were policy conditions, geared to free up resources for debt service. These policies were designed in close collaboration with the IMF and the World Bank, which also provided their own loans to help with debt service and to offer incentives for policy change. Initially, the new policies involved typical IMF-designed measures to cut domestic spending. The resulting recession lowered imports, which generated trade surpluses allowing the large net transfer of financial resources to take place. During the course of the decade, however, policies evolved toward so-called structural adjustment whereby governments cut their own economic role, liberalized domestic markets, and reduced barriers to foreign trade and capital flows.

The results were mixed. During the 1980s and particularly the early 1990s, some countries (especially in Latin America) saw a resumption of growth, while others (especially in Africa) remained mired in recession or even depression. The Asian countries, by contrast, grew rapidly and quickly overcame whatever debt problems they had. The change in economic policies in Latin America and the increased growth rates in that region helped to fuel the renewed interest of international investors as of the early 1990s, which reversed the negative resource flows that had characterized much of the developing world during the preceding decade. As will be seen later, however, interest rate trends in the industrial countries were an essential complement to events internal to the third world, leaving some question about the durability of the new capital flows.

At about the same time in the early 1980s, when many developing countries were running into severe debt problems that led to capital outflows, trends in the industrial world were moving in a direction that resulted in increased inflows to those countries. Specifically, fiscal and trade deficits began to grow. By far the most prominent case, of course, was the United States. During the Reagan–Bush years, the U.S. budget deficit increased from $76 billion in 1980 to $219 billion in 1990, and the current account of the balance of payments went from a surplus of $2 billion in 1980 to a peak deficit of $160 billion in 1987 before falling to $92 billion in 1990.[11] Given the low and declining savings rate in the private sector, the only way these deficits could be sustained was through foreign borrowing. Thus, by 1984, the United States had become the world's largest debtor, as foreigners became major purchasers of U.S. government securities used to finance the growing budget deficit. These funds were simultaneously the counterpart to the trade deficit.[12]

The trade deficit also stimulated capital flows into the United States in at least two other ways. On the one hand, the most conspicuous part of the U.S. trade deficit was with Japan, and growing calls for protection against Japanese imports brought the establishment of "transplants." Especially in the automobile industry and electronics, Japanese firms set up production facilities in the United States as a substitute for exports. (Nonetheless, their imports of inputs helped to keep the U.S. deficit with Japan at a high level.) On the other hand, attempts to cut the trade deficit led to the Plaza Accords in the fall of 1985, partly designed to lower the value of the dollar in order to make U.S. exports more competitive. The higher value of the yen resulted in more Japanese investment abroad. Some of this investment went to Asia, but most wound up in the industrial countries, especially the United States, thus reinforcing the trend toward transplant industries. (See Chapter 4, this volume, for further discussion of the globalization of industry.)

Other industrial countries also ran large fiscal deficits in the 1980s, as expenditures grew and revenues failed to keep pace. Virtually all had deficits on central government accounts during the decade, and all but Japan

---

[11] Data are from various issues of the IMF's semiannual publication *World Economic Outlook*.
[12] "IMF, *World Economic Outlook* (Washington, D.C.: IMF, April 1988), pp. 88–90.

also had deficits on the broader general government accounts. There were differences in the size of these deficits and the pattern during the decade; more importantly, there were also differences in the capacity to finance the deficits and domestic investment through private savings. With the exception of Germany and Japan, all of the major industrial countries turned to external savings during the 1980s, whereas only the United Kingdom and Canada did so in the 1970s.[13]

It is generally acknowledged that the Reagan budget deficits were a crucial factor in pulling the U.S. economy out of the recession that marked the early 1980s. Indeed, unlike the situation in the earlier postwar period, from 1983 to 1988, the United States grew faster than the major European countries and even Japan. Under the Bush administration, U.S. growth rates fell off, in part because of attempts to cut the deficit. The counterpart was falling interest rates, which declined from relative highs in 1989 to postwar lows in 1993 before turning up again. It was these falling interest rates that led U.S. investors, followed later by Europeans as their rates began to fall too, to look abroad for better returns; Asia and Latin America appeared especially attractive in this context.[14]

As we stated at the outset of this section, these international financial trends and their explanations are very complex and intertwined. Increases in the volume of international capital flows derived from shifts on both the supply side (changes in market structure) and demand side (increased deficits in the industrial countries, especially the United States). Although demand for capital in the third world continued, the inability to pay rendered this demand ineffective in most countries outside Asia until the early 1990s. Sources of supply moved toward the nations with big current account surpluses: no longer OPEC but Japan and also Germany (until reunification absorbed the German surplus). The type of capital exports changed from an emphasis on bank loans to direct and portfolio investment, both as a consequence of demand in the industrial countries but also the

---

[13] For an analysis of fiscal deficits and savings rates in industrial countries during the 1980s and projections for the 1990s, see IMF, *World Economic Outlook* (Washington, D.C.: IMF, October 1993), chap. 4.

[14] It is interesting to note that Eastern Europe and the former Soviet republics have not become significant competitors for Latin America and East Asia, despite fears to that effect with the end of the cold war. As Fred Halliday argues in Chapter 2 of this volume, such competition has not emerged among private investors, although there has been some shift among multilateral and bilateral donors. The latter has involved a movement of personnel as much as financial resources.

interests of suppliers. Thus, the OPEC governments' preference for bank deposits was replaced by German and Japanese private-sector preference for equity shares, real estate, and production facilities, as well as government securities. In the early 1990s, Latin American countries began to join their East Asian counterparts as participants in these new forms of international finance.

Contrasting patterns of external finance for the third world

Flows of capital to the different regions of the developing world in the 1980s and early 1990s have had significantly different features, in terms of their stability and composition. The most positive pattern was found in Asia, where net inflows increased gradually over time; the Asian region also had the largest volume of inflows. Latin America experienced a very volatile pattern of capital inflows, high at the beginning and end of the period but low in between, while Africa's access to external finance stagnated at a relatively low level.[15]

Table 5.4 provides details on these diverging patterns. The most dramatic, by far, was found in Latin America. The average capital flows going to Latin America in 1980–82 were nearly twice as high as those in Asia and three times as high as those of Africa. By mid-decade, with the onset of the debt crisis, these flows had collapsed to only 40 percent of their previous level and remained at similar low levels through the end of the 1980s; they were well below inflows to Asia. By the beginning of the 1990s, however, the flows more than doubled to figures exceeding those before the debt crisis began, but they nonetheless failed to catch up to the Asian level.

There were several determinants of these fluctuating totals. Most obvious in the early years was the behavior of commercial bank loans (the major component of the "other long-term capital" category). These loans had come to account for over half of all capital inflows to Latin America by the early 1980s. From 1983, they were negative, as lenders refused to roll over maturing credits. To some extent, the outflows were compensated for by restructuring loans ("exceptional financing"), but the totals for the two

---

[15] An earlier discussion of differences between the role of foreign capital in Latin America and East Asia is found in Barbara Stallings, "The Role of Foreign Capital in Economic Development," in Gary Gereffi and Donald Wyman (eds.), *Manufacturing Miracles: Patterns of Industrialization in Latin America and East Asia* (Princeton, N.J.: Princeton University Press, 1990), pp. 55–89.

Table 5.4. *Annual average long-term net inflows of foreign capital to developing countries by region, 1980–92 (millions of dollars)*

Type of flow	1980–82	1983–86	1987–90	1991–92
Western Hemisphere				
Official transfers	1,231	1,571	2,219	2,831
Direct investment	6,719	3,470	6,081	13,545
Portfolio investment	2,364	−616	3,980	26,988
Other long-term capital	26,660	−8,971	−18,271	−2,803
Exceptional financing	6,891	23,426	25,597	8,214
Net long-term flows	43,897	18,879	19,606	48,775
Asia				
Official transfers	3,121	3,382	3,908	4,022
Direct investment	3,859	5,043	13,896	24,005
Portfolio investment	1,431	2,771	343	6,219
Other long-term capital	15,299	15,253	11,610	18,863
Exceptional financing	681	866	693	1,453
Net long-term flows	24,391	27,314	30,449	54,562
Africa				
Official transfers	4,077	4,261	6,898	9,806
Direct investment	1,316	900	1,616	2,523
Portfolio investment	−305	47	−422	1,091
Other long-term capital	7,846	1,696	−480	−4,600
Exceptional financing	3,410	4,392	9,176	9,910
Net long-term flows	16,344	11,296	16,817	18,730

Source: Calculated from IMF, *Balance of Payments Yearbook,* Vol. 2, *1987, 1991, 1993.*

types of finance fell from an average of $33 billion in 1980–82 to $11 billion in 1983–90 to only $5 billion in 1991–92. It should be noted that bilateral and especially multilateral loans (the other main components of "other long-term capital") increased in importance during the crisis period of the 1980s, but dropped off again in the early 1990s.[16]

---

[16] The IMF data used to construct Tables 5.1–5.3 do not provide a breakdown of long-term capital by source. Based on World Bank figures, which do offer such a disaggregation, the ratio of commercial bank loan *disbursements* to those of official creditors for the Western Hemisphere was 4.7 in 1980, 0.5 in 1986, 0.6 in 1987–90, and 1.1 in 1991–92. Calculated from World Bank, *World Debt Tables, 1993–94,* Vol. 1, p. 187.

More positive from the point of view of volume of capital inflows were direct foreign investment (DFI) and portfolio investment. DFI to Latin America also fell in the immediate aftermath of the debt crisis, but returned to earlier levels by the end of the decade and more than doubled in the early 1990s as transnational firms regained confidence in the region. Portfolio investment followed a similar but more pronounced trend, becoming negative in the mid-1980s but reaching unheard-of levels — an average of $27 billion per year — by 1991–92. The portfolio investment boom also resulted from increased confidence in Latin America, but an equally important stimulant came from low interest rates in the United States and one-time opportunities for profits in Latin American stock markets. Official transfers doubled between the early 1980s and the early 1990s, but remained as a very small share of overall external finance.

Trends in Asia differed from those characterizing Latin America in many ways.[17] Overall flows started out in the early 1980s at a much lower level than in Latin America, but they continued to increase by modest amounts throughout the decade. In the early 1990s, Asia also witnessed a substantial jump in foreign capital inflows, although the percentage increase was less than that in the Western Hemisphere.

In terms of the composition of flows, several important differences with respect to Latin America should be noted. The first concerns commercial bank lending. With the exception of the Philippines, Asian nations did not confront serious debt crises in the 1980s. Korea had a debt/GDP ratio similar to that of Brazil and Mexico, but the high level of its export revenues meant that the debt could be serviced without serious problems. Furthermore, banks "regionalized" their perceptions, withdrawing credit from all Latin American countries and sustaining it in Asia, even in cases where economic indicators were fairly similar. As a consequence, Asian nations never lost access to commercial bank finance, although the absolute amounts dipped somewhat in the late 1980s. The counterpart is that restructuring finance never reached high levels either. Also important in the Asian

---

[17] In this chapter, unlike others in the volume, Asia includes all three subregions: East Asia, Southeast Asia, and South Asia. They have quite different patterns of foreign capital use. East Asia, especially South Korea and Taiwan, relied heavily on their own domestic savings. Southeast Asia, especially in the past decade, has received large amounts of direct foreign investment in the industrial sector from other Asian countries. Finally, the South Asian pattern is most similar to Sub-Saharan Africa, although the absolute amounts are lower, even before taking per capita criteria into account.

context were bilateral nonconcessional loans, especially from the Japanese government, as well as some multilateral credits.[18]

Second, DFI in Asia increased steadily throughout the period. The rise was slow until the Plaza Accords in 1985 raised the value of the yen with respect to the dollar, thus driving up costs in Japan and lowering the competitiveness of Japanese exports. Japanese firms countered by moving some of their plants to Southeast Asia (mainly Thailand, Malaysia, and Indonesia), from whence they imported a portion of the resulting manufactured items and exported the rest to third countries. A second phase of this process occurred in the later 1980s, when the currencies of South Korea and Taiwan were also allowed to appreciate, and they too began to invest in Southeast Asia. Portfolio investment in Asia also increased substantially in the early 1990s, compared with the 1980s, but it did not reach nearly the volume of similar flows into Latin America. Official transfers were slightly larger than in Latin America (mainly going to the South Asian nations of India, Pakistan, and Bangladesh), but not very significant in overall terms.

Finally, Africa illustrates yet a third pattern of capital flows. Like Latin America, the debt crisis in Africa led to a drop in total flows in 1983–86. By 1987–90, flows again reached the level found at the beginning of the decade, but they rose only slightly in the 1990s. In other words, Africa has not participated in the current foreign investment boom that Latin America and Asia have experienced.

Compositional differences in African capital inflows in comparison with other developing areas are also apparent in Table 5.4. The most obvious difference is the role of official transfers. These grants and concessional loans represented 25 percent of total external finance to Africa in the early 1980s. A decade later, the figure had risen to over 50 percent, as the deep crises of growth and development and several major emergencies led bilateral and multilateral donors to respond. The debt crisis meant that commercial bank and other nonconcessional lending became negative by the second half of the decade, and restructuring finance increased concomitantly. Figures for both categories in the early 1990s – unlike the situation in Latin America – suggest that the debt crisis in Africa still remains serious. Even in Africa, DFI and portfolio investment have increased in the past few years, but the levels are very low compared with the rest of the third world.

---

[18] Ratios of commercial bank disbursements to official credits for the East Asian and Pacific region were 2.0 in 1980, 1.4 in 1986, 1.2 in 1987–90, and 1.6 in 1991–92. Calculated from World Bank, *World Debt Tables, 1993–94,* Vol. 1, p. 179.

In addition to examining differences in the composition of capital flows over the entire period, it is important to focus specifically on the situation as of the early 1990s, since this is the principal basis for projections of future trends. The current composition of flows varies substantially across regions, as seen in the last column of Table 5.4. The dominant component of Asian flows is DFI (44 percent of the total), followed by commercial bank and nonconcessional public-sector loans (35 percent). For Latin America, by contrast, the most important item is portfolio investment (55 percent), with DFI in a distant second place (28 percent). In Africa, official transfers and restructuring loans are of roughly equal importance.

These different kinds of flows have important implications for development prospects. In financial terms, the official transfers from bilateral aid agencies and special programs of the IFIs are the most favorable type of flow, since they either do not have to be repaid at all (grants) or have very low interest rates and long maturities (concessional loans). Precisely because they have such favorable terms, however, such funds are available only to the poorest third world countries, mainly in Sub-Saharan Africa and South Asia. Although Africa is the recipient of the large majority of such flows within the third world, they have generally been insufficient to stimulate much growth given the overwhelming problems in the region. (For discussion of the reasons, see Chapter 10, this volume.)

Coming next in favorability of financial terms have traditionally been bilateral and multilateral nonconcessional loans. The former have usually been export credits tied to the purchase of the exports of the donor nation. In the case of Japan, however, a new type of "untied" loan for middle-income countries was introduced in the late 1980s, as part of Japan's attempt to recycle its large trade surplus and to dampen the complaints of the United States. Although these credits, whether bilateral or multilateral, have shorter maturities and higher interest rates than concessional loans, they have nonetheless tended in the past to carry more favorable terms than those of commercial banks or the bond markets. In the early 1990s, however, very creditworthy developing countries have been able to raise private funding at lower cost (albeit with shorter maturities) than they obtain via multilateral loans.

Commercial bank loans, on the whole, have higher interest rates (and other fees) and, above all, shorter maturities. They also tend to have floating interest rates, which complicates the calculation of service requirements and increases the instability of debt service. Nonetheless, during the 1970s, third world governments thought they offered significant advantages in comparison with other types of finance. Commercial bank loans were seen as superior to bilateral and multilateral loans because they did not have conditions attached to them, and they were regarded as better than DFI because recipient governments could exercise more control over their use. Once these loans expanded to the point where they could not be serviced, however, multilateral conditionality reappeared, as discussed earlier.

Direct investment, shunned in the 1970s in favor of bank loans, came to be seen in a more positive light in the 1980s. Several factors probably accounted for the change of opinion in developing countries, in addition to the fact that bank loans were no longer available except in Asia. First, these flows are perceived as more stable since it is difficult to withdraw fixed capital assets. Second, profit outflows vary with the economic cycle, so that servicing direct investment is easier than servicing loans. Third, direct investment is a way to import technology and know-how. And, fourth, direct investment can facilitate exports. Southeast Asian countries provide good examples of these advantages, as the DFI from Japan and the East Asian newly industrialized countries (NICs) has gone heavily into the production of manufactured exports. The relationship between DFI and exports, however, is less clear in other regions.

Finally, there is the new portfolio investment. These flows can be divided into various categories, as seen in Table 5.5. The largest is bonds, which have accounted for well over half of portfolio investment in recent years. Bonds have the advantage of being mainly at fixed interest rates, but the average maturity for bonds issued by developing countries in the 1990s is very short (e.g., at around four years for Latin America). This implies that a large portion of the stock of bonds could be fairly rapidly run down, should the bonds not be renewed in the future. Less dramatic, but also a cause of concern, is the risk that even if the bonds are renewed, the cost of borrowing will significantly increase. The problem of nonrenewal of bonds played a key role in the Mexican crisis, especially since many of the bonds had maturities of less than a year.

A new form of external private funding is international equity investment, composed of direct equity investment, American and global depository receipts (ADRs/GDRs), and investments via mutual funds. As shown in Table 5.5, they have together provided about a third of the portfolio investment flows to developing countries between 1989 and 1993. Like DFI, these international equity flows have the advantage of a degree of

Table 5.5. *Portfolio investment in developing countries by instrument, 1989–93 (millions of dollars)*

Instrument	1989	1990	1991	1992	1993[a]
Foreign equity investment	3,485.7	3,773.6	7,552.2	13,073.1	13,190.6
Closed-end funds	2,199.4	2,867.4	1,196.0	1,344.1	2,737.3
ADRs/GDRs	0.0	138.0	4,902.2	5,933.0	7,252.0
Direct equity investment	1,286.3	768.2	1,454.0	5,796.0	3,201.3
Debt instruments	4,030.4	5,555.0	12,723.2	23,736.7	42,600.0
Bonds	3,543.1	4,683.0	10,193.5	21,244.7	39,190.0
Commercial paper	327.3	225.0	1,380.0	851.0	1,610.0
Certificates of deposit	160.0	647.0	1,149.7	1,641.0	1,800.0
Total	7,516.1	9,328.5	20,275.5	36,809.8	55,790.6

[a]Figures for 1993 are estimates.
Source: World Bank, *World Debt Tables, 1993–94*, Vol. 1, p. 21.

cyclical sensitivity of dividends, but they also carry important risks for recipient countries. For various reasons, investors could stop investing in equities, and even try to sell their stocks quickly, if they feared worsening economic or political prospects in a country. This could lead to pressure on the exchange rate and/or price falls in domestic stock exchanges. The latter effect could have a negative impact on aggregate demand – via a wealth effect – and on the domestic financial system, especially if banks and securities activities are closely integrated through cross-holdings or investor leveraging.[19] Again, the Mexican-led crisis provides clear examples of these problems, which spread to other parts of Latin America and even to Asia.

It has been argued that the composition of capital inflows into Asia and Latin America has important effects on the impact and reactions to such flows.[20] One type of impact concerns the relationship between capital inflows and investment in the recipient country. Specifically, DFI is directly linked to investment, while other types of flows may go for other purposes. Thus, the fact that DFI predominated in flows to Asia seems to be an important reason why recent capital inflows have been associated with increased investment, whereas the lower proportion of DFI to Latin America in the same period may be an important factor explaining why the surge in foreign capital has not been matched with a corresponding increase in investment. It is interesting in this context to note that Chile, which is one of the countries in Latin America attracting the highest proportion of DFI, also has seen its level of total investment increase far more than the rest of Latin America during this period.

The different composition of flows also helps to explain the differential macroeconomic impact of such flows. As Calvo, Leiderman, and Reinhart show,[21] the recent surge in capital inflows in Latin America has been accompanied by a real exchange rate appreciation; in Asia such an apprecia-

---

[19] See Stephany Griffith-Jones, "European Private Flows to Latin America: The Facts and the Issues," in Ricardo Ffrench-Davis and Stephany Griffith-Jones (eds.), *Coping with Capital Surges: Latin America in the 1990s* (Boulder, Colo.: Lynne Rienner, 1995), pp. 41–73. See also Vittorio Corbo and Leonardo Hernández, "Macroeconomic Adjustment to Capital Flows: Latin American Style versus East Asian Style," World Bank, mimeo, July 1994.

[20] Guillermo Calvo, Leonardo Leiderman, and Carmen Reinhart, "Capital Inflows to Latin America with Reference to the Asian Experience," IMF Paper on Policy Analysis and Assessment (Washington, D.C.: IMF, 1993).

[21] Ibid.

tion is less common. Excessive appreciation of local currencies is undesirable because it discourages production of tradeable goods. Such appreciation has been partially avoided in Asia because DFI has led to higher investment, which requires large-scale imports of capital goods (in a far higher proportion than do consumption increases).[22]

Also, DFI would seem to pose less problematic effects for the conduct of monetary policy. Since DFI is not usually intermediated through the domestic banking system, there is no accompanying expansion in domestic credit, and therefore the difficult issue of the sterilization of such monetary expansion is less important.[23] Thus, the different composition of capital flows, as well as the different historical stability in the evolution of such flows, may help explain why concerns over "hot money" and a sudden reversal are more prevalent among Latin American policy makers than among their Asian counterparts.

In addition to their possible impact on investment and macroeconomic policy in recipient countries, financial flows also have an impact via conditionality. In the 1980s, an important by-product of the debt crises of Latin America and Africa was the increased role that the IMF, the World Bank, and the regional development banks played in assembling restructuring packages for countries in those two regions. As discussed earlier, attached to the packages were a large number of policy conditions, which greatly influenced the conduct of economic policy in those countries.[24]

At least three types of conditionality need to be briefly distinguished. The first is macroeconomic conditions, oriented mainly to eliminating budget and balance-of-payments deficits. While macroeconomic conditions had long been advocated by economists in the IFIs, their impact became much more pervasive in the 1980s because a consensus on their advisability emerged among donors, both public and private. In the preceding decade,

---

[22] Other sources, however, suggest that a more important reason for the lack of currency appreciation in Southeast Asia may be government purchase of foreign currency. See "Malaysia's Problems with Prosperity," *Economist*, July 16, 1994.

[23] See Robert Devlin, Ricardo Ffrench-Davis, and Stephany Griffith-Jones, "Surges in Capital Flows and Development: An Overview of Policy Issues," in Ffrench-Davis and Griffith-Jones, *Coping with Capital Surges,* pp. 225–60.

[24] For different interpretations of the importance of conditionality, see Miles Kahler, "External Influence, Conditionality, and the Politics of Adjustment," pp. 89–136, and Barbara Stallings, "International Influence on Economic Policy," pp. 41–88, both in Stephan Haggard and Robert Kaufman (eds.), *The Politics of Economic Adjustment* (Princeton, N.J.: Princeton University Press, 1992).

private creditors had undermined the influence of the IFIs by providing large amounts of finance to the wealthier developing countries in Latin America and East Asia with virtually no strings attached. Consequently, only the African region was generally subject to strict conditionality in the 1970s. During the debt crisis, the Latin Americans joined the queue for conditioned finance although most of the Asian countries did not. Again in the early 1990s, IFI conditionality to Latin America was weakened by increased access to private sources, as several Latin American countries became "reluctant borrowers" from the IFIs.

The second type of conditionality involved structural reforms, designed to create market-oriented economies in recipient countries. Particular emphasis was placed on opening up third world economies to international trade and capital and on limiting the role of the state. The latter was related to the shrinking of fiscal deficits mentioned earlier, but also extended to liberalization, deregulation, and the sale of state firms. These structural conditions had been part of IFI programs for Africa throughout the 1980s, but they did not become generalized to other regions until the announcement of the Baker Initiative in the fall of 1985. With this initiative, then–U.S. Treasury Secretary James Baker also tried to move debt policies beyond austerity and toward growth. The basic idea was that freer markets and an active role for the private sector would be the motor of renewed growth. The main instrument for these policy conditions became the structural adjustment loans of the World Bank.

A brief review of the main policy conditions advocated by the IFIs and others in Washington, as seen by an influential think tank, will serve to summarize the quid pro quo that accompanied official loans in the 1980s.[25] Later we will discuss the likelihood that they will continue in the 1990s. The policy conditions were said to include: (1) elimination of large fiscal deficits, mainly through a reduction in government spending; (2) reorientation of public spending, especially toward education and health, and perhaps infrastructure; (3) establishment of a broad tax base with moderate rates; (4) market determination of interest rates, preferably at a positive but

---

[25] Together these policies have been dubbed the "Washington Consensus." They were first enumerated in the volume edited by John Williamson, *Latin American Adjustment: How Much Has Happened?* (Washington, D.C.: Institute for International Economics, 1990). Later Williamson differentiated some policies as generally accepted and others as more controversial. See John Williamson, "Democratization and the 'Washington Consensus,'" *World Development* 21, 8 (August 1993), 1329–36.

moderate level; (5) maintenance of a competitive exchange rate, so as to promote exports and bring about a current account that can be financed; (6) promotion of exports, especially nontraditionals, and the liberalization of imports; (7) encouragement of DFI to provide capital, skills, and technology; (8) sale of public enterprises, both to relieve the demand for subsidies and because private ownership is believed to be more efficient; (9) deregulation to increase competition and make it easier for the private sector to engage in economic activities; and (10) guarantee of property rights in order to stimulate private investment, both domestic and foreign.

Finally, in the 1990s, a third type of conditionality has emerged that goes beyond economic performance.[26] Typical of this new trend are conditions to encourage pro-poor policies, reduced military expenditures, respect for human rights, good governance, democracy, and environmental protection. These conditions were mainly introduced by bilateral donors; the IFIs have been somewhat more reluctant. There is much less consensus with respect to these noneconomic goals, and individual donors emphasize different aspects. The United States, for example, has placed a special stress on democracy, while some Europeans (especially the Dutch and Scandinavians) have emphasized the alleviation of poverty. Japan and Germany have taken the lead on trying to reduce military expenditures. According to a recent analysis,[27] the process also varies with the "new" conditionality. Most importantly, both bilateral and multilateral donors have placed more stress on persuasion than on conditionality per se. When conditions are used, they have been selective, focusing on cuts in aid to particularly egregious offenders or rewards to outstanding performers. Not surprisingly, the results have been mixed.

Implications for development and development strategies

Having examined trends in international capital flows in the 1980s and early 1990s, we now turn to our final task and ask about the impact of external

---

[26] Various types of political conditionality have been analyzed in a series published by the Overseas Development Council. See, e.g., Joan M. Nelson with Stephanie Eglinton, *Encouraging Democracy: What Role for Conditioned Aid?* (1992); Nicole Ball, *Pressing for Peace: Can Aid Induce Reform?* (1992); and Maurice J. Williams and Patti L. Petesch, *Sustaining the Earth: Role of Multilateral Development Institutions* (1993). The summary volume of the series is Joan M. Nelson and Stephanie J. Eglinton, *Global Goals, Contentious Means: Issues of Multiple Aid Conditionality* (1993).

[27] See Nelson and Eglinton, *Global Goals, Contentious Means,* especially Part 4.

financial trends on development prospects during the rest of the decade. First, we outline three ways that international financial flows can influence development strategies and prospects. Then we focus on regional differences among Africa, Asia, and Latin America.

A first way in which international finance has an impact on development strategy is via explicit conditionality imposed by the IFIs. The most explicit conditions are those on IMF and World Bank loans, but other financial institutions, such as regional development banks and bilateral donors, also impose policy conditions. In fact, the abundance of institutions and conditions involved, leading to what has been called "cross-conditionality," often makes negotiations quite cumbersome.[28]

Among the various types of conditionality reviewed in the preceding section, it is the structural conditions that are particularly potent in shaping development strategies. They were designed to move third world countries away from their traditional import-substitution industrialization policies – featuring high levels of protection and a strong role for the state – toward the market-oriented policies advocated by the IFIs. Although there is disagreement on how effective these conditions have been, and they are certainly not the only reasons for the shift, it is hard to deny that IFI conditionality has had a role in the dramatic change in development strategies that occurred in some parts of the third world during the past decade. This role was particularly important in the early 1980s, when there was often strong disagreement between the IFIs and developing country governments. By the late 1980s and early 1990s (particularly in Latin America), there was much more agreement between policy makers and IFIs. Conditionality has thus become both less controversial and less influential, but it is still very time-consuming for donors and recipients alike.

Although more low key, the IFIs are likely to continue to influence policy in the rest of the 1990s. In particular, the IMF and the World Bank can be expected to continue in their role as powerful advocates of market-oriented policies, both in providing incentives for new countries to undertake such reforms and especially in trying to prevent "backsliding" among countries that already have done so. Nonetheless, these organizations were in the early 1990s providing a smaller proportion of external finance to developing countries than they did in the mid-1980s, so their direct influence

---

[28] See, e.g., Enio Rodriguez and Stephany Griffith-Jones (eds.), *Cross-conditionality, Banking Regulation and Third World Debt* (London: Macmillan, 1992).

declined. For example, the IMF and the other IFIs provided slightly over 20 percent of the total external finance for Sub-Saharan Africa in 1992–93, compared with 40 percent in the mid-1980s. For Latin America, they provided 16 percent in 1992–93, versus 33 percent in the earlier period; for East Asia the figures were 7 and 14 percent, respectively.[29] In the particular case of Latin America, the IFIs have regained a significant role in the mid-1990s. The large IMF loans to Mexico and Argentina, as part of the synchronized international attempt to deal with the foreign exchange crises following the Mexican devaluation, are the most dramatic examples. Nonetheless, the conditionality accompanying these loans was essentially to ratify policies already underway.

A second type of influence exerted by the providers of foreign capital is what might be called implicit conditionality. This concept refers to the requirement by private investors and lenders that recipient nations follow certain kinds of policies in order to be deemed "creditworthy." Such requirements are rarely laid out in the explicit form assumed by agreements with the IFIs. Rather they are the factors that transnational corporations, managers of mutual funds or insurance companies, and private bank officers take into account in allocating their investments.

It will be recalled that, in the 1970s, private banks were willing to lend to any third world country that was growing rapidly and appeared able to service the loans. With the return of private capital through DFI, bond issues, and the stock markets, the possibility exists that investors will forget the problems of the 1980s and put their money wherever profit opportunities appear, regardless of policies. Our assumption, however, is that memories are likely to linger at least for the rest of the decade, so that private investors will pay substantial attention to the policies in recipient countries. This seems particularly true for more long-term as well as more prudent investors, such as the Japanese.

Of particular concern to investors are likely to be the macroeconomic context (especially the fiscal balance); the role of the state in the economy; tariff and other trade policies; foreign investment regulations, including rules on profit remittance; and intellectual property codes, property rights, and other aspects of the legal framework. In addition, of course, investors are also worried about political stability as well as stability in economic

---

[29] These percentages were calculated from World Bank, *World Debt Tables, 1993–94,* Vol. 1. Data cited as mid-1980s correspond to the year 1986.

management. It should be mentioned, however, that for very short-term flows, these types of conditions are less important than the yield differentials that can be obtained.

If economic (and political) conditions change in ways that are perceived as negative by investors, it is now much easier for foreign money to be withdrawn, as seen in the outflow of funds from Mexico following the 1994 devaluation, exacerbated by political instability and the rise in U.S. interest rates. The fact that the Mexican problem spread so quickly to other countries was especially troubling. Nonetheless, as discussed earlier, some types of investment are more difficult to withdraw than others. Stocks can be sold quickly, but direct investment projects cannot be rapidly liquidated. This is an important reason why countries prefer to attract DFI and are less enthusiastic about (or even try to discourage) very short-term flows.

Both explicit and implicit conditionality can have an important impact on the type of development strategies and policies selected by third world governments, and indeed they have helped reinforce the move toward market-oriented approaches. In addition, however, external financial flows can also influence these strategies and policies by helping determine whether or not they are successful. Obviously the new market-oriented policies will not be continued indefinitely if they are not perceived as having a positive impact on growth rates and (at least in the medium term) as improving the lives of individual citizens in developing countries.

In this sense, external finance can promote success by providing additional resources for investment, channels for marketing abroad, technological know-how, and so on. Nonetheless, if financial flows are very volatile, and especially if this volatility operates in a pro-cyclical fashion, their positive impact will be diluted. Likewise, if such flows lead to a significant appreciation of the local currency, they can undermine attempts to increase exports, an important aspect of the new development models. Or, even more problematic, if they basically go to increase consumption or speculative activities, then they will distort local prices and make market-based decisions more difficult. Furthermore, in this case, they will not create the productive capacity that will help the country to service these flows in the future. This could risk a future debt crisis.

Therefore, the impact of foreign flows on countries' long-term growth will depend both on the type of flows and their sustainability, but also to an important extent on how governments adapt their macroeconomic management to maximize the positive impact of those flows and minimize negative effects, such as an overheating of the economy and/or overvaluation of exchange rates. Naturally, the range of maneuver for governments to define macroeconomic policy has become more limited by the very magnitude of these international financial flows and, more generally, by the process of economic globalization. This is true not just for developing countries, but also for developed ones. For example, major changes in the European Union's exchange rate system were caused largely by private international financial flows.

In principle, all three types of influence – explicit conditionality, implicit conditionality, and influence on policy success – will affect the different regions of the developing world in similar ways. In practice, however, some important distinctions can be seen. For example, the percentages cited earlier on external finance provided by the IFIs vary significantly by region. Thus, we would expect the IFIs, with their explicit conditionality, to be most important in Africa, somewhat important in Latin America, and relatively insignificant in East Asia. This could change if, for example, Latin America were to see its access to private funding significantly reduced.

With respect to the implicit conditionality associated with private investors, we need to look at the main sources of such investment to see if they embody different policy preferences. Here it makes sense to concentrate mainly on Asia and Latin America, since private capital is rare in Africa. As shown in Chapter 3 (see especially Tables 3.3 and 3.4), most investment in the Asian developing countries comes from the region itself (Japan and the East Asian NICs). In Latin America, by contrast, most investment, especially in the recent boom of the 1990s, has come from the United States with Europe as a secondary source.

Asian investors, as well as their governments, tend to favor economic policies that are somewhat different from those advocated by the IFIs. For example, in the past several years, the Japanese have begun to question some of the structural conditions typically attached to IFI loans.[30] Likewise, the policies associated with Japanese and other Asian investment have not been of the type advocated by the IFIs. Rather, they have included fairly

---

[30] The most important early document is Overseas Economic Cooperation Fund (OECF), "Issues Related to the World Bank's Approach to Structural Adjustment: Proposal from a Major Partner," OECF Occasional Paper No. 1, October 1991. See also World Bank, *The East Asian Miracle: Economic Growth and Public Policy* (Washington, D.C.: World Bank, 1993).

high tariff barriers, and they have been promoted in various ways by active governments. If most of the foreign capital in the Asian region is provided by that region itself, then a bifurcated situation might occur where IFI conditions are reinforced in Latin America and Africa, while other policies are followed in Asia. Moreover, these differences between Latin America and Asia (especially East Asia) are not due only to the different level of IFI influence. Of increasing importance is the fact that many Latin American policy makers have become convinced of and committed to "pure" market development strategies, while Asian policy makers prefer a somewhat more active role for the state, although of a selective type. The empirical question of interest, then, is which of the sets of policies produces better results in terms of development outcomes. These issues will be explored in the final chapter of the volume.

A final source of regional differences focuses on the types of external finance and their impact on the success of whatever package of policies is chosen. Table 5.4 showed that a different "profile" of financial flows characterizes Africa, Asia, and Latin America in the 1990s. Specifically, we saw that direct investment is the dominant form of external finance in East Asia, portfolio investment is the most important type of inflow to Latin America, while official transfers predominate in Africa. Insofar as these types of flows have different impacts on policy, we can expect additional regional variation.

We argued earlier that, since DFI is more long term and uses more imported inputs, it is less likely to be subject to problems of volatility and to cause an overvaluation of the exchange rate. It is also more closely associated with increased investment, possibly including investment in the export sector. Portfolio investment, by contrast, has a much greater chance of causing appreciation of the currency, being used for purposes other than productive investment, and entering and leaving the country in response to very short-term criteria. Although official transfers can also lead to an overvaluation of the currency, they are not generally subject to the other problems mentioned. Since they are frequently provided in the context of enormous economic, social and political problems, the mere lack of negative impact on policy instruments does not automatically lead them to have a clear positive impact on production or other outcomes. Nonetheless, the overall effect of official transfers is generally deemed to be positive.

In summary, external financial flows can be expected to continue to have an important influence on economic development prospects in the third world. Based on the composition of flows as of the early 1990s and the history over the last 15 years, our analysis of the future leads us to predict that foreign capital will play a somewhat more positive role in Asia than in Latin America. From the purely financial characteristics of financial flows to Africa, the impact there should be even more positive, but it is likely to be more than offset by the deep-rooted structural problems facing that region.

CHAPTER 6

The "triumph" of liberal economic ideas in the developing world

THOMAS J. BIERSTEKER

Since the beginning of the 1980s most of the developing world has moved unevenly but undeniably toward liberal, market-oriented economic reforms. The 1960s and 1970s were decades of unprecedented economic national-ism, a growing role for state intervention in the economy, and experimenta-tion with variants of socialism and self-reliance. Comprehensive develop-ment planning was widespread, and the prevailing model of development throughout much of Latin America, Asia, and Africa was a variant of a statist, largely inward-oriented import-substitution industrialization. It was also socially redistributive, at least in rhetoric. The 1980s and 1990s, by contrast, have provided a nearly complete reversal in economic policy. Virtually everywhere, developing countries have begun restructuring the nature of their intervention in the domestic economy, liberalizing their domestic trade and investment regimes, privatizing state-owned enterprises, and pursuing a variety of economic reforms.

Behind these policy changes was a new set of ideas. According to some observers, the striking convergence in the pattern of economic (and politi-cal) reform efforts reflects a "triumph" of liberalism on a global scale.[1] It is the "end of history," ushering in a new period of liberal ascendance. This theme has been popularly restated by the U.S. media during the past several years. The extent to which this vision of the new world order is globally shared is subject to serious debate and will be considered in further detail later in this chapter. Nevertheless, there is little doubt that there has been a major change in the language used, the distinctions promulgated, and issues considered important during the past fifteen years.

The political power of ideas and of ways of thinking about development

---

[1] Francis Fukuyama, *The End of History and the Last Man* (New York: Free Press, 1992).

can be considerable and far reaching. A system of ideas, a revised conceptual framework, or even a simple slogan or mobilizing phrase can effect significant changes in the definition of interests, which in turn can influence both individual and group behavior. Ideas and the conceptual frameworks that accompany them help to frame issues and define what is an important problem. They provide critical distinctions, convey the basis for new categorizations, and may determine the very nature of core units of analysis. The language employed in their dissemination has the power to determine what appears to be "natural," taken for granted, unquestioned, or not requiring any further explanation. Thus, ideas can define away problems as much as they define them.

The reception of ideas in a particular national context is rarely identical from country to country. Rather, it tends to be contingent at least in part on the institutional configuration of the state, its prior policy experiences and recent failings, as well as the political viability of new ideas, where that viability is determined by the ability to mobilize support among existing political coalitions or to forge new ones.[2] Ideas can have an independent political effect, but they also need an enabling environment in which to take root and flourish. As Peter Hall has suggested, "Ideas have real power in the political world, [but] they do not acquire political force independently of the constellation of institutions and interests already present there."[3]

The purpose of this chapter is to begin an exploration of the apparent "triumph" of liberal economic ideas in the developing world. Just what is the nature of the change in economic thinking? How did it take place as quickly and as extensively as it did during the 1980s and 1990s? How deeply is it rooted in developing countries today, and what are the implications for our current thinking about development?

The nature of change

To get a better sense of the change in ideas about economic policy, it is useful to reflect back on the nature of the discourse on development that

---

[2] Margaret Weir and Theda Skocpol, "State Structures and the Possibilities for 'Keynesian' Response to the Great Depression in Sweden, Britain, and the United States," in Peter Evans, Dietrich Ruschemeyer, and Theda Skocpol (eds.), *Bringing the State Back In* (Cambridge University Press, 1985), pp. 107–63.

[3] Peter Hall, *The Political Power of Economic Ideas* (Princeton, N.J.: Princeton University Press, 1989), p. 390.

prevailed in the mid-1970s. Although there was tremendous variation in the details of economic policy thinking in different countries, it is still possible to discern a general set of concerns and issues under discussion at the time. It was the era of OPEC price shocks, the formation of cartels modeled after OPEC, the nationalization and indigenization of multinational corporations, and a perceived threat from the developing world.[4] Third world solidarity was not an entirely empty slogan, and the creation of a "new international economic order" was the agenda of the day. Developing countries were united (to various degrees) in an attempt to stabilize commodity prices, gain preferential access to developed-country markets, obtain less restricted access to international finance, and secure easier terms for development assistance. The United Nations was leading the effort to negotiate a code of conduct for transnational corporations operating throughout the world.

A basic premise of much development thinking during this period was that the structure of international economic relations was biased against the countries of the developing world. The structure of the international system, rather than characteristics internal to developing countries, was identified as the principal source of underdevelopment. Development was viewed as qualitatively, even profoundly, different in the North and South, to the extent that the laws of neoclassical economics were assumed not to apply equally in the developing world.[5] That is, while in theory there might be nothing wrong with the operations of markets, in practice, imperfections tended to impede their effectiveness in the developing world.[6] These were views commonly associated with structuralist and dependency thinking, but they were also widespread in development economics more generally. Although the more radical ideas were never implemented as development policy, these perspectives were listened to and set the terms for much of the discourse about development – in the centers of world economic power as well as the periphery.

The very definition of development common to the period is useful to recall when trying to place the current development discourse in perspective. In its discussion of the meaning of development, the Brandt Commis-

[4] See, e.g., C. Fred Bergsten, "The Threat from the Third World," *Foreign Policy* 11 (1973), 102–24.
[5] Albert O. Hirschman, "The Rise and Decline of Development Economics," in his *Essays in Trespassing: Economics to Politics and Beyond* (Cambridge University Press, 1981), pp. 1–24.
[6] Gerald K. Helleiner, *International Economic Disorder: Essays in North–South Relations* (Toronto: Toronto University Press, 1981).

sion Report, published in 1980, argued that "we must not surrender to the idea that the whole world should copy the models of highly industrialized countries."[7] It continued:

Over recent years experts and international observers have become aware that development strategies which used to aim at increasing production as a whole will have to be modified and supplemented in order to achieve a fairer distribution of incomes taking into account the essential needs of the poorest strata and the urgency of providing employment for them.[8]

There was widespread criticism of the IMF for the stringency of its conditions and for its monetarist approach to balance-of-payments crises,[9] and there was also a great deal of concern about the inflationary effects of exchange rate devaluation.[10] Trade policy debates were more focused on preferential access to developed-country markets and the dangers of protectionism than on the promotion of exports. There was virtually no reference to reducing the role of the state or privatizing state-owned enterprises. On the contrary, the state was rediscovered as a unit of analysis and widely regarded as central to directing the development process.[11]

The development discourse of the 1990s is profoundly different. Although there remains great variation in the details of economic policy ideas in different countries, the discourse has changed on many key issues. The basic premise of new thinking about development introduced in the early 1980s was the idea that the principal obstacle to development was to be found within the developing countries themselves. Decades of unwise government intervention in the economy, not the structure of the international economic and political system, were held principally responsible for the failures of development. Violation of the basic (universal) laws of neoclassical economics was considered the source of the main problems of

---

[7] The Brandt Commission, *North–South: A Programme for Survival* (London: Pan Books, 1980), p. 23.
[8] Ibid., p. 24.
[9] Ibid., p. 215. See also Sidney Dell, "Stabilization: The Political Economy of Overkill," *World Development* 10, 8 (August 1982), 597–612, and Tony Killick, Graham Bird, Jennifer Sharpley, and Mary Sutton, "The IMF: Case for a Change in Emphasis," in Richard Feinberg and Valerianna Kallab (eds.), *Adjustment Crisis in the Third World* (Washington, D.C.: Overseas Development Council, 1984), pp. 59–81.
[10] Carlos Díaz-Alejandro, "Southern Cone Stabilization Plans," in William Cline and Sidney Weintraub (eds.), *Economic Stabilization in Developing Countries* (Washington, D.C.: Brookings Institution, 1981), pp. 119–47. See also Louka Katseli, "Devaluation: A Critical Appraisal of the IMF's Policy Prescriptions," *American Economic Review* (May 1983), 359–63.
[11] Evans, Rueschemeyer, and Skocpol (eds.), *Bringing the State Back In*.

development, and it was pronounced important to remove distortions, eliminate rent-seeking practices, and establish market relationships throughout the economy. Development was increasingly defined in terms of the growth of productive capacity, and concerns with distribution and the provision of basic needs were shunted to the side – at least for the time being. The first imperative of development was to eliminate the distortions of state intervention and enable the "magic of the market" to run its course.

At the most general level, the economic ideas being pursued as policy throughout the developing world today include a reduction *and transformation* of state economic intervention, from production and distribution toward increased mediation and a redirection of regulation, an important revision of a principal component of Keynesianism in the postwar developing world.[12] In a very influential summary statement, John Williamson described this change in discourse as the emergence of a "consensus" (or "universal convergence") around the objectives of fiscal discipline, adjustment of public expenditure priorities, tax reform, financial liberalization, exchange rate adjustment, privatization, deregulation, and support for property rights.[13]

While plenty of controversy exists on the margins of this consensus, the terms of discourse reflect a significantly changed acceptance of market mechanisms and a shift in public–private relations in the direction of greater support for (and increased reliance on) the private sector. There has been a major shift away from inward-oriented import substitution toward export promotion, whether or not it involves industrial products. In dramatic contrast to widespread opposition to the use of devaluation as a policy instrument, currency devaluations are relatively common today, and many countries have accepted the idea that it is important to institutionalize nominal devaluations of the currency in order to generate and sustain competitive exchange rates.[14]

---

[12] Thomas J. Biersteker, "Reducing the Role of the State in the Economy: A Conceptual Exploration of IMF and World Bank Prescriptions," *International Studies Quarterly* 34, 4 (December 1990), 477–92, at 488.
[13] John Williamson, *The Progress of Policy Reform in Latin America* (Washington, D.C.: Institute for International Economics, 1990), p. 59.
[14] In some instances, a routine currency auction system might be instituted. In others, an active form of exchange rate management such as a crawling peg system might be introduced, following the initial devaluation undertaken during the stabilization period. The unification of multiple exchange rates might also be undertaken as part of a structural adjustment effort. Each of these measures entails an institutionalization of exchange rate adjustment in an effort to "get the prices right."

There is also now widespread acceptance of the idea that major fiscal policy reform is needed for development. Ordinarily, this means that countries are reducing (or at least constraining) the rate of growth in government spending, reforming the tax structure, rationalizing expenditure, phasing out or reducing government subsidies, and improving the efficiency of public investment by scaling down and shifting the focus from production to infrastructure and social sectors.[15] There is much wider acceptance of the use of monetarist instruments, even for longer-term financial reform.[16] Liberalizing foreign exchange controls is a common policy objective, as is the effort to reduce or eliminate subsidized credit, either by removing or by simplifying existing ceilings on interest rates and credit.[17]

Although there continue to be important debates about its pace and sequencing, trade liberalization has also become a central aspect of developing-country economic policy discussions. Exchange rate flexibility, the elimination of trade licensing systems, the introduction of export incentives, the replacement of quantitative restrictions by tariffs, and the general lowering of tariff levels are all being advocated, as developing-country economies are opened to the international market. A variety of other policy reforms are also being pursued, depending on the particular country context. Specific measures include reducing price controls, ending or reducing government subsidies, adjusting agricultural pricing policy, introducing new incentive schemes, reforming public enterprises, eliminating state marketing boards, liberalizing restrictions on foreign investment, and limiting wage indexation. Privatization has also been frequently prescribed as a component of World Bank–sponsored structural adjustment programs, at least since the mid-1980s, but many countries are experimenting with privatization even without World Bank encouragement.

The general nature of this change in the discourse of development is captured well by recent statements coming from institutions like the United Nations Development Program (UNDP), long recognized as a paragon of structuralist development thinking. At the launching of the UNDP's 1992 *Human Development Report,* Mahbub ul Haq said:

---

[15] World Bank, *Adjustment Lending: An Evaluation of Ten Years of Experience,* Policy and Research Series, No. 1 (Washington, D.C.: World Bank, 1988), pp. 38–41. Institutional reform of public sector management is also included in many World Bank adjustment efforts.
[16] José Antonio Ocampo, "New Economic Thinking in Latin America," *Journal of Latin American Studies* 22, 1 (February 1990), 169–81, 179.
[17] World Bank, *Adjustment Lending,* p. 47.

The South must recognize that the sterile dialogue of the 1970s must give way to a more enlightened dialogue on new patterns of development cooperation in a changing world – mutual interests, not unilateral concessions; two-sided responsibility, not one-sided accusations; more equitable access to global opportunities, not massive transfer of financial resources; more open markets, not more managed markets.[18]

As John Williamson has suggested, the general approval for opening up the economy in the developing world (involving trade liberalization, incentives for direct foreign investment, and realistic exchange rates) "marks a striking change from attitudes that prevailed as recently as 1986."[19]

In their recent work on the impact of ideas on policy, Judith Goldstein and Robert Keohane distinguished between ideas as general worldviews, as principled beliefs, and as causal beliefs.[20] The change in development discourse just described comes closest to their conception of ideas as causal beliefs, beliefs that derive their authority from a shared consensus and provide guides for individuals to achieve their objectives. But the change is not restricted to that domain and includes elements of principled beliefs and worldviews as well. This dramatic change in economic policy thinking in the developing world has not been gradual, uniform, or evenly distributed across different countries. Like the spread of Keynesian ideas at the middle of the century, the process has been lumpy, jerky, and uneven in important respects.[21] Nevertheless, the change in development ideas has been profound.

The spread of liberal economic ideas

On first consideration, there are a number of plausible explanations for the dramatic change in economic thinking. First, it is possible that developing countries may have finally been "educated" and accepted the superiority of the liberal economic ideas they resisted for decades. This could be best

[18] Mahbub ul Haq, "Human Development in a Changing World," speech delivered at the launching of the UNDP's annual *Human Development Report*, Stockholm, Sweden, April 23, 1992.
[19] Williamson, *The Progress of Policy Reform*, p. 60.
[20] Judith Goldstein and Robert Keohane, *Ideas and Foreign Policy: Beliefs, Institutions, and Political Change* (Ithaca, N.Y.: Cornell University Press, 1993).
[21] John Odell, *U.S. International Monetary Policy: Markets, Power and Ideas as Sources of Change* (Princeton, N.J.: Princeton University Press, 1982), p. 368, describes the uneven spread of Keynesian ideas. Hall, *The Political Power of Economic Ideas*, also provides extensive analysis of the phenomenon.

described as a variant of the "social learning" explanation.[22] Second, it is possible that the changes in economic policy simply reflect the power of international financial institutions (most notably, the IMF and the World Bank), which have enforced a new market orientation in the developing world. Although their influence is subject to much debate, their power was undoubtedly enhanced significantly after the onset of the 1981 global recession, the ensuing global debt crisis, and the continuing debt overhang.[23] Third, perhaps changes in the global economy (such as the globalization of production and increased competition), along with the evident success of export-oriented development regimes, have forced countries to engage in a fundamental rethinking of their economic policy. Or fourth, perhaps it is the exhaustion of prior models of accumulation (notably import-substitution industrialization)[24] and/or the collapse of socialism as an alternative model of development that has encouraged the recent policy transformation.

While any one of these explanations is no doubt at least partially correct and might be a useful place to begin to understand the change in particular countries, none alone can provide a complete explanation of the phenomenon. Moreover, they pay insufficient attention to the important role of ideas. In an effort to evaluate different explanations, I will begin by attempting to trace the introduction of ideas central to the transformation in development thinking. Next, I will differentiate between ideational explanations, systemic explanations, domestic interest explanations, and international institutional explanations. Each of these should be considered as an idealized construction, designed to identify and differentiate between different explanations on the basis of their *principal* point of departure. At the end of this section, I will suggest a more integrated explanation synthesizing core elements from several of them.

The basic ideas of the 1990s development discourse have been around for some time and are by no means entirely new. For the most part, they were articulated within the central banks and finance ministries of many develop-

---

[22] Miles Kahler, "Orthodoxy and Its Alternatives: Explaining Approaches to Stabilization and Adjustment," in Joan Nelson (ed.), *Economic Crisis and Policy Choice: The Politics of Adjustment in the Third World* (Princeton, N.J.: Princeton University Press, 1990), pp. 33–61.

[23] Barbara Stallings, "International Influence on Economic Policy: Debt, Stabilization, and Structural Reform," in Stephan Haggard and Robert Kaufman (eds.), *The Politics of Economic Adjustment: International Constraints, Distributive Politics, and the State* (Princeton, N.J.: Princeton University Press, 1992), pp. 41–88.

[24] Alain Lipietz, "How Monetarism Has Choked the Third World," *New Left Review* 145 (1984), 71–87.

ing countries during the 1960s and 1970s, but they are probably best considered to have been recessive discourses in the larger framework of national macroeconomic policy at the time. It is useful to recall that although these ideas emerged as dominant in a few countries (such as Chile) during the 1970s, the Chilean experience was the exception, not the rule.

It was also during the 1970s that the East Asian newly industrialized countries (NICs) began differentiating themselves from the rest of the developing world with their export-oriented industrialization policies. These policies enabled them to expand their exports dramatically in the essentially liberal (and still expanding) world trading system of the 1970s. The highly influential National Bureau of Economic Research (NBER) studies on the advantages of liberal exchange regimes provided a theoretical explanation and played an important role in writing the dominant narrative explaining the success of the NICs.[25] The NICs came to be interpreted as striking evidence of the bankruptcy of structuralist and dependency thinking, and of the potential benefits of turning away from import-substitution industrialization, of relying more directly on market mechanisms, of reducing the role of the state in the economy, and of greater integration into the world economy. This dominant narrative omitted reference to the fact that the NICs were strongly interventionist regimes, with a high degree of state guidance and direction of economic activity. It has taken the revisionist literature of the 1980s to identify the extent to which the NICs relied historically on state intervention, as well as restrictions on imports of goods and capital, and to elaborate the narrative more fully.[26]

It was around the same time, at the end of the 1970s, that Margaret Thatcher and Ronald Reagan came to power and began to play a significant role in reorienting the domestic and foreign economic policies of their respective countries. Reagan made a deliberate effort to export his economic policy ideas to the developing world in his "magic of the market" speech delivered at the last major North–South conference in Cancun in late 1981. During its first term in office, the Reagan administration reached far

---

[25] See Jagdish Bhagwati, *Anatomy and Consequences of Exchange Control* (Cambridge, Mass.: Ballinger, 1978), and Anne Krueger, *Liberalization Attempts and Consequences* (New York: National Bureau of Economic Research, 1978).

[26] Alice Amsden, "The State and Taiwan's Economic Development," in Evans, Rueschemeyer, and Skocpol (eds.), *Bringing the State Back In*, pp. 78–106; Stephan Haggard, *Pathways from the Periphery* (Ithaca, N.Y.: Cornell University Press, 1990); Robert Wade, "East Asia's Economic Success: Conflicting Perspectives, Partial Insights, Shaky Evidence," *World Politics* 44, 2 (1992), 270–320.

down into the bureaucracy to replace career civil servants out of step with the new thinking. The atmosphere was highly politicized, and there was little reluctance on the part of the new administration about using U.S. power and influence in international organizations to assert the ideological hegemony of its ideas.

It is not necessary to rely on assertions of U.S. hegemony, however, to illustrate the persuasive power of ideas. Within the social sciences, liberal economic ideas gained new force, visibility, and legitimacy in the late 1970s and early 1980s through a series of influential publications critical of the prevailing economic policy thinking. In addition to the NBER studies already cited, the influential Berg report on African development in 1981,[27] studies of the urban bias in development,[28] and forceful rational choice analyses of the distorting effects of government policy intervention[29] contributed to the critique of prevailing development policy thinking. Economists like Peter Bauer turned many dependency arguments on their head with polemical treatises on the importance of further integration with the world economy and calls for a rethinking of basic development issues.[30] These ideas within development economics joined the arguments of international trade theorists and public choice economists, which had become increasingly influential within neoclassical economics taught in the United States and Europe during the 1970s.[31]

Ideas may have an important independent explanatory role by way of a number of different transmission mechanisms. First, there may be contagion effects and policy emulation, or what John Ikenberry terms "policy bandwagoning."[32] Generally shared events or examples of effective policy performance and "success" may make a series of policy reforms conceivable or more acceptable politically. Second, there may be a "trickle-up" process, where ideas gain initial acceptance among academic economists, who sub-

---

[27] World Bank, *Accelerated Development for Africa* (Washington, D.C.: World Bank, 1981).

[28] Michael Lipton, *Why Poor People Stay Poor: Urban Bias in World Development* (Cambridge, Mass.: Harvard University Press, 1977).

[29] Robert Bates, *Markets and States in Tropical Africa* (Berkeley: University of California Press, 1983).

[30] Peter Bauer, *Equality, the Third World, and Economic Delusion* (Cambridge, Mass.: Harvard University Press, 1981).

[31] I am indebted to Chris Barrett of the University of Utah Economics Department for this insight.

[32] John Ikenberry, "The International Spread of Privatization Policies: Inducements, Learning, and 'Policy Bandwagoning,'" Center for International Studies, Princeton University, 1988.

sequently press their policy advice on the political leadership. The influence of the "Chicago boys" in Chile would be a good example of this phenomenon.[33] The World Bank has recently developed a new training program "to build African institutional capacity" in what could be considered an effort to create a transnational epistemic community around economic policy reform.[34] Its emphasis on governance, institutional accountability, and the transparency of economic transactions is also evidence of an effort to institutionalize liberal economic ideas.[35] Third, the bargaining or negotiation that takes place routinely between international financial institutions (the World Bank and the IMF) and developing countries over the terms of assistance, adjustment, or debt relief can provide an effective mechanism for the transmission of new ideas.

Goldstein and Keohane have usefully suggested three causal pathways through which ideas can influence policy choice. They argue that ideas can serve as "road maps" or understandings of the causal connections between a given set of objectives and different political strategies for achieving them. Alternatively, ideas can influence the choice of policy in situations where there exist multiple solutions to a given problem. Finally, once they become embedded in political institutions, ideas can influence policy choice long after the interests that founded those institutions have changed.[36]

While the scholarly works produced by the NBER and within the rational choice tradition exhibited high academic standards, there is little evidence that it was the particular academic expression of the ideas alone in the late 1970s and early 1980s that influenced decision making within developing countries. Developing-country decision makers are not likely to have read Peter Bauer and been immediately persuaded about the need for policy change. Indeed, a World Bank publication like the 1981 Berg report was roundly criticized by state elites throughout Africa when it first appeared. Nonetheless, those same elites might have been persuaded by the arguments articulated by local economists. In general terms, ideas that have the

---

[33] Patricio Silva, "Technocrats and Politics in Chile: From the Chicago Boys to the CIEPLAN Monks," *Journal of Latin American Studies* 23, 2 (1991), 385–410. But there was also a similar process among the opponents of the Chicago boys. See the enlightening article on links among Latin American finance ministers, established while they were students in U.S. universities, in Matt Moffett, "Seeds of Reform," *Wall Street Journal,* August 1, 1994.

[34] World Bank, *The African Capacity Building Initiative: Toward Improved Policy Analysis and Development Management* (Washington, D.C.: World Bank, 1991).

[35] World Bank, *Governance and Development* (Washington, D.C.: World Bank, 1992).

[36] Goldstein and Keohane, *Ideas and Foreign Policy,* pp. 12–13.

capacity to empower or enhance the position of nascent local allies (often groups who had long been advocates of a particular policy position or view) are likely to have greater influence and potential impact than those that are entirely imported.

Thus, although they are necessary for defining the content of change, ideas alone cannot provide a sufficient explanation for the dramatic transformation in developing-country economic policy during the 1980s. Rather, they need to be examined along with systemic changes in the global political economy, the actions of domestic interests, and the activities of international financial institutions.

Systemic changes in the world economy provided an important foundation for the transformation in economic policy in the developing world. Increased competition, the globalization of production, and a drying up of financial resources forced developing countries to focus more intensely on their relationship with (and competitiveness within) the rest of the world economy. This provides a background for, but not a sufficient explanation of, the transformation of thinking. In a great many countries, it took a particular system-wide shock to prompt a major reversal of thought.

The global recession that afflicted the economies of the advanced industrial world between 1980 and 1983 provoked a depression throughout much of the developing world. It was a critical event, a shock that reverberated throughout Africa, Latin America, and Asia, with different manifestations in each region. For Africa, the recession triggered a collapse in commodity prices, followed by an unsustainable debt burden. For Latin America (and some parts of Africa and of Asia), the monetarist response to the recession in the United States forced interest rates to record highs, triggering the global debt crisis and the lingering debt overhang. For countries of East Asia, the recession increased competition, reduced the total volume of world trade, prompted protectionism, and slowed growth. Because this system-wide shock was transmitted to different parts of the developing world through various filtering mechanisms, depending on their mode of integration with the world economy, it affected different countries in different ways and at different times.

Nonetheless, the 1980s recession provoked a rethinking of economic policy throughout the developing world. In a great many countries there was already a growing sense of failure, a belief that the policies of the past had not worked and something new should be considered. There was also serious disillusionment with the outcome of economic nationalism. Cartels (outside of OPEC) had proved disappointing, nationalized firms had become fiscal burdens for the state, indigenized enterprises yielded little effective managerial control, and national self-reliance had proved virtually unattainable. Thus, the direction of the dramatic change in policy was at least partially a product of a dialectical reaction against the economic policy practice of the past. The shock further undermined the prevailing policy order in many countries and enabled a radical shift in economic policy. In short, there was a crucial opening for new ideas.

"New" ideas were plentiful in the early 1980s, largely built upon critiques of traditional approaches to development. These ideas emanated from the centers of world power (especially the United States and the United Kingdom) as well as from the powerful international financial institutions, the IMF and the World Bank. The NICs provided successful role models for the international demonstration effects of these ideas.

Before they could be realized as development policy practice, however, these ideas needed both interests and institutional bases of support. The individuals who articulated the critiques of the policy failures of the past became crucial interests, located principally within the state, pushing for economic reform. In most instances, the "demand" for policy reversal came from technocratic groups (partially formed epistemic communities) within the state, many of whom had been educated at leading research universities in the United States and Europe during the 1970s. Although their factions were present in some form before the early 1980s, the magnitude of the economic crisis, along with the failure of past policies, provided these technocratic groups with an opportunity to articulate an alternative set of ideas. These nascent interests were given a crucial international backing from the IMF and the World Bank. There was a pronounced increase in the willingness, especially on the part of the U.S. government, to use the Fund and the Bank to force changes in developing-country economic policy during the early 1980s. In general terms, ideas backed with power, and a willingness or eagerness to use that power, are most likely to be influential.

Thus, systemic changes, recently mobilized interests within the state, international institutions, and ideas all played a role in explaining the dramatic change in developing-country economic policy that began in most countries in the early 1980s. But they did not play an equal role. On reflection, three factors were especially important: (1) the shock of the early 1980s recession, (2) the fact that the system-wide shock coincided with a historical opening because of the perceived failure of the policies of the past, and (3) the presence of a reinvigorated set of liberal economic ideas, backed by critically placed domestic interests within the state and reinforced strongly by international institutions. In the language of Goldstein and Keohane, these ideas served as road maps for the emerging international economic order.

The dismantling of the socialist regimes in East and Central Europe, followed by the disintegration of the Soviet Union at the end of the decade (part of a process Fred Halliday terms the end of European socialism in Chapter 2, this volume), dramatically reinforced the changes in the discourse of development already underway in many countries. The virtual elimination of a rival, state-based alternative to liberal economic ideas accelerated the institutionalization of the new ideas. The discrediting of the policies of social democratic coalitions in power in Western Europe earlier in the decade (particularly the French experience under Mitterrand, but also the Swedish redefinition of the welfare state over the course of the decade) further reinforced the sense that there were few, if any, alternatives to economic liberalism. These developments have triggered an ideological crisis of the "Left" throughout the world today.

If liberal policies succeed and produce sustained, noninflationary economic growth in developing countries, the new ideas (along with the policies they provoked) should ultimately begin to create and mobilize their own interests. Interests therefore are not just potential sources of ideas, they can also be the product of ideas. Potential interests simultaneously exist within most states for a number of different policy directions. For example, advocates of state intervention remain within most developing countries to this day, but their ideas are recessive for the time being. They might become mobilized and influential again, if given voice by new external shocks, new resources of financial assistance, or the "heavy hand" of historical experience (i.e., the perceived failure of liberal economic policies). Indeed, if countries pursuing economic reforms cannot soon demonstrate significant accomplishments in performance terms and mobilize the beneficiaries politically, another system-wide shock could well trigger yet another shift or, at the very least, a significant adjustment in the current policy direction.

The depth of change in development discourse

Although many states are simultaneously moving in the same direction, they are not necessarily traveling on the same road and may not ultimately end up in the same place. We may be experiencing a momentary, transitory convergence, a phase en route to an as yet uncertain future. Multiple possibilities for ways of ordering the world coexist, and we have not reached the "end of history." The disappearance of many socialist, authoritarian regimes at the end of the 1980s will not necessarily lead to the emergence of liberal, democratic capitalism in the 1990s. Many other alternatives are possible: neofascism, revised corporatism, new forms of populist collectivism, a resurgence of authoritarianism, ethnocentrism, or novel combinations of several of these.

There is a legitimate question about the depth of commitment of developing countries to many of the liberal economic reforms. The World Bank and the IMF staffs consistently reflect rather pessimistically (from their standpoint) on the extent to which policy agreements will eventually be implemented fully.[37] After all, governments under extreme financial pressure will often agree in principle to meet any number of obligations in exchange for assistance. The implementation of policy reform, and its institutionalization in government practice, will be the ultimate test of the extent of the "triumph" of economic liberalism. It is quite possible that the change in thinking that appears to have emerged is *not* genuinely shared across different countries. Indeed, the precise meaning of economic and political liberalization tends to vary considerably from country to country.

Moreover, a recurring problem with the shift in development discourse away from statist models toward economic liberalization is the difficulty (or, some pessimists would suggest, the inability) of economic liberalism to provide for basic subsistence needs of the majority of the population (i.e., its historic difficulty with equality both within and between states). The materialism associated with capitalist developmentalism is also increasingly at odds with ecological preservation and environmental protection. A related difficulty for economic liberalism is its association with individualism, technical achievement, and hyperrationality, and its undervaluing of the collective dimension of human existence, a point some recent feminist theorizing has also identified.[38]

These tensions are especially visible in the developing world, where an

---

[37] Stephan Haggard, "The Politics of Adjustment: Lessons from the IMF's Extended Fund Facility," *International Organization* 39, 3 (1985), 505–34.

[38] Christine Sylvester, "Feminists and Realists on the Concepts of Autonomy and Obligation," Center for International Studies Working Paper, University of Southern California, March 1991.

increasing number of countries are engaged in the simultaneous pursuit of forms of both economic and political liberalization. Throughout the 1980s a great deal of optimism was expressed about the extent to which liberal policy reforms could solve virtually all outstanding problems of the economy and the polity. Expectations were raised to an unprecedented degree, and if they are dashed, a major reaction can be anticipated.

The depth and sustainability of the new direction in economic policy in the developing world is largely contingent on its success in economic performance terms. As suggested earlier, if they succeed in improving performance, the economic reforms should be able to create domestic interests dedicated to defending the programs. It is in this sense that interests can be created by ideational change. If the new policy directions do not succeed, however, they are not likely to be sustained over the medium to longer term.

There is already some evidence that policy disappointments and failures are emerging in several critically placed African countries. The military regimes that introduced economic reforms in both Ghana and Nigeria have increasingly found themselves with a narrowing of their political bases.[39] Without any significant economic successes to their credit, the legitimacy of their rule is increasingly under challenge. Nigeria, in particular, moved sharply away from economic reform in 1994. African countries face the additional burden that increased efficiency in their production of primary products is likely to be rewarded with lower prices. The collapse of international cocoa prices following the recent expansion of exports from the countries of West Africa is a good illustration of this problem.[40]

The future course in much of Latin America is also uncertain. While Chile, Mexico, and Argentina seem likely to continue with their economic reforms, since successes of various kinds have produced substantial agreement on the advantages of the new policies, Brazil has been slow to embark on a similar course, and Venezuela has begun to backtrack. More generally, two kinds of problems have to be overcome to institutionalize reform in

[39] E. Gyimah-Boadi, "Economic Recovery and Politics in the PNDC's Ghana" (unpublished paper), Department of Political Science, University of Ghana, Legon, 1989.

[40] It is also a good illustration of a failure on the part of the IFIs to think in regional or systemic rather than individual country terms. In the example of the collapse of the international market in cocoa, the glut on the world market was caused in part by the export-oriented development policies simultaneously pursued by Ghana, Nigeria, and the Ivory Coast. Each of these countries was undergoing a World Bank structural adjustment program, which encouraged them to increase exports. While each individual program may have made sense in isolation, the combination led to a glut on the world market and a collapse of international prices.

Latin America: economic efficiency must rise to the point where the region's goods can compete both at home and abroad, and the fruits of the resulting growth must be distributed widely enough to include the large majority of the population in the consensus about the advantages of reform. The Chiapas rebellion in Mexico is a dramatic example of how a failure on the distributional issue can undermine apparent economic success. A full year after the initial outbreak of rebellion, external concerns about the Mexican government's control of the region helped trigger the country's peso devaluation and financial crisis in early 1995.

The situation in East Asia appears relatively more promising for the continuation of the economic reform measures. The successful NICs (Hong Kong, Singapore, South Korea, and Taiwan) have the longest experience with export-oriented economies, have already benefited from them, and have developed influential domestic coalitions for their continuation.[41] Major questions, however, remain about the "second-tier" NICs, such as Thailand and Malaysia. Easy access to the world's largest integrated market (the United States) was crucial for the success of the first-generation NICs and was one of the consequences of the cold war. With the end of the cold war, there is no guarantee similar market access can be replicated – particularly with a declining rate of growth in the volume of world trade. While an increasing share of the trade of the second-generation NICs is within the Asian region, the continuation of Japan's recession in the early 1990s renders the depth and sustainability of their economic reform programs far less certain.

Even one of the strongest institutional advocates of liberal economic ideas, the World Bank, has adjusted its emphasis in recent years away from penetrating critiques of the state, of government policy failures, and administrative mismanagement. Although there is no departure from the core of its calls for greater reliance on the market and the pursuit of international economic openness, recent volumes of the Bank's annual *World Development Report* have emphasized the alleviation of poverty, investment in people, the environment, and human capital. The general disposition of its 1989 study, *Sub-Saharan Africa: From Crisis to Sustainable Growth*, provides a stark contrast to the more ideological tone of the Berg report published at the beginning of the decade. Perhaps a more significant indication

---

[41] Michael Shafer, *Sectors, States, and Social Forces: Towards a New Comparative Political Economy of Development* (Ithaca, N.Y.: Cornell University Press, 1994). See also Haggard, *Pathways from the Periphery.*

of changes in Bank thinking is the 1993 study *The East Asian Miracle: Economic Growth and Public Policy,* which acknowledges that the objective of macroeconomic stability ("getting the prices right") needs to be supplemented with effective institutional development, investment in human capital, and perhaps even some types of sectoral policies.

Thus, the apparent "triumph" of liberal economic ideas throughout the developing world may prove to have been a transitory phenomenon that peaked sometime during the late 1980s. Much depends on whether the policy measures begin to yield some tangible successes in economic performance terms. If they do, they may be able to create the interests necessary for their long-term institutionalization. If they do not, the present trends in economic policy may prove to be ephemeral. Although many countries have been moving in the same direction (away from the statist, inward-oriented, economic nationalism of the 1970s), it is important to remember that they began at very different starting points, have achieved different successes to date, and may eventually end up in very different places.

Implications for development thinking

Even if liberal economic ideas are not yet fully institutionalized in policy practice throughout the developing world, the general movement away from statist, inward-oriented development models has profound implications for our thinking about development issues. As the world economy becomes more fully integrated and the intense, ideological cold war competition between capitalism and socialism begins to fade, there is a real narrowing of the range of economic policy choice for developing countries. Accordingly, the very categories that have historically defined the central debates about development alternatives require substantial revision.

It is time to move beyond the "three worlds of development" that have dominated the discourse of development since the 1960s. The implosion of the socialist bloc has erased the principal contradiction of the post–World War II order, and the world can no longer be divided into capitalist West and socialist East. Nonalignment has lost its meaning as a distinct alternative. At the same time, the end of the opposition between East and West does not lead automatically to a new opposition between North and South. The South is not a cohesive entity, and it has become increasingly differentiated, a point evident from a reading of the regional chapters included in this volume. The idea of "the South" only gained force and meaning historically out of its temporarily unified opposition to the liberal-capitalist North from the late 1960s through the mid-1970s.

While the spread of capitalism on a global scale appears to be continuing apace, it is likely that different forms of capitalist organization may emerge as the basis for new categorizations and debates over development policy alternatives in the future. One of the principal distinctions among capitalist state forms is between societal corporatism and pluralism.[42] Societally corporatist, hierarchically organized modes of interest aggregation can be identified readily in the newly industrialized countries, beginning with Japan, while more pluralist modes of interest aggregation have been historically associated with the decentralized liberal order found in the United States, the United Kingdom, and parts of Latin America.

The general development model characteristic of Japan and East Asian political economies (with their selective state intervention, high levels of savings, and low levels of consumption) can be contrasted with their U.S. (and Latin American) counterparts, with their variable degrees of state intervention, low levels of savings, and high levels of consumption.[43] There is already some evidence that Japan and the United States are beginning to differ in their prescriptions about the most appropriate role of the state in development, a divergence emerging in discussions about the application of IMF and World Bank conditionality – both economic and political.[44] Some of the key differences between the Anglo-American (and Latin American) and the Japanese-East Asian models of development with regard to international trade orientation and the role of the state in the economy are well specified by Barbara Stallings in Chapter 11 in this volume. Stallings argues that while both models stress exports, the Asian model emphasizes more active steps to promote exports, which entails greater state intervention to enhance both human capital and physical facilities.

[42] Philippe Schmitter, "Still the Century of Corporatism?" *Review of Politics* 36, 1 (1974), 85–131.

[43] Fernando Fajnzylber, "The United States and Japan as Models of Industrialization," in Gary Gereffi and Donald Wyman (eds.), *Manufacturing Miracles: Paths of Industrialization in Latin America and East Asia* (Princeton, N.J.: Princeton University Press, 1990), pp. 323–52.

[44] Kenichi Ohno, "Market, Government, and Long-Term Real Targets: A Different Perspective from Japan," Institute of Socio-Economic Planning, University of Tsukuba, Tsukuba, Japan, March 1993. See also "Issues Related to the World Bank's Approach to Structural Adjustment," OECF Occasional Paper No. 1, Overseas Economic Cooperation Fund, Tokyo, October 1991.

Other alternatives within the category of societal corporatism are also possible to imagine in the emerging post–cold war order, especially if one considers the different degrees of state intervention that exist under current corporatist structures. Robert Wade has suggested a fruitful typology for thinking about the possibilities, with his distinction between the simulated free market model (where state intervention simulates a free market but protects the interests of national producers) and the governed market model (where the state nurtures the activities of individual firms with specific incentives and disincentives).[45] Jean Oi has recently suggested that contemporary China exemplifies yet another form of corporatist model: local state corporatism. Local (not national) government has emerged as a principal economic agent and begun to assume a direct entrepreneurial role in the country's economy, especially as it "coordinates economic enterprises in its territory as if it were a diversified business corporation."[46]

European regulation school theorists employ a different terminology to capture the emerging variation within capitalist state forms of production. Rather than contrasting the antistatism of Anglo-American liberalism with forms of East Asian neocorporatism, they suggest the emergence of a European social democratic alternative: what one writer has termed the Kalmarian model.[47] For regulation theorists, the dominant mode of organization of production in the post–World War II period was global Fordism, a regime of accumulation characterized by mass production, a sharing of value added between capital and labor, and corporate profit stability.[48] This regime of accumulation was accompanied by a mode of regulation that included Keynesian intervention, extensive social legislation, and the construction of the welfare state, a compromise John Ruggie has described as "embedded liberalism."[49]

For regulation school theorists, the two decades following World War II constituted the "golden age" of global Fordism, whose crisis (beginning

---

[45] Robert Wade, *Governing the Market: Economic Theory and the Role of Government in East Asian Industrialization* (Princeton, N.J.: Princeton University Press, 1990), pp. 22–29.
[46] Jean C. Oi, "Fiscal Reform and the Economic Foundations of Local State Corporatism in China," *World Politics* 45, 1 (1992), 99–126 at 100–1.
[47] Alain Lipietz, *Towards a New Economic Order: Postfordism, Ecology and Democracy* (New York: Oxford University Press, 1992), pp. 66–76.
[48] David Harvey, *The Condition of Postmodernity* (Oxford: Blackwell Publishers, 1989).
[49] John Ruggie, "International Regimes, Transactions and Change: Embedded Liberalism in the Postwar Economic Order," *International Organization* 36, 2 (Spring 1982), 379–415.

with the stagflation of the 1970s) led to the introduction of several alternative models in the 1980s. The Thatcher and Reagan governments produced
what some regulation theorists characterize as "liberal productivism," a
societal paradigm that tried to maintain profitability by attacking the welfare state and was associated with hierarchical individualism and societal
polarization. In contrast, the Kalmarian model, which derives its name from
a Volvo plant located in Kalmar, Sweden, entails a labor process in which
line operatives are less alienated and become directly involved in the search
for quality improvements and the regulation of production flows. In contrast
to liberal productivism, the Kalmarian model entails a mutualization of
responsibility for employment – among firms, unions, local governments,
banks, and educational institutions.[50] Regulation school writers contend
that the Kalmarian model has already won out over the liberal productivism
of the United States and the United Kingdom, at least in part because it is
better suited to the flexible accumulation (described in greater detail by
Gary Gereffi in Chapter 4) that has generally succeeded global Fordism.
While the Kalmarian model shares some basic similarities with the East
Asian models, it has a distinctly less hierarchical authority structure.

    In addition to forms of capitalist organization emanating out of the ad-
vanced industrial world, it is also possible to imagine quite different kinds
of development models or alternatives emerging out of the developing
world, the arena where economic liberalism is likely to encounter the most
disappointments over the next decade. The reactions to and potential disappointments stemming from unfulfilled expectations following the embrace
of liberal economic ideas could produce a variety of alternatives. The former Soviet Union and countries of East and Central Europe should be
included in the developing world for purposes of this analysis.

    One alternative political economic model might emerge out of the Is-
lamic world, with its distinctive history of integrating state and religion,
extensive state intervention in the economy, and a transnational ideology.
Revolutionary Iran rejected the materialism of both the capitalist West and
the socialist East during the last decade of the cold war and has pursued a
variant of national self-reliance since the 1979 revolution that brought the
Ayatollah Khomeini to power. Iran has defined the world in terms of a
conflict between oppressors and the oppressed, and its leaders have decried

---

[50] Lipietz, *Towards a New Economic Order*, p. 76.

the unjust global economic order that has emerged.[51] Its concepts of Islamic justice and the pursuit of Islamic universalism strive for the formation of a non-state-based, Islamic society and community whose development is measured not in terms of materialist GNP per capita growth rates, but in terms of the creation of a social and political order governed by Islamic values. Godliness is valued over prosperity, growth is pursued in order to provide subsistence for all, and the development strategy is adjusted to match spiritual needs.[52] These are ideas that have a scope far broader than the limits of revolutionary Iran, as indicated by the growth of Islamism in contemporary Egypt and Algeria, two of the most thoroughly Westernized countries in the region. They could form the basis of a development alternative at the margins of the capitalist world economy.

Other alternatives to liberalism might emerge from other parts of the developing world, possibly out of what Jowitt has termed "movements of rage," such as the Shining Path in Peru, the Khmer Rouge in Cambodia, the Maitatsine in Nigeria, the Mulele uprising in Zaire, the indigenous Muslim groups in the Philippines, or the Zapatistas in Mexico.[53] Increasingly, the principal bases of individual political identification in some parts of the developing world are not with the state, but with other entities. Primary loyalties have shifted in those areas, as evidenced by the importance of ethnicity in the Soviet Union, Eastern and Central Europe, as well as increasingly (and depressingly) throughout Africa (Rwanda, Liberia, Somalia, Ethiopia, and the Sudan) and South Asia (India and Sri Lanka). Religion has also become an important primary identification. It is quite possible that these new identifications will form a basis for still other counterdiscourses and reactions to economic and political liberalism that might emerge in the future. The emergence of new political-economic orders is ultimately contingent on the development of new vocabularies, languages, discourses, and ideologies, often articulated and led by a determined minority and directed by a charismatic leader.[54] It is striking to consider the degree to which the location of these potential counterdiscourses corresponds geographically to those countries (or regions within

---

[51] Tahir Amin, "Iran: From Bi-Colonialism to Islamic Revolution," in Hayward Alker, Tahir Amin, Thomas Biersteker, and Takashi Inoguchi, *The Dialectics of World Order* (forthcoming).
[52] Ibid.
[53] Kenneth Jowitt, "After Leninism: The New World Disorder," *Journal of Democracy* (Winter 1991), 11–20.
[54] Ibid.

countries) most significantly marginalized from the flows of global trade and finance, described in greater detail elsewhere in this volume.

We live in dynamic and uncertain times, and the basic discourse of development is undergoing change. The fundamental opposition between the capitalist West and the socialist East no longer defines the boundaries of development discourse, having been displaced by attention to a variety of forms of capitalist development, along with some as yet inchoate alternatives from marginalized regions. It no longer makes sense to describe the range of development policy choice in terms of the swings of a pendulum between public and private (of more or less state intervention), but rather in terms of different mixes of public and private initiative within an increasingly integrated global capitalist mode of production. While the range of options has for the most part narrowed to choices within capitalism, our consciousness of the range of choice within capitalism has broadened appreciably. Hence, it is increasingly useful to characterize development choices by differentiating among Anglo-American liberalism (liberal productivism), forms of Asian corporatism, the social democratic Kalmarian model, and a variety of other forms of flexible production within capitalism – all the while keeping an eye on developments at the margins of the world economy that may provide an empirical basis for some of the discursive alternatives of the future.

PART II

Regional responses

CHAPTER 7

The East Asian NICs: a state-led path to the developed world

YUN-HAN CHU

The East Asian newly industrialized countries (EANICs) – Hong Kong, Singapore, South Korea, and Taiwan – occupy a distinctive position in the international system. In the 1960s and 1970s, they were the chosen few that seized the structural opportunities for upward mobility in the international political-economic system. During the second half of the 1970s and early 1980s, they launched effective economic adjustment programs that enabled their economies to ward off the looming competition from the "second-tier NICs" of Southeast Asia and to moderate the new protectionist pressures in the OECD countries. As a result, in the mid-1990s, the EANICs are poised to become the first group of postcolonial states to join the ranks of the developed countries in the postwar era.

Since the mid-1980s, however, the EANICs have been facing a new set of challenges that threatened their established modes of capital accumulation and patterns of state intervention. Beginning in the early 1980s, both economic officials and business leaders in the EANICs found themselves operating in a very different international environment due to the epic changes in the global political system, the tumult in the international monetary regime, and the discord in the management of multilateral economic relations. To strike a balance between the need to harmonize their economic relations with their major trading partners and the need to facilitate the structural adjustment of their economies, EANIC governments were compelled to reset their policy priorities and retool their policy instruments.

In this chapter, I concentrate on the policy redirection in the two largest EANICs, namely, South Korea and Taiwan, beginning with the Plaza Accords in 1985, a watershed that initiated a major realignment in global monetary relationships and precipitated a redirection of trade flows and capital movements in the Asia–Pacific region. The analysis goes through the break-up of the Soviet Union in 1991, which put a conclusive end to the postwar era and transformed a long-standing East–West confrontation into a South–North dependency, and the end of the Uruguay Round of the General Agreement on Tariffs and Trade (GATT) in 1994, which ushered in a new era of global trade liberalization.

I begin the chapter with a brief review of the EANICs' postwar economic development and some salient aspects of past economic performance up to the mid-1980s. Next, I outline the important changes in the international system that precipitated the policy redirection and constrained the selection of adjustment strategies of the EANICs. Adopting a useful scheme first developed by Susan Strange,[1] I organize my discussion of the new international development context in five domains: changes in the international trade regime, finance regime, production structure, security structure, and ideological structure.

Then I present a documented account of the policy responses of the two EANICs and evaluate their effectiveness in the late 1980s and early 1990s. I place my focus on patterned and coherent – in contrast to sporadic and ad hoc – responses with long-term implications. Also, I put more emphasis on the convergence rather than diversity of policy responses between South Korea and Taiwan. Consequently, changes in the international system, rather than domestic structures, constitute the primary explanatory source for the adjustment strategies of the private agents and the governments in the EANICs. In the conclusion, my analysis moves beyond the nation-state level to address the larger issues with regard to the policy implications and regional impact of EANIC adjustment strategies, especially for the ASEAN countries and China.

History of postwar economic development

The development sequences in the EANICs are well known. After World War II, they moved from primary commodity exporters under colonial control to import-substitution industrialization (ISI) to export-oriented industrialization (EOI), shifting production from land-intensive to labor-

---

[1] Susan Strange, "Cave! hic dragones," in Stephen Krasner (ed.), *International Regimes* (Ithaca, N.Y.: Cornell University Press, 1983).

intensive to capital-intensive industries and decisively turning from domestic to international markets in the early 1960s.[2]

Most economists have observed that South Korea and Taiwan pursued an ISI strategy in the early 1950s via the usual policy package of tariffs, import licensing, low interest rates, and so on. Nonetheless, they chose a milder version of the strategy than is typically the case, which meant that the undesirable consequences of ISI were less pronounced than in other less-developed countries (LDCs). During this phase of labor-intensive industrial growth or primary import substitution, the production of nondurable consumer goods for the domestic market expanded rapidly. This process lasted until the end of the 1950s and the beginning of the 1960s, when the supply of foreign exchange and the size of the domestic market became a constraint on growth.

At that time, South Korea and Taiwan began to export these labor-intensive, nondurable consumer goods, rather than following other LDCs toward the production of durable consumer goods, as well as intermediate and capital goods. Though ISI policies were still selectively applied during the export-expansion phase, protection was clearly superseded by export promotion. Tax and tariff burdens on exports were systematically offset; hence, the exporters enjoyed a level playing field in their competition with foreign producers.

The EANICs' experiences with ISI also differed from most other developing countries in three important ways. First, South Korea and Taiwan inherited from Japanese colonial rule a modern infrastructure, well-educated populace, and effective agricultural extension system. Also, they were endowed with an elaborate state bureaucracy, built by the colonial government to penetrate the society and extract resources. Second, due to their privileged status in the postwar U.S. security arrangements, both South Korea and Taiwan received an unusually large amount of foreign aid during their ISI phase. U.S. aid was crucial for stabilizing the Korean and Taiwanese economies during the 1950s. Aid was a major source of domestic capital formation and enabled the two countries to grow without the usual balance-of-payments constraints.[3] With minimal involvement by transna-

[2] Tun-jen Cheng, "Political Regime and Development Strategies: South Korea and Taiwan," in Gary Gereffi and Donald Wyman (eds.), *Manufacturing Miracles: Paths of Industrialization in Latin America and East Asia* (Princeton, N.J.: Princeton University Press, 1990).

[3] David Cole, "Foreign Assistance and Korean Development," in David Cole, Yonil Lim, and Paul Kuznets (eds.), *The Korean Economy: Issues of Development* (Berkeley: Institute of

tional corporations in their early stage of industrialization, the EANICs avoided most of the distortions in consumption patterns and misallocation of productive resources typically associated with direct foreign investment (DFI).[4] Third, the decolonization process produced the necessary political conditions for the two regimes to carry out extensive land reform, which laid the groundwork for sustained growth of agriculture and generated the surplus rural savings needed to support industrialization.

There is little disagreement about the benefits of the EOI strategy. It underlay both the hypergrowth and the improved income distribution in the EANICs during the 1960s and 1970s. Average annual growth in both countries exceeded 9 percent, and their economic structures changed radically. In Taiwan, between 1960 and 1979, agriculture's share of net domestic product declined from 37 to about 10 percent, while the share of manufacturing increased from under 17 to 35 percent. The change was equally dramatic in Korea. As a share of GNP, exports increased from 5 percent in 1960–62 to 20 percent in 1970–72 in Korea, and from 11 percent in 1960 to 45 percent in 1972 in Taiwan. In both countries, the share of manufactured goods in total exports rose from 20 percent in the early 1960s to over 80 percent by the end of the decade.[5] (For summary statistics on the 1970–92 period, see Table 7.1.)

Partly because of the extensive land reform that preceded the postwar industrialization, rapid economic growth in South Korea and Taiwan has been unusually egalitarian. Income distribution in the two countries in the mid-1970s was among the most equal in the world. The ratio between the income share of the lowest and highest quintiles of households was 7.9 in South Korea around the mid-1970s compared with 9.5 in the United States and 19.9 in Mexico. For Taiwan, the ratio in 1980 was only 4.2.[6] This equality was both cause and consequence of an emphasis on education. The resulting highly skilled population then reinforced the possibilities of rapid economic growth (Table 7.2).

East Asian Studies, 1980), and Neil H. Jacoby, *U.S. Aid to Taiwan* (New York: Praeger, 1966).

4 On this point, see Peter Evans, "Class, State, and Dependence in East Asia: Lessons for Latin Americanists," in Frederic Deyo (ed.), *The Political Economy of the New Asian Industrialism* (Ithaca, N.Y.: Cornell University Press, 1987).

5 Samuel P. S. Ho, "South Korea and Taiwan: Development Prospects and Problems in the 1980s," *Asian Survey* (December 1981).

6 See Medhi Krongkaew, "Income Distribution in East Asian Developing Countries: An Update," *Asian Pacific Economic Literature* 8, 2 (November 1994), 58–73.

Table 7.1. *Economic indicators, East Asia, 1970–92*

Country	1990 GDP ($ billions)	1990 Population (millions)	1990 GDP per capita (dollars)	Real GDP per capita, annual increase (percent) 1970–80	1980–90	1991–92	Merchandise exports, annual increase (percent) 1970–80	1980–90	1991–92	Inflation, annual rate (percent) 1980–90	1992
Hong Kong	70.1	5.8	12,084	6.7	5.7	4.4	21.0	7.8	20.6	7.7	9.4
Korea	236.4	42.9	5,514	6.7	9.0	5.7	35.6	14.0	9.1	6.1	6.2
Singapore	34.6	3.0	11,537	7.3	5.3	4.1	28.7	10.5	10.3	2.4	2.3
Taiwan	155.8	20.4	7,652	7.6	7.0	5.8	29.6	13.0	10.0	3.0	4.5
Total	496.9	72.0	6,899	7.0	8.0	5.4	28.1	11.8	13.3	5.1	5.9

Sources: Calculated from World Bank, *World Tables* tapes, *1992*, and Republic of China, *Taiwan Statistical Data Book, 1992* (for 1970–90); Asian Development Bank, *Asian Development Outlook, 1994* (for 1991–92).

Table 7.2. *Social indicators, East Asia, 1965–89*

Country	1965	1980	1989	Annual growth (percent)	
				1965–80	1980–89
Daily calorie supply per capita					
Hong Kong	2,486	2,898	2,853	1.0	-0.2
Korea	2,178	2,957	2,852	2.1	-0.4
Singapore	2,285	3,158	3,198	2.2	0.1
Taiwan	2,411	2,812	2,993	1.0	0.7
Total	2,270	2,919	2,906	1.7	0.0
Infant mortality per 1,000 live births					
Hong Kong	27	10	7[a]	-6.4	-3.5
Korea	62	33	17	-4.1	-6.4
Singapore	26	12	7	-5.0	-5.2
Taiwan	na	na	na	na	na
Total	56	29	15	-4.3	-6.3
Primary school enrollment (percentage of eligible age)					
Hong Kong	103	109	105	0.4	-0.4
Korea	101	107	198	0.4	0.1
Singapore	105	107	110	0.1	0.3
Taiwan	98	101	102	0.2	0.1
Total	100	105	106	0.3	0.1
Secondary school enrollment (percentage of eligible age)					
Hong Kong	29	62	73	5.2	1.8
Korea	35	85	86	6.1	0.1
Singapore	45	55	69	1.3	2.6
Taiwan	33	68	81	4.9	2.0
Total	34	77	83	5.5	0.8

Sources: World Bank, *World Development Report, 1983, 1992;* Republic of China, *Taiwan Statistical Data Book, 1992.*

During the 1970s and early 1980s, the EANICs managed to cope with both recurring worldwide stagflation and long-term challenges associated with protectionism, rising labor costs, and automation and technological change in the advanced industrial nations. Despite similar shocks from the international environment, the EANICs experienced higher levels of growth, more rapid expansion of exports, and fewer debt-servicing prob-lems than their Latin American counterparts. (For comparisons, see Chapter 1, especially Table 1.1.)

The prevailing explanation about the "East Asian miracle" emerging from neoclassical economics is that these countries adopted more rational, market-oriented policies by liberalizing imports, adopting realistic ex-change rates, and providing incentives for exports; above all they managed to get factor prices right so their economies could expand in line with their comparative advantage. Governments in these countries helped create and sustain an economic environment in which price signals in the international market drove industrial change.[7] The shift of the EANICs toward EOI absorbed much unskilled labor, given the relatively unlimited opportunities for growth in the world market. This, in turn, led to more equitable income distribution as employment opportunities expanded rapidly, and a more robust and flexible development process as further import and export sub-stitution took place in more capital- and technology-intensive commodities. Thus, it is argued, the advantages of lower capital/output ratios, fewer demanding infant industries that refused to "grow up," and the stimulus of greater competitiveness from a world-market orientation gave the EANICs a decisive edge in terms of growth rates and capacity to adjust to the shocks in the world market.

The neoclassical interpretation of East Asia's growth did not go un-challenged. The most compelling criticisms followed two lines.[8] The first concerned the importance of a particular international context for the suc-cess of export-led growth; the second focused on the role of the state in bringing about industrial change.[9]

Patterns of industrial change in the EANICs, the critics contended, had to

[7] Good examples of the neoclassical account of East Asian growth include Bela Balassa, *The Newly Industrializing Countries in the World Economy* (New York: Pergamon Press, 1981); Jagdish Bhagwati, *Foreign Trade Regimes and Economic Development: The Anatomy and Consequences of Exchange Control Regimes* (Cambridge, Mass.: Ballinger, 1978); and Gustav Ranis, "Employment, Income Distribution and Growth in the East Asian Context: A Comparative Analysis," paper presented at the Conference on Experiences and Lessons of Small Open Economies, Santiago, Chile, 1981.

[8] For a review of the debate, see Stephan Haggard, *Pathways from the Periphery: The Politics of Growth in the Newly Industrializing Countries* (Ithaca, N.Y.: Cornell University Press, 1990), chap. 1.

[9] See, e.g., Bruce Cumings, "The Origins and Development of the Northeast Asian Political Economy: Industrial Sectors, Product Cycles, and Political Consequences," *International Organization* 37 (Winter 1984), and William Cline, "Can the East Asian Model of Develop-ment be Generalized?" *World Development* 10 (February 1982).

be understood, at least in part, as the result of the promotion and steering of "developmental" states.[10] These authors argued that South Korea and Taiwan were far from liberal market-oriented economies; rather their states typically exercised a wide range of policy instruments and forms of pervasive intervention that lay outside the neoclassical policy analysis. Moreover, they said that the neoclassical approach tends to ignore the social and political dimensions of development. In downplaying the social, political, and historical dimensions of comparative advantage, error results in both the attribution of causality and in more narrowly prescribing the limits within which developmental choices can be made.

As an alternative explanation, the developmental state view emphasizes that the policy of the EANICs has been strongly reminiscent of Japan, with major decisions taken on the basis of long-term development objectives and in disregard of short-term efficiency as indicated by existing prices. The state responds to and anticipates opportunities in the international economy and dynamically directs capital and labor out of declining sectors and into more competitive ones, continuously adjusting its sector-specific policies to changing international market conditions. The state is capable of intervening on both the demand side through restriction on foreign competition or captive procurement policy and the supply side through the manipulation of factor prices. By exercising direct and indirect influence on the level of profit and investment, the state can modify, enhance, or create competitiveness. In short, development strategies in the EANICs were pursued on the premise of "acquired dynamic comparative advantage" rather than "endowed static comparative advantage."

The developmental state interpretation also gives a central role to state autonomy. Implementing national planning priorities and exercising direct and indirect control over investment, production, and marketing depend on an elaborate, resourceful, and efficient administrative apparatus for their success. Furthermore, the effectiveness of state action is rooted in its overall relationship to society. It is important that the state acquire the political ability to resist penetration by special interests, to circumscribe the auton-

---

[10] Perhaps the clearest analytical account along the developmental statist line is provided by Robert Wade and Gordon White (eds.), "Special Issue on Developmental States in East Asia: Capitalist and Socialist," *IDS Bulletin* 15 (April 1984). See also David Evans and Parvin Alizadeh, "Trade, Industrialization, and the Visible Hand," *Journal of Developmental Studies* 20 (December 1984), and Alice Amsden, *Asia's Next Giant: South Korea and Late Industrialization* (New York: Oxford University Press, 1989). All attribute East Asia's successful late industrialization to a development-oriented dirigiste state.

omy of economic actors, to subordinate labor through direct control over unions and outright repression, and to assert an independent national development interest. Without such autonomy, policy instruments would simply play into the hands of rent-seeking economic agents, resulting in a considerable loss of macroeconomic efficiency.[11] In a nutshell, the EANIC governments organize the societies they control. The policy process is typically state-dominated and socially segmented. The authoritarian political systems of these countries, while not identical, resemble each other in most of these essential aspects.

The new development context

The EANICs' concern with economic restructuring is nothing new. The basic issue is the state's role in steering industrialization, facilitating adjustment, and maintaining international competitiveness in a world economy dominated by advanced industrial countries and transnational corporations, and characterized by rapid technological change. The challenges confronting the EANICs in the late 1980s and early 1990s, however, were quite different. In large part, the new crises were created by their own past successes, meaning that their existing development strategies had reached their limits.

The changes in the global trade and finance regimes during the late 1980s exerted the most direct pressures on the EANICs for policy redirection and imposed new constraints on their development strategies. It was the changing nature and dynamics of the global production, security, and ideological trends, however, that restructured the power relations in the global political economic system, shaped the evolution of the international trade and financial regimes in the long run, and mediated the impact of the changes in these regimes in the short run.

The most significant change in the global production structure in the 1960s and 1970s was a rapid diffusion of production technology and facilities from the United States and Western Europe to Japan, the EANICs, and a select group of Latin American countries. The diffusion was brought about by a focused allocation of foreign aid based on security considerations, the

---

[11] See, e.g., Anne Krueger, "Political Economy of the Rent-Seeking Society," *American Economic Review* (March 1973), and Mancur Olson, *The Rise and Decline of Nations: Economic Growth, Stagflation, and Social Rigidities* (New Haven, Conn.: Yale University Press, 1982).

investment and sourcing strategies of the OECD-based transnational corporations, and state-sponsored industrialization programs.[12] The diffusion process was accelerated in the 1980s. Since the mid-1970s, when the reservoir of surplus labor was exhausted and real wages were pushed up by a tight labor market, the EANICs have carried out effective economic adjustment strategies to diversify and upgrade their manufactured exports and deepen ISI.[13] Their move toward higher-value-added manufacturing has created opportunities for other lower-wage economies in the region to enter relatively labor-intensive industries and segments of the production process. Thus, in the past decade, a second tier of NICs was formed through the emulation of the EANIC export-oriented strategies by the ASEAN countries and more recently China. The uneven spread of productive capital created economic frictions among sovereign states and economic dislocation in the OECD countries. It prompted national governments to seek trade adjustment and monetary realignment.

Changes in the trade regime

Since the early 1970s, the access of the EANICs to the OECD market has been threatened by the rise of a new wave of protectionism. Multilateralism and nondiscrimination, the two organizing principles of the postwar free trade regime, gradually gave way to the rising demand in the advanced industrial countries for specific reciprocity and differential treatment.[14] Multilateralism was gradually replaced by minilateralism (trade blocs) and bilateralism.[15] The orderly marketing arrangements (OMAs) and voluntary export restraints (VERs) that proliferated in the 1970s and 1980s have been directed primarily against the EANICs and Japan. By the mid-1980s, the proliferation of product-specific trade arrangements had reached the point of saturation. Close to 60 percent of the manufactured exports from Taiwan and South Korea to the United States were covered by these arrange-

---

[12] Cumings, "The Origins and Development of the Northeast Asian Political Economy," and Deyo (ed.), *The Political Economy of the East Asian Industrialism.*

[13] Yun-han Chu, "State Structure and Economic Adjustment," *International Organization* 43 (August 1989).

[14] Judith L. Goldstein and Stephan D. Krasner, "Unfair Trade Practices: The Case for Differential Response," *American Economic Review* 74 (1984).

[15] Beth Yarbrough and Robert Yarbrough, "Cooperation in the Liberalization of International Trade: After Hegemony, What?" *International Organization* 41 (Winter 1987).

ments.[16] Nonetheless, the surge of the imports from the EANICs showed no signs of abatement.

Facing mounting domestic pressure for more effective actions to reduce the trade deficit, the U.S. government changed its approach in the second half of the 1980s. The United States took the lead among the OECD countries in forcing the EANICs to graduate from the class of LDCs by taking away their Generalized System of Preference status beginning in 1989. The priority in the bilateral negotiation also shifted from erecting new VERs and OMAs to the protection of intellectual property rights and, more importantly, to the removal of tariff and nontariff barriers, unfair trade practices, and the entry barriers to foreign suppliers in the service sector and government procurement. This policy redirection was best exemplified by the passage of the U.S. Trade Act in 1986, which identified a broad pattern of unfair trade practices and required the U.S. Trade Representative to take punitive measures, including mandatory trade reduction, against the violating nations under the so-called Super Section 301 of the Trade Act.

In recent years, both Taiwan and South Korea were among the most salient targets of Section 301. In 1986, Taiwan's trade surplus accounted for 10 percent of GDP, a world record. In 1987, Taiwan ran the second largest trade surplus against the United States and accumulated the second largest volume of foreign reserves after Japan. In 1988, South Korea piled up a current account surplus of nearly $14 billion or almost 9 percent of GDP. Reserves rose to over $10 billion in 1988.[17] To defuse an imminent trade war with the United States, both governments began to take decisive actions to overhaul their trade regimes.

Toward the close of the 1980s, the anxiety of the EANICs over future access to OECD markets had built up further. The formation of regional trade blocs in Europe and North America prompted the EANICs to take some proactive responses, including redirecting their trade flows and reducing their overall trade dependency on the United States in the second half of 1980s. At the same time, the ominous signs of regional protectionism also prompted the EANICs to engage in serious negotiation and make major concessions in the Uruguay Round and to play a highly supportive role in

---

[16] Vinod Aggarwal, Robert Keohane, and David Yoffie, "The Dynamics of Negotiated Protectionism," *American Political Science Review* 81, 2 (June 1987).
[17] Economist Intelligence Unit (EIU), *Country Report: South Korea* 1 (1989), p. 10.

the formation of the Asia-Pacific Economic Cooperation (APEC) forum in the early part of 1990s.

Changes in the finance regime

The most significant development in the international finance regime has been the synchronized liberalization of capital controls in OECD countries and the trend toward international capital market integration. Recent changes in regulations and technology have made it possible for money to travel across borders almost instantaneously, giving rise to massive increases in international financial transactions. Moreover, DFI has been dwarfed by new types of arm's-length portfolio flows, which in 1991–92 accounted for half of the long-term capital outflows from the 13 leading industrialized countries. Short-term flows have also risen in importance. (See Chapter 5, this volume.)

Increased capital mobility can severely limit or contravene national policy. The trend also threatens the viability of the long-standing national financial regime of the EANICs. In the past, South Korea and Taiwan could maintain highly stable fixed exchange rates, monetary policy autonomy, and stringent regulation on both short- and long-term capital mobility. Starting in the second half of 1980s, the EANICs confronted increased U.S. pressure to force the opening of their domestic banking and insurance sectors and stock markets. The Riegle–Garn bill authorizes the U.S. government to take retaliation against the recalcitrants that close their markets to U.S. financial institutions. This meant it would no longer be possible for the EANIC governments to maintain a wall between their domestic capital markets and the international markets, an institutional condition that has been essential for the effectiveness of state macroeconomic management and sectoral planning in the past.[18]

The trend toward international capital market integration also shifted the policy debate. The exchange rate has emerged as an important intermediate or ultimate policy instrument for the adjustment of current account balances and the coordination of macroeconomic policy. In the second half of the 1980s, the United States utilized its power as the lender of last resort to build up market pressures for an appreciation of the German mark and Japanese

---

[18] Robert Wade, *Governing the Market: Economic Theory and the Role of Government in East Asian Industrialization* (Princeton, N.J.: Princeton University Press, 1990).

yen. This led to a monetary realignment among the major OECD nations, culminating in the 1985 Plaza Accords. The EANICs were beneficiaries of the relative loss of Japanese exchange rate competitiveness, but not for long because the situation immediately triggered a ballooning surplus in their own bilateral trade with the United States. Beginning in 1986, U.S. officials picked the EANICs as the targets for next-round currency adjustment. The U.S. government set an implicit target zone for individual EANICs and came forward with an explicit demand for the deregulation of foreign exchange controls.

Between September 1985, when the dollar was at its highest level ever, and the beginning of 1989, the New Taiwan dollar appreciated 49 percent against the U.S. dollar and the Korean won rose 27 percent. As it turned out, monetary realignment was a more effective instrument than trade sanctions and bilateral trade negotiations in redirecting trade flows and correcting chronic trade imbalances. The phenomenal currency appreciation of the late 1980s virtually wiped out the cost advantage of the Taiwanese and South Korean producers in many labor-intensive manufacturing sectors. At the same time, it undermined the effectiveness of tariff policy. In the end, it intensified the market pressure for industrial upgrading and precipitated a wave of capital outflow from the EANICs and a search for low-wage sites for transplant production and off-shore sourcing.

Related developments

To gauge the full implication of these new developments in the international trade and financial regime for the EANICs' development strategies and to make sense of their policy responses, we must take into account some concurrent changes in global production, security, and ideological structures. In the following, I will concentrate my discussion on changes in production, while making some passing reference to the security and ideology dimensions.

First, the global economy is undergoing an industrial restructuring. A wide range of industrial branches have been restructuring their production process, with an emphasis on higher-value-added, knowledge-intensive market segments. The conditions that govern and shape best-practice industrial accumulation are changing, and new types of economic structures are now required for nations to achieve competitiveness. There have recently been many attempts in the academic literature to record and explain this transition, which is often referred to as a transition from Fordism to post-Fordism.[19]

Post-Fordism presents a range of new opportunities and challenges for the EANICs. First, it diminishes the competitive advantage of cheap labor and places the emphasis on skill creation. The EANICs with their relatively skilled labor force are favored. Second, it allows for the manufacture of better quality and more income-elastic products and a reinvigoration of declining, traditional export industries. Third, the gains arising from horizontal collaboration between small firms and vertical cooperation with transnational giants means that small and medium-sized firms can be dynamic instigators of industrial development in many sectors and major potential producers for world markets.[20]

At the same time, the race for technological innovation was forced upon the EANICs. Acquisition of skills, productive assets, and comparative advantage in the production and utilization of three major technological families – microelectronics, advanced material components, and biotechnologies – are critical for the entry of the EANICs into the high-tech industries and for the adaptation of sophisticated manufacturing technologies. For this, they must vastly increase their indigenous research and development (R&D) and design capacity, as well as accelerate the transfer of new technologies across borders.[21] This means the EANICs must either attract a new flow of foreign investments by the U.S. and European transnational corporations or buy into foreign high-tech industries because, by the late 1980s, the flow of new technology from Japan to the EANICs had virtually dried up. Given the current level of development of South Korean and Taiwanese skills and technology, Japanese firms are reluctant to provide key advanced technologies and inputs to potential competitors.[22] Also, the two EANICs have faced increased difficulty in copying foreign technology, given tougher enforcement of intellectual property rights.

---

[19] Raphael Kaplinsky, "Industrial Restructuring in the Global Economy," *IDS Bulletin* 20, 4 (1989); Herbert Kitschelt, "Industrial Governance Structures, Innovation Strategies, and the Case of Japan: Sectoral or Cross-national Comparative Analysis?" *International Organization* 45, 4 (1991), 453–94; E. Schoenberger, "From Fordism to Flexible Accumulation: Technology, Competitive Strategies, and International Location," *Environment and Planning D: Society and Space* 6 (1988).

[20] Kaplinsky, "Industrial Restructuring."

[21] Lakis Kaounides, "The Material Revolution and Economic Development," *IDS Bulletin* 21, 1 (1990).

[22] *Business Week,* November 11, 1991, p. 35.

Thus, for a rapid transition to post-Fordism, the EANIC governments have a critical role to play in industrial restructuring. The states must provide the umbrella institution within which the acquisition and diffusion of the new technologies can take place, as well as set priorities for reforming the education, training, banking, legal, and trade regimes. The degree of liberalization of the domestic economy, protection of property rights, and open-door policy to foreign investment and technology flows are becoming critical. Restructuring requires the generation of a sector-based industrial policy involving more than just a battery of protectionist devices and fiscal incentives; close collaboration between state and industry in the research, development, dissemination, and commercialization of new technologies, as well as in the diffusion and assimilation of new work practices, is also necessary.

Even without U.S. pressures, then, the EANIC states would have had to make major adjustments in their approach to macroeconomic management and sectoral guidance. The elements of the EANICs' international competitiveness had to be retooled and areas of deficiency redefined. From this perspective, the impact of U.S. pressures was circumscribed. In responding to the more immediate U.S. demands with respect to trade liberalization and financial deregulation, the EANIC governments have tried to assert control over the scope and sequence of policy reforms and have given priority to measures that would also facilitate the desired industrial restructuring.

While these economic changes were occurring, the melting-down of the security demarcation in the post–cold war era has redrawn the economic map of East Asia. As security considerations gave way to the development imperative, market forces opened vast and hitherto unexplored opportunities for economic integration in the Asian region. The receding military threat from their old rivals and the economic reform in the socialist countries, in particular the former Soviet Union, China, and Vietnam, not only significantly reduce the security dependence of the EANICs on the United States, but open up new hinterland for their next round of economic expansion. This development leads EANIC firms to impart an Asian orientation in their business strategies and freshens the interest of Asian countries in building up a stronger multilateral cooperative institution.

A final element of international change of particular relevance to the EANICs is the global move toward democracy. In the 1980s, the triumph of liberal democracy as the predominant mode of legitimation threatened the viability of the preexisting authoritarian arrangements that underwrote the past mode of economic accumulation in South Korea and Taiwan. Political liberalization and democratization of the 1980s meant a realignment of power relations among state institutions and a transformation of the power base of the state elite in the two EANICs. In both countries, national representative bodies emerged from rubber-stamp institutions and turned into important policy-making arenas, while the military-security arms of the state were facing an irreversible decline. The coherence of the state apparatus suffered from the persistent internal conflicts over political succession, which were entangled with divisions over the scope and speed of political reform. The resourceful business elites moved to capitalize on the strategic opening brought about by the split within the state and the strengthening of representative institutions.[23]

Democratization also meant changes in the larger state–society relations. The penetration of the state into the organized sectors of the civil society has receded. EANIC governments became politically more vulnerable to socioeconomic grievances of groups that had failed to benefit from the economic boom, and they felt obliged to be more responsive to demands for a more balanced development strategy from newly mobilized social sectors. Enterprise owners were also confronted with various new contenders. The acquiescence of labor to low wages and inhuman working conditions, consumers to collusive business practices, and the community to pollution can no longer be taken for granted.[24] To protect its economic interests in the political contest over development priorities, the business elite has learned to take a more active role in politics. Their degree of success in managing these new tasks will be important determinants of economic policy outcomes during the coming decades.

National responses

Trade liberalization

In the late 1980s, the most dramatic changes in the approach of the EANIC states to economic adjustment took place in the trade regime, the focal point

---

[23] Yun-han Chu, "The Realignment of State–Business Relationship in Taiwan's Regime Transition," in Andrew MacIntyre (ed.), *The Changing Government–Business Relations in the Industrializing East and Southeast Asia* (Ithaca, N.Y.: Cornell University Press, 1994).
[24] Yun-han Chu, *Crafting Democracy in Taiwan* (Taipei: Institute for National Policy Research, 1992), chap. 4.

of U.S. pressure. The Korean government announced its trade liberalization plan in 1985. The average tariff on all items was scheduled to fall to 18.1 percent in 1988 and to 12.7 percent in 1989.[25] The trade regulations for all strategic sectors including automobiles, however, were to be governed by a new Industry Development Law enacted in 1986. Part of the trade liberalization involved the removal of certain nontariff barriers to trade. The system of import monitoring was abolished by the end of 1988, and the Import Recommendation System was ended in early 1989. As part of the Uruguay Round negotiations, in late 1993 the South Korean government announced the reduction or elimination of tariffs on 253 industrial products, bringing the average trade-weighted tariff to 8.3 percent by 1999.

Taiwan's economic planners have also engaged in drastic tariff cuts since 1987. In 1988, tariffs on 4,619 items were reduced by an average of 50 percent. In 1988, there was a further 29 percent cut on average covering 62 percent of imports listed in the customs tariff regulations.[26] The average tariff rate was cut to 8.9 percent in 1990. The prospect of GATT membership has led Taiwan to promise to open up its domestic market even further. On GATT (or now World Trade Organization) accession, the average tariff on industrial good would fall to 4 percent.

South Korea and Taiwan wasted no time in expanding new trade relationships with the former socialist countries and even their respective political rivals – North Korea and mainland China, respectively. A strengthened International Private Economic Council of Korea was entrusted to coordinate business with the socialist countries. South Korea approved the resumption of direct trade with North Korea in all but military goods in October 1988; it opened its first trade office in Beijing in June 1989. South Korea and the People's Republic of China signed a trade agreement in December 1991 in which the two conferred most favored nation (MFN) status on each other. In early 1994, South Korea's National Unification Board, for the first time, approved nine joint-venture projects destined for North Korea.

Taiwan liberalized its trade with Eastern Bloc countries in August 1987 and with the Soviet Union in 1990. Taiwanese authorities also adopted a very pragmatic approach to economic exchange with mainland China. The government legalized indirect trade from Taiwan to mainland China in

---

25 EIU, *Country Report: South Korea* 1 and 4 (1994).
26 EIU, *Country Report, South Korea* 2 (1989), p. 24.

1985, with the restriction on imports substantially eased in 1989. By the end of 1994, some 5,000 products (out of a total customs list of 9,000-plus items) were on the permitted list, including most intermediate and semi-finished goods, and there were even fewer restrictions for imports going through the bonded export-processing zones.

Financial liberalization

Dramatic changes also took place in the area of the financial regime.[27] On the surface, the liberalization of the financial regime was precipitated by persistent U.S. demands, but two underlying economic forces have also played a critical role. First, the external pressure for financial liberalization coincided with a rising domestic call for modernization of the banking sector, which had been minimally internationalized and was ill-equipped to provide logistic support for business expansion abroad. Second, especially in the case of Taiwan, the accumulation of a trade surplus and domestic savings built up tremendous demand for nontradeable goods and financial assets. The excessive demand started to wreak havoc on the real estate and stock markets around 1987–88. In the end, the government was compelled to loosen its control over the outbound flow of capital. In essence, the accumulation of wealth in the private sector eventually overflowed the dam of a dirigible state.

Despite the trend toward global financial integration, the EANIC states are determined to exercise some control over the inbound and outbound flows of capital and to set their own monetary policy targets. As soon as the U.S. Trade Representative put the spotlight on the undervalued local currencies at the beginning of 1986, the central banks of South Korea and Taiwan responded by initiating a controlled currency appreciation. Both governments opted for a gradual appreciation and took measures to prevent a free fall of the U.S. dollar to ease the adjustment pain of the export sectors. At the same time, the monetary authorities in Seoul and Taipei began to nurture the growth of a foreign exchange spot market and later a futures market, so that the burden of currency fluctuation could be shifted from the state to the private sector.

---

[27] For a detailed account of the financial liberalization in South Korea and Taiwan, see Kazutaka Kodama, "Financial and Capital Markets in South Korea and Taiwan – Present Conditions and Prospects for Liberalization," *Pacific Business and Industries* 3 (1992).

In July 1987, the Central Bank of Taiwan removed most restrictions on the private holding of foreign exchange. In March 1990, the Korean authority introduced a "market average rate" system of determining the price of the won. In theory, this provides a reasonable approximation to market forces, but in fact it does not because of the panoply of official controls on the financial market and capital flows.[28] While both the national banks and the local branches of foreign banks were permitted to trade in foreign exchange, the monetary authorities did not allow the market forces to create chaos.

Both the Bank of Korea and the Central Bank in Taiwan continued to intervene heavily to prevent excessive short-term fluctuation. At the same time, by setting the interest rate and exchange rate to closely approximate market prices, the monetary authorities manipulated the foreign exchange markets to make them look as if they were, de facto, liberalized. This practice also mitigated possible criticism from the U.S. Treasury, but both governments adamantly prevented the internationalization of local currency. Both prohibited their banks from offering local currency accounts for their customers abroad and restricted the outbound movement of their own currencies. In particular, they are keen to curb the growth of an offshore foreign exchange market of the New Taiwan dollar or won, so that the central banks in Seoul and Taipei can retain their position as the sole market makers for local currency.

The currency appreciation precipitated a new wave of capital outflow on an unprecedented scale. First, currency appreciation forced ill-adjusted domestic producers to relocate their production facilities to lower-cost sites in order to lengthen the life of their traditional export products. Second, the appreciation generated a rising demand for foreign assets. The EANIC governments moved swiftly to revise their policies on outbound capital flows.

The old restrictions on capital outflow were lifted one by one, beginning in early 1987 in the case of Taiwan and early 1989 in South Korea. Taiwan's Central Bank lifted the ban on individual investments in the foreign securities market and simplified the review process of overseas investment in March 1987. Starting from July 1987, Taiwan residents can remit up to $5 million per year without specific Central Bank approval. Also both individuals and firms were allowed to make direct investments in overseas real

---

[28] *Far Eastern Economic Review,* June 13, 1991, pp. 67–68.

estate. The Korean authority abolished restrictions on investment in overseas real estate in early 1989. Investment in foreign securities was opened to institutional investors in 1989, to all business enterprises in 1990, and to individual investors in 1992 under the principle of reciprocity.

A strong surge in overseas direct investment immediately followed the removal of restrictions. South Korea registered a 35 percent increase in approved direct investment abroad in 1988. The approved amount of direct investment increased from $357 million in 1987 to $820 million in 1990, $1.06 billion in 1993, and more than $2 billion in 1994. In 1990, South Korea also registered its first *net* capital outflow in its postwar history, despite a concurrent surge in incoming direct investment.[29] The largest proportion of Korean direct foreign investment is located in the United States, primarily for establishing sales networks and manufacturing facilities. The second largest recipient region is Southeast Asia. Investment in the ASEAN countries went mostly into labor-intensive manufacturing ventures, such as textiles, wood and rubber products, and electronics.[30] To avoid protectionism in the European Union, South Korean firms have also made substantial investment in Europe since 1990. Their cumulative investment in Europe, mostly in electronics, rose 60 percent in the four years through 1993, to $560 million. The investment by Korea's large conglomerates (*chaebol*) in China surged after South Korea signed an industrial cooperation pact with China in the early part of 1994.

The rise in outward investment was even more dramatic in the case of Taiwan. Official figures show the amount of approved investment abroad increased from only $66 million in 1986 to about $7 billion in 1989.[31] Taiwan and South Korea suddenly emerged as the major sources of foreign investment in Southeast Asia (Table 7.3). The rise pushed the EANICs ahead of Japan as the largest source of foreign investment in Indonesia, the Philippines, and Malaysia between 1986 and 1990. The total direct investment made by the four EANICs amounted to 43.3 percent in Malaysia, 36.8 percent in the Philippines, 21.5 percent in Thailand, and 28.2 percent in Indonesia between 1986 and 1990.

---

29 EIU, *Country Report: South Korea* 1 (1992), p. 22.
30 Junko Sekiguchi, "Transformation of the ASEAN Manufacturing Industry," *Pacific Business and Industries* 4 (1991).
31 The actual figures should be much larger than the official figures because many of the investments were unreported. Usually the official statistics of the recipient countries are more accurate.

Table 7.3. *Investment in ASEAN countries by EANICs and Japan,*
1986–90 (millions of dollars)

Investing country	Indonesia	Thailand	Philippines	Malaysia
Taiwan				
1986	18.0 (2.2)	35.7 (6.2)	0.4 (0.5)	1.9 (1.5)
1987	7.9 (0.5)	299.2 (15.3)	9.0 (5.4)	47.0 (15.8)
1988	910.2 (20.5)	849.9 (13.6)	123.4 (27.3)	146.7 (19.1)
1989	158.2 (3.4)	867.9 (10.9)	148.7 (18.5)	373.8 (29.8)
1990	618.0 (7.1)	766.1 (5.4)	140.7 (14.6)	869.9 (37.8)
1986–90	1,712.3 (8.5)	2,818.8 (9.1)	422.2 (17.2)	1,439.3 (30.3)
South Korea				
1986	12.0 (1.5)	0.9 (0.2)	0.0 (0.0)	0.6 (0.5)
1987	23.0 (1.6)	12.9 (0.7)	0.7 (0.4)	0.8 (0.3)
1988	209.0 (4.7)	109.0 (1.7)	1.5 (0.3)	8.9 (1.2)
1989	466.1 (9.9)	170.7 (2.1)	17.5 (2.2)	29.1 (2.3)
1990	723.0 (8.3)	269.7 (1.9)	21.2 (2.2)	60.6 (2.6)
1986–90	1,433.1 (7.1)	563.2 (1.8)	40.9 (1.7)	100.0 (2.1)
NICs total,[a]				
1986–90	5,698.8 (28.2)	6,651.1 (21.5)	906.9 (36.8)	2,074.7 (43.7)
Japan	4,117.4 (20.4)	10,101.5 (32.7)	629.8 (25.6)	1,378.7 (29.0)

Note: Figures in parentheses are percentages of total foreign investment in the respective countries.
[a]Taiwan, South Korea, Hong Kong, and Singapore.
Source: Sakura Institute of Research, *Pacific Business and Industries,* Vol. 4, *1991.*

Overall, during the 5-year period between 1988 and 1992, on a contract and approval basis, of the total $82.4 billion of DFI committed to the ASEAN countries, 36 percent came from the four EANICs, 26 percent from Japan, and 20 percent from Europe, with less than 10 percent from the United States. The rise of outward expansion to Southeast Asia slackened in 1991 and 1992, since the rush of new investment had saturated the infrastructure capacity in Thailand and Malaysia, but it picked up again in 1993 and 1994, with Vietnam and Indonesia emerging as the new frontier. More than $1.9 billion had been invested in Vietnam by Taiwanese firms by the end of 1994, far more than Hong Kong and Japan, the second and third largest investors, respectively.

Most of the Taiwanese investment in Southeast Asia, like that of South Korea, was concentrated in labor-intensive manufacturing, such as garments, textiles, footwear, electronics, and toys. The only difference between the two EANICs is that, in the South Korean case, the *chaebol* took the lead in overseas expansion. Large firms accounted for more than three-quarters of all foreign investment.[32] Taiwan's foreign investment was carried out by both big business groups and small and medium-size firms. The former took the lead in investment in the OECD countries, while the latter played the major role in ASEAN and mainland China.

With the acceleration of economic reform in mainland China, the coastal area across the Taiwan Straits has become more attractive than Southeast Asia to Taiwanese firms for its geographic proximity and cultural affinity. The coastal provinces were attractive especially to Taiwan's small and medium-size firms because most of them lacked the financial resources and managerial skills for a full-fledged internationalization strategy. Thus, despite the legal ban imposed by the government, Taiwan's investment capital flowed rapidly into Fujian and Guangdong Provinces through a third country, usually Singapore or Hong Kong.

Once the government lifted the restrictions on capital outflows, it also lost control over the final destination of investment capital. Between 1987 and 1990, in the coastal area of China, Taiwan has emerged as the second largest source of incoming investment after Hong Kong. Of the 15,000 projects, worth $20 billion, approved in Guangdong up to the end of June 1991, 80 percent came from Hong Kong, with Taiwanese firms second. In Fujian, of nearly 4,000 investment projects, worth $3.5 billion, approved by the end of 1990, Taiwan accounted for a third, Hong Kong for only 30 percent.[33] As the economic reform shifted into high gear in the early part of 1992, Taiwanese capital was pouring into all major industrial centers, especially Shanghai and other large cities along the Yangtze River.

During the first 10 months of 1994, of the 820 projects approved by Taiwan's Investment Commission, 49 percent were destined for the Yangtze River Delta area (Shanghai Municipality and Jiangsu and Zhejiang Provinces), while 36 percent went to Guangdong and Fujian Provinces. By the end of 1993, according to the PRC official statistics, Taiwanese investors had committed more than $25.6 billion, with more than 25,800 projects

[32] EIU, *Country Report: South Korea* 2 (1990), p. 26.
[33] *Economist,* October 5, 1991.

approved. Thus, between 1986 and 1991, Southeast Asia had been the top recipient region of Taiwan's DFI, and the United States the second most favored destination. But after Deng Xiaoping's symbolic southern trip in the early part of 1992, mainland China surged to the top.[34]

The vibrant capital flows effectively contravened state policy, eventually forcing the state to modify its policy to accommodate the fait accompli. To prevent themselves from being made to look powerless, Taiwanese authorities moved to legalize the indirect investment in the early part of 1990. The Ministry of Economic Affairs published a list of 1,000 products that Taiwanese firms may in the future manufacture on the Chinese mainland. The list of industries in which "indirect" investment is permitted was quickly expanded to 3,922 in August 1990.[35] Still, the official policy is to steer investment away from the mainland to Southeast Asia. Investments in mainland China are subject to stricter financial regulations by the Securities and Exchange Commission. For example, listed companies are not allowed to earmark funds raised from share issues for mainland projects. With the market opportunities in mainland China looming increasingly large, however, most business elites are preparing for a new era of cross-straits economic integration. Since late 1994, all the leading Taiwanese shipping companies have been making plans as if direct transport links with mainland China were just around the corner.

The South Korean and Taiwanese governments not only moved to abolish most of the restrictions on outbound capital flows, but they also took supplementary measures to facilitate the globalization strategies of national firms. Under the directive of the Finance Ministry, the Export–Import Bank of Korea shifted its emphasis from the provision of export financing to the support of overseas investment.[36] Taiwan's government also aided overseas investment by providing funds for expansion abroad. Since April 1990, the Central Bank has been lending U.S. dollars to Taiwanese enterprises via the Bank of Communications, the Export–Import Bank, the International Com-

---

[34] For the geographic distribution of Taiwanese investment in China, see the Investment Commission, Ministry of Economic Affairs, *Statistics on Overseas Chinese and Foreign Investment Monthly* (October 1994). For the volume of investment flows, see the Mainland Affairs Council, *Cross-Strait Economic Statistics Monthly* 26 (October 1994).

[35] Lee-in Chen Chiu and Chin Chung, "As Assessment of Taiwan's Indirect Trade toward Mainland China," Occasional Paper, Chung-Hua Institute for Economic Research, Taipei, 1992.

[36] For instance, in 1989, of the 700 billion won available, 100 billion were earmarked to finance overseas investment. See EIU, *Country Report: South Korea* 1 (1989), p. 12.

mercial Bank of China, and the China Development Corporation to cover up to 80 percent of the cost of individual investment projects abroad.[37] Priority was given to establishing sales and marketing networks and the acquisition of technology. The financial support of the state was behind every major merger and takeover plan of Taiwanese firms in the U.S. high-tech industries, including the acquisition of Altos by Acer Computer and the acquisition of WYSE by a consortium organized by the semipublic Taiwan Semiconductor.

The state also encouraged national firms to finance investment projects through the overseas issuance of corporate bills and convertible bonds, but in both countries, government approval to do so was required. By 1991, more than 100 Korean firms were given permission to raise money in foreign capital markets. The monetary ceiling on bond issues overseas was steadily lifted to $900 million in 1993 and $1.2 billion in 1994. Taiwanese companies were even more aggressive in using this new vehicle.[38] Taiwanese firms were permitted to issue $2.0 billion of corporate bonds in 1994. The most celebrated case was the $335 million purchase of Wyndham Biscuits (the third largest cookie maker in the United States) by Taiwan's President Enterprise, the island's leading food-processing group.

For business expansion in the developing countries, private investment was supplemented by official development assistance (ODA). Both Taiwan and South Korea began to launch mini–foreign aid programs. The South Korean government budgeted $125 million in 1988, $200 million in 1989, and up to $500 million by 1992 for its ODA.[39] The Korean government pledged to increase its ODA volume to $920 million, or 0.2 percent of GNP, by 1996, when the seventh development plan will end. Taiwan's development aid loans are extended by the International Economic Co-operation Development Fund, which was established in 1988 and had a paid-in capital of $400 million by the end of 1993. The capital endowment is expected to reach an interim target of $1.13 billion in the next few years. Aid disbursement rose from $37 million in 1989 and $60 million in 1990, to more than $120 million in both 1992 and 1993. Following the past practice of Japan, the management of the fund was closely tied to the expansion of trade and investment. The allocation of the fund concentrates on infrastructure projects in areas where the investment activities of national firms cluster.

[37] EIU, *Country Report: Taiwan* 2 (1990), p. 24.
[38] EIU, *Country Report: Taiwan* 1 (1990), p. 17.
[39] EIU, *Country Report: South Korea* 2 (1989), p. 13.

With regard to the inbound flow of capital, both governments took much more cautious steps in relaxing the existing restrictions. As a rule, DFI is always favored over portfolio investment because the former facilitates the cross-border mobility of use-specific capital, such as technological and managerial knowledge and networks while the latter does not. Also, both governments have been keen to control the sequence of financial liberalization. The deregulation of the financial sector took precedence over internationalization, that is, opening up for foreign participation.

South Korea launched its program of banking deregulation in 1984. Major commercial banks were denationalized. Foreign banks enjoyed the same rediscount facilities with the Bank of Korea as of 1986. In 1988, commercial bank interest rates were formally decontrolled, but the move toward privatization was cautious. Before the government proceeded with selling its nonperforming bank shares, it had tackled the problem of loans and called upon the *chaebol* to put their financial houses in order. Also, since no single investor was allowed to own more than 8 percent of a bank, the Finance Ministry inevitably became the major shareholder. The government continued to keep tight control, guiding the banks' lending and routinely placing former Finance Ministry officials in management positions. There are few signs of interest competition among banks. The Central Bank in Taiwan formally decontrolled the commercial bank interest rate in 1987. The privatization program was accelerated in 1990, when the government announced plans to sell off some of its shares in three commercial banks and enacted the new Banking Law that opens up the banking sector for private participation. The share of a single corporate investor is limited to 5 percent, however, and that of a diversified business group to 15 percent.

Despite the persistent urging of the U.S. government, South Korea and Taiwan have moved slowly in opening up their securities markets to foreign investment. In the beginning, both governments provided foreign investors with indirect access to the local stock markets through investment trusts.[40] From the beginning of 1991, foreign institutional investors were allowed to invest directly in securities on the Taiwan Stock Exchange, but strict limitations applied. Initially, each institution could invest up to $50 million, and the total quota was set at $2.5 billion. Between 1991 and 1994, the stipulated maximum was steadily raised to $7.5 billion, which still represented

---

[40] Namely, the Taiwan Fund, Korea Fund, and Europe Korea Fund. The first two are openly traded on the New York Stock Exchange.

less than 5 percent of total market capitalization by the end of 1994. Each institution is allowed to buy up to 5 percent of a single company, while total foreign ownership of a company is limited to 10 percent.[41] The South Korean government took a similar move. From the beginning of 1992, foreign institutional investors were allowed to make portfolio investment directly, but a single foreign investor may own no more than 3 percent of a company. Total foreign ownership may not exceed 10 percent in most cases, with certain strategic industries declared off-limits. The Ministry of Finance has been very reluctant to raise the ceiling too fast, worrying that a sudden influx of foreign funds will either inflate the money supply or drive up the value of the won. The ceiling was raised one more time in December 1994 to 12 percent, and may be raised to 15 percent by the end of 1995.[42]

Despite the financial reform, both governments are still keen to prevent their national industrialists from acquiring a financier mentality, that is, being more attentive to short-term financial gain than long-term profitability. Thus, it is considered important to limit the transnational liquidity of their assets.

The state-orchestrated industrial-upgrading program

The EANICs in the late 1980s and early 1990s have adopted a more open policy toward DFI in the most advanced sectors. The South Korean government revised its stringent policy on DFI. Restrictions on inward investment were eased in 1984. A new Foreign Inducement Law specified a list of areas in which foreign investment is restricted or prohibited, all others being considered open to investment, theoretically up to 100 percent ownership although informally there may be pressure in favor of local equity participation. Out of 999 industries, the law specified 339 that were prohibited or restricted. In 1985, the list was shortened to 237; by 1989, 93 percent of all manufacturing and 58 percent of all service-sector groups were opened.[43]

The Taiwanese government has been even more aggressive in attracting new waves of DFI. In the early part of 1994, the government launched a new pitch for foreign investors, unveiling an all-encompassing plan to develop Taiwan into a regional operational center for the transnational corporations (TNCs). Six functional areas, where Taiwan may build up its competitive

---

[41] EIU, *Country Report: Taiwan* 4 (1990), p. 19.
[42] EIU, *Country Report: South Korea* 4 (1994), pp. 17–18.
[43] EIU, *Country Profile: South Korea, 1989–1990*, pp. 49–50.

edge, were identified in the plan. It is hoped that Taiwan, competing with Hong Kong and Singapore, can become a production center for video and audio programs, an air passenger and freight trans-shipment hub in greater China, a regional distribution and service center, a financial center, a tele-communication, data-processing, and software development center, and re-search and development center. To this end, the government moved to slash virtually all sectoral restrictions on DFI in January 1995. So far, Texas Instruments, Ericson (the Swedish telecommunication giant), and CSR (the Australian building materials firm) have located their regional headquarters in Taipei. IBM, Motorola, Microsoft, and Federal Express have expressed similar intentions.

Further, the governments of South Korea and Taiwan have taken a range of measures to channel foreign investment into strategic sectors and en-hance the capability of local firms in these sectors to develop strategic alliances with transnational firms. First, the EANIC states used government procurement to enable local firms to enter technical cooperation relation-ships or joint ventures with TNCs. Take the aerospace industry, for exam-ple. In the case of South Korea, in a military craft procurement decision in early 1990, McDonnell Douglas's F/A 18 was preferred to General Dynamics' F-16 because McDonnell Douglas offered better terms on tech-nology transfer. The deal was tied to a joint venture between Samsung Aerospace Industries and McDonnell Douglas in the assembly of 36 fighters from imported kits and a co-production of 72. It provided an impor-tant stimulus to the nascent industry, whose exports increased from $210 million in 1988 to more than $1.8 billion in 1990. More recently, Korean companies have been contracted to manufacture parts for all major commer-cial jets and military craft producers, including Boeing, Lockheed, Pratt and Whitney, British Aerospace, and General Electric.[44]

Taiwan's aerospace industry took off from the development and produc-tion of the indigenous defense fighter with technical assistance from North-rop Corporation. The project involved the production of 250 fighters over 10 years. Many local firms were signed up to supply parts and components, which laid the foundation of an indigenous aerospace industry. In 1991, a new joint venture, Taiwan Aerospace, was established by the former direc-tor of the IDF project with the participation of state development funds and five leading business groups. With assistance from the government, Taiwan

44 EIU, *Country Report: South Korea* 1 (1990), pp. 22–23.

Aerospace successfully piggybacked a technology transfer agreement to a business deal between Boeing and a newly licensed airline, the Eva Airline, over the purchase of 22 jumbo jets. Also, with its sale of 150 F-16 fighter jets in 1992, Lockheed was required to purchase $600 million worth (10 percent of the total sales) of parts and components from Taiwan.

In most cases, joint ventures between TNCs and local firms in strategic sectors received strong financial backing from the EANIC states. In Taiwan, the economic planners have set up various instruments to finance joint ventures in strategic industries. The funds from the Executive Yuan Development Fund, China Development Corporation, and the Bank of Communications were used to facilitate joint ventures between Taiwan Microelectronics and Semi-Conductor and the Netherlands' Philips; a $250 million project between Acer and Texas Instruments to make dynamic random-access memory (DRAM) chips in 1990; a joint venture among the U.S.-based Swearingen Aircraft Co., Taiwan Aerospace, and four other Taiwanese business groups to build SJ-30 corporate jets in 1994; and a $770 million joint venture between Taiwan's Umax Data Systems and Japan's Mitsubishi Electric to produce the cutting-edge 16-megabit DRAM chip in 1995.

In early 1992, the Taiwan Industrial Development Bureau launched a more extensive program that provides a panoply of policy incentives for the formation of strategic alliances between national firms and U.S.–based TNCs. The new program not only targeted 10 sunrise industries for special promotion, but in each industry 2 to 4 leading U.S. firms were identified as the favored candidates, including most of the blue-chip high-tech firms in the United States, such as AT&T, IBM, Intel, SUN, DEC, Rockwell, Du Pont, USS, and Johnson & Johnson.[45]

More significant is the effort of the South Korean and Taiwanese govern-ments to accelerate the acquisition of skills, productive assets, and compara-tive advantage in the production and utilization of critical technologies. First, both governments hired foreign consultant firms, for example, Arthur D. Little and Data Quest, to identify points and level of entry and set up priorities for focused state support. Second, both governments vastly ex-panded public-sector budget allocations for R&D. Large amounts of gov-ernment funds are channeled into state research labs, universities, and state-

---

[45] The 10 industries are communications, information, consumer electronics, semiconduc-tors, precision machinery, aerospace, high-grade special materials, special chemicals and pharmaceuticals, and medical equipment. See *Commercial Times,* April 4, 1992.

sponsored R&D consortia or are used to subsidize the R&D activities under-taken by private firms.

During the 1980s, both governments have enhanced the existing fiscal incentives for R&D investment in the private sector. In South Korea, total R&D expenditure (exclusive of national defense spending) as a percentage of GNP had increased from 1.19 in 1984 to 1.98 percent by 1992, which approached the OECD average of 2.0. In Taiwan, the percentage had increased from 0.95 in 1984 to 1.70 percent in 1992; more than 50 percent of the increase came from the government budget. In a bid to promote corporate R&D activities, the South Korean government planned to invest a total of $4.6 billion between 1992 and 2001 in the development of eleven key technologies, including nuclear reactors, advanced materials, high-definition television, broad integrated services digital networks, and very large-scale integration chips. Thirty percent of the required funds will come from the government budget.

The government of Taiwan played an even stronger role in the develop-ment and diffusion of key industrial technologies due to a more de-centralized industrial structure. In strategic industries, the government sub-sidized private R&D projects up to 60 percent of the total cost. The state research labs and parastatal research organizations under the Ministry of Economic Affairs, Ministry of Communications and Transportation, Minis-try of Defense, and National Science Council were entrusted with the re-sponsibility to serve private industry and carry out research projects for developing prototype technologies targeted by the Strategic Industries Pro-gram established in 1982, from microelectronics, telecommunications, bio-medical engineering, special chemicals, material science, precision machin-ery, and nuclear energy, to aerospace. These research organizations transferred developed technologies to qualified private firms or more likely to new semipublic joint ventures for commercialization.

In both South Korea and Taiwan, all the most complex and expensive research projects, such as the submicron microelectronics technology and high-definition television, were carried out by state-sponsored R&D con-sortia, which were typically organized around state research organizations such as the Korean Institute for Advanced Technology and Taiwan's Indus-trial Technology and Research Institute. In Taiwan, the state research organ-izations and state financial institutions were also intimately involved in the commercialization of newly acquired technologies. A series of semipublic firms were established to commercialize the prototype product technologies developed at the state research labs in the 1980s and early 1990s.[46] In addition, both governments have made a concerted effort to reduce their dependence on Japanese industrial technology, manifested by their chronic large trade deficits with Japan. Both governments have put technology transfer on the top of their demand list in bilateral trade negotiations with Japan. In 1994, Taiwan's Industrial Development Bureau rounded up more than 200 shareholders – mostly large Taiwanese corporations – to establish Asia-Pacific Investment Co. with initial capital of $615 million. The company was entrusted with the mission to facilitate the transfer of technologies from Japan primarily through joint ventures. A similar arrangement, under the name of the Japan–Korea Technology Cooperation Foundation, is currently being planned in South Korea.

The government also nurtured the growth of private venture capital funds. Starting in 1985, the Bank of Communications invested a total of $20 million in eight funds; in 1990, a further $60 million was made available. Twenty venture capital firms now operate in Taiwan, with some $420 million invested in more than 200 enterprises, ranging from computers and electronics, specialty materials, biotechnology, environmental products, to electro-optics.[47]

An overall assessment

Of course, it is still too early to reach definitive conclusions about the effectiveness of the EANICs' adjustment strategies in the recent decade. Nonetheless, there are some unmistakable signs indicating that they are working. First, the EANIC producers in many traditional export sectors have effectively circumvented their major partners' trade barriers by taking the route of indirect export: transplanting low-value-added manufacturing or the final assembly phase of the production to lower-wage countries. The states have effectively fostered the rationalization of the production in traditional export sectors by creating a bottom layer of international subcontracting in the region and nurtured the growth of higher-value-added export activities by pushing local producers to move upward in the hierarchy of

---

[46] Notable examples included United Microelectronics (in 1979), Taiwan Microelectronics and Semiconductor (in 1986), Taiwan Photomask (in 1988), Lifeguard Pharmaceutical (in 1988), Taiwan Aerospace (in 1991), and Vanguard Semiconductor (in 1994).

[47] *Far Eastern Economic Review,* January 17, 1991, p. 49.

international subcontracting networks or develop strategic alliances with the TNCs. These activities are clear examples of the process of advancing in the production hierarchy, as advocated by Gary Gereffi in Chapter 4.

Of course, the industrial restructuring process is not free from adjustment pains. Both South Korea and Taiwan suffered an export slump in 1989–90, but the export sectors in both nations registered a strong recovery in the early 1990s. The economic performance of the two EANICs has remained impressive. The annual average growth rate of South Korea and Taiwan in the period between 1980 and 1992 was 9.3 and 8.2 percent, respectively. The annual growth rate of merchandise exports in the period stayed at a respectable 12.2 and 12.5 percent, respectively (see Table 7.1).

The overall effectiveness of the recent adjustment experiences of the two EANICs is best summarized by a well-known economist, Schive Chi, who characterized the recent experience of Taiwan in the following terms:

Taiwan has come out of the "Dutch disease" during the 1980s in surprisingly good shape and recovered its economic vitality at record speed. It is a miracle recovery considering the magnitude of the external shocks – a 50 percent currency apprecia-tion, a severe macroeconomic disequilibrium, and a record rise in wage level in dollar terms between 1985 and 1988. It is unprecedented in terms of compressed time. The government was called upon to deal with five major obstacles in one decade – labor unrest, industrial deepening, economic restructuring, environmental protection, and trade and financial liberalization. Nevertheless, the total industrial output grew at an annual rate of 6 percent with 5 percent loss of labor input.[48]

Implications for the regional economy

The economic restructuring of the EANICs carries important implications for the regional economy. The new wave of DFI from the EANICs to Southeast Asia and China stimulated intraregional trade and accelerated the intraregional division of labor to create a regional production system that lined up Japan, the EANICs, and the second-tier NICs. (A complementary discussion of the regional economy, from the Southeast Asian perspective, is found in Chapter 8, this volume.)

Basically, three mutually reinforcing economic trends have redirected trade flows in East Asia. The first is the relocation of production facilities from Japan and the EANICs to the Southeast Asian countries and China

---

[48] Quoted from the *United Daily,* February 29, 1992.

through DFI. An essential feature of this new foreign investment is its trade-creating, rather than trade-diverting, nature. Most of these investments concentrated in the export-oriented manufacturing sectors, which required capital goods and intermediate inputs from Japan and the EANICs. The net result can be seen as a form of indirect export from the EANICs to the advanced industrialized countries. According to one recent survey, the transplant firms set up by Taiwanese businessmen in mainland China obtained on average 54 percent of their raw materials and intermediate inputs from Taiwan.[49] The second is the steady removal of trade barriers among the East Asian economies. Under the pressures of their OECD trading partners, both the EANICs and their neighboring economies took decisive action to slash their tariffs and abolish many nontariff barriers in the latter half of the 1980s. An unintended consequence was to accelerate trade flows among the East Asian economies themselves. Finally, the strong growth in the region also generated a rising demand for imported consumer goods, which can be partially met by the products of the EANICs.

The importance of the developing Asian region as an export market for the EANICs has steadily increased, especially since the second half of the 1980s. In 1983, total trade among Japan, the EANICs, ASEAN, and China was worth $106 billion, while their total trade with the United States amounted to $132 billion. By 1993, the positions had been reversed. Intraregional trade had increased by 3.9 times to $420 billion, while trade with the United States had increased by 2.7 times to $363 billion. In 1993, the region absorbed more than 47.7 percent of the exports from the ten East Asian economies, while the United States took only 32.4 percent.[50]

Also the bilateral trade between the EANICs themselves has grown significantly in recent years. Hong Kong became the second largest export market for Taiwan and the third largest for South Korea in 1992 because of its entrepot status in the region (Figure 7.1). The amount of bilateral trade between Taiwan and Korea is rapidly approaching that between South Korea and mid-sized OECD countries, such as Canada. More importantly, the trade among the EANICs increasingly looks like the trade pattern

[49] *Far Eastern Economic Review,* March 5, 1992, p. 54.
[50] Center for Pacific Business Studies of Sakura Institute of Research, "Economic Outlook of the Asian Economies for 1995," *Pacific Business and Industries* 4, 26 (1994); and Ken Iijima, "The Current State of the East Asian Economies and Issues for the Future," *Pacific Business and Industries* 4, 25 (1994), 7. The data were compiled from IMF, *Direction of Trade Statistics.*

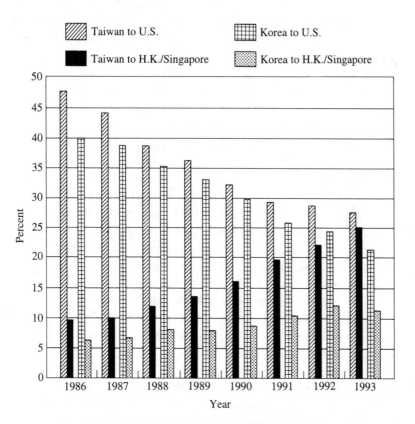

Figure 7.1. Exports to the United States and city NICs from Taiwan and South Korea, 1986–93. From IMF, *Direction of Trade Statistics Yearbook,* and Republic of China, *Taiwan Statistical Data Book.*

among the OECD countries – predominantly intraindustry as opposed to interindustry trade.[51]

The most dramatic rise is in bilateral trade with China. The bilateral trade between South Korea and China has grown from a little more than $1 billion to $11.7 billion between 1985 and 1994, making China South Korea's third largest trading partner. The triangular trade between Taiwan and the mainland, mostly via Hong Kong, rose from $0.6 billion to $13.6 billion between 1980 and 1993. By the end of 1994, Hong Kong, accounting for more than

[51] EIU, *Country Report: South Korea* 2 (1989), p. 27.

22 percent of the island's total exports, is set to overtake the United States as Taiwan's largest trading partner. In 1994, mainland China absorbed close to 17 percent of Taiwan's total exports and the gross volume of the cross-straits trade has risen to $16.3 billion.[52]

The new wave of investment has shifted some of the EANIC exports previously going to North America toward Southeast Asia and China. For instance, the diversion of Taiwan's production capacity has reduced its dependence on the U.S. market (Figure 7.1) and effectively shifted the island's formerly huge trade surplus with the United States to the mainland. Taiwan's surplus with the United States has narrowed from $19 billion in 1987 to $10 billion in 1992. Over the same period, China's surplus with the United States grew from $3 billion to $20 billion, the second largest source of the U.S. trade deficit after Japan.[53] An unintended consequence of the expanded U.S.–China trade is the increased economic leverage that U.S. policy makers can wield against Beijing in policy areas of human rights and economic reform, as exemplified in the political bickering on Capitol Hill surrounding the annual extension of MFN status for China.

In contrast to the European Community, the acceleration of intraregional trade and investment flows was mostly driven by private adjustment strategies and assisted by Japanese business organizations and the informal overseas Chinese business networks.[54] It received little help from regional economic cooperative institutions or multilateral arrangements.

The new wave of investment flows and the formation of an intraregional division of labor are redrawing the economic borders in the region and rendering the existing political demarcations and ideological barriers increasingly meaningless. The emerging East Asia is best viewed as a collection of dynamic growth zones. Complex networks of production and distribution link local firms to a subregional metropolis, and through it to the regional and world market. Singapore's new growth zone links the city-state's service industries to an industrial park that encompasses the Southern

---

[52] See Yun-wing Sung, "Hong Kong and the Economic Integration of the China Circle," paper prepared for the Economic Working Group of the China Circle Project, sponsored by the University of California Institute on Global Conflict and Cooperation, Hong Kong, September 1–3, 1994. The 1994 figures are reported in *Commercial Times*, January 28, 1995.

[53] *Far Eastern Economic Review*, March 5, 1992, p. 54. Update for data from IMF, *Direction of Trade Statistics Yearbook*.

[54] Ken Iijima, "The Outlook for Industrial Cooperation between ASEAN and Japan," *Pacific Business and Industries* 1 (1992).

Malaysian state of Johor and Indonesia's Batam Island. Hong Kong's new growth zone now encompasses the entire Pearl River delta.[55] The investment binge of Taiwanese firms in the coastal area will eventually integrate Fujian Province and much of the Yangtze River delta into a complex network of production. In a similar vein, South Korea's new growth zone will cover the entire Korean Peninsula and much of the Tumen River delta, which sprawls over the boundaries of North Korea, Russia, and China's Jilin Province.[56] Another significant development is the economic integration among Hong Kong, Taiwan, and the coastal provinces of mainland China. The growth potential of China and its future slot in the emerging "Greater China" economic community deserves special attention as the thriving overseas Chinese pull forward the homeland.

In the last decade, China has carved out its own pathway from the socialist quandary. By gradually shifting toward an outward-looking and market-oriented development program since 1979, it has achieved the same very high growth as the EANICs did in the 1960s and 1970s.[57] China's average annual growth rate between 1980 and 1992 was 10.1 percent, one of the fastest in the world. The total value of its GDP increased from $21 billion in 1978 to more than $170 billion in 1992. Exports grew at a 15.6 percent annual rate during this period, so that foreign trade is now equivalent to more than a third of China's GDP, compared with less than 10 percent before 1979.[58]

The transformation of the economic system is characterized by a thorough privatization of farm production based on a household responsibility system,[59] decentralization of industrial planning and foreign trade decisions, bold experiments with capitalist institutions in isolated test sites

55 In the Pearl River delta, from 2.5 to 3 million workers are employed in Hong Kong–invested plants. See John Thoburn et al., "Investment in China by Hong Kong Companies," *IDS Bulletin* 22, 2 (1991).

56 *Far Eastern Economic Review,* January 16, 1992, pp. 16–20.

57 George Crane, *The Political Economy of China's SEZ* (Armonk, N.Y.: Sharpe, 1990); Christine P. W. Wong, "Between Plan and Market: The Role of Local Sector in Post-Mao China," *Journal of Comparative Economics* 11, 3 (1987); Ezra Vogel, *One Step Ahead in China: Guandong under Reform* (Cambridge, Mass.: Harvard University Press, 1989); Victor Nee and Su Sijin, "Institutional Change and Economic Growth in China: The View from the Village," *Journal of Asian Studies* 1 (February 1990).

58 Xiao Zuoji, "The Acceleration of Reform and the Prospect of Taiwan–Mainland Economic Cooperation" [in Chinese], paper presented at the conference Changing Economic and Trade Relationship between Taiwan and Mainland, sponsored by the *China Times,* Taipei, November 18–20, 1992.

59 Peter Nolan, *The Political Economy of Collective Farms: An Analysis of China's Post-Mao Rural Reform* (Oxford: Polity, 1988).

before their widespread adoption, and the phenomenal expansion of the private and collective sectors.[60] Much of the export expansion was achieved by national firms that utilized domestic savings but tried out new labor practices and management techniques. Just as in the case of Taiwan and South Korea, foreign capital played a significant, but far from dominant, role in the export-led industrial growth. In 1993, the foreign invested enterprises contributed 27.5 percent of the PRC's exports, bringing their total value to $25.3 billion.[61]

As market-oriented reforms moved beyond the Special Economic Zones to the entire coastal and border provinces, however, the relative importance of DFI rose rapidly. The average share of DFI in China's gross fixed capital investment during the 1980s was a mere 2.5 percent. It went up to 4.5 percent in 1991, 8 percent in 1992, and 13 percent in 1993. Inflows increased from $11.1 billion in 1991 to $38.5 billion in 1994. By the end of 1994, there were more than 100,000 foreign-invested enterprises operating in China, employing more than 14 million workers. Private foreign investment is even being used as a main way of building infrastructure.

The latest wave of foreign investment to China is less interested in its comparative advantage in labor, energy, and land costs or generous fiscal incentives, but increasingly concerned for the vast potential in the growth of the domestic consumption power and the minimally commercialized but relatively advanced military and science technology. Until 1991, ASEAN had been the leading recipient of DFI, but China moved into first place since 1992. China's share of total DFI in developing countries was 24 percent in 1992 and 27 percent in 1993, making China by the largest recipient of DFI among developing countries. The largest part of the investment capital is coming from overseas Chinese. Since the Tienanmen bloodshed, Hong Kong and Taiwan together have accounted for three-fifths of the direct

---

[60] The contribution of the state-owned enterprises to gross industrial production dropped from 78 percent in 1981 to 55 percent in 1991. By this measure, mainland China in 1991 is no more socialist than Taiwan at the early stage of its EOI. On the other hand, the private sector, which consists of the privately owned, privately run, and foreign-invested enterprises, made up only 0.7 percent of gross industrial production in 1981, but accounted for 10 percent in 1991. The collective sector (the enterprises owned by townships and villages) now accounts for 35 percent of gross industrial production and absorbs more than half of the surplus labor in the countryside. See *Minpao*, August 7, 1992, p. 9.

[61] See Zhang Xiaoji, "Prospect of Economic Integration Among Mainland, Hong Kong-Macau and Taiwan of China," paper prepared for the Economic Working Group of the China Circle Project, sponsored by the University of California Institute on Global Conflict and Cooperation, Hong Kong, September 1–3, 1994.

investment flows.[62] The Chinese of Southeast Asia add another 10–15 percent.

Thus, in a unique way, overseas Chinese – ethnic Chinese living outside China – are the major external force helping drive the modernization of this poverty-ridden land of continental size. The 51 million overseas Chinese in Asia command resources far beyond their number. Of Asia's four "tigers," only South Korea is not Chinese. Almost all the citizens of Taiwan and Hong Kong are Chinese; so are three-quarters of Singaporeans. Another four ASEAN countries – Malaysia, Thailand, Indonesia, and the Philippines – have Chinese minorities that account for an astonishing share of their economies.[63] In this sense, China enjoys a development resource that Russia can only dream about, and India can only partially copy. (See Chapter 8, this volume, for further discussion of the crucial role of overseas Chinese in Southeast Asia.)

The EANICs are serving an important role in this change. They are not only an important source of investment capital, production technology, and managerial know-how, but the wellspring of development strategies and capitalist institutions. The diffusion of modern economic institutions and legal infrastructure from Hong Kong and Taiwan to China is accompanying their investment capital. The presence of Hong Kong and Taiwanese influence is most visible in the creation of a market-based real estate sector, the stockmarkets in Shanghai and Shenzhen, and the adoption of modern accounting systems.

The economic transformation in China carries extraordinary significance not only because the Chinese model exemplifies a pathway from the socialist conundrum, but also because of its sheer size. An effective market-oriented reform in China will transform the social and economic life of more than 1.1 billion people. After 15 years of miraculous growth, China's real per capita income, based on the purchasing power parity (PPP) measure, approached $2,470 in 1992, about the same level achieved by Taiwan

---

[62] For example, Hong Kong and Taiwan accounted for, respectively, 44 and 19 percent of realized DFI in mainland China in 1993. See Zhang Xiaoji, "Prospect of Economic Integration."

[63] For example, a recent study found that Indonesian Chinese, 4 percent of the population, controlled 17 of the 25 biggest business groups. In Thailand, ethnic Chinese, 8–10 percent of the population, own 90 percent of commercial and manufacturing assets, and half of the capital of the banks. See Yozo Tanaka, Minako Mori, and Yoko Mori, "Overseas Chinese Business Community in Asia: Present Condition and Future Prospect," *Pacific Business and Industries* 2 (1992).

around the mid-1970s. This made China the third largest economy in the world, after the United States and Japan. If China can keep up its current speed of economic growth, it will become the single largest economy of the world in 20 years. This sea change may well be the most significant economic transformation in human history since the Industrial Revolution.

Conclusion

The policy reorientation undertaken by the two EANICs in the second half of the 1980s and the early 1990s was largely driven by external forces. The past patterns of state intervention and macroeconomic management were no longer sustainable because of the profound changes taking place in the EANICs' external economic environment and their elevated economic position in the international division of labor. The changes in the global trade and finance regimes exerted the most direct pressures on the EANICs for liberalizing their economies. Nonetheless, in both countries the movement toward economic liberalism was checked by a legacy of state activism, yielding both continuity and discontinuity.

The economic rationale for state intervention and the approach to macroeconomic management and sectorial guidance changed, but the initial objectives that state policies addressed and, more importantly, the centrality of the state in the process of economic restructuring, remained. In responding to U.S. demands for trade liberalization and financial deregulation, the EANIC governments have tried to maintain control over the scope and sequence of policy reforms and give priority to measures that would also facilitate desired industrial restructuring. Nor was there any rush to undo their past learning and experiences in economic management and industrial steering. The EANIC governments continued to exert a tight control over inbound capital flow and put limits on foreign participation in the domestic equity market, thus limiting integration with the global securities market, despite the trend toward globalization of finance.

Therefore, it is most useful to conceive of the policy reorientation of the EANICs as a mediated response. The impact of the new development context on national government and domestic firms was mediated through existing modes of incorporation into the global economy and domestic structures. On the domestic front, the impact and the search for appropriate responses emanated from existing structural conditions, institutional arrangements, and a repertoire of policy instruments.

The epic changes taking place in the global economic and political system and the national adjustment strategies undertaken by the EANICs in the past decade carry great long-term significance. Decisions made by various national governments at this crucial juncture will set the parameters for the future evolution of both their national economies and the emerging Asian regional economy for decades to come. The reorientation of the EANICs' development strategies, the emergence of EANIC-based transnational corporations, and the diffusion of their proven development model to the neighboring countries are increasingly becoming new factors that shape the flows of trade and investment in the region and redefine the development context for the rest of the developing countries.

CHAPTER 8

Southeast Asia: success through international openness

LINDA Y. C. LIM

After nearly three decades of steady economic growth, the six capitalist countries of Southeast Asia today constitute the world's fastest-growing regional economy. The six (Indonesia, Malaysia, the Philippines, Singapore, Thailand, and Brunei) form the Association of Southeast Asian Nations, known as ASEAN. In contrast to their relatively homogeneous Northeast Asian neighbors, the ASEAN countries are characterized by extreme ethnic, cultural, and religious diversity.[1] Their European colonial heritage is equally diverse.[2] Yet unlike other ethnically diverse, European-colonized developing regions such as Africa, the Middle East, and South Asia, the ASEAN countries have maintained ethnic harmony and political peace for decades.[3] Their sustained economic success challenges popular ideologies that, for example, Confucianism is conducive to capitalist economic development while Islam is not, or that colonialism is the primary cause of economic development failure in postcolonial societies. In contrast to ASEAN's success, the four socialist countries of Southeast Asia –

[1] For example, Islam is the dominant religion in Malaysia, Indonesia, and Brunei; Theravada Buddhism in Thailand, Burma, Laos, and Cambodia; Catholicism in the Philippines; and Confucianism in Vietnam and Singapore. In addition, each country has significant ethnic and religious minorities. Indonesia alone, the world's fourth most populous and largest Muslim nation, has more than 200 different ethnolinguistic groups. There are large Muslim minorities in Thailand, the Philippines, and Singapore, and some 25 million overseas Chinese dominate the commercial sector in nearly all the countries.

[2] Thailand was never colonized by an external power, but Burma, Malaysia, Singapore, and Brunei were colonized by Britain, Indonesia by the Netherlands, the Philippines by Spain and the United States, and Vietnam, Laos, and Cambodia by France. The periods of colonial rule ranged from 50 to 350 years.

[3] While there have been occasional ethnic and political disturbances during this period, these have not been frequent, prolonged, sustained, or disruptive of the general political and social order. Nor have they involved large numbers of casualties. The one exception is the Philippines in the first half of the 1980s.

238

Vietnam, Cambodia, Laos, and Burma (Myanmar) – have been counted among the world's poorest and least successful economies, with their 120 million citizens suffering decades of war and civil strife. Tables 8.1 and 8.2 document the economic contrasts between these two groups of countries. The ASEAN countries' economic success is particularly distinctive for its heavy dependence on the world economy, continuing the region's more than 1,000-year history of widespread participation in maritime-based trade.[4] This is the result of Southeast Asia's distinctive geography, which consists of peninsular and archipelagic territories lying astride the major world sea-trading route between the great empires of China to the north and India to the west. This long trading history has arguably fostered an out-ward- and market-focused economic orientation in the region's population that persists to the present day. (It contrasts vividly with the lingering inward-focused, protective orientations of the once "hermit" national econ-omies of Northeast Asia.) As we will see later, geography remains an important factor underlying the ASEAN countries' accelerated economic growth and industrialization in the 1990s.

The ASEAN countries are also more heavily dependent on international trade, in terms of export shares of GDP, than most other developing regions (see Table 4.1). With respect to trade policy, the World Bank ranked most of the ASEAN countries as either strongly or moderately outward-oriented between 1963 and 1985, with the more outward-oriented nations experienc-ing higher real income growth over this period.[5] These countries have also always received a disproportionately large share of the direct foreign invest-ment (DFI) going to developing countries.[6] They have remained major

---

[4] See, e.g., Kenneth R. Hall, *Maritime Trade and State Development in Early Southeast Asia* (Honolulu: University of Hawaii Press, 1985); and Anthony Reid, *Southeast Asia in the Age of Commerce, 1450–1680, Vol. 1: The Lands below the Winds* (New Haven, Conn.: Yale University Press, 1988).

[5] World Bank, *World Development Report, 1987* (New York: Oxford University Press, 1987), chap. 5. The Bank divided this period into two: 1963–73 and 1973–85. Out of 41 developing countries considered, Singapore ranked with South Korea and Hong Kong as "strongly outward-oriented" in both periods, while Malaysia and Thailand were among only 4 countries ranked as "moderately outward-oriented" during both periods. Indonesia was ranked as "moderately outward-oriented" in the earlier period and "moderately inward-oriented" in the later period, while the Philippines, the ASEAN group's weakest economic performer, was " moderately inward-oriented" in both periods. Note that the period under study precedes the market-oriented liberalization that all the ASEAN countries embarked on in the second half of the 1980s, which makes them even more outward-oriented now.

[6] In 1983, Singapore, Indonesia, and Malaysia (in that order) were already the largest developing country hosts of cumulative DFI stocks after Brazil and Mexico (World Bank, *World Development Report, 1987*, p. 117). With the huge post-1987 influx of new DFI to

world producers and exporters of a variety of primary commodities, while simultaneously becoming increasingly important as exporters of manufactures and services.[7]

Much of this sustained outward-oriented, externally dependent economic success is due to skillful state management of external dependence in the ASEAN countries. They have survived and even prospered through many changes in the world economy that devastated other regions: the oil shocks, the third world debt crisis, periodic slumps in commodity prices, and the recent recession in the industrialized countries. They have achieved these economic successes under different, and changing, domestic political regimes. Moreover, as the region's socialist economies embarked on market-oriented economic reforms in the 1980s, they too experienced similar economic successes. The recent economic performance of Vietnam, Cambodia, Laos, and Burma surpasses that of other industrial and developing countries undergoing similar transitions from socialist to market economies (e.g., Eastern Europe, Russia, and Africa), despite the continuation of authoritarian governing regimes and the added burden for some of international economic embargoes. While it would be interesting to examine the reasons why the people of this region manage to be economically successful in diverse ethnic and cultural contexts and under different political and economic regimes, a full exploration of this subject goes beyond the scope of this chapter. Here the focus will be the impact of recent international economic changes on the region and its responses.

Historical background

During World War II, all of Southeast Asia was invaded and occupied by Japanese military forces, which severed economic ties with the West and

the region (see text upcoming), these countries were joined by Thailand, and their absolute and relative positions as DFI hosts increased.

[7] For example, over 90 percent of the world's exports of natural rubber, tin, palm oil, and tropical timber come from the ASEAN countries, which are also important exporters of coffee, cocoa, tropical fruits and vegetables, and seafood. Malaysia alone is the world's largest exporter of palm oil (with two-thirds of the world market), as well as of semiconductors, room air-conditioners, color TVs, VCRs, and phone answering machines. Singapore is usually the fifth or sixth largest exporter of computer products in the world, with a 60 percent world market share in hard disk-drives; it typically exports 50 percent more electronics products to the United States than Britain and Germany combined. Indonesia is the world's largest exporter of liquified natural gas and plywood, while Thailand is the world's largest exporter of natural rubber, frozen shrimp, and tuna, and vies with the United States as the world's largest exporter of rice (Vietnam ranks third). The region as a whole is also a major exporter of textiles, garments, and footwear. Overall, electronics and petroleum products are its largest exports by value.

Table 8.1. *Economic indicators, Southeast Asia (ASEAN), 1970–92*

Country	1990			Real GDP per capita, annual increase (percent)			Merchandise exports, annual increase (percent)			Inflation, annual rate (percent)	
	GDP ($ billions)	Population (millions)	GDP per capita (dollars)	1970–80	1980–90	1991–92	1972–80	1980–90	1991–92	1980–90	1992
Brunei	4	0.3	13,333	na	na	na	na	na	na	-6.9	na
Malaysia	42	19.0	2,211	5.4	2.7	5.8	4.7	10.3	17.6	1.6	4.7
Philippines	44	61.5	715	3.5	-1.4	-3.1	6.0	3.6	9.6	14.9	8.9
Singapore	35	3.0	11,666	5.9	4.5	4.1	28.7	10.5	10.3	1.7	2.3
Thailand	80	55.8	1,434	5.2	6.1	6.4	10.5	14.8	18.8	3.4	4.1
Total	312	317.8	982	5.0	5.0	4.1	13.1	8.6	13.4	8.3	7.0

Sources: World Bank, *World Tables tapes, 1992* (for 1970–90); Asian Development Bank, *Asian Development Outlook, 1994* (for 1991–92).

Table 8.2. *Economic indicators, socialist Southeast Asia, 1989–92*

| Country | 1990 | | | Real GDP per capita, annual increase, 1980–92 (percent) | Merchandise exports, annual increase, 1980–92 (percent) | Inflation, annual rate, 1989–92 (percent) |
	GDP ($ billions)	Population (millions)	GPD per capita (dollars)			
Myanmar	37.7	41.6	907	2.2	43.8	24.8
Cambodia	na	8.5	na	1.7	73.3	118.9
Laos	0.6	4.1	220	4.5	23.5	29.6
Vietnam	9.5	66.3	200	4.5	24.4	63.3

Source: Asian Development Bank, *Asian Development Outlook, 1994.*

resulted in severe economic dislocation and hardship largely unknown during the preceding European colonial era. After the war, each country became independent of its respective colonial power – Indonesia, the Philippines, and Burma in the late 1940s; Vietnam, Cambodia, Laos, Malaysia, and Singapore in the 1950s; and the tiny oil-rich sultanate of Brunei in the 1980s. Postwar and postindependence communist insurgencies in all the ASEAN countries were essentially extinguished or diminished by the 1960s (with the partial exception of the Philippines). But communist regimes did come to power in Vietnam, Cambodia, and Laos, which remained war-torn for another two decades or more, during which time socialist Burma was riven by internal ethnic and ideological strife (in effect a 40-year civil war).

During the colonial era, Western enterprises dominated the "commanding heights" – the large-scale, capital-intensive sector – of these primary-commodity-exporting economies. Immigrant ethnic Chinese (and in the case of Burma, Indian) minority middlemen monopolized most lower-level commercial operations. Indigenous populations functioned mainly as peasants, laborers, and colonial servants until the small educated indigenous elite took over the reins of government at independence. In the immediate postcolonial period, nation building was the primary political task of governments of territories that in most cases had previously been unified only by Western colonial rule.

Primary production for export continued as the main modern economic activity, but all the ASEAN countries also gradually embarked on programs of import-substitution industrialization. Import barriers were erected to protect nascent industries manufacturing for the domestic market, and ownership restrictions were imposed on foreign and local-Chinese-owned enterprises everywhere except Malaysia and Singapore, which retained essentially laissez-faire policies as late as 1970. State enterprises were set up as an indigenous alternative to European- and Chinese-dominated private enterprise, rather than as reflections of socialist ideology, and various economic policies were implemented favoring indigenous ethnic groups and discriminating against foreigners and Chinese in the private sector.[8]

The shift to labor-intensive export manufacturing began in the late 1960s as a response to political rather than economic imperatives. The predominantly Chinese island city-state of Singapore embarked on this development

---

[8] See, e.g., Frank Golay, Ralph Anspach, Ruth Pfanner, and Eliezer Ayal, *Underdevelopment and Economic Nationalism in Southeast Asia* (Ithaca, N.Y.: Cornell University Press, 1969).

strategy (based on the earlier examples of Hong Kong and Puerto Rico) when its separation from the Federation of Malaysia in 1965 made import-substitution industrialization unrealistic for a home market of less than two million. Because Singapore, a trading entrepôt for the region since its founding by the British in 1819, lacked local industrialists, multinationals were assiduously courted and the U.S. electronics industry in particular began locating offshore assembly facilities there beginning in 1968.

This development had a demonstration effect both on Singapore's neighbors and on foreign multinationals, which became educated about the region's potential as an efficient low-cost export platform to world markets. Malaysia, responding to domestic tensions over a continued ethnic division of labor, and the Philippines, responding to the political and economic needs of the Marcos martial law regime, sought high growth rates by shifting to export-oriented manufacturing in the early 1970s.[9] Thailand and Indonesia did not follow suit in a major way for another decade, when a severe downturn in primary commodity prices provided the major impetus for large-scale export-oriented industrialization. Meanwhile, commodity exports continued in Malaysia, Indonesia, Thailand, and the Philippines, boosted by newly discovered oil and natural gas resources in the first two countries.

By the mid-1980s, manufactures exceeded commodities to account for more than half of the foreign exchange earnings for all the ASEAN countries except oil-exporting Indonesia and Brunei. Except in Malaysia and Singapore, however, this was less the result of a conscious strategic national policy shift toward export-oriented manufacturing than of external factors. These factors included Multifiber Arrangement quota limitations on the East Asian NICs (EANICs), which helped spur the textile and garment export industry, and multinational corporate strategies, which helped spur the electronics export industry in the region.

Southeast Asia suffered less from the third world debt crisis than did other developing regions, although because of their economic size the Philippines, Indonesia, and Thailand all ranked among the top dozen developing

---

[9] For economic policy analyses of the shift to export manufacturing in the ASEAN countries, see Eddy Lee (ed.), *Export-Led Industrialization and Development* (Singapore: Maruzen Asia for the International Labour Organisation, 1981); Eddy Lee (ed.), *Export Processing Zones and Industrial Employment in Asia* (Bangkok: Asian Employment Programme of the International Labour Organisation, 1984); Mohamed Ariff and Hal Hill, *Export-Oriented Industrialisation: The ASEAN Experience* (London: Allen & Unwin, 1985).

country debtors in terms of the absolute size of their debt in the early 1980s. With the collapse of commodity prices and a regional recession in the mid-1980s, these external debt burdens (incurred for projects ranging from rural infrastructure to the development of heavy industry) became onerous, resulting in the successful implementation of conventional structural adjustment policies.[10] With the partial exception of the Philippines, and in contrast to the much richer and more industrialized Latin American nations, the ASEAN countries were "model debtors." Their market-oriented economic reforms included phased-in trade and investment liberalization, privatization, and deregulation,[11] all of which contributed to making their economies more efficient and more attractive and accessible to foreign investment – thereby facilitating the shift to export-oriented industrialization.

This shift was immeasurably enhanced by the worldwide currency realignment initiated by the Plaza Accords of September 1985. The sharp rise of the Japanese yen, followed in succession by the New Taiwan dollar, the Korean won, and the Singapore dollar, added to the competitive cost pressures already faced by export manufacturers in these increasingly labor-short, high-wage economies. The result was a massive outflow of industrial investment from Japan and the EANICs to the now more hospitable and low-cost ASEAN economies in the late 1980s. The 1989 withdrawal of U.S. Generalized System of Preference privileges for the EANICs further contributed to this process, which has spurred economic and industrial growth in the ASEAN host countries to record levels since 1987.[12]

[10] See Ungku A. Aziz (moderator), *Strategies for Structural Adjustment: The Experience of Southeast Asia* (Washington, D.C.: IMF and Bank Negara Malaysia, 1990); David G. Timberman (ed.), *The Politics of Economic Reform in Southeast Asia: The Experiences of Thailand, Indonesia and the Philippines* (Manila: Asian Institute of Management, 1992); Andrew MacIntyre and Kanishka Jayasuriya (eds.), *The Dynamics of Economic Policy Reform in South-East Asia and the South-West Pacific* (Singapore: Oxford University Press, 1992).

[11] In addition to the sources in note 10, see *ASEAN Economic Bulletin,* Special Issue on Privatization and Deregulation in ASEAN, 5, 3 (March 1989); Jacques Pelkmans and Norbert Wagner (eds.), *Privatization and Deregulation in ASEAN and the EC* (Singapore: Institute of Southeast Asian Studies, 1990); Ng Chee Yuen and Norbert Wagner (eds.), *Marketization in ASEAN* (Singapore: Institute of Southeast Asian Studies, 1991).

[12] For more on DFI in ASEAN through the late 1980s, see Soon Lee Ying (ed.), *Foreign Direct Investment in ASEAN* (Kuala Lumpur: Malaysian Economic Association, 1990); Pasuk Phongpaichit, *The New Wave of Japanese Investment in ASEAN: Determinants and Prospects* (Singapore: Institute of Southeast Asian Studies, 1990); Eric D. Ramstetter (ed.), *Direct Foreign Investment in Asia's Developing Economies and Structural Change in the Asia–Pacific Region* (Boulder, Colo.: Westview, 1991); and Linda Y. C. Lim and Pang Eng Fong, *Foreign Direct Investment and Industrialisation in Malaysia, Singapore, Taiwan and Thailand* (Paris: OECD Development Centre, 1991).

International changes since the late 1980s

Since the late 1980s, the ASEAN economies have been affected by several major international changes. The most important change has been the rapid evolution of increasingly *integrated regional production* and *trade networks,* which link the ASEAN countries closer to their other Asian neighbors – Japan, the EANICs, China, and Vietnam – and are reducing their dependence on Western industrial nations. These networks reflect the new intraregional investment flows, which began in the late 1980s in response to changing national comparative cost advantages, and they have continued to develop as internal markets within the region itself have grown.[13] The data presented in Tables 8.3 and 8.4 do not yet capture the full impact of these developments, but they do show the following: (1) Japan and the EANICs dominated investment flows into the ASEAN countries in the late 1980s, accounting for the bulk of DFI inflows into Indonesia (44.8 percent), Malaysia (65.5 percent), and Thailand (66.5 percent). Inflows from the EANICs exceeded those of Japan in Indonesia and Malaysia, but declined dramatically in the early 1990s. (2) This has increased the ASEAN countries' import dependence on both Japan and the EANICs, turning healthy ASEAN bilateral trade surpluses in 1985 into large deficits (especially with Japan) in 1991.[14] (3) Over the same period, the United States has remained the largest single market for ASEAN exports, and the ASEAN bilateral trade surplus with the United States has remained fairly stable.[15] At the same time, the European Community increased in impor-

---

[13] Linda Y. C. Lim and Nathaniel Siddall, "Foreign Investment, Trade and Technology Linkages in Asian Developing Countries in the 1990s," in John Dunning (ed.), *Globalization and Developing Countries* (London: Routledge & Kegan Paul for the United Nations Conference on Trade and Development, forthcoming).

[14] Note that these bilateral deficits are readily covered by a combination of the following: compensating bilateral trade surpluses with the United States and other countries; service income inflows, especially from tourism and worker remittances; and long-term capital inflows.

[15] On an individual country basis, the United States in 1991 was the largest export market for Singapore (19.8 percent of its total exports), Thailand (21.7 percent), and the Philippines (36.4 percent), while Japan was the largest export market for oil-exporting Brunei (53.8 percent) and Indonesia (37.1 percent). Although Singapore – which accounts for about 40 percent of ASEAN's total trade – was Malaysia's largest export market (23.3 percent), this is largely due to trans-shipment of Malaysia's exports through Singapore's sea- and airports. (Singapore also serves the same middleman function for Indonesia, but its trade figures with Indonesia are classified by the Singapore government; the figures used in Table 8.4 are Indonesia's, which may represent a substantial undercounting due to smuggling.) If oil exports are excluded, the United States would account for a much larger share

tance as a market for ASEAN exports. In short, industrial relocation from Japan and the EANICs to ASEAN countries has led to a triangular pattern of trade, in which the ASEAN countries import machinery, equipment, parts, and supplies from the Asian home countries of foreign investors, use these to manufacture final products, and then export them to Western markets. (For further discussion of triangular trade, see Chapter 4, this volume.)

Nonetheless, it should be noted that ASEAN trade and investment patterns are quite diversified geographically; they also vary by country. For example, the stock of EC investment in Malaysia and Singapore exceeds that of Japan, because of heavy British and Dutch investments in plantations, mining, and petroleum that date back to the colonial era, while the United States continues to dominate DFI stocks and flows in the Philippines, its former colony. Despite some shifts in the early 1990s,[16] ASEAN trade and investment patterns of the late 1980s are consolidating into complex regionally integrated production and distribution networks.

Japanese and Western multinationals have established vertically integrated divisions of labor in the region, based on the different comparative advantages of different locations. For example, electronics companies like Sony (a late-1980s newcomer) and Texas Instruments (a 25-year veteran) combine capital-intensive manufacturing and highly skilled research and design activities in Singapore and (increasingly) Malaysia with lower-skilled, labor-intensive assembly operations in Thailand and Indonesia. They often use Singapore additionally as a regional operational headquarters and as a site for training, servicing, parts procurement, warehousing, marketing, and distribution activities. Automobile companies like Toyota, Nissan, and Mitsubishi also operate regionally integrated production networks with different auto parts and components being made in and ex-

of total ASEAN exports than the 18.7 percent shown in Table 8.4, which is still the largest single country share (the larger ASEAN figure being the summation of five country shares, including Singapore's import–export middleman function).

[16] In 1992, DFI from both Japan and the EANICs into the ASEAN countries declined – in some cases precipitously – as Japan went into recession and both Japanese and EANIC firms turned to China for cheap-labor investments that earlier went to the ASEAN countries, which now face rising costs and infrastructural bottlenecks resulting from DFI-induced rapid growth. At the same time, U.S. investment into the region, which declined in the late 1980s, recovered strongly in 1992 to overtake investments by Japan. This is the result of recovery in the U.S. economy, strengthening global markets in high-tech industry, and the growing attraction of the ASEAN market itself. By 1994, Japanese DFI flows rebounded strongly as the Japanese economy recovered and the strong yen encouraged further industrial relocation to ASEAN.

Table 8.3. *Distribution of direct foreign investment stock in ASEAN, 1980s*

		Source country/region share of direct foreign investment (percent)				
Host country	Year	European Community	United States	Japan	EANICs[a]	ASEAN
Indonesia	1980	8.3	4.3	33.7	10.3	2.0
	1988	12.1	5.8	18.4	8.5	2.6
Malaysia	1981	26.6	6.4	17.6	8.7	28.0
	1987	24.0	6.1	20.1	6.1	31.2
Philippines	1980	9.3	54.6	16.8	5.1	0.4
	1989	11.2	55.7	14.3	8.7	1.2
Singapore	1980	39.6	29.6	16.7	—	—
	1989	28.7	33.2	30.7	—	—
Thailand	1980	15.9	32.8	29.0	12.7	7.5
	1988	12.4	24.2	36.7	15.1	5.6

[a]EANICS include Hong Kong, Korea, Taiwan; Singapore is included in ASEAN. *Source:* UN Centre on Transnational Corporations, *World Investment Directory, 1992, Vol. 1, Asia and the Pacific.*

Table 8.4. *Distribution of ASEAN trade, 1985–91 (percent)*

	Exports		Imports		Total trade	
Trade partner	1985	1991	1985	1991	1985	1991
European Community	9.3	12.0	13.3	11.2	11.2	11.5
United States	19.7	18.7	15.7	14.5	17.9	16.5
Japan	25.4	18.3	20.7	24.0	23.2	21.3
EANICs	13.9	10.8	6.8	10.9	10.6	10.8
ASEAN	19.5	19.9	20.0	17.7	19.7	18.7
China	1.3	2.0	5.2	2.9	3.1	2.5
Total ($ billions)	71.5	161.7	64.0	181.1	135.5	342.9

Source: International Monetary Fund, *Direction of Trade Statistics Yearbook, 1992.*

changed between plants in different ASEAN countries.[17] But multinational regional integration also extends beyond ASEAN. For example, Matsushita exports room air conditioners from Malaysia to China, Guardian Industries exports glass from Thailand to China, and AT&T exports telecommunications equipment from Thailand and Singapore to China.

Japanese companies have begun developing networks of local suppliers.[18] In addition to transferring technology and raising local content, this development increases the integration and interdependence of multinationals and local enterprises within the region. By contrast, investments by companies from Korea, Taiwan, and Hong Kong tend to more closely resemble the traditional pattern characteristic of earlier export-oriented offshore investments by Japanese and Western multinationals, with most supplies and equipment being imported from the home country of the parent firm.[19]

A second type of regional network is the horizontally diversified network of Southeast Asian Chinese family-based companies, which began expanding internationally after the financial liberalizations of the early 1990s.[20] They include many large conglomerates, which both extend their core activities to, as well as enter into new activities in, neighboring countries as part of new corporate strategies of diversification and internationalization.

[17] Lim and Pang, *Foreign Direct Investment and Industrialisation.*

[18] See, e.g., Pasuk Phongpaichit, "Japanese Investment in ASEAN after the Yen Appreciation"; Shojiro Tokunaga (ed.), *Japan's Foreign Investment and Asian Economic Interdependence* (Tokyo: University of Tokyo Press, 1992); Doug Tsuruoka, "In the Same Mould," *Far Eastern Economic Review,* December 30, 1992; Richard Doner and Patcharee Siroros, "Contending with Fragmented Markets: Firm and Group in the Toyota Parts Industry in Thailand," case study prepared for the Southeast Asia Business Program, University of Michigan, April 1993 (mimeo).

[19] Exports from these EANIC firms go mainly to third countries, as has long been the case for export-oriented Japanese multinationals and for Western multinationals over the past 10 years. Previously, exports from Western subsidiaries in the region tended to go back to their parent companies and home countries.

[20] See Linda Y. C. Lim, "The New Ascendancy of Chinese Business in Southeast Asia: Political, Cultural, Economic and Business Implications," Association for Asian Studies, New Orleans, Louisiana, April 14, 1991; Linda Y. C. Lim, "Southeast Asia and the Overseas Chinese" and "Organizational Relationships in East Asia," comments presented at the Wharton International Forum, Kyoto, Japan, May 21–24, 1992; Linda Y. C. Lim, "The Role of the Private Sector in ASEAN Regional Economic Cooperation," in Lynn K. Mytelka (ed.), *South–South Cooperation in a Global Perspective* (Paris: OECD Development Centre, 1994), pp. 125–68; Linda Y. C. Lim and L. A. Peter Gosling, "Economic Growth, Liberalization and Chinese Ethnicity in Southeast Asia in the 1990s," in Daniel Chirot and Anthony Reid (eds.), *Entrepreneurial Minorities and Modern Nationalism in Central Europe and Southeast Asia* (forthcoming for the Social Science Research Council).

Sectors in which Southeast Asian Chinese investors are particularly active in the ASEAN countries include agribusiness (shrimp farming, chicken processing), tourism (hotels, recreational developments), banking, and property development.

Changes in the *competitive position* of the major international capitalist powers since the 1980s have generally benefited Southeast Asia. One example is continuing exchange rate realignments, as the currencies of Japan and the EANICs appreciate against that of the United States. In the late 1980s, most ASEAN currencies depreciated with the U.S. dollar, increasing their nations' competitiveness and attractiveness to new foreign investment. This has continued in the 1990s, except for Singapore and, increasingly, Malaysia, whose currencies have been appreciating against the dollar. At the same time, relative economic decline is driving all the major international capitalist powers – Western Europe, North America, and Japan – to seek to counter the stagnation of their own mature markets by venturing into the world's fastest-growing regional economy. The Clinton administration, for one, sees Asia (primarily China and Southeast Asia) as presenting a "new primacy of economic opportunity" for the United States and is focusing considerable attention on its trade and investment relations with the region. And U.S. and European automakers are beginning to mount serious challenges to the long-established Japanese domination of the ASEAN car market, the fastest growing in the world, by committing major new manufacturing investments in the region.[21]

Thus, both the relative rise of Japan, compared with other mature capitalist powers, and the relative decline of all these powers (including Japan) has benefited the ASEAN countries. They have received large supplies of investment capital from the developed countries, especially Japan, because of their attractiveness both as world-competitive production locations and as growing markets. For the ASEAN countries, there has not yet been a shrinking of international development financing. But this may change in the later 1990s, given the projected continued rapid economic growth of the region, the increasing capital requirements and technological intensity of this growth, and the huge needs for public infrastructure and human capital development. Moreover, intensified competition for international capital from other emerging capitalist countries (especially China and Vietnam),

[21] Bruce Stokes, "Driving East," *National Journal,* November 14, 1992; "Asia in the Driver's Seat," *Asiaweek,* February 24, 1993.

inadequate domestic savings (though high by other developing-country standards – see Table 1.3), and still underdeveloped local capital markets may exacerbate problems of financing.

Southeast Asia has also benefited from the emergence of *new regional economic actors,* which reflects shifts in international competitiveness. Japanese export-oriented industry moved to the ASEAN countries following the 1985–86 yen appreciation in response to the declining competitiveness of Japanese home-based production relative to that of the EANICs, in industries like consumer electronics and household appliances. The later relocation of EANIC industries was a response to their subsequent currency appreciation and the Japanese move. The major relocated industries in both cases were those in which U.S. companies were not major players, and in which European companies were similarly affected by rising home currencies and responded also by relocating to ASEAN countries. More recently, the emergence of rapidly growing China, and of Vietnam and Burma, as markets for ASEAN commodity and manufactured exports and destinations for ASEAN-originating outward investment (mostly by overseas Chinese companies), is contributing to regional growth and increased regional integration.[22] Singapore, for example, is Vietnam's largest trade partner, while its main foreign investors are from Taiwan and Hong Kong, with significant representation also by Korean, Malaysian, and Singapore investors. China is also beginning to invest in Southeast Asia, with more than 50 companies expected to set up shop in Singapore alone in 1993 and a state-owned weapons manufacturer announcing the establishment of assembly operations in Malaysia for the local market and for export.

Besides market-determined global economic forces and the emergence of new regional actors, *international political developments* have also propelled the ASEAN countries toward closer regional integration with each other and with their Asian neighbors. These include the emergence of new potential capitalist competitors for Western markets, capital, and technology in the reforming economies of Eastern Europe, Russia, and Latin America; the movement toward more closely integrated regional economic blocs in Western Europe and North America; and the long and difficult negotia-

---

[22] See, e.g., Linda Y. C. Lim, "Models and Partners: Singapore and Malaysia in Vietnam's Economic Reforms," in Scott Christensen and Manuel Montes (eds.), *Marketization in Southeast Asia* (Honolulu: East–West Center Press, forthcoming); "The Yen Bloc Breaks Open," *Economist,* May 8, 1993.

tions that preceded the conclusion of the Uruguay Round of the General Agreement on Tariffs and Trade (GATT).

The end of the cold war is also affecting the ASEAN countries. First, the demise of the Soviet Union led to the evaporation of its financial support for Vietnam, accelerating that nation's market-oriented economic reforms and development of its economic relations with ASEAN and other Asian neighbors.[23] Second, the feared withdrawal of U.S. military forces from East Asia generally (and the accomplished withdrawal from the Philippines) – in response to both the end of cold war hostilities and the emergence of a more inward-looking, budget-cutting U.S. administration – has led to an arms race in the region. Korea and Japan are striving to protect themselves from Russian and North Korean nuclear arsenals; China is vastly expanding its military capability with hardware purchases from Russia and other former Soviet republics, while aggressively positioning itself in the South China Sea (the crucial international sea-lane for the ASEAN countries and oil and natural gas trans-shipments to Japan); and Taiwan continues to arm itself against an ever-powerful China. At the same time, however, a Taiwan-government-led consortium is developing the former U.S. naval base at Subic Bay in the Philippines into an industrial estate, and a similar fate may be in store for the former Soviet military base at Cam Ranh Bay in Vietnam. Third, as the U.S. military clout in the region declines, so will its political influence. Relations between the United States and Japan in the region may be characterized by greater economic competition and perhaps more hostility, since they will be less mediated by the need for military cooperation.

The ASEAN countries stand to be hurt by the second and third developments, especially if the military withdrawal of the United States (which is favored as a benign distant power able to fend off closer and more unpredictable regional powers) is accompanied by a relative economic withdrawal. This would remove a valuable counterweight to the Japanese economic presence (in terms of an alternative source of capital, technology, and

---

23 See Do Duc Dinh, "Vietnam's Foreign Economic Policies before and after 1986," paper presented at the conference, Political Economy of Foreign Policy in Southeast Asia in the "New World Order," Department of Political Science, University of Windsor, Ontario, October 30–November 1, 1992; Do Duc Dinh, "Marketization and Economic Cooperation between Vietnam and ASEAN Countries," paper presented at the Social Science Research Council conference Marketization in Southeast Asia, Chiang Mai, Thailand, January 14–16, 1993; Do Duc Dinh, "Vietnam's Economic Renovation toward the Market Mechanism," paper presented at the Fourth Southeast Asia Business Research Conference, Southeast Asia Business Program, University of Michigan, Ann Arbor, May 22–23, 1993.

markets for the region), especially at the high-tech end of the industrial spectrum that cannot or will not yet be supplied by the EANICs. So far there are no indications that this will happen, but in the meantime, the ASEAN countries are also (defensively) purchasing sophisticated armaments.[24]

In 1993–94, the Clinton administration also introduced other uncertainties into the international policy environment facing the ASEAN countries. In addition to the fear of further U.S. military pullouts from the region, there was anxiety that the administration would increasingly tie U.S. aid and access to the U.S. market to human rights and environmental issues; that it would be more aggressive in trade policy, including pushing for accelerated "market-opening" measures in Asian countries; that it would withdraw China's most favored nation privileges, which would adversely affect the entire regional economy; and that it would adopt a more active and nationalistic industrial/technology policy. This last policy might reduce high-tech investment outflows to the ASEAN countries by increasing the competitiveness of U.S. production sites for such products as Intel semiconductors and Motorola telecommunications equipment now made in Malaysia for world markets, by restricting "the export of jobs" from the United States, by "temporarily" protecting the U.S. market in certain strategic sectors, or by diverting other international capital and technology to the United States. These fears have since been mitigated by the administration's new focus on developing U.S. economic links with Asia, in particular its recent push to strengthen the Asia–Pacific Economic Cooperation (APEC) forum, of which the United States and its Asian trade partners are members, and by the Republican takeover of majority control of the U.S. Congress in November 1994.

Finally, the ASEAN countries have only been marginally affected by *new ideological currents* favoring market-oriented reforms. Pragmatism and domestic political pressures have always had a stronger influence on ASEAN economic policy than have foreign ideologies. Thus, ASEAN gov-

---

[24] The ASEAN countries are also developing their own arms industries, to the extent that Paul Beaver of the definitive military publication *Jane's Sentinel* says that "by the turn of the century, the main providers of all but Asia's most sophisticated weaponry may come from ASEAN arms industries" (*Asian Wall Street Journal Weekly,* May 17, 1993). In the meantime, Malaysia, for one, has contented itself with playing desperate U.S. defense contractors off against Russian arms merchants to upgrade its military equipment at low cost. During a recent such negotiation, the U.S. Navy even offered to relinquish its own order of new F-18 planes to Malaysia, so that their U.S. producer could make the sale. Malaysia is also importing Russian scientists and technicians for its skills-short, mostly multinational-owned, high-tech industry.

ernments (except for that of the Philippines) have always accorded high priority to macroeconomic stability and have always been more open to external trade and investment than have other developing countries. Indeed their success following this path has been one of the factors leading to the new policy orthodoxy worldwide. They embarked on deregulation, privatization, and further trade and investment liberalization in the mid-1980s in response to domestic economic concerns and political pressures rather than to foreign ideological currents. And they are not likely to reduce the strong government role in their economies as much as these ideologies recommend. For example, regional trade liberalization under the ASEAN Free Trade Area (AFTA) agreement is proceeding very slowly, and governments are actually increasing their economic role in areas such as technology policy,[25] albeit mostly in collaboration with the private sector.

In general, international economic developments since the late 1980s have been mostly favorable to Southeast Asia's economic development, while international political developments are more threatening. The exception is Vietnam's enhanced embrace of market economics and closer relations with its neighbors, following the demise of its communist mentor, the Soviet Union.

Responses to international changes

Regional-level responses

Because ASEAN is an established regional organization, its member nations have turned in part to regional-level responses to these new international circumstances. There is a historical precedent for this in the spurt of ASEAN cooperation that followed the end of the Vietnam War in 1975. In the 1990s, the most important impetus for enhanced regional economic cooperation has come from two primary international sources: the apparent solidification and likely expansion of regional blocs in Europe and the Americas, and the emergence of newly market-oriented developing coun-

[25] Linda Y. C. Lim, "Technology Policy and Export Development: The Case of the Electronics Industry in Singapore and Malaysia," paper presented at the conference New Technologies and Developing Countries, United Nations University Institute for New Technologies, Maastricht, June 21–23, 1993; Marcus Brauchli, "Indonesia Is Divided over How to Compete: Low Cost or High Tech," *Wall Street Journal,* March 25, 1993.

tries now willing and able to compete with the ASEAN countries for international markets and finance.

In Europe, the single market integration, the joining of the European Free Trade Area with the European Union and the prospect of EU membership being extended to Eastern European countries, and in the Western Hemisphere, the NAFTA grouping of the United States, Canada, and Mexico and its possible extension to other Latin American and Caribbean countries, both raise the prospect that market access to and foreign investment from the advanced industrial countries of Western Europe and North America might favor competing developing countries in those blocs over ASEAN.

To counter possible reduced trade and investment flows from the West by developing closer economic relations with their neighbors, and to increase their own attractiveness to Western investors as a single large integrated regional market, the ASEAN countries decided upon accelerated formation of AFTA, which began on January 1, 1994. Manufactured products with an ASEAN-wide content of at least 40 percent will qualify for a Common Effective Preferential Tariff in member countries. Unprocessed agricultural goods and service industries are not included. Current tariffs on manufactures are to be reduced to no more than 20 percent in five to eight years, and to no more than 5 percent by January 1, 2008. Progress on this tariff liberalization varies by country, however, and is proving to be disappointing,[26] although the completion date for AFTA was recently moved up from 2008 to 2003.

Singapore and Brunei are already virtually tariff-free, and Malaysia is accelerating its tariff cuts ahead of the agreed-upon AFTA schedule, but Indonesia, the Philippines, and especially Thailand are delaying their cuts, and in certain highly protected but strategic industries like automobiles, vested business interests have postponed the *start* of tariff reductions to 2008. Singapore and Malaysia are the largest trading nations in ASEAN, with the most open economic policies and the most internationally competitive manufacturing sectors, hence their eagerness and willingness to implement tariff liberalization. In Indonesia, the Philippines, and Thailand, by contrast, protected import-substitution industries are entrenched in the individual countries' political as well as economic power bases, and therefore are successfully resisting increased competition.

[26] Michael Vatikiotis, "Market or Mirage," *Far Eastern Economic Review,* April 15, 1993. Originally planned to start on January 1, 1993, AFTA's inauguration was set back a year by the failure of member countries to agree on scheduled tariff cuts.

A faster and more flexible alternative to a region-wide free-trade area is the development of subregional cooperation zones, known as "growth triangles."[27] These involve the national or provincial/state governments of geographically contiguous territories working together to attract external investments – for example, through joint infrastructure development, joint investment promotion missions to third countries, and coordination of national investment policies. It is left to private-sector investors to decide where their investments should go, according to the comparative advantage of the different areas. The first cooperation zone that has been fully developed is the Johor (Malaysia)–Singapore–Riau (Indonesia) triangle, in which cheap land and labor from Johor State and Riau Province are combined with Singapore's abundant human skills, managerial expertise, technology, transportation, and communications infrastructure to attract investment to all three locations. Singapore is a free port, and Riau has been declared a free-trade zone, so that trade between factories located there and in Johor's bonded factories and free-trade industrial zones is free of most trade restrictions; in addition, export-oriented enterprises may be 100 percent foreign owned in all three territories. Investors in the zone currently include companies from Hong Kong, Taiwan, Singapore, and Indonesia, as well as Japan, the United States, and Europe. Besides manufacturing, there are cooperative subregional investments in large tourist projects to serve Singapore and other Asian markets. Singaporeans already constitute the largest group of foreign tourists in Malaysia and Indonesia, while Malaysians are second to Singaporeans in Indonesia.

In July 1993, a second subregional growth triangle emerged within ASEAN, based on the northern Malaysian port city and industrial center of Penang and its northwestern peninsular Malaysian hinterland, the city of Medan and north Sumatra across the Straits of Malacca in Indonesia, and southern Thailand up to the city of Phuket. A dozen cooperative projects have been announced in the infrastructure, agribusiness, and tourism sectors. Like Singapore, Penang (known as "Silicon Island" because of its large semiconductor manufacturing base) is faced with extreme labor shortages and would like to relocate some of its more labor-intensive export manufacturing industry to its neighbors, while maintaining and expanding the high-tech and services aspects of such industry. One such relocation of elec-

[27] Lee Tsao Yuan (ed.), *Growth Triangle: The Johor–Singapore–Riau Experience* (Singapore: Institute of Policy Studies and Institute of Southeast Asian Studies, 1991); Lim, "The Role of the Private Sector."

tronics assembly to Medan has reportedly already taken place. A third triangle is developing between the southern Philippines, Sabah in Malaysia, and northeastern Kalimantan, Sulawesi, and Maluku in Indonesia, with tourism the most likely area of cooperation.

Subregional cooperation zones like these have several advantages over region-wide trade liberalization. They involve smaller-scale, decentralized negotiations among fewer parties, which are more committed to the partnership because of closer geographical proximity and associated historical ties. Commitments are locally based, looser, and more informal, avoiding both complex national-level politics and the time-consuming and cumbersome bureaucratic machinery of the full ASEAN organization. As such zones proliferate and expand, they may eventually coalesce into one another, bringing about "creeping regionalization," since to function as unified entities the zones require free movement of goods and services, including some labor, across their boundaries. The zones institutionalize private- and public-sector cooperation on a decentralized, local basis to facilitate exploitation of the complementary comparative advantages of neighboring territories. They can thus form single market entities for the purposes of multinational corporate strategic planning and investments.

Subregional cooperation zones can also include non-ASEAN members. One such zone has already been proposed that would link the port city of Kuantan on the east coast of peninsular Malaysia with Cambodia and southern Vietnam. The focus of this triangle would likely be oil and liquid natural gas exploration and recovery from the South China Sea, an activity in which Kuantan is already heavily involved. A "golden quadrangle" is evolving between northern Thailand, Burma, southern China, and Laos, and plans are underway to accelerate Vietnam's becoming a member of ASEAN.

Despite its slow progress toward formal economic regionalization, ASEAN remains the most coherent and established regional economic grouping in the Asia–Pacific area and plays a prominent role in other proposed groupings in the region. The ASEAN countries are members of APEC, which was formed in December 1989 as a broader regional response to the then-perceived threat of a "Fortress Europe" emerging out of the EC-1992 single-market integration effort. In addition to the six ASEAN countries, APEC now includes Japan, Korea, China, Hong Kong, Taiwan, Australia, New Zealand, Papua New Guinea, the United States, Canada, Mexico, and Chile. From the ASEAN perspective, it has the advantage of including both the United States and Japan, thus providing a forum that could mitigate trade tensions between these two major ASEAN trade partners, and of providing a means for ASEAN and other smaller trading nations in the region to press for greater cooperation from the larger members in bilateral and multilateral trade matters (e.g., the GATT). It also includes all "three Chinas" – China, Taiwan, and Hong Kong – which are particularly important as growing trade and investment partners for ASEAN.

In response to the formation of NAFTA, Malaysian Prime Minister Mahathir in late 1990 proposed the formation of an alternative Asia-only group, called the East Asia Economic Group (EAEG). The EAEG would include all Asian members of APEC, but exclude Western members. The proposal received a lukewarm reception at best from most of the other Asian countries (including Japan). They felt that it did not make sense to exclude the United States, which was in most cases their largest export market and still a major foreign investor that could provide a counterweight to Japanese economic domination of the region. Mahathir's EAEG was thus downgraded to a caucus within APEC, but U.S.–Japan and U.S.–China trade conflicts in the mid-1990s may have given it a new lease on life.[28]

The competing APEC organization, meantime, has been given a boost with the establishment of a small secretariat in an ASEAN country (Singapore) and with the sudden interest and leadership shown by the Clinton administration since the annual APEC meeting in April 1993, which was held for the first time in the United States. An unprecedented summit meeting of all APEC heads of government took place in Seattle in November 1993, where Mexico, Papua New Guinea, and Chile were admitted, and a framework for cooperation on trade and investment issues was approved. (Mahatir did not attend.) At a second summit meeting held in Jakarta in November 1994, government heads agreed to the establishment of an APEC-wide free-trade area within the next 25 years.

National-level responses

National-level responses to new international circumstances in the economic sphere include continued moves toward economic liberalization and

---

[28] Business and government leaders in Asia are now "confident that the region will be able to withstand the threat of protectionism in Europe and North America without forming its own exclusive trade bloc." Laurence Zuckerman, "Regional Bloc Doesn't Foresee an Exclusive Trade Bloc in Asia," *Asian Wall Street Journal Weekly,* May 17, 1993.

internationalization, as well as increased government efforts to accelerate domestic technological development. There is now recognition that the ASEAN countries' ability to benefit from favorable international economic circumstances in the late 1980s was largely predicated on their ability to offer political and financial stability, attractive tax incentives, and at least selectively open trade and investment policies. Investment liberalization in Indonesia, Thailand, and Malaysia contributed to large inflows of DFI. Domestic political uncertainty and a slower pace of liberalization in the Philippines resulted in that country largely missing out on the wave of Japanese and EANIC investment in the late 1980s and early 1990s. Following a steep decline in DFI in early 1994, the Indonesian government liberalized ownership requirements for DFI in May. By the end of the year, it had received a record U.S. $25 billion of new investment commitments, more than double the previous record, in 1992.

In the 1990s, the ASEAN countries face greatly increased competition from newly liberalized developing countries and transitional market economies the world over for trade with, and investment from, advanced industrial countries and the EANICs. China, and eventually Vietnam, are or will be the strongest competitors with the capacity to divert investment flows from ASEAN countries and to displace some ASEAN producers in world markets.[29] To continue attracting and retaining foreign companies, and to maximize their benefits from foreign investment and trade growth, the ASEAN countries need to invest in enhancing their domestic absorptive capacity for new capital and technology.

In particular, there is a pressing need for state action to build up infrastructure and human skills, as current rapid economic growth has created severe infrastructural bottlenecks and extreme shortages of unskilled as well as skilled labor. It is arguable that some ASEAN countries relied too much and for too long on resource- and cheap-labor-based exports, which

---

[29] Examples abound here. For example, the U.S. agribusiness company Dole is deciding between Vietnam or Sulawesi, Indonesia, for a major new investment in a fruit plantation; it is already investing in a new plantation in Guangdong Province, China. The U.S. consumer products company Procter and Gamble may also decide to concentrate new investment resources and marketing effort in China rather than in Indonesia. Some labor-intensive Taiwan investors in industries like Christmas tree lights have apparently already moved from Thailand, to which they ventured only in the late 1980s. And Indonesia is competing directly with China for export-oriented footwear manufacturing subcontracted by international design companies like Nike, Reebok, and Adidas. The Philippines in particular is afraid that it will quickly "fall behind Vietnam" in its efforts to attract foreign investment, especially from the EANICs, Japan, and other ASEAN countries.

can now be sourced from other, cheaper developing countries. They need to develop specific national competitive advantages, especially technology and skill-based advantages, which will enable them to compete with these other countries, not only for foreign, but also for their own, increasingly outward-oriented, domestic capital sources.

As in other policy areas (e.g., trade and investment liberalization), Singapore and Malaysia have taken the most aggressive steps in the direction of industrial upgrading.[30] They have launched national government policies that are vigorously expanding investments in infrastructure development through both the public and private sectors. Both countries are actively engaged in the privatization of state agencies and enterprises involved in infrastructure development, and Malaysia has the distinction of having implemented more privatizations than any other developing country.[31] Both nations are investing heavily in education and training, in both the public and private sectors, to improve industrial skills. Both are establishing – often jointly with the private sector – publicly initiated or funded research institutes, science parks, technology centers, and programs to foster linkages between multinationals and local suppliers, as well as to accelerate technology transfer and local technological development and enterprise growth. Both offer investors tax incentives, which favor capital- and skill-intensive projects utilizing new technology and encourage research and development as well as training activities.[32]

Besides Singapore and Malaysia, Indonesia has seriously considered promoting indigenous technology development and high-tech industry. But so far this has been confined largely to the state-operated resource extraction and transportation equipment sectors, especially aircraft. Because Indonesia

---

[30] There are many reasons for this. British colonialism left both Singapore and Malaysia with competent, development-oriented bureaucracies, as well as good education and training institutions, which could take an active role in industrial upgrading efforts. As relatively small countries, both are highly trade-dependent and forced to be export-oriented and outward-looking, unlike their larger ASEAN neighbors that favor focusing on the domestic market. Both also had limited labor surpluses that have been exhausted, forcing them to ascend the industrial technology ladder in order to maintain international competitiveness in the face of rising labor costs and shrinking labor supplies.

[31] Note that in Malaysia, the establishment and expansion of state enterprises and agencies, mostly in the 1970s, were motivated by ethnic political considerations rather than by ideology. The goal was to use state resources and expertise to develop enterprises that would be owned and run by the Malay community – initially through the state, and now that capital and expertise has been built up within this community, through privatization. Malay politicians and bureaucrats also often have a personal interest in privatization as a source of funds for the ruling Malay Party and of profits for its supporters.

[32] See, e.g., Lim, "Technology Policy and Export Development."

Table 8.5. *Social indicators, Southeast Asia (ASEAN), 1965–89*

Country	1965	1980	1989	Annual growth (percent) 1965–80	Annual growth (percent) 1980–89
Daily calorie supply per capita					
Indonesia	1,791	2,315	2,750	1.7	1.9
Malaysia	2,353	2,625	2,774	0.7	0.6
Philippines	1,875	2,275	2,375	1.3	0.5
Singapore	2,285	3,158	3,198	2.2	0.1
Thailand	2,138	2,308	2,316	0.5	0.0
Infant mortality per 1,000 live births					
Indonesia	128	105	61[a]	−1.3	−5.3
Malaysia	55	30	16	−4.0	−6.1
Philippines	72	53	41	−2.0	−2.5
Singapore	26	12	7	−5.0	−5.2
Thailand	88	53	27	−3.3	−6.5
Primary school enrollment (percentage of eligible age)					
Indonesia	72	98	118	2.1	2.1
Malaysia	90	92	96	0.1	0.5
Philippines	113	110	111	−0.2	0.1
Singapore	105	107	110	0.1	0.3
Thailand	78	96	86	1.4	−1.2
Secondary school enrollment (percentage of eligible age)					
Indonesia	12	28	47	5.8	5.9
Malaysia	28	53	59	4.3	1.2
Philippines	41	63	73	2.9	1.7
Singapore	45	55	69	1.3	2.6
Thailand	14	29	28	5.0	−0.4

[a]Data are for 1990.
Source: World Bank, *World Development Report, 1983, 1992.*

is still cost competitive in resource and cheap-labor activities, and will remain so for many years to come, there is little incentive for private enterprise across a spectrum of industries to invest in accelerated local technological upgrading in the absence of stronger government initiative and support. Thailand also claims to have an interest in upgrading technology, but there is little achievement so far in this area, and education levels remain far below those of its neighbors (Table 8.5).

Besides technology development, internationalization strategies also figure prominently in national-level ASEAN responses to changing international circumstances. Some ASEAN governments have been promoting outward investment by locally domiciled firms, as well as engaging in such investments themselves through state enterprises. In the case of Thailand, it is mostly local private firms that have gone abroad, with government blessing, while in Singapore and Malaysia, state enterprises are also active in internationalization. In Indonesia, by contrast, there is public if not government opposition to such internationalization, which has been undertaken only by private firms.[33] China, Burma, Vietnam, Laos, and Cambodia have been the most prominent target countries in all cases, though Singapore has committed more investments to its ASEAN neighbors and has also attracted investments from them.

At the national level, it is the role of the state that is important. For example, both Prime Minister Mahathir of Malaysia and former Prime Minister Lee Kuan Yew of Singapore have been vigorous promoters of their respective countries' trade and investments with Vietnam, and both have led large delegations of local businesspeople to Vietnam. Part of the motivation may be political – to ensure that Vietnam remains "friendly" and market-oriented – but most of it is economic. For Singapore, especially, the maturing of its small domestic economy is pushing cash-rich government-linked corporations (GLCs) abroad in search of new markets for their technical and managerial expertise in infrastructure provision. In Vietnam, Singapore GLCs are already heavily involved in airport, seaport, and property developments, as well as in venture capital activities. In addition, since the Singapore government lifted its 13-year ban on investment in Vietnam, government agencies have started programs to help local firms invest there.[34] The government is actively promoting links between GLCs and

---

[33] For example, a controversy has arisen for Indonesians over increasing investments in their home provinces in southern China by Chinese-Indonesian business tycoons and their conglomerates, at a time when Indonesia itself needs the capital and could benefit from the same type of enterprises that are being started in China by its own ethnic Chinese businesses. Many of these businesses made their fortunes through political patronage, which granted them monopolistic positions in the protected Indonesian home market. See Lim and Gosling, "Economic Growth, Liberalization and Chinese Ethnicity."

[34] For example, the Trade Development Board organizes and coordinates Singapore firms' participation in industrial trade fairs in Vietnam, Cambodia and Laos, while the Economic Development Board (EDB) operates a Local Enterprises Financing Scheme, which provides local firms with financing to cover the purchase of productive assets abroad and investments "that offer significant economic spinoffs for Singapore." The EDB is also

local private firms to "jointly penetrate regional markets."[35] It has set up a $10 million fund to help with the reconstruction and rehabilitation of Vietnam, Cambodia, and Laos, offering technical help and training in areas such as civil aviation, port management, telecommunications, public housing, health care, urban planning, and management, in which Singapore state agencies and GLCs have a strong competitive advantage. Besides the government of Vietnam, those of Singapore and Malaysia have also long been promoting trade and investment linkages with China.

But the outward-oriented vision of both Lee Kuan Yew and Mahathir extends beyond China and Southeast Asia to embrace the rest of the world, particularly other developing countries. Mahathir is probably the world's leading proponent of "South–South" economic linkages with developing countries as a collective means of countering economic dominance by advanced industrial countries, as well as an outlet for Malaysia's national economic interests. He led major business missions to Brazil and Mexico in 1991, and to Africa in 1992, to promote this vision. Lee Kuan Yew, meanwhile, has ventured to Russia and other former Soviet republics, as well as to southern Africa.

A constant stream of Latin American and African government and business delegations now visit Singapore and Malaysia and vice versa in search of development lessons and closer economic ties.[36] These are not merely ritualistic ventures, as in their wake have come some trade and investment deals, as well as direct communication links via the national air carriers of Malaysia and Singapore. But because of the small size of most Latin American and African trade flows, their relatively slow growth, and their great geographic and cultural distance from Southeast Asia, they are not likely to

training managers to do business in the region using a consortium approach. See Lim, "Models and Partners."

[35] This could be done, for example, by having the state agency Jurong Town Corporation, which builds and runs most of Singapore's industrial estates, build such an estate in Vietnam that would have its utilities provided by the Singapore Public Utilities Board, telecommunications services provided by Singapore Telecoms, workers' housing constructed by the Singapore Housing Development Board, and the facilities themselves occupied by Singapore private manufacturing companies, while imports and exports are handled under service contracts with the Port of Singapore Authority and Changi Airport Transit Services, and the Economic Development Board and its associated training institutes provide worker training. Similar arrangements are being considered or implemented in China (Pudong) and India (a proposed "Madras corridor" for Singapore firms).

[36] See Linda Y. C. Lim, "Foreign Investment, the State and Industrial Policy in Singapore," in Howard Stein (ed.), *Asian Industrialization and Africa: Case Studies and Policy Alternatives to Structural Adjustment* (London: Macmillan, 1995), for a discussion of the possible relevance of Singapore's development experience for Africa.

become very important ASEAN trade and investment partners, compared with the much closer, larger, culturally familiar, and faster-growing economies of Asia, particularly China and Vietnam. Latin America and Africa may, however, become important to individual ASEAN companies that choose to target these regions in particular sectoral niches.

Corporate-level responses

Corporate-level responses in Southeast Asia to changing international economic circumstances are closely intertwined with the regional- and national-level responses discussed earlier. They include the responses of non-Asian multinational corporations as well as regional firms.

The example of the automobile industry will serve to outline the significance for Southeast Asia of this trend of corporate globalization-cum-regionalization strategies. In the early 1980s, dramatic losses of home market share to Japanese imports caused the U.S. Big Three automakers to close down their sometimes decades-old plants in the then-marginal markets of Southeast Asia, in some cases selling them to newly arrived Japanese competitors (e.g., GM sold its Thai plant to Honda, and Ford sold its Philippine plant to Toyota). By 1990, however, it became clear that leaving the Japanese automakers to dominate the ASEAN markets, where they have an estimated 90 percent direct and indirect (through local joint ventures) market share, was giving them a potential "profit sanctuary" from which they could subsidize competitive actions against the U.S. automakers in both North America and Western Europe. At the same time, the ASEAN countries had become the world's most rapidly growing – though still small – vehicle market. Any company without representation there and in China would eventually lose global market share.

A return to the ASEAN market became an urgent strategic imperative for the U.S. automakers, although resource and other limitations have hampered this move. For example, General Motors decided to move its Asia–Pacific headquarters from Detroit to Singapore to coordinate the multiple marketing and assembly ventures it has initiated in nearly all countries of the region, including a $700 million manufacturing joint-venture investment in Indonesia.[37] But GM is not only attacking its Japanese competitors'

---

[37] Sharing a nationality does not, of course, mean that the Big Three have similar strategies. For example, its (until recently) poor financial position has inhibited Chrysler's plans to

potential profit sanctuary in Southeast Asia. It is also penetrating the Japanese home market in order to deny the Japanese a profit sanctuary there, which could support their competitive efforts in ASEAN countries. In other words, to compete globally with the Japanese, GM needs to be in ASEAN countries; and to compete there, it needs to be in Japan. Moreover, GM, Chrysler and, to a lesser extent, Ford have increased production and sales in the ASEAN countries. But their new investment commitments are small, compared with the much larger new investments of Toyota, Mitsubishi, and other Japanese makers.

In another auto-related investment, Dana Corporation, the largest U.S. auto parts maker, has launched major manufacturing investments in Thailand and Indonesia to supply these countries' market leader, Toyota, with whom Dana developed a strong relationship by supplying Toyota's U.S. auto transplants. In electronics, companies such as France's consumer electronics giant Thomson, U.S. companies such as Seagate and Conner Peripherals in disk-drives, and Texas Instruments in semiconductors and computers – whose main competitors are Japanese and EANIC firms – have now become virtually all-Asian in their production for global markets, including major production bases in several ASEAN countries. These countries have become integral to multinational corporate responses to international economic changes, as part of global production networks.

Corporate investments in the ASEAN countries also include more complex joint ventures and strategic alliances between Western multinationals and Asian firms, whose investments need not be located in the Asian partner's country of domicile. Examples include an export joint venture between a Japanese and a Taiwanese electronics firm in Malaysia, and a Korean subcontractor to a U.S. footwear firm manufacturing for export in Indonesia. There are also similar joint ventures with local state as well as private-enterprise partners. An example is the Texas Instruments (United States) – Hewlett Packard (United States) – Chartered Semiconductor (Singapore government) – Canon (Japan) high-tech wafer fabrication joint venture in Singapore. In most of these ventures, the foreign partners provide the technology while the local partners provide access to government support,

---

establish joint-venture operations in Thailand and Indonesia, while Ford's reliance on a global strategic partnership with Mazda, a second-tier Japanese player, has restricted its ability to venture to ASEAN countries, where Mazda has limited capabilities and market share. Ford's global strategy also accords higher priority to Eastern Europe and China than to Southeast Asia.

local market knowledge and business networks, and sometimes venture capital (particularly in the case of capital-rich Singapore).

Local firms from the ASEAN countries, both state and private enterprises, have also been investing in neighboring developing countries.[38] The motivations are many. First, the liberalizations of the 1980s now permit such investments. Second, many ASEAN-based companies have developed firm-specific competitive advantages and cash hordes through operating in their own (often protected or otherwise monopolized) home markets that they are now eager to exploit abroad. Third, many local Singapore and Malaysian companies in particular are labor-intensive, low-tech businesses, which can no longer produce competitively in their own home countries, whose comparative advantage has shifted in the direction of higher-cost, higher-value-added activities in which advanced industrial country multinationals have the edge. This explains the growing interest of Singapore manufacturing firms in Vietnam's and Indonesia's lower-cost labor, and of Malaysian plantation companies in Vietnam's abundant land as well as cheap labor.

Fourth, investment abroad by ASEAN firms can be part of a corporate strategy of geographic diversification in order to reduce dependence on home markets, which are either saturated (in terms of market share) or newly liberalized, increasing the threat of foreign competition. Fifth, most ASEAN private enterprises are owned and operated by overseas Chinese families, which may invest abroad to diversify their political risk at home (being a politically unpopular minority often subject to government discrimination). Many ASEAN Chinese businesses are also investing in China, primarily because of its economic promise, but also in some cases because of sentimental attachment to the "motherland," and especially to the home provinces of origin of these emigrant entrepreneurs. ASEAN state-owned enterprises may have political motivations in investing in their neighbors. In the case of Singapore, for example, these would include ensuring the country's political security by helping Vietnam and China to develop successful market economies and by establishing good relations with the governments of these still-communist nations that are yet considered to be potential aggressors.

Most ASEAN companies investing abroad will be motivated by more than one of these factors. An example is Natsteel of Singapore, now a

---

[38] Lim, "The Role of the Private Sector."

selectively diversified, vertically integrated, steel-based conglomerate that was once state-owned (and subsequently privatized). Faced with the resource and market-size constraints of the very open domestic Singapore steel market, Natsteel has chosen a strategy of geographic as well as industrial diversification. To penetrate the heavily regulated and protected neighboring ASEAN markets, Natsteel has established joint ventures with local steel companies in Malaysia, Thailand, and Indonesia, providing these partners with financing, access to state-of-the-art technology, global information networks, low-cost training, and export market outlets.

It has relocated low-end production to these overseas joint ventures (buying back part of their output), while bringing new high-end products to Singapore. It also uses its core steel business to facilitate subsequent entry into these neighboring markets of its more profitable steel-related businesses like engineering, chemicals, construction, and services, which were first developed in the Singapore market. Its holdings in several different ASEAN countries will position it well as a pan-regional company when the ASEAN steel markets are eventually liberalized. In the meantime, as a regional grouping it can achieve economies for its affiliate companies through joint procurement of raw materials, shared use of spares and equipment for standardized plants, economies of scale, shared research and development, and eventual product specialization by country according to different comparative advantages.[39]

There are many much larger private conglomerates in the other ASEAN countries that are beginning to undertake similar regional, and even international strategies. One notable example is Unicord of Thailand, which in 1990 acquired the U.S. canned-tuna company Bumble Bee in order to control distribution of the processed and canned tuna it exports to the United States and other world markets.[40] This follows the standard corporate strategic practice of moving up the value chain to capture higher-value-added activities, in the same way as Natsteel has moved from commodity steel into construction and, finally, property development of high-value projects like golf courses and leisure marinas. In short, although they may be in different

---

[39] Linda Y. C. Lim, "Natsteel," case study prepared for the Southeast Asia Business Program, University of Michigan, June 1992 (mimeo).

[40] The other major U.S. canned tuna company, Chicken-of-the-Sea, was acquired by the Indonesian company Mantrust, whose beer operations were recently bought by San Miguel. Both Unicord and Mantrust are controlled and operated by ethnic Chinese business families.

sectors, the corporate-level responses of ASEAN-based companies increasingly resemble those of global multinationals that operate in the region. In both cases, strategic corporate responses are based on firm competitive advantage, shifts in country comparative advantages, and the actions of competitors in global, regional, and national markets.

Recent and ongoing changes in the international economic environment have been mostly favorable to the ASEAN countries. The domestic policy trend in these countries is toward privatization and marketization, and their governments are already actively engaged in national-level policy responses to these international changes. These state-level responses are mostly pro-business, and many were developed in consultation and collaboration with the private sector, within which local firms' own responses have been concentrated.[41] As will be further noted later, the harmonious relationship between the state, multinationals, and local capital has been a major factor underlying the ASEAN countries' so far successful response to changes in the international environment.

Conclusions

The international economic and political environments of the 1990s present the countries of Southeast Asia with both challenges and opportunities in their development trajectory for the rest of the decade and beyond. In the economic arena, the emergence of other developing countries offers export and investment opportunities for ASEAN companies, but also creates more competition for them for international capital and export markets. China is the most important competitor and potential market. At the same time, global competitive pressures faced by industrial-country corporations, as well as the maturity and growth stagnation of their own home markets, encourage these multinationals to invest more in Southeast Asia. The difficulties that emerged during the GATT negotiations, and the possibility that economic regionalization in Europe and the Americas might be protectionist, both pose some potential future problems for the ASEAN countries, but even if worst-case scenarios are realized (which is far from assured), they are likely to be more than counterbalanced by positive regional economic developments.

The Asia–Pacific region of which Southeast Asia is a part will continue to be the fastest-growing regional economy in the world, and by early in the

---

[41] See Lim, "Technology Policy and Export Development," for a discussion of state and private-sector technology development responses.

twenty-first century, on current projections, it will also be the largest. Besides the growing strength of the ASEAN economies themselves, the expected economic take-off of China, and perhaps the socialist countries of Southeast and South Asia as well, will add a boost to the region's increasingly integrated growth. Industrial investment in Southeast Asia is more and more oriented to the large and dynamic regional market, which will reduce the relative importance of exports to slow-growing industrialized countries. Technological development within the region, due to the combined efforts of governments, multinationals, and local firms, will also eventually reduce technological dependence. And as domestic incomes and savings rise rapidly, while financial markets and institutions continue to mature, domestic and regional sources may gradually displace nonregional sources of capital.

Thus, the international and regional economic environments facing Southeast Asia are, on balance, positive. Whether these countries manage to make the most of the opportunities presented by this favorable picture depends on national circumstances. There are both political and economic challenges. Political leadership succession and continued democratization in some countries may introduce temporary instability,[42] and government policies in many instances remain hostage to domestic interest group pressures.[43] But the economic liberalizations of the past decade are continuing.

---

[42] The likely consequences of political democratization for Southeast Asia's economic development are complex and vary considerably by country. In general, the expectation is that democratization will not adversely affect economic development because it is occurring at a time of rapid economic growth and continued improvements in mass economic welfare. The highly economically oriented populations of the region are now educated and experienced enough to recognize that political stability is essential for economic prosperity, and they are unlikely to jeopardize this; living together peacefully has also arguably become a habit. On the other hand, democracy is likely to give greater voice to opposition groups such as environmentalists and labor activists, though they are unlikely to either intend to or succeed in derailing economic growth. Democracy is also likely to reduce public tolerance of corruption, which is endemic in many Southeast Asian countries as it is in China, and this should induce changes in traditional business practices. Economic liberalization and the development of modern market institutions should also reduce the opportunity and necessity for corruption, which arose as a solution to the high transactions costs arising from imperfect market mechanisms. A decline in corruption will reduce a major barrier to increased Western business participation in the region, since Western firms have been the most discouraged by its prevalence. The impact of democratization on the ethnic Chinese business community varies by country according to their numbers and degree of cultural assimilation, but here again, major disruption is unlikely (see Lim and Gosling, "Economic Growth, Liberalization and Chinese Ethnicity").

[43] In the Philippines, which has the oldest and strongest indigenous capitalist class and the smallest Chinese presence in the population and the business sector, state autonomy has been lacking, especially given the U.S.-style democratic political system under which local constituencies are routinely captured electorally by wealthy members of entrenched local

The growing and increasingly visible economic power of overseas Chinese business communities, combined with the rise of an increasingly economically competitive and potentially politically threatening and aggressive China, may lead to some ethnic policy backlash, which would be severely detrimental to the current economic growth that is led by the Chinese. The ability of Chinese family businesses to grow, professionalize, and internationalize successfully is also by no means assured.[44] Neither is the ability of the ASEAN public and private sectors to create the domestic technological capabilities that will enable them to achieve a successful transition from low-wage and resource-based to higher-value-added economies. Finally, there are growing public concerns with wealth and income inequities, as well as with rapidly worsening environmental degradation.

Despite these challenges, there are nonetheless good reasons to remain optimistic about the ASEAN countries' economic future in the new international environment. A combination of development-oriented governments, outward-oriented national economic policies, and highly entrepreneurial and market-responsive populations has served the ASEAN countries well in the past and is likely to continue to do so in the future. In an uncertain international economic environment, the capacity to adjust at the national and enterprise levels to changing external forces is what determines success or failure in economic development. Because they have been and remain open to world-market forces and external players in their economies, the ASEAN countries have been able to attract foreign capital and technology for their own development, as well as to help them penetrate world markets and even achieve commanding positions in particular market niches. A remarkable factor in Southeast Asia compared with other developing regions is that there is little if any hostility to the strong foreign economic presence in the region.[45]

and regional elites. One example of this has been the import-substitution industrial elite's successful resistance to trade liberalization initiated by the previous Aquino government.

[44] The weaknesses of Chinese family businesses are well known, and as the founding patriarchs reach retirement or death there is the very real possibility that many of these companies, including large publicly held ones, will collapse. The collapse of the Astra family group, once revered as the best managed of Indonesian Chinese conglomerates, is an instructive case, and there are reportedly many others waiting to happen.

[45] In the other developing regions, antiforeign sentiments tend to be strongest among the indigenous elite, which forms the national capitalist class and is interested in keeping out foreign competition while monopolizing its control of the domestic economy. In the ASEAN countries, however, the dominance of the national capitalist class by the ethnic Chinese minority reduces its political power and increases the willingness of indigenous government groups to tolerate and even welcome foreign capital as a counterweight to Chinese monopoly power and as an alternative source of capital, technology, and employ-

ASEAN governments, however, have not been passive in their outward orientation. They have actively, if selectively, encouraged exports and foreign investments through their domestic policies. It is this capacity to intervene strategically to manage their participation in the world economy and to realize national development goals that is arguably the most distinctive developmental feature of these countries.[46] Having triumphed over much more serious political and economic challenges in the past, and given the much stronger position of their economies and polities today, it is unlikely that they will fail entirely to meet new international and domestic challenges.

Nonetheless, there are now two differences. One is that state control and initiative is likely to give way, in a process that has already begun, to collaborative public/private-sector efforts to develop and facilitate the exploitation of national comparative advantages, as well as to anticipate and adjust to projected shifts in these advantages, which requires both corporate- and national-level actions. The second is the development of regional-level actions as a new means of adjustment or pattern of response to changes in the international economic environment. These regional-level actions include joint efforts to realize complementary national comparative advantages where these exist and the eventual development of an integrated regional market that will strengthen Southeast Asia's ability both to attract, and to offset possible negative aspects of, continued large external participation in its economic development. Both these developments – the increased importance of the private sector and of regional-level actions – will further enhance the ASEAN countries' proven high capacity to respond to and benefit from the (largely favorable) changes in the international economic environment that they will face in the 1990s and beyond.

ment for indigenous groups. It is significant that the Philippines, which has the smallest Chinese minority and the strongest indigenous national capitalist class, has also had the most antiforeign sentiment and policy and the lowest absolute and relative levels of foreign trade and investment.

46 This is not the place to discuss the reasons for this state capacity. Recall, however, that Southeast Asian indigenous communities have had centuries if not millennia of experience in manipulating and/or accommodating to larger external powers – China, Asia, European colonizers – with which they traded for mutual benefit.

CHAPTER 9

Latin America: toward a new reliance on the market

AUGUSTO VARAS

Dramatic international changes are forcing third world countries to adapt their agendas and institutions to become part of a new global political economy. In the case of Latin America, massive shifts in international financial flows, the muting of East–West conflict and renewal of U.S. hegemony, the new primacy of markets, and the return to competitive political systems have been the most significant international changes. Accommodation to these changes is producing multiple tensions and conflicts, and it is not yet clear whether the adjustment will produce competitive economies.

During the post–World War II period, Latin American countries' inward-oriented development strategies – the import-substitution industrialization model – determined their main domestic policies and foreign relations. Now the region is facing new systemic conditions, following a decade of severe economic weakness during the 1980s. Looking back at the "lost decade" and comparing it with the success of the Asian economies, most Latin American leaders have concluded that they have no alternative but to accommodate their domestic policies to the new international context. Their initial success in doing so can be seen in recent economic data: inflation is under control in most countries; financial resource flows and investments have increased, despite the turbulence following Mexico's peso devaluation; and growth is beginning to resume. Nonetheless, Latin America lags behind its East Asian rivals in terms of growth and technological progress. At the same time, inequality is much higher in the Latin American region.

The author thanks Barbara Stallings for her thoughtful and stimulating comments on the content of this chapter, as well as her editorial assistance, and Wilson Peres for his well-informed criticisms.

Why have these problems in economic performance emerged, and in particular why has Latin America fallen behind East Asia when the two regions were frequently linked as successful "newly industrialized countries" (NICs) in the 1970s? While many authors have focused on recent differences in economic policies in the two regions, a basic hypothesis of this chapter is that the combined effects of the historical variations in international linkages and internal relations among ruling elites are at least as important. Indeed, these relationships may well help to explain why policies have differed.

One of the main international factors has been the strategic importance of third world regions during the East–West conflict and the nature of associated economic policies. During the cold war period, Latin American countries were defined as marginal in strategic terms. After the Cuban missile crisis of 1962, the rhetoric of a Soviet threat in the Western Hemisphere lacked credibility. As a consequence, Latin America received neither the political attention nor the massive economic aid that countries such as Taiwan and South Korea did. In the case of the East Asian nations, U.S. economic involvement helped to modernize their traditional economic structures and laid the basis for future growth. Later, U.S. economic input was supplemented by that of Japan, which incorporated East Asia into international networks of production, trade, and finance. Latin America, by contrast, was left mainly to private investors from the United States, with their well-known proclivities toward short-term profit maximization.[1] Aside from the failed Alliance for Progress, U.S. public-sector activities in the region consisted mainly of occasional intervention to punish governments perceived as hostile to foreign capital.[2]

A second set of factors contributing to differences within the third world is the approach of domestic ruling elites to the process of modernization. In East Asia, moves toward modernization were made after severe political crises, which sometimes were so extreme as to result in territorial partition in the context of cold war ideological confrontations. These partitions gave legitimacy to authoritarian governments and enabled modernizing elites to

---

[1] A comparative analysis of the nature and characteristics of foreign investments in East Asia and Latin America is found in Barbara Stallings, "The Role of Foreign Capital in Economic Development," in Gary Gereffi and Donald L. Wyman (eds.), *Manufacturing Miracles: Paths of Industrialization in Latin America and East Asia* (Princeton, N.J.: Princeton University Press, 1990), pp. 55–89.

[2] See G. Pope Atkins, *Latin America in the International Political System* (Boulder, Colo.: Westview, 1989).

impose structural reforms on their economies. By the 1980s, the East Asian nations were able to advance rapidly in economic diversification.[3] In the Latin American case, neither territorial partition nor any other phenomenon brought about elite consensus. Rather, Latin American countries moved from one stage of development to another in a context of permanent intra-elite disagreements and resulting instability. A few seem to have succeeded, also after periods of intense political crisis (e.g., Mexico after the revolution of 1910–17, Costa Rica after the revolution of 1948, Chile after the military government of 1973–89, and Colombia after the domestic violence of 1947–53), but in many cases serious disagreements continue (e.g., Argentina, Brazil, Peru, and Venezuela). Some of these conflicts evolved into military and authoritarian governments; others remained unresolved. As a consequence, it has been much more difficult for Latin American countries than for the East Asian NICs to organize a consensual path of development.

Although the majority of countries in the region have now begun to implement a common set of policies – featuring new reliance on market mechanisms and the private sector, domestic and foreign – these policies are being superimposed on different national situations as a consequence of variation in intraelite relationships and foreign relations strategies. The resulting divergences must also be mapped onto geographic divisions among Mexico, Central America and the Caribbean, and South America. As will be seen, the results are a mixture of similarities and differences in national performance. In elaborating these points, I will first discuss the evolution of Latin American countries through the 1970s; second, I will identify major changes in the 1980s and 1990s and their impact on the region; third, the responses of Latin American countries will be analyzed; and, finally, considerations about the future of the region will be presented.

From the early twentieth century to the debt crisis

Latin America's economic development strategies in the twentieth century can be at least partially understood as a response to the changing international environment, especially capital flows in their various forms. Likewise, some domestic political processes in the region – especially the centrality of the state in economic development – can also be explained as

---

[3] See Robert Wade, "Industrial Policy in East Asia: Does It Lead or Follow the Market?" in Gereffi and Wyman (eds.), *Manufacturing Miracles,* pp. 23–66.

reactions to the presence of foreign capital in local economies. Different types of foreign capital and local responses had given rise to three phases by the early 1980s.

In a first period, from the late nineteenth century to World War II, capital exports by U.S. and European investors went into the primary sector (mainly mining and agriculture) and public utilities (including power, tele-communications, and railroads). The entry of foreign capital in Latin American economies produced two main types of conflicts.

First, there were tensions between Latin American governments and foreign companies, especially over the amount of taxes and the rate of reinvestment in domestic economies by foreign firms. These policies were important since the surplus provided by foreign investors was a major source of state revenue, which could be used to provide subsidies to producers and welfare to the new middle and working classes. These tensions led to confrontations between foreign investors and local governments in Central America, the Caribbean, and some South American countries. Nationalist and anti-U.S. movements arose, aiming to gain control over national resources. These tensions were more or less acute, involving a larger or smaller number of social sectors, according to the type of product and the approach followed by local governments in these conflicts. They tended to escalate into interstate conflicts when investors and host countries confronted each other in protracted ideological clashes and mobilized their respective social bases.[4]

A second type of conflict pitted the ruling elites against each other. As the economies began to grow in response to foreign investment inflows, a nascent group of industrialists developed under the auspices of the state. In trying to promote their own interests, the new industrialists had to challenge the traditional oligarchic rule, producing tension and clashes with the powerful landowning classes. Populist movements aiming for a larger part of the surplus to redistribute to impoverished masses, military groups aspiring to control class tensions, and oligarchic caudillos trying to regain power all contributed to the complex political and economic landscape in Latin America during this first period.[5]

---

[4] See Cole Blasier, *The Hovering Giant: U.S. Responses to Revolutionary Change in Latin America* (Pittsburgh, Pa.: University of Pittsburgh Press, 1985).
[5] Tulio Halperin Donghi, *Historia contemporánea de América Latina* (Madrid: Alianza Editorial, 1972).

In a second stage, from the end of World War II until the late 1960s, foreign investors seeking markets and cheap wage labor, and attracted by successful indigenous efforts to construct an industrial base, diversified into the manufacturing sector. Not being major actors in the war, Latin American countries had taken advantage of the conflict to expand their own industrial base. The increased demand for their primary products led to higher prices, and the resulting rise in income provided support for a growing industrial sector. The war also helped in two other ways. On the one hand, it created a demand for goods that had previously been imported but could not be obtained since foreign factories had been turned to the production of war matériel. On the other hand, the same lack of imports sheltered the new industries from external competition. After the war, tariffs were raised to provide similar protection, and the import-substitution industrialization process quickened its pace. When the hostilities ended, U.S. exporters discovered that Latin American markets were closed by tariff barriers; to continue to sell, they had to invest and produce inside the markets. Some of these new operations were joint ventures with local industrialists, deepening the engagement of foreign investors in domestic politics.[6]

The main conflicts in this period came as a result of the dissatisfaction of elites and the populace, who were not receiving the benefits promised by import-substitution industrialization. This situation again led to political instability, sometimes in the form of guerrilla warfare or more often through nationalist/populist movements. To cope with political instability, leftist governments, and radical nationalist responses, as well as to support some domestic and/or foreign groups, the armed forces took control in several countries, and the United States intervened militarily or through covert operations to support them. Foreign investments fell off in periods of instability but returned once military governments were firmly in control. Domestic elites divided over issues of democracy, but especially over economic policy. Those linked to the production of consumer durable and intermediate goods tended to favor the policies of military rule, with their

---

[6] On these economic trends, see United Nations, *El financiamiento externo de América Latina* (New York: United Nations, 1964). On the political effects, see Elizabeth A. Cobbs, "U.S. Business: Self-Interest and Neutrality," in Abraham F. Lowenthal (ed.), *Exporting Democracy: The United States and Latin America* (Baltimore: Johns Hopkins University Press, 1991), pp. 264–99; Fernando H. Cardoso, "Entrepreneurs and the Transition Process: The Brazilian Case," in Guillermo O'Donnell, Philippe C. Schmitter, and Lawrence Whitehead (eds.), *Transitions from Authoritarian Rule* (Baltimore: Johns Hopkins University Press, 1986), pp. 137–53.

emphasis on growth and regressive redistribution of income. Those who produced basic consumer goods for the domestic market wanted more progressive income distribution policies to expand their sales base.[7]

During the 1970s, Latin American countries moved into a third phase in their relations with the outside world, developing a new type of linkage with the international economy. When oil producers raised their prices in the early 1970s, massive financial liquidity (petrodollars) was created, which in turn was transformed into loans for third world borrowers. Different from both the foreign firms' investments in primary products before World War II and the industrial investments made by transnational corporations during the early postwar years, in the 1970s Latin American countries had to accommodate themselves to the dominant role of private banks. Many Latin American governments became enthusiastic borrowers, matching the banks' desire to lend. The oil-importing countries, of course, needed to borrow to meet their enlarged oil bills. Beyond that, some governments, such as those in Brazil and Mexico, saw the possibility to obtain resources to expand their public enterprises and push forward their high-growth development strategies. In other cases, such as Chile and Argentina, borrowing was concentrated in the private sector and mainly used to finance a consumption boom. In both situations, interest rates were low or even negative in real terms, and no difficulties were foreseen in meeting payments on the resulting debt.[8]

On the surface, the 1970s seemed to produce a truce in both types of conflict that had characterized Latin America in the past. The large volume of loans, which led to a doubling of the volume of foreign resources available to the region in the earlier postwar years, appeared mutually beneficial to lender and borrower alike. Even the Carter human rights policy, intended to moderate military governments, explicitly stopped short of interfering with the lending binge,[9] and U.S.–Latin American relations entered a period of relative quiet. Likewise, relations among elite factions were

[7] See Robert R. Kaufman, "Industrial Change and Authoritarian Rule in Latin America: A Concrete Review of the Bureaucratic-Authoritarian Model," in David Collier (ed.), *The New Authoritarianism in Latin America* (Princeton, N.J.: Princeton University Press, 1979), pp. 165–253. The Peruvian military government was an important exception to these trends.

[8] Rudiger Dornbush, "The Latin American Debt Problem: Anatomy and Solutions," in Barbara Stallings and Robert Kaufman (eds.), *Debt and Democracy in Latin America* (Boulder, Colo.: Westview, 1989), pp. 7–23, at 10.

[9] Lars Schoultz, *Human Rights and United States Policy toward Latin America* (Princeton, N.J.: Princeton University Press, 1981).

smoother in the period of high growth and external abundance. By 1981, however, international conditions changed as the United States raised its interest rates to halt inflation, and the industrial world slid into recession. These changes limited the ability of the Latin American countries to service their now bloated foreign debts, and by the end of 1982, the flow of resources was shut off.[10]

Major international changes in the 1980s and 1990s

The year 1982 marked a major break in Latin America's postwar trajectory. Until 1980, per capita growth rates approached 4 percent annually, but this growth had come at a cost. It had been fueled by deficit spending, which in turn led to high rates of inflation. Budget deficits for the central governments of the region averaged 2.3 percent of GDP in the 1970–80 years. More important were the deficits of public-sector firms, which served the function of providing employment and subsidizing the private sector in addition to producing needed products. The budget deficits were increasingly financed by foreign borrowing as the resulting long-term debt rose from $28 billion in 1970 to $239 billion in 1982. Moreover, by the late 1970s, borrowing was also necessary to meet interest and amortization payments.[11]

In August 1982, as oil prices fell, the Mexican government was no longer able to keep up with this process. It announced that it would have to suspend payments if a rescheduling agreement could not be arranged. The U.S. government together with the IMF arranged a temporary bridge loan, followed later by a longer-term agreement. The latter had three main parts: rescheduling of the principal due, new loans from private banks and multilateral agencies, and new economic policies to assure that Mexico would generate the foreign exchange needed to service its debt.

As discussed in Chapter 5, the Mexican announcement triggered a similar process in other parts of the third world, especially in Latin America. Bankers panicked, fearing that other clients would also be unable to meet payments, and they cut off their loans. The result was precisely what they were trying to avoid: the cutoff led to the cessation of payments throughout

---

10 Ricardo Ffrench-Davis and Richard E. Feinberg (eds.), *Más allá de la crisis de la deuda: bases para un nuevo enfoque* (Buenos Aires: CIEPLAN/Diálogo Interamericano/GEL, 1986).
11 Barbara Stallings, *Banker to the Third World: U.S. Portfolio Investment in Latin America, 1900–1986* (Berkeley: University of California Press, 1987).

the region. (The one exception was Colombia, which had not borrowed as heavily as other countries.) To deal with the expanding problems, policies similar to those followed with respect to Mexico were implemented elsewhere.

The results were twofold. On the one hand, an international banking crisis was avoided as countries cut back sharply on imports and borrowed more money to generate foreign exchange for debt service. On the other hand, a deep recession followed from the drain that debt service represented. Net transfers (the sum of new loans minus repayments and interest) turned negative on the average of $24 billion per year (some 3.5 percent of GDP) between 1983 and 1990, and per capita GDP fell by about 1 percent annually during this period. For some countries, income fell back to the level at the end of the 1970s; for others, conditions were much worse, and income returned to levels not seen since the early 1960s. Investment also declined significantly, from 24 percent of GDP in 1980 to less than 19 percent in 1990, thus endangering future growth.[12] This was the situation commonly described as the "lost decade."

The initial recommendations of the IMF and the industrial-country governments were predicated on the idea that the austerity policies put into place throughout the region would resolve the debt crisis within a few years, and Latin America would again be able to borrow and resume growth. By the middle of the decade, however, it seemed clear that such a positive scenario was not going to occur. In 1985, then–Treasury Secretary James Baker put forward a new strategy that emphasized structural reforms. The new diagnosis was that the overall economic development strategy of the debtor countries needed to be changed before growth would return. Thus, the so-called Baker Plan, in addition to continuing the emphasis on new loans from the banks and multilateral agencies, stressed the need for a set of policies focusing on macroeconomic stability, a reduced role for the state in the economy, and greater openness to international trade and capital flows.[13]

These policies received significant reinforcement from a variety of sources. First, the international financial institutions (IFIs) – especially the IMF and the World Bank – substantially increased their power in the 1980s

---

[12] Inter-American Dialogue, *The Americas in a New World* (Washington, D.C.: Aspen Institute, 1990).

[13] Roberto Bouzas (ed.), *Entre la heterodoxia y el ajuste: negociaciones financieras externas de América Latina (1982–1987)* (Buenos Aires: GEL, 1988).

compared with the preceding decade. The change came about both because of a large increase in the money they had available to lend and because of a new unity on the part of public and private creditors. The power of the IFIs was crucial because they had long been advocates of the types of policies that Baker suggested. A second reinforcement was the arrival on the political scene in the major industrial countries of political leaders who supported such policies: especially Ronald Reagan, Margaret Thatcher, and Helmut Kohl. In an influential analysis by a prominent think tank, the new unity around market-oriented policies was labelled the "Washington Consensus."[14]

By the end of the decade, the growing problems and ultimate collapse of communism in Eastern Europe and the Soviet Union provided support from the other direction for market-oriented policies. That is, with the demise of the only existing examples of an alternative development model, the confidence of groups advocating more radical approaches declined precipitously. In Latin America, the main impact of the Soviet changes fell on Cuba and Nicaragua. While Cuba has thus far been able to survive the drastic decline in material support, Fred Halliday's analysis in Chapter 2 of this volume suggests the hardships it has produced. For the Sandinistas, by contrast, their inability to find sufficient economic backing in the socialist world was partially responsible for their electoral defeat.[15]

In the particular case of Latin America, a regional demonstration effect also served to buttress the Washington Consensus. Two countries in the region became prominent advocates of contending "orthodox" and "heterodox" policies. On the orthodox side was Chile, which by 1985 had begun to recover the economic dynamism of the 1970s after a disastrous crash in 1982. While most other countries in the region remained mired in a mixture of high inflation and negative growth, Chile's economy emerged from its problems to resume growth at a respectable 5 percent during the 1986–90 period. In contrast was neighboring Peru, where Alan García denounced the IMF and set unilateral limits on debt payments. He also implemented economic policies designed to expand the economy by increasing wages and

---

14 John Williamson (ed.), *Latin American Adjustment: How Much Has Happened?* (Washington, D.C.: Institute for International Economics, 1990). An analysis of different views on the "Washington Consensus" is found in Richard Feinberg, "Economic Themes for the 1990s," in North–South Center, *Setting the North–South Agenda* (Miami: North–South Center, 1991), pp. 33–38.

15 Rolando Franco, "Elecciones en Nicaragua: el gallo pinto y el gallo ennavajado," *Cono Sur* 9, 3 (May–June 1990), 18–23.

government expenditure and by stepping up the government's regulatory capacities. In 1987, the private banks were nationalized. After a quick expansion during the first two years of these policies, disaster struck as the balance of payments went into deficit, reserves disappeared, inflation soared, and eventually growth collapsed. These two cases were often portrayed as exemplars of the two types of economic model. Further strength for the argument in favor of orthodoxy came from Argentina and Brazil. There the governments tried heterodox policies on a more limited basis, to attack inflation, and again failed in a dramatic way.[16]

Within the Western Hemisphere, a separate but reinforcing trend came through the new role for the United States. Over the course of the postwar period, Latin America had increasingly lost its importance for its neighbor to the north. Latin America's share of U.S. economic transactions had fallen on a fairly steady basis from a high in the 1950s. In political terms, U.S. attention was attracted only when a particular "problem" arose, generally a government trying to follow an independent policy line. The U.S. response tended to involve some kind of intervention, overt or covert (e.g., Guatemala in 1954, the Dominican Republic in 1965, Chile in 1973, Nicaragua in the 1980s, and Cuba throughout the period). Partly as a reaction to the U.S. approach, Latin American countries diversified their international relations. Europe became more important, particularly as a trade partner; Japan appeared as a significant new source of capital; and, of course, a few countries tried to establish special relations with the socialist bloc.[17]

During the 1980s, and especially after George Bush was elected in 1988, trends began to change in both the northern and southern parts of the hemisphere. Throughout the decade, Latin America's economic reliance on the United States increased, as Europe turned inward and Japan was discouraged by the economic problems of the region. The share of Latin America's exports going to the United States, for example, rose from 30 percent in 1980 to 40 percent in 1990. The U.S. share of foreign capital also increased.[18]

---

[16] Joaquín Vial (ed.), ¿Adonde va América Latina? Balance de las reformas económicas (Santiago: CIEPLAN, 1992).

[17] Augusto Varas (ed.), Soviet–Latin American Relations in the 1980s (Boulder, Colo.: Westview, 1986), and Eusebio Mujal-León, The USSR and Latin America (New York: Unwin Hyman, 1989).

[18] ECLAC, Open Regionalism in Latin America and the Caribbean (Santiago: ECLAC, 1994), p. 24. See also Roberto Bouzas, "U.S.–Latin American Trade Relations: Issues in the 1980s and Prospects for the 1990s," in Jonathan Hartlyn, Lars Schoultz, and Augusto

During the Bush administration, two processes came together. In political terms, Bush adopted a more pragmatic approach to economic and political relations in the hemisphere. In particular, he abandoned the Reagan obsession with Central America, both the attempt to undermine the Sandinista regime in Nicaragua and the support for the military in El Salvador. Instead, attention was shifted to the larger countries and to economic problems created by the debt crisis. From the U.S. perspective, these included dangers to U.S. banks and a precipitous decline in U.S. exports to Latin America.

At the same time, the United States needed to reposition itself to deal with declining U.S. hegemony and the rising economic strength of Europe and Asia. One method was to establish closer economic relations with the rest of the hemisphere. An initial step involved the formation of the U.S.–Canadian Free Trade Agreement in 1986, which was then expanded to include Mexico. Negotiations for a North American Free Trade Agreement (NAFTA) began in June 1991 and concluded in August 1992; by the end of 1993 NAFTA had been approved by the legislatures in all three countries.

On an even grander scale, but with a much vaguer timetable, Bush proposed a hemispheric free-trade agreement. The latter proposal, known as the Enterprise for the Americas Initiative (EAI), was launched in preparation for a Bush trip to Latin America in 1991. The quid pro quo for greater access to the U.S. market was more market-oriented economic policies.[19] Bush's defeat in the 1992 elections put the plan on hold, but the Clinton administration expressed support for the accession of additional Latin American countries to the NAFTA treaty and then for a hemispheric free-trade area by the year 2005.[20]

All of these trends pushed Latin America to consider a change toward the new type of economic strategy embodied in the Washington Consensus. Financing was no longer available on an unconditional basis as it had been in the 1970s. Technocrats within the governments began to argue strongly in favor of the new policies, claiming that the countries with successful growth

---

Varas (eds.), *The United States and Latin America in the 1990s* (Chapel Hill: University of North Carolina Press, 1993), pp. 152–80. One important exception is the case of Chile, which is increasing its trade with Asia at a higher rate than with the United States.

[19] Sidney Weintraub, "The New U.S. Economic Initiative toward Latin America," *Journal of Interamerican Studies and World Affairs* 33, 1 (Spring 1991), 1–18, and Susan Kaufman Purcell, "U.S. Policy toward Latin America after the Cold War," in Douglas W. Payne, Mark Falcoff, and Susan Kaufman Purcell, *Latin America: U.S. Policy after the Cold War* (New York: Americas Society, 1991).

[20] See Inter-American Summit, *Declaration of Principles* and *Action Plan*, December 1994.

records in the 1980s had adopted such an approach. The Bush election in 1988 became a turning point for Latin America, signaling as it did that the United States was unlikely to alter its own stance on these issues. NAFTA and the EAI provided positive incentives for change in the view of most Latin American governments.

At the same time, political leaders in the region were clearly in a bind. Their constituencies, in general, wanted to maintain the old system. That system had proved very lucrative for businesspeople, who could take advantage of their protected markets to keep profits high. Workers also benefited through job creation, even if productivity was not very high. Moreover, the state could finance its own activities at least partially through inflationary means, rather than impose high taxes on business, since tariff barriers meant that business could sell its products regardless of the resulting price increases. Abundant state resources, in inflationary settings, could be used to provide social services to various constituencies as well as employment for a substantial portion of the middle class. With the return to democracy in many Latin American countries, the power of constituent groups increased. Thus, the twin problems identified in the preceding section – international pressures and the lack of an intraelite consensus – continued to define Latin America at the end of the 1980s.

Responses to international change

Not surprisingly, the response in Latin America to the international and hemispheric changes has not been uniform, which makes it is possible to analyze the resulting processes from two different angles. On the one hand, an emphasis can be placed on the variations across countries: in political style, the details of policies followed, their timing and sequencing, their relative success, and the winners and losers that have emerged. Brazil is a crucial case for this argument, as the extreme example of a country that deviates from an alleged regional model. Its trade liberalization has lagged behind that of neighboring countries, to avoid endangering its industrial sector; it has made little progress on privatization; its state continues to play a dominant role as the country strives to become a leading economy of the twenty-first century.

On the other hand, looking back 15 years from the mid-1990s to the early 1980s, it is hard not to be struck by the similarities of the general approach to economic policy that has been followed in Latin America – even by individual leaders and political parties that had advocated other policies for decades. The new emphasis on macroeconomic equilibrium, the sale of public enterprises, the deregulation of the financial sector, the lowering of tariffs, the welcoming of foreign capital, and the delegation to the private sector of tasks ranging from education to infrastructure are found in virtually every country. Again Brazil is a crucial case, but here the argument is that *even Brazil* is committed to policy change that would have been unimaginable only a decade ago.

While both arguments are valid, the nature of this book – in its stress on regional response to international changes – leads to an emphasis on the similarities of the new economic approach in Latin America as opposed to the differences. This clearly does not imply ignoring the latter, but they will be studied within a context that highlights the contrasts with other regions. Moreover, the contrast is not limited to economic choice. As will be discussed later, there also appears to be a growing convergence within the region in terms of economic performance.

Nonetheless, Latin America is composed of a large number of countries (between 19 and 32, depending on the definition), which are spread over a vast geographic space. The geographic factor alone has led to important historical distinctions, especially in terms of foreign relations. Thus, the United States has been much more influential in the northern half of the region: in Mexico, Central America, and the Caribbean, and even Venezuela and Colombia. More independence, as well as more diversified economic and political relations, where Europe and more recently Asia have competed for influence with the United States, has characterized the rest of South America.

These distinctions continue to be important and interact in some ways with national development policies, so that it is possible to identify several clusters within the Western Hemisphere. The first one is the North American space organized around NAFTA, with a Central American and Caribbean concentric area dynamized by the Group of Three (Mexico, Colombia, and Venezuela). For this group of countries, the United States is their main export market and source of external finance. Second, there are the Andean countries, with their newly reinvigorated subregional organization, the Andean Pact. Colombia, which is a bridge between the Group of Three and the Andean group, has taken the lead in promoting Andean integration through foreign investments. The Andean group has a more diversified set of export markets than Mexico and Central America, as well as a particular set of problems involving the drug trade. Third, there is the potentially important Brazilian–Argentine axis, organized through the Southern Cone Common Market, Mercosur. Paraguay and Uruguay have joined the Mercosur leaders in an increasingly integrated economic bloc. Chile, until recently unaffiliated with any regional subgroup, is negotiating a special link with Mercosur at the same time it hopes to join NAFTA. Argentina, Chile, and Brazil have the most diversified export markets, with products going in fairly equal shares to the United States, the European Union, Asia, and the rest of the Latin American region itself.[21]

Thus, as was discussed in the preceding chapter on Southeast Asia, responses to the international changes are occurring at several levels in Latin America. First, there are national-level responses by individual governments, attempting to position their countries to take advantage of the new conditions. Second, at the other extreme, there are hemispheric attempts to deal with the new situation and to buttress the chances of the entire region vis-à-vis other parts of the world. In between are bilateral arrangements, which can be seen as extensions of both of the others. That is, bilateral free-trade agreements are simultaneously a reinforcement of the economic reforms initiated to improve a country's competitive position and the building blocks for a possible hemispheric unit.

National-level responses

The basis of the individual responses are structural reforms of the type supported by the Washington Consensus. These transformations have included extensive reforms of the state (privatization of public-sector enterprises, fiscal reforms, severe retrenchment in compensatory social spending, and elimination of subsidies to consumers and inefficient producers); sweeping market-oriented reforms (deregulation of the private sector, increased flexibility of labor markets); and competitive reinsertion in the world economy (trade liberalization and promotion of foreign investment). Figure 9.1 shows the extent of two of the principal reforms: trade liberalization vis-à-vis average tariff levels and fiscal policy vis-à-vis public-sector budget balances. Successful implementation of these reforms has required important changes in economic ideology by the main economic and politi-

---

[21] Export figures are from Gary Clyde Hufbauer and Jeffrey J. Schott, *Western Hemisphere Economic Integration* (Washington, D.C.: Institute for International Economics, 1994).

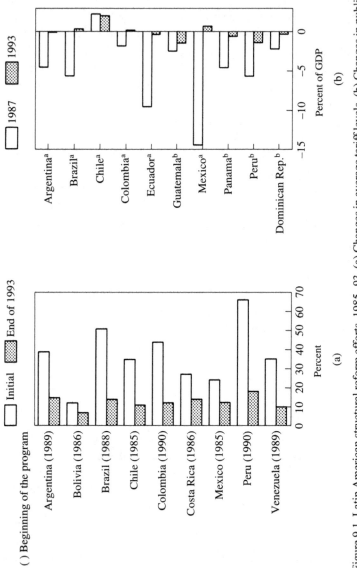

Figure 9.1. Latin American structural reform efforts, 1985–93. (a) Changes in average tariff levels. (b) Changes in public sector budget balances. Superscript a indicates nonfinancial public sector; b indicates central government. From UN Economic Commission for Latin America and the Caribbean, on the basis of official statistics.

cal elites. Behind these changes have been shifts in political culture, which privilege compromise over confrontation and modernization over backwardness.[22]

The two countries that have gone furthest in transforming their own economies are Chile and Mexico. Both succeeded in overcoming the two problems identified earlier in the chapter: intraelite conflicts and clashes with foreign capital. In the Chilean case, the end to intraelite conflict came in two stages. Initially, it was enforced by a military dictatorship; later the impact of the dictatorship led to a broad coalition of leftist and centrist political parties that agreed with the right-wing parties on basic political and economic parameters. In Mexico, over the course of the postwar era, the single-party dominant system created the favorable preconditions – domestic governability – to implement structural changes in the 1980s. International tensions also diminished as both countries sought foreign capital, providing the political stability required by foreign investors as well as attractive economic incentives.

Chile was the first country in Latin America to openly embrace market-oriented policies.[23] After the military coup in 1973 brought an end to the democratically elected socialist-leaning government of Salvador Allende, policies gradually evolved in the direction of a more open economy and a lower role for the state. Under a military dictatorship, characterized by the massive violation of human rights and a particularly rigid set of technocrats, spending was cut and many subsidies were eliminated to the extent that

---

[22] On the importance of cultural aspects in development, see Seymour Martin Lipset, "The Centrality of Political Culture," in Arend Lijphart (ed.), *Parliamentary versus Presidential Government* (New York: Oxford University Press, 1992), pp. 207–11.

[23] The volume of literature on Chile is enormous. A book that summarizes much of the economic analysis is Barry Bosworth, Rudiger Dornbusch, and Raúl Labán (eds.), *The Chilean Economy: Policy Lessons and Challenges* (Washington, D.C.: Brookings Institution, 1994). On the political economy of the Chilean experience, see Barbara Stallings and Philip Brock, "The Political Economy of Economic Adjustment: Chile, 1973–90," in Robert H. Bates and Anne O. Krueger (eds.), *Political and Economic Interactions in Economic Policy Reform* (Oxford: Basil Blackwell, 1993), pp. 78–122; Genaro Arriagada and Carol Graham, "Chile: Sustaining Adjustment during Democratic Transition," in Stephan Haggard and Steven B. Webb (eds.), *Voting for Reform: Democracy, Political Liberalization, and Economic Adjustment* (New York: Oxford University Press, 1994), pp. 242–89. On the transformation of the productive sector, see Alvaro Díaz, "Dinámicas del cambio tecnológico en la industria chilena," and Mario Castillo, Marco Dini, and Claudio Maggi, "Reorganización industrial y estrategias competitivas en Chile," Proyecto Conjunto CEPAL/CIID, "Reestructuración Productiva, Organización Industrial y Competitividad Internacional en América Latina," Santiago, 1994.

Chile's once enormous budget deficit was brought into surplus. Simultaneously, structural reforms were initiated, including the sale of most public-sector firms, the return of expropriated land, the lowering of the country's very high tariffs and quotas, and extensive deregulation of the economy. In the short term, these reforms brought high growth rates, based mainly on speculative activities. At the same time, they increased financial instability and undermined productive capacity, with the exception of a new line of "nontraditional" exports. By the early 1980s, these policies had paved the way for economic collapse. Their impact was exacerbated by an international crisis as credit was cut off, interest rates rose, and the prices of primary products fell.

The postcrisis policies featured a more flexible version of the previous approach and put a premium on the role of foreign capital that had begun to enter Chile in large amounts. In part, it was private capital stimulated by innovative policies, such as debt–equity swaps. The World Bank and the IMF also supported the Chilean policies with large loans and viewed Chile as a model of the structural transformations that other Latin American countries should follow. The transition to a democratic regime took place smoothly between 1988 and 1990, and the new government could take advantage of a stable, growing economy and a sophisticated new private sector. Steps were taken to overcome some serious problems (especially the low investment rate and the high number of people living in absolute poverty), but others remain (exports that rely on low-value-added products and a very unequal distribution of income and social services).

Mexico began its reforms a decade later than Chile, in the mid-1980s. After several years of dealing on a short-term basis with its debt problems and macroeconomic imbalances, the government made the decision in 1986 to apply for membership in the General Agreement on Tariffs and Trade (GATT) with the corresponding obligation to open its economy. Plans were also made to privatize a number of state firms, including the banking sector that had been nationalized in 1982. A qualitative leap in this direction, however, came with the election in 1988 of Carlos Salinas de Gortari as president. Salinas realized that Mexico needed large amounts of new investment if it was to be able to compete internationally. When initiatives toward European and Japanese capital proved disappointing, the new president reversed 70 years of Mexican policy and approached the United States to negotiate a free-trade agreement. The agreement would guarantee Mexico continued access to the crucial U.S. market and, it was hoped, attract investment not only from the United States but from others who hoped to take advantage of Mexico's privileged location.[24]

Opinion to the contrary, Mexico's policies were not totally orthodox; rather they combined some orthodox measures with a substantial dose of heterodoxy. The "Stability and Economic Growth Pact" was based on a tripartite agreement to cut inflation through control over wages and prices, together with strict containment of fiscal deficits and monetary expansion. The achievements of this program are based on three main aspects.[25] First, there was an agreement within the ruling elite that this was the only way to solve the economic crisis. The consensus was possible because of strong governmental leadership operating with a "visible hand." Second, the consensus relied on the defeat of both the trade union and entrepreneurial resistance. Third, the government launched an important social welfare program to compensate for the recessive effects of economic changes: the National Solidarity Program (PRONASOL). Through active community participation, the implementation of PRONASOL was instrumental in overcoming partisan resistance to change.

In addition, Mexican firms have undertaken major restructuring in order to increase their competitiveness in the newly enlarged North American market. Indications are that competitiveness has improved substantially, but the struggle to lower inflation has kept growth rates low.[26] Moreover, Mexico developed an enormous current account deficit, financed by the new private capital flows that suddenly returned to Latin America in 1990. Mexico absorbed about half of these flows, which averaged more than $50 billion per year during the early 1990s. The dangers of such reliance on international capital became clear when an attempt to devalue the peso and so shrink the trade deficit led to a major foreign exchange crisis that caused serious political and economic damage to the Mexican reform process.

[24] On the major changes in the Mexican economy, see Nora Lustig, *Mexico: The Remaking of an Economy* (Washington D.C.: Brookings Institution, 1992). On the political economy of the process, see Robert Kaufman, Carlos Bazdresch, and Blanca Heredia, "Mexico: Radical Reform in a Dominant Party System," in Haggard and Webb (eds.), *Voting for Reform*, pp. 360–410.

[25] Blanca Heredia, "Making Economic Reform Politically Viable: The Mexican Experience," in William C. Smith, Carlos H. Acuña, and Eduardo A. Gamarra (eds.), *Democracy, Markets, and Structural Reform in Latin America* (New Brunswick, N.J.: Transaction Publishers, 1993), pp. 265–95.

[26] On microeconomic transformations, see José I. Casar, "Un balance de la transformación industrial en Mexico," Proyecto Conjunto CEPAL/CIID, "Reestructuración Productiva, Organización Industrial y Competitividad Internacional en América Latina," Santiago, 1994.

Based in part on the success of the Chilean economy in the late 1980s and on expectations for similar success in Mexico, especially with the prospect of NAFTA on the horizon, other Latin American governments began to implement similar policy packages. These have included Argentina, Bolivia, Colombia, Costa Rica, the Dominican Republic, Jamaica, Peru, and Venezuela. Others have announced the intention to follow suit.

The Argentine program required dramatic changes in the ideology and values of the main economic actors, under the leadership of the Peronist president Carlos Menem.[27] In fact, Menem campaigned on a platform that promised policies very different from the ones he implemented. Finance Minister Cavallo's economic plan, "dollarizing" the economy and launching an all-embracing privatization program, brought substantial success during 1991–94, as reflected in the plummeting level of inflation and high growth rates. The budget moved into surplus, and investment increased together with manufactured exports. But intraelite disagreements remain, and labor and lower-class groups have begun to protest their exclusion from the benefits of the new policies through rioting in some provinces and protest marches in the capital. The new economic policy was supported by a Washington-backed rescheduling of the Argentine foreign debt. Like Mexico, Argentina has financed a large current account deficit by importing massive amounts of foreign capital, mainly from the United States. Indeed, the shift from its traditional detachment from the United States to a close alignment has been a key to the Argentine government's economic policies, as the Menem government sought preferential U.S. treatment in exchange for political allegiance.

Beginning with the inauguration of the Fujimori government in mid-

[27] On Argentine reforms, see Carlos H. Acuña, "Politics and Economics in the Argentina of the Nineties (Or, Why the Future Is No Longer What It Used to Be)," pp. 31–73, and Adolfo Canitrot, "Crisis and Transformation of the Argentine State, 1978–1992," pp. 75–102, both in Smith, Acuña and Gamarra (eds.), *Democracy, Markets, and Structural Reform;* Pablo Gerchunoff and Germán Coloma, "Privatization in Argentina," in Manuel Sánchez and Rossana Corona (eds.), *Privatization in Latin America* (Washington, D.C.: Johns Hopkins University Press for the Inter-American Development Bank, 1993), pp. 251–99; José María Fanelli and Mario Damill, "Los capitales extranjeros en las economías latinoamericanas: Argentina," in José Antonio Ocampo (ed.), *Los capitales extranjeros en las economías latinoamericanas* (Bogota: Fedesarrollo, 1994), pp. 41–102; Luis Alberto Beccaría and Bernardo Kosacoff, "La industria argentina: de la sustitución de importaciones a la convertibilidad," Proyecto Conjunto CEPAL/CIID, "Reestructuración Productiva, Organización Industrial y Competitividad Internacional en América Latina," Santiago, 1994.

1990, Peru has also made dramatic economic changes.[28] As was the case with Menem in Argentina, these changes were contrary to what citizens thought they had voted for in the presidential election. Inheriting a country with a combination of hyperinflation, depression, and severed links with the international financial institutions, Fujimori undertook what is perhaps the most radical version of the Washington Consensus reforms of any country in the region. The government budget deficit was slashed, throwing tens of thousands of people out of work, and tariffs were reduced dramatically. The latter also increased unemployment as bankruptcies ensued. Social unrest from these changes, combined with failing efforts to deal with the Sendero Luminoso guerrilla movement, led to the most controversial part of the Peruvian process – Fujimori's "auto-coup" that shut the congress and threatened the improving international relations. A new election appeased most foreigners, however, thus clearing the way for a large influx of foreign capital that has been an essential component of the new program. Privatizations have become an important vehicle for the entry of external resources. Peru's growth rate is now even higher than Argentina's and its inflation rate has also declined substantially, but it seems clear that consensus on the direction of economic policy is much less solid than it is in Chile or Mexico.

Still less consensus exists in Venezuela. There, the government of Carlos Andrés Pérez introduced drastic stabilization and restructuring policies in the late 1980s, trying to reorient the economy in line with new world directions.[29] The recessive effects of the policies, rising prices of consumer goods, and growing unemployment produced generalized social unrest that

---

[28] Background on Peruvian economic policies in the 1980s is found in Manuel Pastor and Carol Wise, "Peruvian Economic Policy in the 1980s: From Orthodoxy to Heterodoxy and Back," *Latin American Research Review* 27, 2 (1992), 83–117. For an overview of the reforms at the beginning of the Fujimori government, see Carlos E. Paredes and Jeffrey Sachs (eds.), *Peru's Path to Recovery: A Plan for Economic Stabilization and Growth* (Washington, D.C.: Brookings Institution, 1991), and Efraín González de Olarte, *Nuevos rumbos para el desarrollo del Perú y América Latina* (Lima: Instituto de Estudios Peruanos, 1991). Evaluations of the first years of the reforms are found in Teobaldo Pinzas, "Cuatro años de ajuste," *Argumentos: Boletín de coyuntura política y económica* (Lima), 21–22 (July–August 1994), 10–14, and John Sheahan, "Peru's Return toward an Open Economy: Macroeconomic Complications and Structural Questions," *World Development* 22, 6 (June 1994), 911–23.

[29] Venezuelan reforms under Pérez are analyzed in Moises Naim, *Paper Tigers and Minotaurs: The Politics of Venezuela's Economic Reforms* (Washington, D.C.: Carnegie Endowment for International Peace, 1993).

erupted in violent riots in early 1989 and the February and November 1992 military coup attempts. After these events, the government's direction was modified and some traditional policies were reintroduced, showing that the new orientation did not pervade the ruling elite and the business community. The 1993 presidential campaign was waged largely on economic issues. The two leading candidates strongly opposed the previous government's economic policies, and the victor, Rafael Caldera, promised to reverse many of them. Once in office, a financial crisis led him to take control of the banking system and enact exchange and price controls. Nonetheless, the controls were declared to be temporary, and the September 1994 economic program returned to stabilization and privatization measures.[30]

Finally, there is the atypical but crucial case of Brazil.[31] Brazil's economic problems have cast a shadow over the continent because of its huge size: the fifth largest territory and ninth largest economy in the world, it represents 35 percent of the Latin American GDP. During the 1980s, its economy experienced modest, though fluctuating, growth with high rates of inflation. Moreover, Brazil is one of the Latin American countries with the highest level of income disparity and poverty. What was most disturbing in the Brazilian case was the lack of change in the political culture of the elites. President Collor promised to combat corruption and to discipline the economy, but his administration ended in a total failure. The successor Franco government proved vacillating and divided, reflecting the lack of consensus on the direction that policy reforms should take. Tensions between elites seeking a more autonomous role in world affairs and those aiming for closer bonds with the United States paralyzed the chances to solve Brazil's main problems.

---

[30] On the Venezuelan elections, see *Latin American Weekly Report,* December 16, 1993. The most recent economic policies are discussed in "Venezuela: Crisis Manager," *Economist,* September 17, 1994.

[31] Brazil's economic strategy, and attempts at stabilization before 1993, are discussed in Winston Frisch and Gustavo Franco, "Los avances de la reforma de la política comercial e industrial en Brasil," in Vial (ed.), *¿Adonde va América Latina?,* pp. 135–57; Deepak Lal and Sylvia Maxfield, "The Political Economy of Stabilization in Brazil," in Bates and Krueger (eds.), *Political and Economic Interactions,* pp. 27–77; Lourdes Sola, "The State, Structural Reform, and Democratization in Brazil," pp. 151–81, and Antonio Barros de Castro, "Renegade Development: Rise and Demise of State-Led Development in Brazil," pp. 183–213, in Smith et al. (eds.), *Democracy, Markets, and Structural Reform;* and Dionisio D. Carneiro and Rogerio L. F. Werneke, "Obstacles to Investment Resumption in Brazil," in Edmar Bacha (ed.), *Savings and Investment Requirements for the Resumption of Growth in Latin America* (Washington, D.C.: Johns Hopkins University Press for the Inter-American Development Bank, 1993), pp. 57–102.

Brazil was able to postpone resolution of its structural problems for two main reasons. Its large trade surplus provided a cushion of foreign exchange, and its indexed economy enabled people to live with high inflation rates. In 1994, however, a new stabilization plan was introduced, with some similarities to the Argentine policies. The initial success of the "Real Plan" paved the way for the election to the presidency of the plan's author, Fernando Henrique Cardoso, together with a broad coalition of center-left and right-wing parties. Cardoso's electoral platform called for a continued stress on stabilization and a major restructuring of the economy, including an increased emphasis on privatizations. This would be combined with programs to combat poverty and improve social services. The declining support for Cardoso's leftist rival in the months before the election may be an indication of a greater convergence of opinion around a set of economic policies with similarities to others in the region.[32]

The Latin American reform programs initially produced quite uneven results. Some countries grew rapidly, others stagnated. In some cases inflation was brought down quickly, in others it lingered on. By the mid-1990s, however, with estimates for economic performance in 1994 and projections for 1995, a common plateau seems to be emerging.[33] On a regional basis, the new situation has three elements. First, economic growth has replaced the contraction of the 1980s, averaging between 3 and 4 percent per year in aggregate terms and about 1.5 percent on a per capita basis. The wide variation in growth rates has begun to converge: nine countries grew more than 5 percent per year in 1992, six in 1993, and only two in 1994. The rapid growth rates that characterized some countries initially were based on recovery from the long recession of the 1980s; that high growth has now begun to subside in most countries. Second, with the exception of Brazil, inflation began to fall on a steady basis. In 1991, prices rose by an average of 49 percent; the figure fell to 22 percent in 1992, 19 percent in 1993, and 16 percent in 1994. As mentioned earlier, Brazil's very high inflation rates have also begun to decline sharply. Third, growth has been accompanied by large and growing current account deficits, financed by huge capital in-

---

[32] On the Real Plan, see Luiz Carlos Bresser Pereira, "A economia e a política do Plano Real," *Revista de Economia Política* 14, 4 (October–December 1994), 129–49. Cardoso's platform in summarized in "Plano Fernando Henrique Cardoso," *Revista de Economia Política* 14, 2 (April–June 1994), 114–31.

[33] UNECLAC, *Preliminary Overview of the Economy of Latin America and the Caribbean* (Santiago: UNECLAC, 1994).

flows. The regional current account deficit in 1994 was about 4 percent of GDP, and capital inflows averaged about $50 billion per year between 1991 and 1994. Unlike the loans of the 1970s, these current financial flows consist mainly of direct investment, bonds, and the purchase of securities (see the discussion in Chapter 5, this volume).

Table 9.1 summarizes some of these trends and reveals that differences still remain, despite converging trends. Per capita GDP growth is especially high in Argentina, for example, while Brazil and Mexico trail the regional average. Three small countries in Central America and the Caribbean continue to suffer problems from political conflicts plus recent drought, leading to negative growth rates. In 15 of the 19 countries covered in the table, inflation is down, often sharply, as compared with the preceding decade. Exceptions include two of the small countries just mentioned – Haiti (political problems) and Honduras (drought) – plus Brazil and Venezuela – the two countries that have been at odds with the region in terms of reforms.

The higher growth and lower inflation, in comparison with the 1980s, represents an important achievement. Nonetheless, growth remains fairly modest, relative both to historical levels in Latin America itself and to growth rates in Asia. In addition to special situations in individual countries, as mentioned earlier, there are several general reasons for low growth. The anti-inflation policies, while laying the basis for stable growth in the future, restrain current performance. Likewise, the structural reforms are expected to increase competitiveness in the longer run, but they can cause severe dislocations as firms adjust. Finally, low investment rates over more than a decade have limited the possibilities to incorporate up-to-date technology. At the same time, it is possible that future growth is being jeopardized by the large-scale capital inflows, which cause appreciation of exchange rates and thus undermine programs to promote exports. The capital, much of which takes the form of short-term flows, also increases the vulnerability to external shocks. A dramatic example was seen in the capital flight and the price gyrations in Latin American stock markets following the peso devaluation in Mexico.

Low growth, in turn, makes it difficult to deal with unemployment and underemployment, as well as accumulated social problems. Indeed, unemployment is increasing, even in countries where the growth of output is relatively high. This is because higher productivity is generally being achieved by dismissing workers rather than by improving their skills or raising the technological capacity of firms. Not surprisingly, there are indicators of increased inequality, although the poor quality of data and lack of comparability make analysis of these trends difficult. For example, among 14 Latin American countries for which data are available, urban poverty increased in 10 of them between the 1980s and 1992. Likewise, 7 of 13 countries saw an increase in the ratio of the income share of the top 10 percent of the urban population to that of the bottom 40 percent; in 3 countries the ratio fell, and in 3 it remained more or less the same.[34]

Both unemployment and inequality are influenced by the record of human capital development; some indicators are shown in Table 9.2. The table indicates that health standards improved substantially for the region as a whole, even during the "lost decade." Nonetheless, several countries experienced setbacks in the 1980s with respect to nutrition; they included Argentina, Bolivia, Chile, and Uruguay. Education indicators also improved, but the growth rate fell in the 1980s compared with the 1965–80 period. Again, a number of countries saw absolute declines in the levels previously reached.

If the Latin American data are compared with those for East Asia, the difference is notable. Perhaps the most significant gap is in the secondary school enrollment rate. In East Asia, 86 percent of the eligible age group was enrolled in high school in 1991, while in Latin America the figure was only 47 percent. (See Table 1.5, this volume.) Even the most successful cases in Latin America fall short of the Asian levels. A related comparison is the number of scientists and engineers in the population plus research and development (R&D) expenditures. In the former category, Uruguay has the highest number of scientists and engineers per 10,000 population in Latin America. The figure is 6.8 compared with 13 in South Korea and Singapore. Argentina, Brazil, and Chile – the next highest group in Latin America – have fewer than 4 per 10,000 population. A similar situation is found in R&D expenditures. Among the major countries of the region, Mexico has the highest R&D expenditures at 0.55 percent of GDP compared with 1.9 percent for South Korea.[35] The possibility of catching up any time soon is small, given the difference in investment rates: over 30 percent in East and Southeast Asia in 1990 but less than 20 percent in Latin America (see Table 1.4).

[34] UNECLAC, *Social Panorama of Latin America, 1994* (Santiago: UNECLAC, 1994), tables 18 and 22.
[35] Inter-American Development Bank (IDB), *Economic and Social Progress in Latin America, 1992 Report* (Washington, D.C.: IDB, 1992), pp. 215–16.

Table 9.1. *Economic indicators, Latin America, 1970–94*

Country	1990 GDP ($ billions)	1990 Population (millions)	1990 GDP per capita (dollars)	Real GDP per capita, annual increase (percent) 1970–80	1980–90	1991–94	Merchandise exports, annual increase (percent) 1970–80	1980–90	1991–94	Inflation, annual increase (percent) 1980–90	1994
South America	761.8	294.1	2,591	3.9	−0.8	1.8	18.8	3.0	6.2	287.3	620.9
Argentina	105.4	32.3	3,265	1.0	−2.5	6.0	16.3	4.4	6.2	438.5	3.6
Bolivia	4.5	7.2	626	1.4	−2.4	1.4	16.5	1.2	3.9	220.4	8.9
Brazil	473.7	150.0	3,158	6.0	−0.6	0.3	22.1	4.5	8.3	330.5	1,294.0
Chile	27.8	13.2	2,110	0.9	1.1	4.6	14.0	6.5	9.1	19.6	8.9
Colombia	41.1	32.3	1,271	3.2	1.4	2.1	18.4	5.5	4.0	25.0	23.0
Ecuador	10.9	10.3	1,058	6.2	−0.3	1.8	28.9	1.2	7.8	37.0	24.5
Paraguay	5.3	4.3	1,220	5.6	−0.4	−0.1	17.1	11.9	−1.8	23.9	18.7
Peru	36.7	21.7	1,693	0.1	−2.5	2.5	12.1	0.0	6.8	313.0	17.5
Uruguay	8.2	3.1	2,656	2.6	−0.8	3.6	16.4	4.8	2.5	60.0	44.7
Venezuela	48.3	19.7	2,446	−0.8	−2.0	0.6	19.7	1.1	−2.2	21.6	70.9

Mexico	237.7	86.2	2,760	3.5	−0.4	0.7	29.1	5.6	6.4	62.3	6.9
Central America and Caribbean	39.7	42.1	937	2.2	−2.0	1.5	15.9	−1.0	6.5	57.5	12.6
Costa Rica	5.7	2.8	2,031	3.0	0.1	2.5	16.1	3.5	12.5	25.8	17.4
Dominican Republic	7.1	7.1	1,005	4.2	−0.4	1.4	16.2	−2.7	−4.6	22.6	11.4
El Salvador	5.4	5.2	1,036	0.8	−1.2	2.3	16.7	−6.5	9.6	16.3	9.4
Guatemala	7.6	9.2	829	2.8	−2.0	1.0	17.7	−2.0	7.6	14.8	12.5
Haiti	2.8	6.5	427	2.6	−2.8	−9.9	18.6	−2.9	−22.0	7.6	na
Honduras	2.7	5.1	536	2.1	−1.3	0.4	17.0	1.2	1.9	6.5	28.0
Nicaragua	3.4	3.9	886	−2.6	−6.8	−3.3	9.0	−0.9	1.8	502.0	12.2
Panama	4.8	2.4	1,965	3.0	−1.6	5.0	12.4	−0.9	14.5	2.4	1.8
Total	1,039.1	422.4	2,460	3.7	−0.8	1.6	19.8	3.2	6.3	227.1	473.9

Sources: Calculated from World Bank, *World Tables* tapes, *1992* (for 1970–90); UNECLAC, *Preliminary Overview of the Economy of Latin America and the Caribbean, 1994* (for 1991–94).

Table 9.2. Social indicators, Latin America, 1965–90

Country	Daily calorie supply per capita			Infant mortality (per 1,000 live births)			Primary school enrollment (percentage of eligible age)			Secondary school (percentage of eligible age)		
		Annual growth (percent)			Annual growth (percent)			Annual growth (percent)			Annual growth (percent)	
	1989	1965–80	1980–89	1990	1965–80	1980–90	1989	1965–80	1980–89	1989	1965–80	1980–89
South America	2,684	0.3	0.5	49	-2.4	-2.9	107	0.1	0.4	47	4.7	1.8
Argentina	3,113	0.7	-1.3	29	-1.8	-4.1	111	0.9	-0.5	74	4.7	3.1
Bolivia	1,916	0.7	-0.9	92	-2.3	-2.0	81	0.9	-0.4	34	4.7	-0.6
Brazil	2,751	0.1	1.3	57	-2.2	-2.7	105	-1.0	1.4	34	4.7	0.7
Chile	2,581	0.5	-0.9	17	-5.5	-8.6	100	-0.4	-1.7	75	3.3	3.5
Colombia	2,598	1.0	0.3	37	-2.9	-3.9	107	2.8	-2.0	52	6.9	1.4
Ecuador	2,531	0.0	1.7	55	-2.2	-3.7	118	1.1	1.1	56	5.9	3.8
Paraguay	2,757	0.4	0.1	32	-3.0	-3.6	106	0.0	0.4	29	4.7	1.2
Peru	2,186	-0.8	0.7	69	-2.8	-2.1	123	0.8	1.0	67	5.5	2.0
Uruguay	2,653	0.2	-1.0	21	-1.2	-6.0	106	-0.1	0.1	77	2.1	2.8
Venezuela	2,582	0.7	0.2	34	-3.2	-1.6	105	0.7	0.1	56	2.5	4.1

Mexico	3,052	0.5	1.0	39	-2.7	-3.2	114	1.8	-0.6	53	5.3	4.1
Central America and Caribbean	2,292	0.1	1.3	59	-3.1	-2.1	91	1.1	0.7	29	5.1	0.9
Costa Rica	2,808	1.0	0.2	16	-6.3	-5.1	100	0.1	-0.9	41	4.7	-1.7
Dominican Republic	2,359	0.5	2.0	56	-3.3	-1.6	95	1.3	-1.2	na	6.8	na
El Salvador	2,317	0.6	1.5	53	-3.1	-3.4	78	-0.7	0.6	26	2.0	1.4
Guatemala	2,235	0.1	1.0	62	-3.5	-0.6	79	2.2	1.5	21	4.7	3.1
Haiti	2,013	-1.5	2.4	95	-2.3	-1.6	84	1.7	3.1	19	6.0	5.2
Honduras	2,247	0.7	0.4	64	-2.6	-2.9	108	0.7	2.2	na	5.1	na
Nicaragua	2,265	-0.5	0.7	55	-2.1	-4.6	99	2.4	0.1	43	7.8	0.0
Panama	2,539	-0.2	1.8	21	-6.3	0.0	107	0.7	-0.6	59	4.4	-1.1
Total	2,720	0.3	0.7	48	-2.6	-2.9	106.7	0.5	0.2	48	4.8	2.5

Source: World Bank, *World Development Report, 1983, 1992.*

Regional-level responses

The other pole of the Latin American response to globalization has been bilateral and multilateral free-trade negotiations, as well as attempts at regional political coordination. In contrast to the integration schemes of the 1960s – which were basically extensions of the domestic ISI models in Latin America, designed to enlarge highly protected markets to encourage further industrialization – regional integration in the 1990s is based on an export-oriented model looking toward increased relationships with the global economy. Also unlike the relatively orderly process of the earlier era, based on a limited set of subregional units under the umbrella of the Latin American Free Trade Area, integration in the 1990s has been described as "a complex patchwork of negotiations."[36]

The largest of the embryonic FTAs is that covered by NAFTA, signed by the United States, Canada, and Mexico. NAFTA brought together a market of 360 million people, larger than the European Union. It provides the potential for integrating production facilities across the three countries, with the resulting products traded freely. Expected benefits center on economies of scale and the ability to locate particular parts of the production process according to comparative advantage (i.e., labor-intensive processes in Mexico and skill-intensive processes in the United States and Canada). The resulting rise in income levels should reinforce the process by increasing the size of the market. While overall benefits could be considerable, and there are claims that these are already beginning to appear through expanded trade, there will nonetheless be losers: those workers whose jobs are transferred, third countries that are excluded, and perhaps the environment with implications for all.[37]

At the same time the U.S.–Canada–Mexico negotiations went forward, three other types of integration initiatives were occurring in the hemisphere. First was a set of "framework agreements" between the United States and many Latin American countries. These agreements established rules and principles for future negotiations of free-trade arrangements. Chile has been declared to be next in line, after Mexico, to move beyond the framework

---

[36] Van R. Whiting Jr., "The Dynamics of Regionalization: Road Map to an Open Future?" in Peter H. Smith (ed.), *The Challenge of Integration: Europe and the Americas* (New Brunswick, N.J.: Transaction Publishers, 1993), pp. 17–49, at 39.

[37] Gary Clyde Hufbauer and Jeffrey J. Schott, *NAFTA: An Assessment* (Washington, D.C.: Institute for International Economics, 1993).

agreement stage to enter NAFTA. The Central American and Caribbean nations, which conduct the large majority of their trade with the United States and fear losing markets to Mexico under NAFTA, are eager to follow suit; given the small size and fragile nature of their economies, however, they hope to obtain preferential status. Response in South America is more mixed but generally positive.[38]

A second strand in the integration web involves subregional groups among Latin American countries themselves. Some are revitalizations of the groups formed in the 1960s: the Andean Pact (Peru, Colombia, Venezuela, Bolivia, and Ecuador), the Central American Common Market (Costa Rica, Guatemala, Honduras, El Salvador, and Nicaragua), and the Caribbean Community (13 English-speaking countries in the Caribbean or adjoining mainland area). A new addition is Mercosur (Brazil, Argentina, Paraguay, and Uruguay, with Chile as a special partner). While all have set ambitious targets for lowering trade barriers and setting a common external tariff, the degree of institutionality varies substantially. For example, the Andean Pact has a large bureaucracy in Lima, while Mercosur has no permanent bureaucrats of its own but "borrows" officials from member countries.[39] The initial motivations of the participants varied (e.g., Brazil and Argentina began negotiating more for political and military than economic reasons), but all are now exploring combinations of preparations for possible links with the United States and defensive alternatives if such links prove impossible.[40]

There are also bilateral and trilateral agreements that reach across the four subregional groups and – to further the complexity – between some members of the groups themselves. Over 20 such agreements have been signed in recent years. Within the Andean Pact, for example, Venezuela and Colombia have signed ambitious agreements to form a customs union and cooperate in various sectors including iron and steel. Colombia and Ecuador have also signed an FTA. Peru has signed bilateral agreements with all its Andean Pact partners – although it temporarily suspended its participation in the Andean Pact in August 1992. Mercosur began with a bilateral pact

---

[38] For an analysis of the potential benefits of a hemispheric FTA, as seen by various groups of countries, see Sylvia Saborio (ed.), *The Premise and the Promise: Free Trade in the Americas* (Washington, D.C.: Overseas Development Council, 1992).

[39] Institute for European–Latin American Relations (IRELA), *Prospects for the Processes of Sub-regional Integration in Central and South America* (Madrid: IRELA/IDB, 1992).

[40] Alberto Van Klaveren, "Why Integration Now? Options for Latin America," in Smith (ed.), *The Challenge of Integration*, pp. 115–45.

between Brazil and Argentina. In general, Mexico and Chile have practiced the most aggressive trade diplomacy in Latin America, reflecting the fact that neither is a member of a Latin American regional subgroup. Chile has signed bilateral pacts with seven countries (including Mexico), while Mexico has become the center of a hemisphere-wide network. It includes a trilateral relationship with Venezuela and Colombia (the Group of Three) and links with the Central American Common Market as well as with Chile.[41]

These new bilateral and multilateral agreements are extremely diverse and overlapping. A few are "deep" trade liberalization agreements, while most are "superficial" ones. The former broaden the range of products, by focusing on lists of exceptions rather than products eligible for trade liberalization, intend to eliminate tariffs rather than reduce them and contemplate the removal of nontariff barriers. A number of problems can arise from bilateral agreements. Their limited geographic coverage could have political and economic costs due to asymmetries in bargaining strength and the negative externalities for smaller countries. Similarly, there is an associated cost to the administration of this variety of agreements to each party involved, possible higher transportation costs if trade is diverted from neighbors, concentration of investments, insecurity and instability of foreign investments, and distortion of the allocation of resources. Governments will have to decide whether to integrate the bilateral agreements into a homogeneous network or to continue them on the current basis.[42]

Finally, there are de facto processes of integration led by private corporations investing abroad. Examples include Chilean investments in the Argentine power industry and in the Peruvian power and financial sectors, as well as in pension funds; Mexican investments in selected countries, especially in television stations, as well as in the agricultural area in selected countries to overcome U.S. sanitary restrictions on some Mexican products; Colombian financial investments in Ecuador and Venezuela as well as industrial investments in Peru; and Brazilian productive investments in Argentina and Chile.[43] These ventures are creating a new profile of economic interactions

---

[41] UNECLAC, *La nueva integración regional en el marco de la Asociación Latinoamericana de Integración (ALADI)* (Santiago: UNECLAC, June 30, 1994).

[42] UNECLAC, *Open Regionalism*, pp. 42–50.

[43] For data on foreign investment by Latin American countries, see UNCTAD, *World Investment Directory: Latin America and the Caribbean* (New York: United Nations, 1994). See also Wilson Peres, "The Internationalization of Latin American Industrial Firms," *CEPAL Review* 49 (April 1993), 55–74.

not necessarily corresponding to governmental FTAs. In some cases, private intraregional investments are forcing governments to revise official trade policies. The Chilean negotiations to establish special links with Mercosur are probably an instance of this process, since the governmental decision followed the dramatic flows of investment to Argentina.

These intraregional processes have been occurring under two umbrellas. One is the old Latin American Integration Association, created by 11 Latin American governments in 1980 to promote linkages among their countries. The plan was to eventually create a free-trade area. The other is a series of U.S. initiatives, beginning with the Bush administration's EAI, which led many Latin American countries to negotiate framework agreements with the United States. Despite the fact that the hemispheric integration movement had begun under the Republicans, the Clinton government pursued it with vigor. Clinton himself took great political risks to gain congressional support for the NAFTA treaty, which comprised the United States, Canada, and Mexico; Chile has now been invited to become the fourth member.

In December 1994, with the encouragement of Latin American political leaders, the U.S. government convened a hemispheric summit, where a Declaration of Principles endorsed the formation of an "American Free Trade Area" by the year 2005 and concrete progress before the end of this century. The 34 participating governments also approved an action plan: (1) to use the OAS Special Trade Commission to carry out studies and discussions of existing agreements, beginning in January 1995; (2) to hold a meeting of regional trade ministers in June 1995 to produce a preliminary report on work accomplished and topics to be dealt with immediately; and (3) to follow up with another trade ministers' meeting in March 1996 to produce a final report and define a timetable to achieve further progress in the integration scheme.

If a hemispheric free-trade area were to come into existence, which is by no means assured, it would probably be a fairly narrow institution in comparison with the European Union. Thus, while the European Union aims to constitute a single communitarian nationality, the American agreement would be limited to the economic realm, especially trade. Moreover, given the structural nature of hemispheric economic relations, intra-American trade would not involve the majority of goods exchanged as happens in the European Union, since export markets in Europe and Asia would continue to be important. In addition, a trade agreement does not necessarily imply integration of financial and investment flows, and it specifically excludes labor mobility. And there will be no attempt to provide special resources to the poorer members of an inter-American FTA, as the European Union has done with the Southern European nations.

These characteristics suggest that, at best, an American Free Trade Area would be a partial relationship. Others have a more negative view, perceiving hemispheric integration as damaging to Latin American economic interests. An influential Canadian economist, for example, has argued that a hemispheric arrangement would be dominated by U.S. interests, preclude the Latin American (and Canadian) governments from following economic policies that promoted development in Asia, and cause social dislocations and increased inequality.[44] Some Latin American experts fear that a hemispheric accord could limit the options for Latin American countries and reduce the scope of the international coalitions these countries could build. Potentially preferable approaches, according to this analysis, would be concentration on subregional blocs or a wider net of trade agreements that would include European and Asian countries rather than concentrating exclusively on relations with the United States.[45]

Because of these difficulties in developing trade agreements and/or reaching integrationist goals, countries in the hemisphere confronting critical issues demanding collective solutions have been restructuring and reordering their regional organizations and extraregional affiliations to deal with the new reality. Organizations like the Latin American Economic System or the Organization of American States face a diminished role in the region. Other multilateral organizations have become more important for Latin American countries, for example, the United Nations to deal with the Haitian issue; the Argentina military interest in NATO; the Chilean and Mexican membership in the Asia–Pacific Economic Cooperation forum; Mexico's recent entry into the OECD; the new role of ad hoc multilateral organs like the Group of Three (Mexico, Colombia, and Venezuela) or the Rio Group.

The Rio Group represents a particularly important attempt at economic and political coordination in the region. The efforts began in the 1980s

---

[44] Bruce W. Wilkinson, "NAFTA in the World Economy: Lessons and Issues for Latin America," paper presented at CIEPLAN conference NAFTA, Latin American Trade Agreements, and Western Hemisphere Integration, Santiago, Chile, January 1995.

[45] See, e.g., Alfredo R. Morelli, "La Iniciativa para la Américas y los intereses argentinos," *América Latina/Internacional* 8, 28 (April–June 1991), 413–19, and Juan Alberto Fuentes, "Reconciling Subregional and Hemispheric Integration," *CEPAL Review* 45 (December 1991), 99–120.

around two sets of issues: ending the civil wars in Central America and dealing with the debt crisis in Mexico and South America. In the Central American case, four countries – Mexico, Venezuela, Costa Rica, and Panama – came together as the Contadora Group to try to prevent the Reagan administration from intervening militarily in the region. Although later joined by a so-called Support Group, consisting of Argentina, Brazil, Peru, and Uruguay, the Contadora Group was not directly influential in the eventual accords that were based on an alternative plan by President Oscar Arias of Costa Rica. Nonetheless, Contadora was successful in a broader context. As one Latin American analyst has said, Contadora's main accomplishment was to revive the spirit of collective diplomacy, independent of the United States.[46]

In the rest of the region, the main problems of the 1980s were economic, led by the massive outflows of funds for debt payments. While a "debtor cartel" was never formed, many informal meetings were held to discuss common problems and potential solutions. The most important were organized by the Cartagena Consensus, which was established at a meeting at Cartagena, Colombia, in June 1984. The 11 largest Latin American debtor countries attended and developed a set of principles calling for political dialogue with the governments of creditor countries and symmetrical adjustment between creditors and debtors.[47]

By the end of 1986, these political and economic initiatives had meshed in the formation of the Group of Eight, which initially consisted of the four Contadora and four Support Group countries (all of which also belonged to the Cartagena Consensus). In December 1986, the eight established the Permanent Mechanism for Political Consultation and Concertation. Its aims were to expand and systematize governmental cooperation, examine international questions of interest to member states, formulate common positions, seek regional solutions to regional problems, and promote the regional integration process together with other means to achieve economic and social development. Rather than a statement of anti–U.S. regionalism, its founders saw the Group of Eight (now better known as the Rio Group) as

---

[46] Alfonso Aguilar Zinser, " Negotiation in Conflict: Central America and Contadora," in Nora Hamilton et al. (eds.), *Crisis in Central America: Regional Dynamics and U.S. Policy in the 1980s* (Boulder, Colo.: Westview, 1988), pp. 97–115.

[47] Barbara Stallings, "Debtors versus Creditors: Power Relations and Policy Response to the 1980s Crisis," in David Felix (ed.), *Debt and Transfiguration? Prospects for Latin America's Economic Revival* (New York: Sharpe, 1990), pp. 83–103.

the regional equivalent of the Group of Seven among industrial countries. The first presidential summit took place in Acapulco in November 1987, the first time in 20 years that such a gathering had occurred without the United States. Gradually expanded to include other democracies, the Group of Eight provides a flexible forum for regional consultation and collaboration.[48]

Toward the future

Globalization is gradually engulfing all national economies and creating a single world economy. To a significant extent, there is consensus on the economic and political institutions associated with this coming world economy: market-oriented policies, privatization of state-owned industries, reduction of the activity and scope of the state, anti-inflationary policies based on reduction of public-sector deficits, deregulation of foreign investment flows and other economic activities, open markets, and free trade. Political institutions identified with this global economy are competitive systems inspired by Western models of democracy.

Nevertheless, the apparent unanimity on the institutions and policies for a new development strategy in Latin America is showing some contradictions under the surface. On the one hand, there is agreement that the institutions of the import-substitution industrialization model are no longer appropriate. But, on the other hand, the new model does not provide institutions able to cope with both economic restructuring and its social effects. Accordingly, as Gary Gereffi argues in the conclusion to Chapter 4, there is a growing tension between globalization and the social problems it creates. These social problems, in turn, lead to political opposition to the new policies. Because of this tension, regional elites favoring the new ideology may not be able to continue economic reforms and, at the same time, secure democratic governance.

It is possible to identify at least three main areas of strain. First is the issue of reducing the role of the state. Latin American governments have generally become less interventionist in the economy and in social issues. But the absence of the state as a social regulator is increasing national structural dualism, as income disparities and job instability increase. The recessive effects of economic reforms are not being compensated through govern-

---

[48] Alicia Frohman, *Puentes sobre la turbulencia: la concertación política latinoamericana en los 80* (Santiago: FLACSO, 1990).

ment programs to ameliorate their impact on those living in extreme poverty. The result is serious tension as seen in Venezuela (military coup attempts), Brazil (nationalist tendencies), Peru and Ecuador (elite dissent), Mexico (Chiapas revolt), and Argentina (riots in the provinces).

Second, to cope with critical social conditions during political as well as economic transition periods, governments have to count on resources to introduce needed structural changes and to cope with the effects of these policies once enacted. In comparative terms, Latin American countries lack modern and efficient tax systems necessary to provide the resources demanded by the simultaneous occurrence of both types of transitions. One of the keys to Chile's successful transition was the multiparty agreement to raise the value-added tax by two points. With the new capital flows into the region, part of the resource constraint has been lifted, at least in the short term. But these flows are creating problems of their own, including increased vulnerability to international shocks and the appreciation of exchange rates, which undermines the export component of the new development strategies.

Third, the agenda for change requested of developing countries is not always observed in the developed world. Large budget deficits in the United States, subsidies in the European Union, and protectionism in Japan run counter to the new world economic agenda. Moreover, these practices can have negative effects on the Latin American economies. The deficits lead the United States to compete with Latin America for scarce international capital, while the subsidies and protectionism limit the potential for exports to the industrial countries. The overall result is likely to be a balance-of-payments constraint that limits growth possibilities.

These problems – internal, external, and institutional – raise serious questions about Latin America's ability to implement the new market-oriented policies, even when governments are in basic agreement with their direction. They suggest that the intraelite disagreements have not disappeared in many countries of the region, nor have the international conflicts been eliminated. While all agree that Latin American economies need to become more competitive, a consensus about the methods of doing so requires a sharing of costs and benefits, nationally and internationally, in a form yet to be devised. Such problems are compounded by opposition from labor and lower-class groups who feel they are expected to pay a disproportionate share of the costs of economic transition and the FTAs. The move toward competitive democratic political systems means that their objections cannot be ignored as they were in the East Asian cases or those of the most successful economies in Latin America.

In a few countries (especially Chile and Mexico), there is a chance for significant progress to be made via Washington Consensus–type policies; these countries are also being incorporated into some type of special relationship with the United States. For others (e.g., Argentina, Colombia, and Peru), greater barriers exist because of internal conflicts. Brazil's resources, human and physical, mean that potential exists, but realizing that potential requires consensus on a viable strategy. Much of the rest of the continent is struggling to prevent marginalization (part of the Andean region as well as most Central American and Caribbean nations). Thus, the counterpart to globalization is a transition period where a new intraelite consensus and an intranational consensus have to be developed; new participative institutions have to be created; and new intraregional relations have to be imagined in order to couple competition and cooperation in the emerging global economy.

CHAPTER 10

Sub-Saharan Africa: underdevelopment's last stand

MICHAEL CHEGE

As the world watches the horror of endemic violence, state disintegration, refugees, and starvation in Somalia and Rwanda, it is worth noting the more disquieting fact that an increasing number of African states are tottering on the brink, threatening to follow Somalia and Rwanda into the abyss. These now include Liberia, Chad, Zaire, Sudan, Togo, and Angola. Nor is the postindependence record elsewhere encouraging. Previous African "success stories," like Ivory Coast and Kenya, are now assailed by chronic political and economic problems. Flickers of hope are few, small, and far between – Botswana, Mauritius, and, perhaps, Ghana, Zambia, and Zimbabwe. And, of course, great hopes are held out for South Africa, but it too can be expected to encounter many difficulties on the road from apartheid to a nonracial democracy.

Against this backdrop, economic performance of most African states south of the Sahara in the past two decades gives little cause for cheer, particularly to the ordinary citizens of the region. After registering average annual per capita growth rates of 2.9 percent in the immediate postindependence period (1965–73), the rate has since experienced consistent decline, stagnating at 0.1 percent between 1973 and 1980, and falling by 0.8 percent on average between 1980 and 1992. At best, therefore, most Africans are as poor as they were at independence 30 years ago. And because the population growth rate in the region has been on the order of 3 percent per annum over most of this period, and is projected to remain at that level for the rest of the century, GDP growth rates must rise to about 5 percent on average before any appreciable reversal in the poverty trend can be made.

To the extent that international calculations of national poverty indices can be trusted, Sub-Saharan Africans are not yet the poorest people in the world. Only 11 percent of the Sub-Saharan population of 420 million in

1985 could be classified as poor.[1] This proportion is nowhere close to the 46 percent poverty-afflicted population among South Asia's 1 billion people. But Africa's consistently declining rates of economic productivity and surging population growth portend deepening impoverishment, compared with South Asia, where an increase in per capita income may finally be beginning. Underdevelopment appears determined to make its last stand in Africa.

This unhappy prospect arises not just from the discouraging prospects of renewed and sustained growth but, more significantly, from disagreement about what development paradigm (and associated policies) might reverse the downward spiral in the region's overall development performance. Considering the economic impact of the national political disasters just mentioned, such a conceptual device must harness stable and efficient governance to proven policies for renewed growth. This is easier said than done. As a recent World Bank report on Sub-Saharan Africa concluded, "The outlook for Africa is potentially devastating. Yet there are no quick fixes, no simple blueprints."[2]

In the past, the debate on the causes of aggravated underdevelopment in Sub-Saharan Africa centered not so much on governance as on where to put the blame. Were endogenous factors at fault, or was economic interaction between the continent and the global economy the critical explanatory variable?[3] Considering the current political and economic events in the region, practical realities have finally arbitrated in favor of giving priority to domestic reforms, with an emphasis on durable and accountable governments and the reintroduction of liberal, market-oriented development policies.

Notwithstanding the uneasy consensus on these recent internal policy reforms, the impact of contemporary international economic changes on African development cannot credibly be discounted. This is primarily because African economies are generally small and highly dependent on foreign aid and trade. Particularly in the conceptualization and funding of the

---

[1] World Bank, *World Development Report, 1990* (New York: Oxford University Press, 1990), p. 2. The report defines poverty as "the inability to attain a minimal living standard . . . calculated on consumption-based poverty measures supplemented with others such as nutrition, life expectancy, under-five mortality, and school enrollment rates" (p. 26).

[2] World Bank, *Sub-Saharan Africa: From Crisis to Sustainable Growth* (Washington, D.C.: International Bank for Reconstruction and Development, 1989), p. 185.

[3] For a valiant attempt to cover this ground, see M. Crawford Young, *Ideology and Development in Africa* (New Haven, Conn.: Yale University Press, 1982).

most important economic policies, external donors and international financial institutions, notably the World Bank and the IMF, play a domineering role. In addition the continent is consistently buffeted by the forces of international commodity trade, erratic global capital flows, external indebtedness, and boom-and-bust cycles originating from the industrialized economies. As African policy makers continue to grapple with severe domestic problems, they cannot ignore the intrusive impact of external forces, despite the region's increasingly peripheral position in the international political economy.

This chapter concentrates on the emerging matrix of international forces and their impact on economic and social progress in Africa. After sketching the historical and contemporary realities behind the marginality of Sub-Saharan Africa in the world economy, it deals with the factors in the new international development regime that have affected Africa most. It then analyzes the policy initiatives African governments have chosen in response to the reconstitution of the global political and economic agenda after the cold war. After commenting on the efficacy of these policies, it then makes some propositions on the most appropriate African responses to domestic and international challenges in national governance, aid, trade, and development.

Origins and dimensions of the crisis

Sub-Saharan Africa is made up of 46 countries with different historical and economic characteristics. The overlay of British, French, Belgian, or Portuguese colonialism is not difficult to detect even in the most anticolonial and revolutionary nations. Like elsewhere in the world, there are disgraced (and sometimes repentant) ex-socialist regimes whose successors are busy retracing the steps back to market-driven economies. Angola, Ethiopia, Guinea-Conakry, Tanzania, and Mozambique are prime examples. And there are free-enterprisers – like the business interests in Ghana, Kenya, Zimbabwe, and South Africa – who feel fully vindicated by the turn of events in Eastern Europe after 1989.

The population size of these countries varies from that of Nigeria (80 million) to the Seychelles (100,000), while per capita GNP in 1992 ranged from Botswana's $2,790 to an estimated $60 for Mozambique. While some countries like Botswana, Mauritius, and Cameroon have weathered the development crisis that has engulfed the region, other national economies –

Zaire, Sudan, Zambia, Ethiopia, Chad, Madagascar, Guinea-Conakry, Benin – have been pulverized by decades of economic mismanagement, perverse dirigiste development policies, and the venality of autocratic governing classes. Some countries like Ivory Coast, Kenya (until recently), Tanzania, Senegal, and Zambia had escaped destabilizing internal conflicts and enjoyed long periods of political stability and sporadic bursts of rapid growth, while at the moment Liberia, Rwanda, Somalia, Southern Sudan, Angola, and Sierra Leone are torn in near-Hobbesian domestic warfare "of every man against every man, and life is solitary, nasty, brutish and short." In these countries, it makes little sense to talk of national economies, let alone their linkages to the global economic concerns in any formal sense.

The economic prospects for Sub-Saharan Africa were not always so bleak. Independence in the early 1960s brought renewed hope and political exuberance on a mass scale. These expectations were generally matched by modest growth in per capita income until the mid-1970s. Between 1967 and the onset of the 1974 oil crisis, African economies benefited from rising commodity prices and increased investment from export earnings, modest external commercial borrowing, and official development assistance. In line with the development orthodoxy of the day, most governments – with donor assistance – introduced five-year comprehensive development plans and regulated exchange rates, domestic prices, and credit in order to strengthen import-substitution industrialization. The average annual per capita growth rate between 1965 and 1973 was 2.9 percent, which was not far below the overall figure for low-income countries of 3.3 percent. It has not exceeded that level since. From the mid-1970s, this trend yielded to a combination of adverse external and domestic factors, leading to a phase of economic stagnation (1973–80), which deteriorated into a secular decline in the average standard of living that still continues.

Explanations differ on the underlying reasons behind this saddening trend. In one of the first major attempts to get to the root of the problem, at the urging of African finance ministers, the World Bank commissioned a landmark but controversial 1981 study, entitled *Accelerated Development in Sub-Saharan Africa* (the Berg report).[4] Its diagnosis focused sharply on "domestic policy inadequacies" and particularly the neglect of agriculture, overvalued exchange rates, price controls, industrial protectionism, poor

---

[4] World Bank, *Accelerated Development in Sub-Saharan Africa: An Agenda for Action* (Washington, D.C.: International Bank for Reconstruction and Development, 1981).

investment choice, and excessive state intervention in the economy. In preparing his case, Professor Elliot J. Berg had not bargained for the torrent of heated counterarguments that the report provoked from Africa.

Based essentially on the perverse consequences of the global economy, these criticisms stressed the crash in primary commodity prices after 1979, adverse terms of trade, falling foreign investment, and a rising external debt burden. Doubts were also expressed about whether "getting prices right" was as important as deep-seated structural reforms, such as diversifying from monoculture, reducing export dependence and foreign monopolies, and lowering military spending. The Nigerian economist Bade Onimode has provided one of the most comprehensive statements of that position.[5] And as Malawi's Thandika Mkandawire has more recently argued, the case for liberal economic reforms in Africa is erected on contestable factual premises, and it will continue to be opposed as long as it subverts the African nationalist agenda in support of an indigenous capitalist class.[6]

Inspired by these structural arguments and the desire for homemade solutions, the UN Economic Commission for Africa (UNECA), based in Addis Ababa, took the lead in promoting the case for a global rescue plan for African economies at the UN General Assembly in 1986. Unimpressed by the World Bank and IMF approach, UNECA produced its "alternative policy framework" for responding to African development needs.[7] Although it provided empirical data demonstrating that economic liberalization of the sort advocated by the Berg report had generally not reversed the cycle of decline, it was short on concrete short-term alternatives, taking refuge in the human dimensions of adjustment and broad long-term structural changes that were required for Sub-Saharan Africa to emerge as a regionally integrated and modern industrial economy.

Perhaps in recognition of the necessity of public institutional reforms and acute human resource needs in Africa, the World Bank in 1989 published a detailed perspective study on the region that conceded these factors and included the first explicit references by the Bank to the need for better governance in Africa. But it remained uncompromising on the immediate relevance of macroeconomic stabilization and market-based economic re-

---

[5] Bade Onimode, *A Political Economy of the African Crisis* (London: Zed Books, 1988).
[6] Thandika Mkandawire, "Crisis and Adjustment in Sub-Saharan Africa," in Dahram Ghai (ed.), *IMF and the South* (London: Zed Books, 1991), pp. 80–94.
[7] UNECA, *African Alternative Framework to Structural Adjustment Programs for Socio-Economic Recovery and Transformation* (Addis Ababa: UNECA, 1988).

forms.[8] In the meantime, economic and political conditions continued to deteriorate, and those national governments that are still functional, together with their international collaborators, are reformulating development strategies to suit their particular circumstances.

The optimal long-term development policy options for African states may in fact be more country-specific than the African development crisis debate suggests. The truth is that generalizations about economic conditions in Sub-Saharan Africa hide a great deal of intercountry variation and should be approached with considerable circumspection. Table 10.1 categorizes Sub-Saharan African countries by level of income and economic performance.

As is evident from this list of 30 countries representing 80 percent of the Sub-Saharan population, only 3 countries – Botswana, Lesotho, and Mauritius – managed a per capita growth record over 3 percent during the 1970–90 period. All have small populations, and they have also enjoyed relatively long periods of political stability. Lesotho and Botswana, it is significant to note, share a common market with South Africa, the largest and most diversified economy in Africa. Botswana's spectacular growth record owes much to diamond production and prudent macroeconomic management, while Mauritius, an Indian Ocean island economy, is the only country in Africa to have broken into comparative prosperity through the export of textiles and other light manufactures. Other strong performers include Congo and Cameroon, which are beneficiaries of oil production and (in the case of the latter) steady agricultural productivity.

Although a number of middle-sized states – Kenya, Ivory Coast, Malawi, Rwanda – managed moderate growth records throughout the 1970s on the basis of export-led agriculture and relatively liberal domestic economic policies, over the recent past, they have succumbed to severe economic mismanagement, political instability, and adverse external conditions. These four countries are also classic cases of how presidential authoritarianism in Africa breeds corruption and institutional decay, together with perverse development policies, which can destroy the benefits of growth accumulated over the years.

This leaves the vast majority of Sub-Saharan countries, among them Nigeria with a fourth of the regional population, facing economic stagnation

---

[8] World Bank, *Sub-Saharan Africa: From Crisis to Sustainable Growth*, pp. 37–62.

or continuous decline in average personal income levels. Most of these countries are victims of ill-advised experimental economic policies (such as socialism in Madagascar, Zambia, Ethiopia, Tanzania, and Mozambique) or rapacious leaders and governing elites as in Nigeria, Ghana, and Zaire. The worst performers – like Uganda, Sudan, Chad, and Angola – have combined those faults with prolonged civil wars with devastating effects on national populations that involve a loss not just in real income, but also in millions of lives.

The declining per capita income statistics from Africa are accompanied by a wide set of deteriorating sectoral indicators. African agriculture, in particular, has been the Achilles' heel of the continent's development. The commonplace caveat is that the Green Revolution bypassed Sub-Saharan Africa on its way to Asia and Latin America. Agriculture accounts for nearly 70 percent of the African labor force, 40 percent of the exports, and 33 percent of the region's GDP. While in the 1960s, agriculture growth rates at 2.7 percent per year matched the population growth rate, the sector's expansion subsequently slowed down to 1.3 percent between 1970 and 1987.[9]

African agriculture is predominantly a rain-fed smallholder variety, so persistent drought explains part of the decline, which manifested itself in food shortages and the widely publicized famines in the Sahel in 1973, southern Africa in 1992, and Ethiopia in 1984 and 1994. But considerable blame must also be assigned to human causes: state-authored agricultural pricing policies that favored consumers and penalized producers, poor credit facilities, corrupt and inefficient marketing boards, overvalued exchange rates, high taxes on farmers, neglect of rural infrastructure, and inadequate agricultural research and extension services.

In addition, the perils of African export crops have sometimes been blamed on unfavorable terms of trade, and there is some truth in that argument. Overall terms of trade fell by 30 percent between 1985 and 1991, but the most precipitous decline (42 percent) involved petroleum exporters. It has not been established, however, that Sub-Saharan Africa as a whole suffered more severely from terms of trade than other developing regions.[10] The immediate cause for Africa's falling external earnings is its declining

[9] Ibid., pp. 224, 244.
[10] Tony Killick, "The Essence of Africa's Development Experiences," *Africa Forum* 2, 2 (1992), 30–5.

Table 10.1. *Economic indicators, Sub-Saharan Africa, 1970–90*

Country	1990			Real GDP per capita, annual increase (percent)			Merchandise exports, annual increase (percent)			Inflation, annual rate (percent)
	GDP ($ billions)	Population (millions)	GDP per capita (dollars)	1970–80	1980–90	1970–90	1970–80	1980–90	1970–90	1980–90
Poor	41.0	46.0	891	2.0	-0.7	0.6	19.3	3.5	11.1	6.0
Mauritius	2.5	1.1	2,288	3.7	4.7	4.2	20.0	10.5	15.2	9.0
Botswana	2.7	1.3	2,156	10.9	7.0	8.9	5.6	12.4	11.1	0.4
Congo	2.9	2.3	1,261	3.9	1.4	2.7	31.7	5.3	23.4	3.0
Cameroon	11.1	11.9	932	4.6	-0.9	1.8	20.6	3.0	17.8	5.5
Ivory Coast	9.9	12.2	812	1.8	-3.5	-0.9	19.7	-1.0	11.4	1.5
Senegal	5.8	7.4	786	-1.1	0.1	-0.5	10.3	7.2	8.9	6.3
Zimbabwe	6.1	9.8	619	-0.2	0.2	0.0	14.6	1.2	8.7	11.8
Poorer	68.6	203.8	336	1.7	-1.3	0.2	25.5	-5.2	9.1	17.4
Mauritania	1.1	2.0	534	-1.1	-0.8	-0.9	7.3	8.2	7.7	8.3
Zambia	3.7	8.1	455	-1.5	-2.5	-2.0	21.5	-1.5	1.4	43.6
Togo	1.6	3.6	446	1.8	-2.5	-0.4	13.0	-1.8	9.2	5.3
Benin	2.0	4.7	431	0.0	-1.1	-0.6	10.0	4.9	7.9	6.5
Central Afr. Rep.	1.3	3.0	429	-0.6	-1.2	-0.9	4.5	0.3	6.4	6.2
Ghana	6.3	14.9	422	-1.8	-1.1	-1.4	16.0	-2.3	3.6	44.1
Kenya	8.8	24.4	359	4.2	0.3	2.2	20.6	-2.2	6.5	9.5
Bourkina Faso	3.2	9.0	352	1.3	1.2	1.3	11.0	6.6	13.4	5.1

Niger	2.5	7.7	329	-0.9	-4.1	-2.5	28.6	-5.9	10.0	3.5
Lesotho	0.5	1.8	307	6.2	1.5	3.8	25.5	-0.2	11.9	12.5
Nigeria	35.5	117.5	302	2.2	-1.6	0.3	35.4	-6.4	12.6	17.9
Rwanda	2.1	7.1	300	1.5	-2.1	-0.3	18.6	-2.0	7.8	3.8
Poorest	30.9	178.8	173	-0.7	-0.7	-0.7	10.5	-1.0	4.6	30.9
Mali	2.5	8.5	290	2.1	1.2	1.7	20.1	5.4	12.5	2.9
Madagascar	3.1	11.6	267	-1.5	-2.3	-1.9	11.6	-3.6	3.7	17.8
Malawi	1.9	8.5	219	3.1	-0.9	1.1	16.9	2.1	9.2	14.8
Sierra Leone	0.9	4.1	217	-0.4	-0.8	-0.6	7.9	-4.0	1.8	51.6
Zaire	7.5	35.6	212	-2.4	-1.8	-2.1	10.5	-0.6	5.0	61.2
Burundi	1.1	5.5	201	3.8	1.5	2.6	11.0	0.9	5.6	4.0
Uganda	3.5	17.4	199	-5.0	0.7	-2.2	6.0	-5.3	-1.7	97.9
Chad	1.1	5.7	194	-4.1	2.5	-0.9	2.0	10.4	8.1	1.8
Somalia	0.9	6.3	144	1.0	-1.2	-0.1	14.1	-7.9	3.2	55.6
Ethiopia	6.0	51.2	118	0.2	-1.3	-0.5	15.7	-3.1	5.2	2.1
Tanzania	2.4	24.5	98	0.4	-0.2	0.1	9.0	-2.5	3.1	23.7
Total	140.4	140.6	328	0.7	-1.0	-0.1	21.3	-2.5	8.7	21.8

Source: World Bank, *World Tables, 1992.*

market share. Between 1970 and 1984, Africa's world market share for its three main agricultural exports – coffee, tea, and cotton – shrank by 13, 33, and 29 percent, respectively.[11] The reasons behind these dramatic falls lie in the factors cited earlier, notably mismanagement, political instability, and drought. The slack in global supply of these commodities – including others like vegetable oils and cloves – was taken up by countries in Asia and Latin America.

In the industrial sector, Sub-Saharan African also put up a disappointing performance. In one of the many ironies arising from the multiple efforts of the UN specialized agencies to promote economic development in Africa, the UN Industrial Development Organization (UNIDO), at the urging of the UN General Assembly, declared the 1980s the "Industrial Development Decade for Africa" (IDDA). In a complex international program predicated on interstate planning by African ministries of industry and various UN agencies, IDDA envisaged some $140 billion in new industrial investment in order to achieve a 1.4 percent share of global industrial production between 1980 and 1990.[12] With emphasis on agroindustrial and basic engineering projects, the program was based on the establishment of a network of African multinational firms that would promote "self-reliant and self-sustaining industrialization."[13]

Notwithstanding IDDA's projections, Sub-Saharan Africa's contribution to global manufacturing value added actually fell to 0.5 percent in 1988. After an encouraging start in the 1960s and early 1970s, when industrial growth rates reached 11 percent on an annual average, African industries fell into a period of declining growth: 0.3 percent annually in 1980–86, 2.7 percent in 1986–89, and –0.2 percent in 1991. With the notable exception of the star manufacturing exporter, Mauritius, and some mineral and oil exporters, the industrial growth rate and manufactured exports made no appreciable progress. For the most part, Africa missed out on the export-led trend now identified with the newly industrialized countries (NICs) of Asia. Mauritius aside, where African countries succeeded in exporting manufactures at all – Ivory Coast, Kenya, and Zimbabwe – these were mostly

---

[11] World Bank, *Sub-Saharan Africa*, p. 19.

[12] UNIDO, *A Programme for the Industrial Development Decade for Africa* (New York: United Nations, 1982).

[13] Ibid., pp. 28–33. The IDDA also included the North African states of Morocco, Tunisia, Algeria, Libya, and Egypt.

destined to traditional neighboring consumers rather than new foreign markets.[14]

The reasons behind Africa's poor industrial progress lie less in declining investment than in falling productivity, resulting from low capacity utilization, constraints in inputs, and poor management practices, often induced by perverse government interference.[15] The rates of return on investment in African states in the 1980s was estimated at 2.5 percent in comparison with 22 percent in South Asia,[16] which further testifies to the rising gap in economic transformation between the Africa region and developing countries previously in similar circumstances or worse.

Not surprisingly, social indicators in Africa also present a depressing picture. For example, Africa's infant mortality rates in 1992 were the highest of any region in the world, at 107 deaths per 1,000 live births, compared with 93 for South Asia at that fatal end of the scale, 4 at the opposite end of the spectrum in Japan, and 7 in Hong Kong, Switzerland, and France. Nonetheless, some African countries within the small group that registered positive economic growth rates, notably Mauritius, Botswana, Kenya, and Zimbabwe, also did well in reducing infant mortality (Table 10.2). As elsewhere, health standards improved with overall development levels. More broadly, there are encouraging indications of success in rural child immunization in the 1980s under the auspices of the UN Children's Fund (UNICEF); some 22 countries are now immunizing 75 percent of their infants.

One reason for the poor social profile is low expenditures in this area. Thus, Africa's mid-1980s per capita public health expenditure amounted to only $7 in comparison with $28 in Latin America and $75 in Asia. In addition, there were (in 1990) 19,690 people per physician on the continent compared with 2,930 for South Asia. This situation is now bound to be aggravated by fiscal cutbacks in health spending mandated by structural adjustment programs in most countries of the region and, even more significantly, by the outbreak of the AIDS pandemic, whose global epicenter is

---

[14] Roger C. Ridell, "Manufacturing in Africa: An Overview," in Roger C. Riddel (ed.), *Manufacturing Africa: Performance and Prospects in Seven Countries in Sub-Saharan Africa* (London: James Currey, 1990), p. 35.

[15] Gerald M. Meier and William F. Steel (eds.), "Overview," in *Industrial Adjustment in Sub-Saharan Africa* (New York: Oxford University Press, 1989), p. 8; World Bank, *Sub-Saharan Africa*, pp. 9–11.

[16] World Bank, *Sub-Saharan Africa*, p. 26.

Table 10.2. Social indicators, Sub-Saharan Africa, 1965–90

Country	Daily calorie supply per capita 1989	Annual growth (percent) 1965–80	Annual growth (percent) 1980–89	Infant mortality (per 1,000 live births) 1990	Annual growth (percent) 1965–80	Annual growth (percent) 1980–90	Primary school enrollment (percentage of eligible age) 1989	Annual growth (percent) 1965–80	Annual growth (percent) 1980–89	Secondary school (percentage of eligible age) 1989	Annual growth (percent) 1965–80	Annual growth (percent) 1980–89
Poor	2,381	0.5	0.1	76	-2.0	-2.6	99	0.6	0.7	29	6.2	6.8
Mauritius	2,887	na	na	20	-4.6	-4.4	103	0.4	-0.5	53	4.2	1.1
Botswana	2,375	na	na	37	-3.8	-5.0	111	2.3	2.1	37	13.9	6.5
Congo	2,590	0.0	1.4	113	-0.2	-0.9	na	2.1	na	na	13.7	na
Cameroon	2,217	1.3	-1.1	88	-2.0	-1.9	101	0.7	-0.3	26	8.9	4.2
Ivory Coast	2,577	1.0	-0.7	91	-2.0	-1.9	na	1.6	na	20	7.2	1.8
Senegal	2,369	0.1	-0.2	80	-2.9	-2.5	58	0.6	3.1	16	2.4	5.4
Zimbabwe	2,299	-1.0	2.8	42	-1.5	-6.4	125	0.3	0.9	52	5.3	16.7
Poorer	2,271	0.8	-0.6	98	-1.9	-1.7	70	5.5	-2.2	20	8.1	1.8
Mauritania	2,685	0.1	3.7	121	-1.5	-1.6	51	6.4	5.0	16	16.6	5.4
Zambia	2,077	-0.1	0.1	74	-1.9	-2.0	95	4.0	0.0	20	6.1	1.8
Togo	2,214	-1.0	0.6	88	-2.2	-2.2	103	5.1	-1.3	22	13.4	-4.4
Benin	2,305	0.8	0.1	111	-1.9	-1.1	65	4.1	0.5	na	11.8	na
Central Afr. Rep.	2,036	0.4	-0.8	98	-1.9	-1.8	64	1.5	-1.0	11	11.3	1.1
Ghana	2,248	0.1	1.5	84	-1.2	-1.6	75	0.0	0.9	39	7.0	0.9
Kenya	2,163	-0.4	0.4	66	-2.0	-2.3	94	4.7	-1.5	23	10.5	2.8

Bourkina Faso	2,288	-0.3	2.8	133	-1.4	-1.5	35	3.1	7.0	7	7.6	9.9
Niger	2,308	1.0	-0.1	128	-1.2	-1.6	28	5.0	2.2	6	9.7	4.6
Lesotho	2,299	1.2	-0.7	93	-1.4	-2.1	110	0.7	0.6	26	10.1	4.8
Nigeria	2,312	1.2	-1.3	98	-2.1	-1.8	70	7.7	-3.7	19	8.1	1.9
Rwanda	1,971	1.6	-2.0	116	-0.3	-1.5	69	1.9	-0.2	7	0.0	14.9
Poorest	1,983	0.0	-0.2	113	-1.2	-1.9	64	3.4	0.9	8	7.2	1.0
Mali	2,314	-0.2	2.4	166	-0.8	-1.1	23	0.8	-1.8	6	13.9	-15.7
Madagascar	2,158	0.1	-1.5	116	-2.5	-1.7	92	5.4	-4.8	19	2.7	5.2
Malawi	2,139	-0.5	0.2	146	-1.1	-1.4	67	2.1	1.2	4	4.7	0.0
Sierra Leone	1,799	0.1	-1.5	146	-1.3	-1.5	53	4.0	0.2	18	6.0	4.6
Zaire	1,991	0.0	-1.0	91	-1.6	-1.9	78	2.0	-2.1	24	10.7	0.5
Burundi	1,932	-0.1	-1.0	68	-1.5	-5.0	71	0.7	10.5	4	7.6	3.2
Uganda	2,153	-1.9	2.3	96	-0.4	-1.6	77	-1.9	4.9	13	1.5	11.2
Chad	1,743	-2.0	-0.2	125	-1.4	-1.7	57	0.2	5.6	7	7.6	9.9
Somalia	1,906	0.9	-0.3	126	-0.8	-1.4	na	6.8	na	na	7.6	na
Ethiopia	1,667	-0.4	-0.4	131	-0.4	-1.6	38	9.5	-1.4	15	12.0	3.5
Tanzania	2,206	0.8	0.8	110	-0.8	-1.0	63	7.4	-4.2	4	4.7	0.0
Total	2,163	0.5	-0.3	102	-1.6	-1.9	71	3.9	-0.7	16	7.6	2.5

Source: World Bank, World Development Report, 1983, 1992.

located in central and eastern Africa. The World Health Organization estimates that at least 10 million African adults – a third of the global total – are infected with the AIDS virus. Since it is the better educated, urbanized, and most economically productive sections of the population that are affected in Africa, the long-term growth consequences of AIDS cannot be overstated. Despite this gloom, some countries like Uganda have launched effective AIDS public education programs, and AIDS awareness in the region is near total.

These problems in the health sector are unfortunately replicated in the field of education. Although primary and secondary school enrollment made phenomenal gains after independence, there is growing evidence of deterioration in quality due to poor school infrastructure and declining real budgets in education. Comprehensive statistics are not yet available, but there is evidence of a decline in regional primary school enrollment from 78 percent in 1980 to 72 percent in 1990.[17] Although again there are significant exceptions to this trend among the better economic performers, similar disquieting developments have been observed in secondary education, and there are now ample indications of degeneration in standards of university education in all parts of the region.[18] Furthermore, at all three levels of formal education – primary, secondary, and university – women continue to be proportionately underrepresented, despite growing statistical evidence that investment in women yields higher rates of private and social returns than most competing development project alternatives.[19] (For comparative statistics on health and education levels among African countries, see Table 10.2.)

All considered, the diminution of human capability resulting from the degradation in health, education, and skills amounts to the single most enduring handicap to the continent's long-term economic recovery. For in the light of current theories of economic growth, expounded most explicitly by Paul Romer and Robert Lucas, the strongest and most sustained prospects for national productivity growth are premised on positive rates of change in human capital combined with steady augmentation of physical assets.[20]

---

[17] Global Coalition for Africa, *1993 Annual Report* (Washington, D.C., 1992), p. 78.
[18] William Saint, *Universities in Africa: Strategies for Stabilization and Revitalization,* Technical Paper No. 194 (Washington, D.C.: World Bank, 1992).
[19] World Bank, *World Development Report, 1991,* p. 55.
[20] Paul Romer, "Increasing Returns and Long-Run Growth," *Journal of Political Economy* 94, 5 (October 1986), 1002–37, and Robert E. Lucas Jr., "On the Mechanics of Economic Development," *Journal of Monetary Economics* 80, 2 (June 1988), 3–42.

Exacerbating all of the problems discussed, economic as well as social, is the increase in population, which cuts across policy initiatives country-wide and regionally. While population growth rates have been falling in Asia and Latin America since the early 1970s, those of Africa continued to soar at a historic high of 3.1 percent a year in the past decade. The total Sub-Saharan population is expected to rise from 490 million in 1991 to 611 million in the year 2000. One need only juxtapose this grim demographic reality with the decrease in economic growth to appreciate the nightmarish scenario in store for the region, unless decisive remedial progress is made on one or both fronts.

Fortunately, recent information suggests that fertility decline is now an established reality, beginning with Mauritius in the 1970s, Botswana, and Cameroon in the early 1980s, and Kenya, Zimbabwe, Ivory Coast, and Nigeria in the late 1980s. Not surprisingly, most of these countries are the same ones that have demonstrated superiority in economic growth. Once development gets going, it eliminates more than poverty. This gives ground for the optimism that notwithstanding the depressing conditions on the African continent, not only are solutions available, but a critical number may have appeared on the scene already – a lesson that African experts and international donors should never lose sight of.

To conclude this overview of contemporary developments in Sub-Saharan Africa, we must return to the crucial issue of governance. Political instability and mismanagement are the best predictors of economic regress in Africa. The number of countries afflicted with debilitating governance crises among the poor economic performers in Africa, and even among medium and better performers, speaks to the obvious need to introduce effective political reforms in order to provide a hospitable medium for African economic recovery. Indeed, efficient and legitimate governance is the organizational bedrock of any economic reforms, and its absence ex-plains much of the intercountry variation in development performance. For that reason, resurgent popular demands for democratic government since 1990, in the name of a "second independence," may be the best news out of Africa for a long time. Although so far only eight authoritarian governments have been voted out in multiparty elections – Cape Verde, São Tomé and Principe, Benin, Lesotho, Niger, Central African Republic, Malawi, and Zambia – the popular tumult has shaken out concessions from such pre-viously unassailable tyrants as Mobutu of Zaire, Moi in Kenya, and Eyadema in Togo. To these good tidings, one must add peaceful accords terminating civil war in Ethiopia in 1991, Mozambique in 1992, and Angola in 1994, as well as reconciliation and the establishment of democratic administrations in South Africa and Mozambique. These positive changes, however, cannot make up for the resumption of war in Angola after the September 1992 elections, the abrogation of June 1993 democratic elections in Nigeria, the Somalian and Rwandan disasters, and continuing civic violence in such key states as Sudan, Liberia, Sierra Leone, and Zaire. Even once-promising nations like Senegal, Kenya, Nigeria, Ivory Coast, and Zimbabwe are either tottering on the brink of political disaster or demonstrating a lack of resolve in formulating stable and accountable governance systems.

The controversial human freedom index adopted by the UN Development Program lists only two African states – Botswana and Senegal – above the international mean.[21] Although there are exceptions like Kenya, Ivory Coast, and Malawi in the 1960s and 1970s, there is ample evidence that incumbent one-party regimes in Africa have squandered opportunities for promoting growth. There is as yet no evidence that democratic governance will do better, but most bilateral donors and the World Bank have argued strongly in favor of uncorrupted, efficient, and accountable governance as a correlate of renewed growth.

Looking at the tenuous statistical relationship between growth and democracy in Africa, as well as the abundant evidence of spectacular economic growth under authoritarian governments in the Asian NICs, Chile under Pinochet, and Brazil under the military, it may be unrealistic to place too much stress on the link between democracy and Africa's economic recovery. For the purposes of economic development, what Sub-Saharan Africa really needs is the replacement of current administrative chaos, managerial incompetence, and corruption with efficient and reliable governance structures. This has been the advice of Singapore's Lee Kwan Yew to several groups of African leaders. The case for African democracy rests on entirely different premises: after the collapse of communism and colonialism, popularly elected governance and the rule of law ought to be demanded as human values in their own right, irrespective of whether they promote economic growth.

---

[21] UNDP, *Human Development Report, 1991* (New York: Oxford University Press, 1991), p. 20.

International impact on African development

Instances of human disaster like those in Africa invite two opposing social impulses: the inclination to flee (or exit) and the determination to stay on and salvage the situation by articulating or taking ameliorative action.[22] Within Africa, the respective alternatives are symbolized by the continent's record refugee population (estimated at 10 million), as well as the outmigration of 100,000 skilled Africans to the wealthier world, and governments and independent actors who are engaged in the recuperation of African economies.

Among international agencies concerned with Sub-Saharan Africa, a similar dichotomy is to be found among those who have quietly walked away in horror and many others who have remained convinced that, with hard work, solutions can be found.[23] The latter include numerous relief agencies and nongovernmental organizations, as well as multilateral and bilateral donors from the OECD countries. In the past decade, none of these had a greater impact on African development than the Bretton Woods institutions – the World Bank and the IMF. This section begins with a discussion of these two agencies before proceeding to the impact of bilateral donors (principally the United States, the EU countries, and Scandinavia), the global trading system, Africa's external creditors, and the ex-communist world.

The World Bank and the IMF: economic policy reform

If the World Bank and the IMF have earned themselves undue criticism and resentment in Africa over the past decade, it is primarily because they have taken initiatives in the formulation, financing, and implementation of socially painful economic liberalization programs in a frontal effort to meet the onerous development problems discussed earlier. The two institutions

---

[22] The most nuanced rendition of this phenomenon, of course, is Albert O. Hirschman, *Exit, Voice and Loyalty: Responses to Decline in Firms, Organizations and States* (Cambridge, Mass.: Harvard University Press, 1970).

[23] A good example of "exit" at the international level is the following newspaper report on a high-level UN meeting in September 1991 to deliberate on African development: "It is the first time in five years the world has sat down to talk about Africa, and the reports are anything but encouraging . . . (but) . . . there is little enthusiasm for Africa's problems. In the meeting room, empty chairs from every region offer testimony of how little the rest of the world cares" (*Toronto Globe and Mail,* September 14, 1991).

now set the pace for most bilateral lending. While the IMF has concentrated its efforts on short-term balance-of-payments support, contingent on specific market-based sectoral and policy reforms, the World Bank seems to have staked its reputation on successful long-term African recovery on its own terms. "Our institutional fate is at stake here," said the Bank's vice-president for Africa, Edward Jaycox. "If we fail in Africa, our fundamental *raison d'être* can be questioned."[24]

In 1992, IMF gross lending to Sub-Saharan Africa was $527 million, down from $1 billion in 1988. This decline is the result of difficulties the borrowing countries had in complying with IMF loan conditions. These states include those that lack effective governance; hence, in 1995, volatile Sierra Leone, Cameroon, Somalia, Sudan, Zaire, and tranquil Zambia had overdue obligations. Still, in 1992, the IMF had 27 Structural Adjustment Facility arrangements in Sub-Saharan Africa, 15 Enhanced Structural Adjustment Facility arrangements, 5 standbys, and 1 Extended Fund Facility arrangement. Their effectiveness was mixed at best. Moreover, because the IMF has become a net recipient of resources from Africa, as debt service exceeds new loans, it is viewed with suspicion even by the most cooperative governments.

The World Bank, in contrast, has attempted to win the confidence of African policy makers as demonstrated in its 1989 long-term perspective study, which, as we have seen, took account of its African critics. The 1992 disbursements by the main members of the World Bank Group (the International Bank for Reconstruction and Development [IBRD] and the International Development Association [IDA]) amounted to $2.6 billion, down from $2.9 billion in 1990. Like the IMF, the IBRD's net resource transfers from Sub-Saharan Africa were negative (–$1 billion) in 1992, and as a result there was a conscious attempt to increase soft-term IDA lending. In 1992, IDA disbursements amounted to 79 percent of World Bank disbursements in the region, up from 67 percent in 1989.[25]

IDA funding was the largest source of concessional loans to Africa, and it went hand in hand with structural adjustment support, which the Bank argues is an essential component for productive project investment. But as with the IMF, there was growing dissatisfaction with the supply-side re-

---

[24] *Newsweek*, September 16, 1991.
[25] World Bank, *World Debt Tables, 1993–94*.

sponse from the poorest African countries – the stagnating group that requires a turnabout most urgently.

In its most recent evaluation of structural reform in Africa,[26] the Bank studied 26 Sub-Saharan countries. It identified 6 as showing large improvements in macroeconomic policy, 9 as showing small improvements, and 11 as deteriorating. Comparing various measures of economic performance in 1981–86 and 1987–91, its data show a positive relation between reform and outcome during the two periods. That is, the strong reformers performed best, the moderate reformers next best, while those countries that did not reform performed worst, generally with negative growth. Touching on governance, the Bank concludes that "most African countries still lack policies that are sound by international standards" (p. 8).

Special effort is recommended on achieving macroeconomic stability (cutting budget deficits and setting realistic exchange rates), encouraging competitiveness (domestic deregulation, trade reform, and privatization), and using scarce institutional capacity wisely. In line with the Bank's reasoning, the 50 percent devaluation of the African (CFA) franc by Francophone states in February 1994 was by 1995 already producing a positive supply response among farming and pastoralist communities of West Africa. At an average of 26 percent, the resulting inflation rates were not as high as initially feared.

Bilateral donors: the link between aid and democratic governance

By eliminating East–West competition in Africa, the end of the cold war has made it unnecessary for Western states to sustain African clients on the basis of sheer loyalty, avoiding embarrassing questions about internal repression, corruption, and the abuse of human rights. At the same time, the new context has strengthened the advocates of democracy, human rights, and the rule of law inside Africa and elsewhere. The Eastern European revolutions, after all, vindicated the doctrine of liberal democracy, which was celebrated by Francis Fukuyama as the "end of history."[27] All these events conspired to derail old patron–client networks in external aid policy

---

[26] World Bank, *Adjustment in Africa: Reforms, Results, and the Road Ahead* (New York: Oxford University Press, 1994).

[27] Francis Fukuyama, "The End of History?" *National Interest* 16 (Summer 1989), 3–18.

and (as discussed in Chapter 5, this volume) to introduce accountable governance, the rule of law, and respect for civil liberties as new criteria of eligibility for development assistance.

France, which has consistently been the leading source of official development assistance to Africa, used the opportunity of the Francophone summit at La Baule in 1990 to warn that it would henceforth be "more lukewarm" to countries that do not observe democratic principles.[28] And although French gendarmes in Africa have not intervened to support beleaguered democrats in Togo or Congo, they have not moved to protect France's favorite dictators as unabashedly as they once did. Almost simultaneously with the French decision, Britain's foreign secretary, Douglas Hurd, announced in June 1990 that his country's external aid would henceforth be restricted to countries that observe democratic practice and human rights. At the end of that year, the U.S. Agency for International Development (USAID) produced a "Democracy Initiative," linking aid to individual liberty. By November 1991, the head of USAID's Africa Bureau, Scott M. Spangler, informed Congress that "the highest priority on limited U.S. aid for Africa would be given to democratic and honest governments."[29] In the same month, the EC external aid ministers announced similar measures. In an unprecedented move, the World Bank produced a turgid, belabored paper on governance and development.[30] It skirted the issue of democracy and laid emphasis on competent management of development programs by public institutions, indicating that political liberalization might assist that process.

As expected, skeptical pro-democracy lobbies in the West and in Africa waited for a chance to put the policy to test. This came in November 1991 when the Kenyan government – a favorite recipient of Western aid and private capital – engaged in yet another of its many brutal crackdowns against peaceful opposition meetings. The Kenya government's record on internal repression and violation of human rights had already been extensively publicized, and the opposition used the opportunity to put the donors on the defensive. On November 25, 1991, the Consultative Donors Meeting in Paris delayed additional aid pledges to Kenya for six months, pending "social and economic reforms." Meanwhile Sweden cut part of its aid to Tanzania, its leading development finance recipient, demanding an end to

---

28 *Newsweek,* July 30, 1990.
29 Quoted in *Daily Nation* (Nairobi), November 14, 1991.
30 Ismail Serageldin and Pierre Landell-Mills, *Governance and the External Factor* (Washington, D.C.: World Bank, 1991).

corruption and enhanced political accountability. The United States and Belgium thereafter cut off official development assistance to Zaire on human rights grounds. Western bilateral donors have since given the same treatment to despotic regimes in Malawi, Togo, and Cameroon. Program aid was not restored to Kenya and Malawi until late 1993, after both governments had permitted considerable political liberalization.

Despite the emerging consensus on the linkage between official development finance and democracy, there were strong differences between and within governments. In the United States, for instance, Congress discontinued aid to Zaire against opposition from the Bush administration. Britain was a reluctant participant on the demarche against the Moi government in Kenya, which Whitehall continued to support, and France has not withheld development aid from Cameroon or Kenya. Indeed, by 1995 Paris had upgraded its relations with autocratic regimes like Zaire and Togo. Among the European donors, Germany has been the most consistent in applying the democracy criteria in its aid programs.

Furthermore, skepticism within donor countries has increasingly been fueled by the incapacity of African opposition parties to rally around forward-looking reformist political and economic strategies for replacing erstwhile dictators. The lethal factionalism of the previously antidespotic movements in Somalia and Liberia are exaggerated forms of this phenomenon, but neither have democratic opposition movements in Kenya, Malawi, Zaire, Togo, Tanzania, Zambia, Nigeria, and Cameroon inspired confidence as credible alternatives. The retreat from Africa by the old cold war patrons – the United States and the former Soviet Union – may have therefore unleashed internally disruptive rather than democratic politics. And the use of aid as a catalyst for democracy may prove less potent than policy makers assumed in the euphoric days following the demise of European communism.

Changes in the global trading system

One of the most adverse changes Sub-Saharan Africa has encountered in its trade relations was the already-mentioned precipitous drop in prices of its export commodities in the 1980s. Although there is agreement among concerned international agencies about this basic fact, there are also strong differences about the magnitude of swings in the terms of trade, and hence on their impact in African development. This, in turn, translated into policy differences on what ought to be done to alleviate their effect.

In making the case for more aid to Africa, UN agencies argued that the terms of trade for African nonoil commodities fell by 35 percent between 1980 and 1990. This cost Africa some $50 billion between 1986 and 1990.[31] By this yardstick, Africa was worse off than other developing regions. Since the compensation mechanisms for such losses under the STABEX system of the European Community or the IMF's Compensatory and Contingency Financing Facility were inadequate, the United Nations argued that there was a case for an export diversification fund for Africa. This is also the position of the Organization of African Unity.

Using 1961 as the base year, however, the World Bank reckons that although African terms of trade dipped to their lowest level in 1986 and 1987, they were still higher in the first half of the 1980s than in the 1960s.[32] The post-1985 income losses could therefore be offset by earlier gains. In any case, other regions – including South Asia – have coped better with more adverse terms of trade, principally because of lower population growth and higher GDP growth. The policy implications of this perspective as opposed to that of the United Nations are clear: give priority to domestic policy reforms rather than commodity income stabilization programs.

While the issue of worsening terms of trade has excited African states, they have not given sufficient attention to two imminent historical changes in the international trading system that have far-reaching economic implications for them. These are the creation of the Single European Market and the Uruguay Round of the GATT that was concluded in December 1993.

For historical reasons, the European Union is the Sub-Sahara's leading external trading partner. The creation of a unified internal market in Europe, combined with probable agreements on textile and agricultural imports to Europe, will likely wipe out most of the preferences accorded to Sub-Saharan Africa under the successive Lomé Conventions between Europe and its former colonies.[33]

---

[31] UN Secretariat, *Economic Crisis in Africa: Final Review and Appraisal of the UN Programme of Action for African Recovery and Development 1986–1990* (New York: United Nations, 1991), pp. 17–18.

[32] World Bank, *Sub-Saharan Africa*, pp. 24–25.

[33] For a detailed account of the Lomé Convention, consult John Ravenhill, *Collective Clientelism: The Lomé Convention and North–South Relations* (New York: Columbia University Press, 1985).

Although there are chances that the Lomé Treaty, with its preferential treatment of African exports to Europe, will be renewed yet again in 1995, there is little evidence that its regime of trade favors will offset the advantages the East Asian NICs enjoy by dint of sheer competitiveness. In a recent study on the Single European Market and the developing countries, Michael Davenport and Sheila Page have estimated that the value of trade diverted from the latter will exceed that created within Europe under uniform European tariffs.[34] For Sub-Saharan Africa specifically, primary commodity producers will compete with each other and with non-African developing-country suppliers. In general, African manufactured exports (particularly textiles) will be at an even greater disadvantage than they are now, especially if the Multifiber Arrangement (MFA) is gradually phased out as specified in the Uruguay Round agreement. The impact on African agricultural goods is mixed, and the more diversified exporters – Ivory Coast, Kenya, and Zimbabwe – will have better market prospects than their poorer monoculture neighbors.[35] Just as there is increasing trade-driven differentiation across third world regions, future European–African trade may increase income differences among African states, and the beneficiaries are likely to be economies that have performed better in the past.

With regard to the implementation of the Uruguay Round, available research is less equivocal. Of all the developing regions, Africa stands to gain the least, again because it has diversified less into commodities scheduled for enhanced trade liberalization.[36] With the exception of fruit, tobacco, and textiles, which face high tariffs in developed markets, Sub-Saharan exports are predominantly raw materials and beverages, which face relatively low barriers because of the preference accorded to them under the Lomé Convention and the Generalized System of Preferences. Asian countries – and the East Asian NICs first and foremost – stand to benefit most from the abolition of the MFA, while the larger and richer Latin American countries – Argentina and Brazil – would gain the most from a freer agricultural trading system. As net food importers from Europe, African nations are likely to suffer a further decline in terms of trade following the proposed cuts in food exports under the Uruguay Round, a loss esti-

---

[34] Michael Davenport with Sheila Page, *Europe: 1992 and the Developing World* (London: Overseas Development Institute, 1991), p. 7.

[35] Ibid., pp. 10–11, 63, 84–94.

[36] Sheila Page with Michael Davenport and Adrian Hewitt, *The GATT Uruguay Round: Effects on Developing Countries* (London: Overseas Development Institute, 1991).

mated at $2.6 billion. If anything, these developments will reinforce Africa's global marginality, but their ominous prophecy must always be balanced against the probability that such a loss could be turned into a gain if current trade liberalization policies in Africa trigger higher domestic productivity, as they had by 1995 among farmers and beef producers in West Africa.

External debt and debt-relief efforts

In aggregate terms, the total long-term external debt of Sub-Saharan Africa's 46 countries is much less than that owed by other developing areas. It was $155 billion in 1992 compared with a $99 billion total external debt in the same year for Brazil alone. Unlike most other developing-country debt, nearly three-quarters of Africa's debt is owed to official bilateral and multilateral creditors rather than private banks. It has also been acquired on softer terms – lower interest rates and longer maturity periods – than the Latin American debt. In addition, it should be remembered that Sub-Saharan nations receive higher grant aid per capita than any other developing area. (For more details, see Chapter 5, this volume.)

Despite these facts, the region faces some of the harshest difficulties in servicing its debt. This is especially the case with the low-income category (i.e., the majority) of African economies with a per capita income of $580 or less. The external debt/GDP ratio for these countries is just short of 100 percent on average, and it is twice that for some countries like Congo, Guinea-Bissau, São Tomé, and Somalia. (Latin American debt by comparison is about 40 percent of GDP.) The debt-service ratio is nearly 20 percent and would have been higher if the full payments had been made as scheduled and if there had been no recent debt cancellation.[37] Against the backdrop of poor export prospects described earlier, the constraint on renewed growth imposed by external indebtedness is not difficult to understand.

Because most of Africa's creditors are Western governments (France, Germany, Britain, and Italy) and international financial institutions (principally the IMF and the World Bank), one would expect easier consensus on lowering the debt burden in order to spur economic growth in Africa. It has not proved to be so. Some European states (France, the Netherlands,

[37] World Bank, *World Debt Tables, 1993–94.*

Britain, the Scandinavian countries), as well as Canada and the United States, have canceled an estimated total of $7.6 billion that was owed by the poorest reforming African economies. The Group of Seven Toronto Summit of June 1988 agreed on a relief program that includes partial write-offs, longer maturity periods, and enhanced concessional rates of interest. All this is subject to a demonstrated capacity to implement corrective economic policies on the part of African governments. Strict adherence to a World Bank–IMF structural adjustment program is the usual proxy for that criterion. Since the Toronto initiative, 20 African states have benefited from the new facility, but this has not reduced the debt burden enough to meet the estimated net resource inflows consistent with a 4–5 percent growth rate.

There has been no subsequent consensus on a debt policy approach to Africa. The Trinidad terms, agreed upon at the Commonwealth Finance Ministers Conference in 1990, propose an immediate two-thirds debt write-off and longer grace repayment periods for the outstanding amount. While Britain has implemented it for keen African economic reformers, the U.S. Treasury has pleaded the need for a special congressional appropriation to cover debt forgiveness. The United States, however, has approved debt relief on a case-by-case basis to credible African reformers. In the meantime, France has announced a "conversion fund" that would allow its West African creditors to transform nearly $1 billion in debt into infrastructural and environmental projects.

In short, each creditor is responding to African debt needs on an ad hoc basis. The World Bank estimates that Sub-Saharan economies will require net resource transfers of $20 billion a year (at 1990 prices) throughout the 1990s to meet their minimum growth needs. This amount would include annual debt relief amounting to $9 billion (on the Toronto terms). So far, the target has yet to be met and it is unlikely to be.

The collapse of communism in Eastern Europe

The height of the cold war rivalry in Africa south of the Sahara probably reached its peak in the open Soviet/Cuban military intervention and U.S. undercover counteraction in Angola's civil war beginning in 1975. Subsequently, the Soviet Union's strongest collaborators in Africa were socialist Angola, Mozambique, and Ethiopia (which took over from Somalia in 1977). Geostrategic and Soviet military priorities underpinned these alliances. Once Mikhail Gorbachev decided on a rapprochement with the West, however, the USSR facilitated peaceful resolution of the Namibian, Angolan, and Ethiopian civil wars, primarily by withdrawing military support from its clients. This was reassuring to the government of South Africa, then seeking a way out of apartheid, and after initial contacts, diplomatic relations between South Africa and Russia were reestablished in April 1992. The rapprochement brought to an end four decades of acrimony between the two countries, during which time the USSR supported the antiapartheid African National Congress. The new-found friendship ushered in new technical cooperation between the two countries in gold mining, diamond marketing, and manufacturing.

The greatest collaboration between the USSR and the African countries with which it had close ties was in the supply of armaments on a loan basis, resulting in massive debts to Moscow. With a $2.9 billion debt, Ethiopia now owes the Russian Republic the most, followed by Angola ($2.0 billion), Mozambique ($809 million), and Somalia ($261 million).[38] Russia's other significant debtors include Tanzania, Mali, and Guinea-Conakry. Given the perilous state of African economies, the chance of recovering these debts is minimal, as the former Soviet republics have realized, and there is unrealistic talk of a debt–food swap.[39]

This is just one aspect of the deteriorating relations between Africa and the former Soviet states. As Fred Halliday explains (Chapter 2, this volume), resentment arising from the belief that African countries were a drain on Soviet resources, and that this must end, runs deep in high official circles and among ordinary citizens in Eastern Europe. African students on Soviet bloc scholarships have been at the receiving end of this.[40] They have also been victims of racist attacks in Russia, the former GDR, and in the Caucasus. Russia and the other republics, however, know they can only go so far in distancing themselves from Africa, where they see prospects of future trade and investment, particularly in the once-derided capitalist "neo-colonies," including Nigeria, Kenya, Ivory Coast, and South Africa. The full nature of these commercial and investment relations remains to be

---

[38] *Africa Analysis* (London), January 10, 1992.

[39] Charles Quist Asade, "Russia to Swap African Debts for Food," *New African* (July 1992), 31–32.

[40] In the face of resurgent racism, the fate of African students in Hungary is described in the *Weekend Gazette* (Harare), April 10, 1992. Such reports came in regularly from the old COMECON countries.

worked out. With the possible exception of South Africa, they are not a priority issue to the continent.

African responses to the new international context of development

Africa's response to these international changes has been of several sorts. First, multilateral diplomacy has been used to try to gain benefits for the region as a whole. Second, regional economic integration has reappeared on the African agenda. Third, individual countries, firms, and citizens have taken the initiative in new approaches to development. A fourth approach, looking to a postapartheid South Africa for assistance as recommended by some observers, does not seem promising.

Multilateral development diplomacy

Over the past two decades, African countries have sought on a collective basis to publicize their economic plight in various international forums. This strategy has not borne much fruit. And, as mentioned earlier, one must always remain alert to the variations in individual country responses to new global realities, because these often contradict joint "African" positions in multilateral negotiations. Take commodity trade, for example. Coffee, cocoa, and tea are among the region's top agricultural exports. The received African position, repeated at the most recent UN Conference on Trade and Development (UNCTAD) meetings in Cartagena, Colombia, in March 1992, is that tropical agricultural commodity producers must receive guaranteed prices (or incomes) to stem the tide of economic deterioration set in motion by rapid downswings in exports earnings, such as those experienced by all tropical beverages since the 1970s. International commodity agreements are another way of arriving at the same end, and African coffee producers have been active lobbyists for the resurrection of the International Coffee Agreement since it collapsed in 1988.

But individual country policies differ. With a 25 percent share of the world's supply of cocoa, the Ivory Coast tried restricting the quantity of its exports in 1979–80 to raise world prices. This is essentially what a buffer stock policy under the International Cocoa Agreement would do. The Ivory Coast failed mightily and incurred the wrath of its donors in subsequent attempts because of its higher producer prices and the storage (and hence fiscal) costs involved.[41] Kenya and Malawi, by contrast, both efficient and high-quality producers of tea, have increased their global share of the product without much recourse to the International Tea Agreement, and Kenya has successfully diversified its agricultural exports through horticulture. In the coffee industry, differences exist between the producers of higher-quality arabicas in East Africa (Kenya and Tanzania) and lower-quality robustas in West Africa and Uganda. When coffee prices paid to African producers doubled between 1991 and 1994, the high-quality producers benefited the most. Thus, beneath the African demand for the resurrection of the International Coffee Agreement, there looms a potential disagreement on quotas in which arabica producers have the upper hand. Overall, each country is likely to pursue a policy that would maximize its own export gains in the long run, even though continent-wide remedial initiatives are likely to remain on the table.

The most common of these strategies now originate from the Organization of African Unity (OAU), whose member states include the North African states of Egypt, Libya, Tunisia, Algeria, and Morocco in addition to Sub-Saharan Africa. The OAU seeks economic redress through multilateral diplomacy, culminating in nonbinding policy documents adopted by the UN General Assembly. The process normally begins with canvassing for an African consensus on a pressing international development issue affecting most of the countries of the region. With the technical support from concerned UN specialized agencies and the UNECA, a program dependent on international donor support is formulated. The OAU ministers and heads of states subsequently debate and adopt it, with or without modification. The document is tabled at the UN General Assembly, and immediate support is urged from the "international community." The UN agencies and African governments then proceed to implement the program, and they await the goodwill of the international community in dollar terms. This is the procedure that was followed in the adoption of the IDDA of the 1980s. As discussed earlier, evidence shows that industrial capacity in Sub-Saharan Africa over the decade took the opposite turn. Nonetheless, neither the OAU nor UNIDO were deterred, and a second Industrial Development Decade was announced in 1990.

---

[41] Mathurin Ghetibouo and Christopher Delgado, "Lessons and Constraints of Export-Led Growth: Cocoa in the Ivory Coast," in I. William Zartman and Christopher Delgado (eds.), *The Political Economy of the Ivory Coast* (New York: Praeger, 1984), pp. 115–47.

Perhaps the most ambitious of such initiatives was the UN General Assembly's adoption of the UN Program of Action for African Economic Recovery and Development (UNPAAERD) in September 1986. At an estimated cost of $128 billion, $82.5 billion of which was to be mobilized in Africa, UNPAAERD was a comprehensive economic recovery program for the continent, covering all major sectors. Like the IDDA, it was intended to promote "self-reliant and self-sustaining" African economies. When the UN Secretariat evaluated it in 1991, it diplomatically concluded that "the goals set in the UNPAAERD are far from being realized."[42] The reasons behind that judgment rested predictably on the weak growth of African economies due to adversities encountered in the world economy and insufficient external aid inflows. Nonetheless, the UN General Assembly proceeded to adopt a "new compact" for African development in the 1990s based on "the political and human solidarity with Africa, to which the General Assembly gave expression in 1986 [within UNPAAERD]."[43] As with the IDDA, a failed strategy was once again adopted uncritically under new terminology.

Regional economic integration

Even before the concept of regional trading blocs became the popular institutions they are today, the UNECA was planning regional common markets for Africa. Such economic integration was seen by UN experts and some African economists as the most expeditious way of expanding the continent's domestic market, given the small size of African economies. There is not much evidence that African political leaders shared this view. The most advanced regional economic grouping on the continent – the East African Community comprising Kenya, Uganda, and Tanzania – collapsed amidst nationalist and ideological acrimony in 1977.

A few regional economic institutions, like the Central African Customs Union and the Dakar-based Central Bank of West Africa, managed to soldier on. On an ad hoc basis, African states and nongovernmental organizations also continued to create regional economic institutions often with overlapping functions with such zeal that by 1989 there were over 200 organizations concerned with regional economic cooperation. The lessons

---

[42] UN Secretariat, *Economic Crisis in Africa,* p. 2.
[43] Ibid., p. 32. This was the session where the *Toronto Globe and Mail* observed widespread indifference to African development issues.

behind failure in regional integration and the multiplication of institutions appear to have gone unlearned.

When the African development crisis set in after the 1970s, the UNECA decided it was time for collaboration with the OAU in organizing economic integration at the continental level, to counteract the impending recession. The Lagos Plan of Action, which arose from those efforts, was adopted by African heads of states and governments in 1980.[44] Much like UN-PAAERD, the Lagos Plan of Action was geared to the modernization of African agriculture, industrialization, and human resource development. The linchpin in its strategy was the creation of an African Economic Community (AEC) by the year 2000. The building blocks towards the AEC were the major regional integration groupings in each of the continent's sub-regions: North Africa, West Africa, central Africa, eastern and southern Africa. A cursory review of these groups at the subregional level would have demonstrated how unrealistic that target was.

In West Africa, the Economic Community of West African States, created in 1975, had by 1992 made little progress in reducing tariff barriers or overcoming the Anglophone and Francophone divide. It also faced strong competition from the Francophone customs union in the region, headquartered in Bourkina Faso, whose trade liberalization program was more advanced. In central Africa, the Union Douanière et Économique de l'Afrique Centrale (UDEAC), with Cameroon as its base, resisted the creation of an UNECA-inspired Central African Economic Community, whose treaty remains little more than a document of good intentions. Nonetheless, the UDEAC began fiscal and customs reforms to establish uniform tariff and tax rates and agreed to harmonize investment codes.

In eastern and southern Africa, the Preferential Trade Area for Eastern and Southern African States (PTA) had made some progress in lowering tariff barriers among its members, but it is now facing stiff competition from the Southern African Development Co-ordination Conference (SADCC), most of whose members also belonged to the PTA. Though created in 1978 to consolidate economic isolation of South Africa by strengthening infrastructure across the African-ruled states neighboring South Africa, SADCC was gradually assuming some customs union characteristics, especially with the imminent end of apartheid. In August 1992, SADCC in fact converted itself by treaty to a regional common market. This brought it into

---

44 OAU, *The Lagos Plan of Action* (Addis Ababa: OAU, 1980).

frontal conflict with the PTA, an issue that remains to be solved. To compli-
cate matters, the PTA converted itself into the Economic Community of
Eastern and Southern Africa in November 1993, without resolving its long-
standing differences with SADCC.

As if these political and organizational problems were not enough, the
Lagos Plan of Action had not bargained for the similarities in structures of
African economies, which – combined with nontariff barriers – severely
hindered regional trade. Recorded intra-African trade is estimated at an
average 5 percent of total African international trade. Particularly for these
reasons, professional assessments indicate that the prospects for regional
integration in Africa are bleak, as one of the most recent studies on the
subject demonstrates.[45]

But since trading blocs in Europe, North America, Latin America, and
Southeast Asia had been planned, it was politically imprudent for Africa to
remain isolated. At the June 1991 summit of the African heads of state in
Abuja, Nigeria, a treaty was signed leading to the creation of an African
Economic Community by the year 2025, thus postponing the old deadline
by a further 25 years. Nothing was said about problems in the existing
economic integration initiatives, much less what had happened to the
deadline of the year 2000 established in 1980. As with the IDDA and
UNPAAERD, the failed objectives were unquestioningly grafted into the
new program. There is little reason to believe that the new deadline stands a
better chance than the previous ones.

Political and economic liberalization at state and popular levels

The recent link between aid and governance has not provoked as much
controversy in Africa as it would have done a decade earlier. The major
reason is that by the time communism collapsed, the incumbent one-party
regimes in Africa had by and large been so highly discredited that it was
thought legitimate and desirable for the new opposition groupings to request
Western donors to distance themselves financially and diplomatically from
dictatorial regimes. This was the case in Kenya, Malawi, Zaire, Cameroon,
Togo, and Madagascar. It is now no longer fashionable to advocate one-
party rule as an institution best suited to African cultural conditions, even in

---

[45] Faezeh Foroutan, "Regional Integration in Sub-Saharan Africa: Past Experience and
Future Prospects," paper presented at World Bank-CEPR Conference on Regional Integration, Washington, D.C., April 2–3, 1992, p. 1.

such once-staunch advocates of this approach as Tanzania. It remains to be seen how the new democracies in such countries as Zambia and Benin will cope with the democracy and human rights conditionalities on external aid, which the parties in power there demanded when they were in opposition.

Although, as mentioned earlier, African governments have grudgingly acquiesced to IMF- and World Bank–sponsored economic reform programs, African citizens have adopted markets as a means of raising personal incomes with much more enthusiasm, particularly after the removal of official restrictions or the collapse of obstructive state authority. The popular regeneration of individual enterprise in Africa could provide yet another avenue to African economic recovery if it is undergirded by the revamped infrastructure, market-supportive planning, internal security, and rule of law, which governance reforms are expected to achieve.

Despite the official harassment to which African small-scale entrepreneurs – the so-called informal sector – have been subjected in the past, their activities are now acknowledged to be more efficient than larger enterprises in generating income and employment. Against the dearth of direct foreign investment that characterizes Africa, it is now estimated that 95 percent of Sub-Saharan labor by the year 2020 will be employed in the smaller business enterprises of this kind. From cities as different as Dakar, Nairobi, and Luanda, the mushrooming of informal markets in the background of the crisis provides living testimony that, given the opportunity, African entrepreneurs would flourish on their own steam.

The prospect of basing an economic turnaround on the informal sector, however, requires a critical reappraisal, given the high social costs of petty unregistered business – urban squatting, high externalities, tax avoidance – which enthusiasts of the informal sector tend to discount. At the same time, there is evidence, again confined to the small group of successful economies, that under appropriate business environment, African medium-scale investors earn identical or better returns than resident foreign private firms.[46] They also tend to generate more jobs per unit of investment than the large multinationals, and they are easier to tax. This provides hope for a vigorous tertiary business sector in the efforts to initiate long-term changes in Africa.

---

[46] Keith Marsden, *African Entrepreneurs,* Discussion Paper, International Finance Corporation, Washington, D.C., 1990.

The role of postapartheid South Africa

Because the Republic of South Africa has the largest and most diversified economy in Africa south of the Sahara, there were expectations inside and outside the region that after dispensing with apartheid in April 1994, South Africa might constitute the economic engine that will pull the rest of the continent out of its current crisis. Comparing South Africa's GDP of $91 billion to $163 billion for the rest of Sub-Saharan Africa in 1990, it is easy to understand the a priori basis of such an assumption. Yet although the South African economy is now poised for greater integration with the rest of the continent, there are internal and regional handicaps that militate against the short- to medium-term realization of such an objective. This is because for all its impressive size, South Africa remains essentially a mineral-export-based economy with a complex but protected and internationally uncompetitive manufacturing sector. In early 1995, the new South African government commenced deregulating its farming and industrial sectors to make them more export oriented. But the absorptive capacity of African states for South African goods and investments will remain limited for some time. As a result, the value of trade between South Africa and the nations outside its captive market in southern Africa – Namibia, Lesotho, Botswana, Swaziland, Zimbabwe – amounted to 9 percent of total South African trade in 1991 and was barely rising.

The weak linkages between the South African economy and its poorer counterparts in the region are also a limiting factor. The role played by gold, diamonds, platinum, and other minerals in the founding of the modern South African economy is well known. These constitute the bulk of the country's export trade, which is directed primarily to the OECD nations. Like all primary producers, South Africa has been buffeted by declining commodity prices and sluggish economic growth since the mid-1980s, which has been aggravated by years of international sanctions and domestic political instability. In the period 1991–92, for example, the South African economy contracted by around 3 percent.

More significantly, the political transition to a nonracial democracy, and the continuing social instability associated with it, have sapped business confidence and curtailed domestic investment just when it is most needed to cater for the economic needs of the African majority: employment, education, housing, health, and infrastructure. Considering the legacy of apartheid, these expenditures must claim priority on domestic savings. Provided the democratic constitutional arrangements produced by the April 1994 elections hold steady, it is likely that a massive economic rehabilitation, involving the private sector, will be undertaken to assuage the legitimate grievances of the black majority. How much of this the new government can undertake without upsetting stable fiscal and monetary policies to which it is pledged remains a big question. There is also the looming specter of violent backlash from right-wing forces of various stripes. Despite positive rating of South Africa by international credit agencies, foreign private capital has been held back by political uncertainty – especially after the exit of Nelson Mandela – and the generally poor image of Africa in world money markets.

And although South Africa is in a strong position to supply consumer goods to new markets outside its traditional catchment area in southern Africa, it has to reckon with competitive substitutes – like textiles and electronics from East and Southeast Asia – in a new era of liberalized trade. South Africa appears to have a cost advantage in supplying mining, transport, and allied equipment, but the limitation here is the shortage of convertible currency in the depressed economies of the continent and, equally important, the high cost of conducting business in an uncertain political environment. As many South African businesspeople had found out by 1995, administrative delays, corruption, and the incapacity to enforce contracts can be more difficult to overcome than the economic sanctions with which their country had to live for so long.

Conclusions

This chapter began with extended discussion of the social disaster in many parts of Sub-Saharan Africa and the marginal role the region has assumed in the unfolding international drama produced by the end of the cold war and the collapse of Marxism–Leninism as an intellectually credible foundation of alternative economic organization. These historic events have pushed Africa even further to the margin than its own internal economic mismanagement and misrule would have done. Even among those who have not given up and are still concerned with the development fate of the region, this has led to a sense of foreboding and increasing uncertainty about the most appropriate development policies in response to this new context. Taking into account the analysis in the foregoing narrative, this conclusion attempts a preliminary conceptual repertoire that might contribute to the search for that solution.

Despite the pessimism generated by the gravity of the economic and political conditions in Africa, an objective view cautions about unmitigated gloom. As we saw in our baseline effort to categorize African states by economic performance, a small number of countries confirm that judicious liberal-oriented development policies, combined with sound public-sector management and political stability, can produce the same favorable results they have elicited elsewhere in the developing world.

Stable and efficient governance appears to be the key explanatory variable in understanding intercountry variations in growth. Considering the widespread acceptance of market-based development policies, not least among ordinary Africans, the predominant handicap for economic recovery almost certainly lies in the incompetent, corrupt, authoritarian, and eccentric regimes, which are gradually yielding to popular uprisings in the name of democracy. Because Western governments had a hand in the installation of some of these unsavory regimes, and to the extent that OECD donors are committed to contributing to the reversal of the continent's decline, they will be inevitably called upon to take a firmer stand than they have yet done in favor of a peaceful transition to accountable governance and development-friendly public administration.

Against the backdrop of Asian development success stories, which by and large avoided democratic governance, the question must be raised about whether Sub-Saharan Africa requires the elaborate paraphernalia of liberal constitutionalism to which African activists and donors are now committed. As the Japanese and other Asian development specialists remarked in the October 1993 Tokyo International Conference on African Development, the "Asian model," combining pragmatic autocratic rule, macroeconomic stability, and liberal market policies, is one option Africa might consider. Such advice, however, ignores the strongly pro-democracy temperament of African societies in the 1990s and the brutal fact that for a vast number of countries the most urgent priority is to create functioning and durable national governance structures, rather than reinforcing existing ones (as in China or Vietnam) in the context of liberal markets. The improvisation of such state institutions, in turn, is a constitution-making process, which is best done in consultative national forums. With some luck, African states could then make the transition from democratic governance to economic growth, while parts of Asia move in the opposite direction, from new prosperity to democracy (as has happened in South Korea and perhaps Taiwan).

Even then, the long-term success of such new African governments cannot be assured without renewed growth prompted by macroeconomic reforms and complementary sectoral policies. The most urgent among the latter is the rehabilitation of human resources together with a resurgent agricultural sector – the natural engine of economic change for most of the continent. These policies must be matched by efforts to lower the population growth rate to get more mileage from growth. As we have seen, evidence from a number of the growing economies suggests that this objective is already being met.

After addressing priority issues at the national and sectoral levels, attention must turn to widening the income-generating opportunities available to individual citizens. Such a strategy must capitalize on the resourcefulness of the informal sector by providing it with the requisite public amenities, but – something seldom mentioned – requiring it to internalize the heavy social costs it presently avoids. Identical policies must be pursued in smallholder agriculture as has been done with success in Ghana and Tanzania under the encouragement of the IFIs. At the same time, there is now ample reason to suggest that medium-scale indigenous enterprises provide another avenue for productive investment and are perhaps a safer bet in the long run than the amorphous and unruly informal sector.

All this calls for considerable liberalization of domestic markets and exploitation of international markets. As Mauritius has proved, such a path remains a viable option, notwithstanding the export pessimism that is prevalent in so many African states. As we have seen, trade barriers to African goods are less of a problem than declining productivity. Answers to new markets may lie more in this international direction than in continental common markets, which have proved so difficult to organize, or salvation from the powerful but problem-ridden South African economy.

As long as some African economies, however few or small, have crossed the development threshold, there must be hope for the others. Useful formulas of success that have worked in Africa are already at hand, indicating to policy makers where to begin. African successes are a beacon to which Afro-pessimists must be encouraged to look in the search for realistic alternatives. At present, there is a dearth of public servants who can assume that role. Political calamity, administrative venality, and economic collapse have conspired to drive off the skills, capital, and entrepreneurship that are needed to implement such policy turnabouts. And they will only return with good governance. The task, therefore, is enormous, and there is every likelihood that things will get worse before they get better. Amidst the gloom that now stalks Sub-Saharan Africa, reality speaks to the urgent need for factually based policy options and the installation of leadership willing to implement them. Outsiders can help, but the principal tasks must be carried out by the Africans themselves.

PART III

Conclusions

CHAPTER 11

The new international context of development

BARBARA STALLINGS

This book documents two sets of interrelated changes that have taken place since the early 1980s. One resulted in a dramatic transformation of the international political economy. The political divisions of the world shifted significantly, while economic interdependence increased sharply. The second led to a rapidly growing differentiation among third world countries. The average per capita GDP of the East Asian newly industrialized countries (NICs), for example, now exceeds $8,000, more than that of some European nations. At the opposite extreme, per capita GDP in Sub-Saharan Africa is only around $300, and it has been shrinking for more than a decade. Indeed, the differences are now such that the composite term "third world" has become an anachronism.

The aim of this final chapter is to suggest an approach to specify the causal relationships between the international changes and third world performance. It centers on the role of geography and regions.[1] "Region" is admittedly a vague concept; the geographic boundaries of a region can be drawn or redrawn at the whim of an observer. Nonetheless, geographic location is important because it is associated with shared historical and contemporary experiences. Especially important for our purposes here are links with external actors and processes. The argument is that groups of

---

The author thanks Peter Evans, Gary Gereffi, and Alice Amsden for comments on earlier drafts of the chapter and Phil Ruder for research assistance.

[1] MIT economist Paul Krugman has recently called attention to the importance of geography for economics: "About a year ago I . . . realized that I have spent my whole professional life as an international economist thinking and writing about economic geography, without being aware of it. By economic geography I mean the location of production in space; that is, that branch of economics that worries about where things happen in relation to one another. . . . [T]he tendency of international economists to turn a blind eye to the fact that countries both occupy and exist in space . . . has had some serious costs." See Paul Krugman, *Geography and Trade* (Cambridge, Mass.: MIT Press, 1991), pp. 1–2.

countries sharing a geographic space will be exposed to international influences through a regional prism. The result leads to characteristics that skew chances of achieving development, defined as rapid economic growth with relative equity of distribution.

Five international changes were analyzed in Part I of the book: the end of the cold war, increasing competition among capitalist powers, globalization of production and trade, shifting patterns of finance, and new ideological currents. Although the presentation implied that the five are separate processes, they really constitute a coherent whole. The first task of this chapter is to show how they fit together and how the resulting structure and mechanisms differ from those that reigned in the earlier period after World War II.

The second task is to analyze the impact on third world countries of the new international context of development and their responses to the challenges posed. Authors of the regional chapters dealt with these issues in Part II. Occasional comparative statements were made in those chapters, but we are now in a position to make an explicit comparative analysis. We will distinguish among the policies followed in East Asia, Southeast Asia, Latin America, and Sub-Saharan Africa, the four regions that constitute the main focus of the book. Then we will look at the differences in growth trajectories. Finally, we will link the different levels of performance to the international influences that each region experienced, showing how the latter accelerated the differences among groups of countries, creating both winners and losers. More specifically, we will explain why the Japanese-dominated Asian region has provided a more supportive environment for development than has the U.S.-dominated Western Hemisphere, and why the marginalization of Africa is especially prejudicial to development possibilities.

To conclude, we look briefly at trends in other regions (South Asia, the Middle East, and Eastern Europe) and then at future prospects. Insofar as the current regional biases continue, the future portends increased polarization in the third world. Some processes may be underway to spread the advantages that Asian countries have enjoyed in recent years, but these are not likely to encompass all regions. For much of Africa, parts of South Asia and the Middle East, and even sections of Latin America, major unforeseen changes will have to occur if poverty and exclusion are to be avoided.

A new political-economic structure

The end of the cold war and the changing relations among capitalist powers are together leading to a new international political-economic structure. The most basic change was the shift from a bipolar system of military opponents to a tripolar system of economic competitors. Among the major powers in the 1990s – the United States, Europe, and Japan – military struggle is highly unlikely; thus, the premium on military might that characterized the cold war period has been substantially downgraded. It has not been eliminated, since regional conflicts of various types will surely continue and nuclear proliferation cannot be ruled out, but it no longer carries the apocalyptic weight it once did. At the same time, economic power has increased in importance.[2] Those countries that run large trade surpluses through their technological superiority and achieve high domestic savings rates have capital surpluses at their disposal. Likewise, countries with large high-income populations have market access to offer. These assets can be used in a variety of ways to acquire influence over others.

During the cold war (the old international context of development), the United States and the Soviet Union constructed parallel hierarchies of allied nations. In the East, the Warsaw Pact members played a secondary role to the Soviet hegemon, while various third world countries were allies of lesser prestige. A parallel structure could be identified in the West, consisting of a U.S. hegemon, Western Europe and Japan in a second tier, and a disparate group of third world countries at a tertiary level. The two superpowers were able to maintain control over their allies through appeal to the military threat from the other side; ideological influence was also important. Internal disagreements within the two alliances, whether economic or political, were subordinated though never eliminated, and some third world countries managed to increase their political power by playing the superpowers off against each other.

The breakup of the Eastern Bloc and the collapse of the Soviet Union not only ended the cold war but also changed the structure of the system itself. In economic terms, Russia plummeted to third world status, while maintaining political leverage through a still powerful (though rapidly shrinking) military apparatus. The other republics of the former Soviet Union and Eastern Europe also became competitors of the traditional third world for markets and resources. At the same time, the disappearance of the Soviet military threat brought about a realignment of forces within the Western alliance; the economic power of Japan and Germany rose in value, while the

---

[2] As early as the mid-1980s, well before the collapse of communism, Richard Rosecrance made a major statement on the shift from military to economic power. See *The Rise of the Trading State* (New York: Basic, 1986).

military power of the United States declined. The symbolic representation of the change was seen during the Gulf War, when U.S. troops did most of the fighting but were financed by Japan, Europe, and the Middle Eastern oil potentates.

Given the new tripolar structure, the question being heatedly debated is how the system will work. International political economists have put forward two competing answers. The first group projects a continuation and deepening of the multilateral, interdependent global system that emerged after World War II. There are at least two complementary variants of this argument. One focuses on market forces, with investment and trade flows uniting the various parts of the globe. The other is more political, concentrating on trilateral management of the world by the United States, Japan, and a unifying Europe. A second group of analysts argues that regionalism is the dominant trend of the future. Three blocs, centering on the same three powers, will be the dominant structure. The zones will be further differentiated by different models or "styles" of capitalism prevailing there.

In Chapter 3, Stallings and Streeck suggest that both the globalist and the regionalist perspectives are correct.[3] They present data showing that trade and investment are increasing both within the so-called triad area (the United States, Europe, and Japan) and within the three regional blocs. Other areas are being marginalized in the process. Focusing on a concept they call "nonhegemonic interdependence," they argue that the different types of capitalisms that exist in the three regions have given rise to differential economic performance. The result is conflict *and* cooperation, divergence *and* convergence. Less successful systems try to assimilate international "best practice," but for domestic sociopolitical reasons, this may be impossible. A system unable to converge toward a superior model has two alternatives: pull the others down to its level (as Japan and Europe see the United States trying to do) or restructure the rules to restrain competition (as embodied in the process of "managed trade").

For the purposes of this volume, however, we need to go further than the preceding paragraphs take us. The crucial question is how the third world is linked to a relatively integrated but differentiated world economy. A concept that is useful in portraying this contradictory reality is Japanese eco-

---

[3] An analysis that is complementary to this point and many others in this chapter and the book more generally is Charles Oman, *Globalisation and Regionalisation: The Challenge for Developing Countries* (Paris: OECD, 1994).

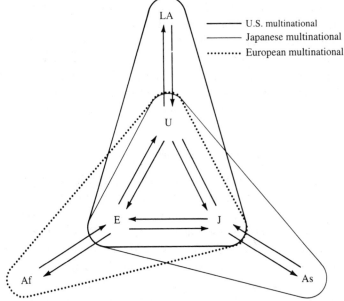

Figure 11.1. The tetrahedron. Af, Africa; As, Asia; E, European Union; J, Japan; LA, Latin America; U, United States. Reprinted with the permission of the Free Press, a division of Simon & Schuster, Inc., from *Triad Power: The Coming Age of Global Competition* by Kenichi Ohmae. Copyright © 1985 by Kenichi Ohmae and McKinsey & Company, Inc.

nomic consultant Kenichi Ohmae's "tetrahedron."[4] As shown in Figure 11.1, the tetrahedron combines the process of dense economic flows uniting the three poles of the contemporary world economy with flows tying each to a particular peripheral area. Thus, in addition to its economic connections to Japan and Western Europe, the United States is also portrayed as having an important relationship with Latin America. Japan's strongest third world links are with East and Southeast Asia, while Europe's main third world connection has been with Africa.

What we have portrayed here is a semiregionalized world economy – regionalized from the viewpoint of the third world countries, but much less so from the triad perspective. It is clear that the links between triad powers

[4] Kenichi Ohmae, *Triad Power: The Coming Shape of Global Competition* (New York: Free Press, 1985).

and third world areas have powerful historical, cultural, and geographic roots; in the next section, data are provided on current economic connections and their implications. The four regions on which we have concentrated – East Asia, Southeast Asia, Latin America, and Sub-Saharan Africa – appear to fit well into this schema. Later we address the situation of other regions, both in the traditional third world (South Asia and the Middle East) and the new third world (Central and Eastern Europe). They, too, are being affected by the new international context of development.

Mechanisms of influence

While two of the five international changes highlighted in this book – the end of the cold war and new relations among capitalist powers – have led to a new global structure in the 1990s, the other three – production and trade networks, finance, and ideology – constitute the main links that unite the triad as well as the regional blocs. Using the tetrahedron concept, we can study the relative importance of regional versus global ties and the differences across regions. In particular, the different degrees of symmetry within regions will be highlighted. But trade, finance, and ideology are not merely "neutral" glue binding the system together. They are also mechanisms whereby the most powerful actors in the international economy can influence less powerful elements and so increase the homogeneity of the resulting blocs.

Figure 11.2 focuses on trade flows within the tetrahedron in the early 1990s. These data show wide disparities in the importance of trade links between poles of the triad: 42 percent of Japan's trade is with the United States and Europe; 35 percent of U.S. trade is with Japan and Europe; but only 10 percent of Europe's trade is with Japan and the United States. Thus, the trade links within the triad, which are a core element of the theory of the multilateral integration of the world economy, are reasonably strong for Japan and the United States but weak for Europe.

At the periphery of the triad, the degree of symmetry also varies. Sub-Saharan Africa conducts nearly half of its trade with the European Union, but European trade with Africa is a minuscule 3 percent of its total. U.S.– Latin American commercial relations are a less extreme version. Some 43 percent of Latin American trade is with the United States, but only 15 percent of U.S. trade is with Latin America. The situation in Asia is quite different. While a third of Japan's exports and imports are with its Asian

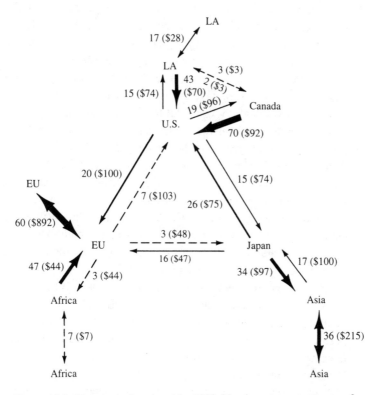

Figure 11.2. The tetrahedron in trade, 1992. Numbers are percentages of total trade (exports plus imports); numbers in parentheses are absolute values (billions of dollars). From IMF, *Direction of Trade Statistics Yearbook, 1993.*

neighbors, only 17 percent of developing Asia's trade is with Japan. Much more significant for developing Asian countries is trade among themselves (36 percent). Intra-Latin American trade has been growing but still represents only 17 percent of regional flows; Africa engages in very little intra-regional commerce. These regionalized patterns have gained importance over the past decade.[5]

---

[5] For example, only 33 percent of Latin American trade was with the United States in 1980, compared with 43 percent in 1992. Likewise, intra-Asian trade (excluding Japan) rose from 21 percent of total Asian trade to 36 percent in the same period. (Calculated from IMF, *Direction of Trade Statistics Yearbook,* various issues.)

Trade as a mechanism through which triad powers can exert influence has many forms; they also have been changing during the past 15 years. One type of trade leverage comes through the negotiation of privileged access to the markets of developed countries. While these agreements are sometimes broadly based, such as the Generalized System of Preferences (GSP), more targeted agreements can have greater significance. The latter tend to reinforce regional links. For example, the Lomé Conventions have provided special entry to the EU market for former European colonies; the Caribbean Basin Initiative offered a similar opening to the U.S. market for Central American and Caribbean nations.[6] The North American Free Trade Area (NAFTA), comprising the United States, Canada, and Mexico, is the most important agreement between a triad country and its peripheral region. Such access to markets has conditions. At a minimum, it usually requires reciprocity (the GSP is an exception), and other conditions are typically imposed. In the case of the NAFTA negotiations, for example, conditionality not only included reciprocal entry for exports, but also investment guarantees, environmental safeguards, and (informally) political concessions.[7] More generally, bilateral trade conditionality provides an opportunity for triad countries to promote policies in third world countries that mirror their own preferred style of development, and the greater regional integration that has emerged over the past decade in Asia and the Western Hemisphere increases these opportunities.

Another kind of trade leverage operates through multinational corporations. Those third world countries that provide adequate incentives – ranging from political stability to cheap and/or skilled labor to infrastructure – will be incorporated into the two new types of trade and production networks discussed by Gary Gereffi in Chapter 4. They are producer-driven networks incorporating third world countries to manufacture components and assemble finished goods, and buyer-driven networks where international retailers supply design specifications and markets to

---

6 On the Lomé Conventions, see John Ravenhill, *Collective Clientelism: The Lomé Conventions and North–South Relations* (New York: Columbia University Press, 1985). A brief update is John Ravenhill, "Africa and Europe: The Dilution of a 'Special Relationship,'" in John W. Harbeson and Donald Rothchild (eds.), *Africa in World Politics* (Boulder, Colo.: Westview, 1991). On the Caribbean Basin Initiative, see U.S. Senate, Committee on Finance, Subcommittee on International Trade, *Hearings on Caribbean Basin Initiative,* February 9, 1990, and Wilfred Whittingham, "The United States Government's Caribbean Basin Initiative," *CEPAL Review* 39 (December 1989), 73–92.

7 Gary Clyde Hufbauer and Jeffrey J. Schott, *NAFTA: An Assessment* (Washington, D.C.: Institute for International Economics, 1993).

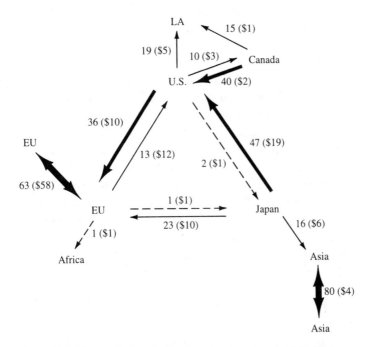

Figure 11.3. The tetrahedron in direct foreign investment, 1990–92 (average). Numbers are percentages of total direct investment; numbers in parentheses are absolute values (billions of dollars). From OECD, *International Direct Investment Statistics Yearbook, 1994,* and author's estimates for intra-Asian investment.

third world countries that produce finished goods. These networks, in turn, transmit the home country's way of doing business to firms in host countries. Although systematic data are hard to obtain, fragmentary evidence suggests that an increasing amount of international trade is carried on within firms.[8] Intrafirm trade raises barriers to entry, thus increasing the value of links with multinational corporations for obtaining access to markets. These channels are especially important for countries trying to break into the world market for manufactured exports, so leverage on policies can be significant.

[8] On intrafirm trade, see Magnus Blomström, *Transnational Corporations and Manufacturing Exports from Developing Countries* (New York: United Nations, 1990). See also OECD, "Intra-Firm Trade Study," unpublished ms., Paris, 1992.

Figure 11.3 provides a parallel analysis of direct foreign investment (DFI) flows within the tetrahedron. Direct investment among the triad countries is much more unevenly distributed than is trade. Although Japan sends the large majority of its investment to the United States (47 percent) and Europe (23 percent), it is the recipient of minimal return flows. The United States sends 36 percent of its DFI to the European Union but only 2 percent to Japan. Similarly, 13 percent of European direct foreign investment goes to the United States and about 1 percent to Japan. As with trade, over 60 percent of European foreign investment takes place within the European Union itself.[9] This enormous disparity – whereby Japanese investment is almost all financed domestically through its high savings rate, European countries invest in their own region, while the United States becomes increasingly reliant on outsiders – is a source of international instability and friction. It also puts the United States at a disadvantage as the recipient of residual (and thus volatile) funds to supplement its own low savings rate, leading to investment rates below those of either Japan or the European Union.

Investment flows between the triad countries and their regional partners are largely one way.[10] U.S. firms locate 19 percent and Japanese firms 16 percent of their direct investment in Latin America and Asia, respectively. Africa receives very little DFI from any source and less than 1 percent of European flows. In the past few years, intra-Latin American investment has begun to increase but still remains low as a share of total foreign investment.[11] In developing Asian countries, by contrast, very substantial intra-

---

[9] Although 63 percent of the European Union's direct investment *outflows* were to other EU nations during the period 1990–92, estimates of investment *stock* were much lower. In 1992, only 38 percent of DFI stock from EU members was in other parts of the Union. (For France and Germany, the stock figures were 62 and 50 percent, respectively.) See OECD, *International Direct Investment Statistics Yearbook, 1994* (Paris: OECD, 1994).

[10] Nonetheless, Asian and Latin American countries have also begun to invest in the industrial countries, especially the United States. No systematic data are available, but Korea and Taiwan have been especially active investors, and Mexico has recently stepped up such activities to increase its competitiveness in NAFTA. On Taiwan and Korea, see Yun-han Chu, Chapter 7, this volume. On Mexico, see Alvaro Calderón, Michael Mortimore, and Wilson Peres, "Mexico's Integration into the North American Economy: The Role of Foreign Investment," in Institute of European–Latin American Relations (IRELA), *Foreign Direct Investment in Developing Countries: The Case of Latin America* (Madrid: IRELA, 1994), pp. 183–213.

[11] For data, see UN Conference on Trade and Development (UNCTAD), Division on Transnational Corporations and Investment, *World Investment Directory: Latin America and the Caribbean* (New York: United Nations, 1994). Chile appears to be the largest investor, with nearly $3 billion sent abroad between 1990 and 1994, mainly to neighboring

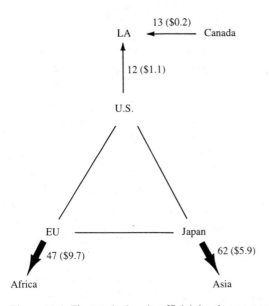

Figure 11.4. The tetrahedron in official development assistance, 1991–92 (average). Numbers are percentages of total bilateral and imputed multilateral ODA; numbers in parentheses are absolute values (billions of dollars). From OECD, *Development Cooperation, 1993.*

regional investment has been taking place, especially in the past decade. For example, in Chapter 7, Yun-han Chu reports that the East Asian NICs invested some $30 billion in the ASEAN countries between 1988 and 1992, surpassing investment there by Japan, Europe, or the United States. Taiwan and Hong Kong are also the top investors in Vietnam, and substantial amounts of investment are going into China.

Finally, Figure 11.4 provides data on official development assistance (ODA) flows from the three triad members. As partial compensation for the lack of foreign investment, Africa is the largest recipient of ODA. Most of it comes from the European Union; 47 percent of EU countries' ODA goes to Africa. This share, but not the absolute amount, is more than matched by the 62 percent of Japan's ODA that is sent to Asia; of this share, 42 percent goes to East and Southeast Asian nations. In the case of the United States, only 12

Argentina and Peru. See Mario Benavente, "La inversión de capitales chilenos en el mundo," Comité de Inversiones Extranjeras, Santiago, 1994.

percent of its ODA monies go to Latin America since the largest share (nearly half) is earmarked for Israel and Egypt.[12]

A complementary analysis to the one just discussed has been carried out in the past several years by the Division on Transnational Corporations and Investment of the UN Conference on Trade and Development (UNCTAD). In its annual *World Investment Report,* the concept of the triad is also employed. Rather than reporting the share of triad countries' investment in third world nations, however, UNCTAD focuses on the share of a third world country's total DFI flows coming from a particular triad country. This analysis also reveals clusters of countries with strong regional links.[13]

The 1994 report shows three "investment clusters." The U.S. cluster includes seven Latin American countries (Argentina, Bolivia, Chile, Colombia, El Salvador, Mexico, and Venezuela), three from South Asia (Bangladesh, India, and Pakistan), plus the Philippines from Southeast Asia. The Japanese cluster is made up of six East and Southeast Asian nations (Hong Kong, Korea, Malaysia, Singapore, Taiwan, and Thailand) plus Sri Lanka and Fiji. Europe's cluster is composed of three countries from Sub-Saharan Africa (Ghana, Kenya, and Zambia), three from Latin America (Brazil, Paraguay, and Uruguay), and four from the Middle East (Egypt, Jordan, Morocco, and Tunisia). In addition, Europe is the main investor in the former Soviet Union and four East European countries (Hungary, Poland, and the former Czechoslovakia and Yugoslavia).[14]

Financial flows, managed at global and regional levels, are again both links and potential mechanisms of influence. At the global level, the triad countries provide loans through the international financial institutions (IFIs), especially the IMF and the World Bank. As the counterpart to the loans, pressure is brought to bear on third world countries to follow certain

---

[12] In 1991–92, 47 percent of gross disbursements of U.S. bilateral ODA went to Egypt and Israel. For data on ODA, see the annual publication of the OECD's Development Assistance Committee, *Development Cooperation* (Paris: OECD).

[13] An economy is in the cluster of a triad member when the latter dominates annual investment flows, either through absolute dominance over a host country (with more than 50 percent of total investment) or relative dominance (where its investment exceeds the share of the next largest investor by at least 10 percent).

[14] UNCTAD, Division on Transnational Corporations and Investment, *World Investment Report, 1994* (New York: United Nations, 1994). Data are for the 1987–91 period and are based on the flow definition cited in note 13. UNCTAD has now added an alternative definition of clusters, which focuses on investment stocks rather than flows. This latter definition is more related to historical relations than contemporary links.

types of economic policies. The focus of conditionality was vastly expanded during the 1980s. On the one hand, it increased from macroeconomic policy (on the part of the IMF) and specific project feasibility (the World Bank) to structural adjustment policies. The latter embody the market-oriented approach described in the upcoming section on ideology. On the other hand, conditionality was also extended to issues such as democracy, human rights, and environmental safeguards.[15] In the 1990s, by contrast, the importance of the IFIs as a source of finance has declined. In Chapter 5, Griffith-Jones and Stallings report that World Bank and IMF loans as a share of total international finance was cut in half: to 7 percent in Asia, 16 percent in Latin America, and 20 percent in Africa. The role of IFI conditionality can thus be expected to decline commensurately, if the trend itself continues.

While IFI loans (with their respective conditions) are available to all third world countries that are members of the organizations, other types of finance are more restricted. For example, Figures 11.3 and 11.4 demonstrate the links between triad members and associated third world areas with respect to DFI and ODA. As Japan and Europe became more important international players in the 1980s and 1990s, their share of DFI and ODA began to overtake that of the United States. Japan now prides itself on being the "number one donor" of ODA, and its DFI outflows surpassed those of the United States for several years during the 1980s. Europe as a whole, of course, exports far more capital than either the United States or Japan.

Like multilateral loans, bilateral ODA generally involves explicit economic and/or political conditionality whose features depend on the criteria of individual donor governments.[16] Other public monies also tend to have regional biases. The most important example was Japan's $65 billion program to "recycle" its trade surplus during the 1988–93 period. Although original expectations were that most of the money would go to Latin Amer-

---

[15] Various types of political conditionality have been analyzed in a series published by the Overseas Development Council. See Joan M. Nelson with Stephanie Eglinton, *Encouraging Democracy: What Role for Conditioned Aid?* (1992); Nicole Ball, *Pressing for Peace: Can Aid Induce Reform?* (1992); and Maurice J. Williams and Patti L. Petesch, *Sustaining the Earth: Role of Multilateral Development Institutions* (1993). The summary volume of the series is Joan M. Nelson and Stephanie J. Eglinton, *Global Goals, Contentious Means: Issues of Multiple Aid Conditionality* (1993).

[16] For information on bilateral conditionality, see Nelson and Eglinton, *Global Goals, Contentious Means*, especially Table 1.

ica, as the main locus of the debt crisis, the majority of the bilaterally dispersed funds eventually went to Asia.[17] These bilateral flows are a means for transmitting a donor country's economic approach to recipient nations.

Private sources of funds also carry conditions, although they are likely to be more implicit than those of the IFIs or bilateral donors. That is, decisions on the "creditworthiness" of particular investment sites are based on economic and political characteristics of the respective countries, ranging from macroeconomic stability to legal frameworks governing foreign investment to the political ideology of governments. This private conditionality serves as another way to export the economic model of the home country to third world recipients, either through the direct control of investments (via DFI) or leverage over economic policies (via purchase of securities or various types of loans). In the case of Japan, private firms have played an important role in the generation of their government's ODA projects, thus providing coordination between the various types of capital flows and increasing the likelihood of incorporating the Japanese style of operation. U.S. firms have been less involved in the foreign aid area.[18]

A third mechanism whereby the United States, Europe, and Japan can influence third world countries is through ideology. During the cold war period, anticommunist ideology played an important role in maintaining loyalty within the Western alliance; the reverse was the case in the Soviet bloc. During the 1980s, a different sort of ideology – pro-capitalist rather than anticommunist – became increasingly prevalent. Dubbed the "market friendly" approach by the World Bank or the "Washington Consensus" by the Institute for International Economics, this new ideology proclaimed the primacy of market-based economics.[19] In the extreme case, it was even said to constitute the "end of history."[20] As discussed by Thomas Biersteker in

---

[17] On the recycling program, see Toshihiko Kinoshita, "Developments in the International Debt Strategy and Japan's Response," *EXIM Review* 10, 2 (1991), 62–80. Figures for the commitment of bilateral funds as of June 30, 1992, show 55 percent of loans going to Asia, 25 percent to Latin America, and 20 percent to Africa, the Middle East, and others.

[18] See Richard E. Bissell, "The Role of the Private Sector in Development Promotion," in Barbara Stallings (ed.), *Common Vision, Different Paths: The United States and Japan in the Developing World* (Washington, D.C.: Overseas Development Council, 1993), pp. 33–59.

[19] John Williamson (ed.), *Latin American Adjustment: How Much Has Happened?* (Washington, D.C.: Institute for International Economics, 1990); World Bank, *World Development Report, 1991* (Washington, D.C.: World Bank, 1991).

[20] Francis Fukuyama, *The End of History and the Last Man* (New York: Free Press, 1992).

Chapter 6, these new policy ideas included a small state and an open economy, as well as macroeconomic stability. The IFIs were very important in popularizing the new approach; they were reinforced by the backing of their chief shareholders under the administrations of Reagan, Thatcher, and Kohl. Together, these bilateral and multilateral forces created an environment that exerted powerful pressure on third world countries to implement market-oriented policies.

Under the rubric of market orientation, however, important variations can still exist, as has become increasingly clear in the 1990s. For example, the Japanese insist that their brand of capitalism is as market-oriented as that of the United States, but the institutional bases have been quite different, as discussed in Chapter 3. Thus, while the U.S. model of capitalism relies on flexibility (unregulated market transactions, limited state intervention, short time horizons), the Japanese model is based on long-term commitments. Markets in Asia are embedded in political and social institutions and relations; hierarchy and authority constitute the glue that binds the structure. In Western Europe, a third variant reigns, although defining it is more difficult than defining the other two because of the diversity on the Continent. While it also features long-term commitments, these are based on politically negotiated social compacts rather than traditional loyalties.

As we will discuss in the next section, it is the Japanese version of market orientation that has guided Japanese foreign assistance, complemented by the activities of the Japanese trade and production networks in East Asia. Likewise, the U.S. brand of laissez-faire became increasingly influential in Latin America during the 1980s, propagated by investments of U.S. firms, loans from the IFIs, and strong ideological links. In Africa, by contrast, a European model of capitalism has not been followed. The lack of European influence can be explained by low levels of European private-sector activity in Africa, whether trade or investment.[21] The main European presence in Sub-Saharan Africa has been via ODA, which was closely coordinated with the IFIs and, thus, closely attuned to the U.S. style of capitalism.

---

[21] An additional factor is that insofar as there has been investment from European countries, the most important source has been the United Kingdom. In the 1990–92 period, for example, 53 percent of EU direct investment in Africa came from the United Kingdom. (See OECD, *International Direct Investment Statistics Yearbook, 1994.*) As was discussed in Chapter 3, many analysts believe that the British model of capitalism is much closer to that of the United States than to its EU counterparts.

Implications for the third world: Asia, Latin America, and Africa

The influence of the new international context of development in the 1980s and the 1990s can usefully be disaggregated into two stages: the impact on economic policy choice and the impact on economic outcomes.

Policy choice

The 1980s saw dramatic changes in economic policies and, more important, in development strategies or models. As discussed in Chapter 1, a crucial narrowing of options characterized policy choice across the third world during the past 15 years compared with the earlier postwar era. The most significant narrowing came from the virtual abandonment of support for socialist economics: central planning, extensive state ownership, and distribution based primarily on need rather than material incentives. Only in Cuba and North Korea are such policies still openly defended. Even nations that continue to be ruled by communist parties, such as China and Vietnam, have turned away from socialist economic policies.[22] Likewise, support for nationalist/populist policies has also largely disappeared. Peru's Alan García was one of the last third world leaders to openly advocate and attempt to implement a development strategy based on large wage increases, expanded government deficits, administered prices, and confrontation with the international financial community.[23] Today, leftist party leaders, such as Cuauhtémoc Cárdenas in Mexico and "Lula" in Brazil, strive to assure businesspeople that they would respect market mechanisms.

Socialist and populist policies have disappeared from the third world map partially as a consequence of several of the trends discussed in earlier chapters. They include the end to the moral and material support of the Soviet bloc, the explicit and implicit conditions for obtaining international finance, the need to meet economic requirements to gain access to markets and production networks, and the increased ideological support for liberalization and privatization. These international factors alone cannot explain

---

[22] See, e.g., Linda Y. C. Lim, "Models and Partners: The Role of Singapore and Malaysia in Socialist Economic Reforms in Vietnam," in Scott Christensen and Manuel Montes (eds.), *Marketization in Southeast Asia* (Honolulu: East–West Center Press, forthcoming).

[23] Manuel Pastor Jr. and Carol Wise, "Peruvian Economic Policy in the 1980s: From Orthodoxy to Heterodoxy and Back," *Latin American Research Review* 27, 2 (1992), 83–117.

the entire movement toward market-oriented policies during the 1980s and early 1990s, but their effect is clearly to buttress such an orientation.[24]

At the same time, a substantial amount of diversity is also found among third world development models. Although economic policies are now much more uniform than they were 10–15 years ago, they are far from identical. One way to account for diversity is to rely on domestic sources of policy making.[25] This approach is a helpful complement to the analysis of international factors, but diversity is also inherent in the structure of the post–cold war world. As discussed earlier, the United States, Japan, and Europe are characterized by different "styles" of capitalism, and those third world countries in their spheres of influence are likely to be similar to the regional hegemons. Specifically, the hypothesis behind the analysis of policy choice in this chapter and the book more broadly focuses on the three mechanisms of influence introduced earlier. It says that the policy packages (models) selected by third world countries will resemble those advocated by the countries that buy their goods, supply their finance, and provide their ideological guidance.

As shown in Table 11.1, there are two main "clusters of influence" in the 1990s: (1) an Asian cluster, centered on Japan but with an increasingly active role for the East Asian NICs, and (2) a U.S./IFI cluster, dominated directly and indirectly by the United States.[26] For some individual countries in several regions, a Soviet/East European cluster was important at the beginning of the 1980s, but its salience had disappeared by the end of that decade. The European influence that might have been expected in Sub-Saharan Africa has been largely absent, since policy guidance was entrusted to the IFIs, in the absence of a strong interest in the region by the European private sector, but a significant Western European role is already emerging in Central and Eastern Europe (as will be discussed later).[27]

---

[24] For a discussion of the impact of international changes on the demise of populism, see Robert R. Kaufman and Barbara Stallings, "The Political Economy of Populism," in Rudiger Dornbusch and Sebastian Edwards (eds.), *The Macroeconomics of Populism in Latin America* (Chicago: University of Chicago Press, 1991), pp. 15–43.

[25] An example of the argument for domestic causation is found in Joan M. Nelson, "Introduction: The Politics of Economic Adjustment in Developing Countries," in Joan M. Nelson (ed.), *Economic Crisis and Policy Choice* (Princeton, N.J.: Princeton University Press, 1990), pp. 3–32.

[26] Indirect domination refers to the fact that the IFIs have traditionally advocated policies championed by the United States as their major shareholder. There was a particular congruence during the Reagan and Bush administrations in 1981–92.

[27] For a comparison of various aspects of the U.S./IFI versus Asian approaches, see Stallings

Table 11.1. *International influence on policy choice in the third world, 1980–92*

Region	Markets	Finance	Ideology
East Asia	Asia	Internal	Japan
Southeast Asia	Asia	Japan/East Asia	Japan
Latin America	United States	United States/IFIs	United States/IFIs
Sub-Saharan Africa	Europe (USSR: various)	Europe/IFIs (USSR: various)	IFIs (USSR: various)
South Asia	Diversified	IFIs (USSR: India)	IFIs (USSR: India)
Middle East	Diversified	Internal (USSR: various)	Islamic (USSR: various)
Eastern Europe	Europe (USSR)	Europe/IFIs (USSR/Europe)	Europe/IFIs (USSR)

Note: Entries indicate *main* international links, not the only ones; entries in parentheses indicate links that were important until the late 1980s.

Among the elements that distinguish the Asian and U.S. models are trade orientation and the role of the state. Although both the Asian and U.S./IFI models stress exports, there are two major differences in approach. First, the Asian models emphasize active steps to *promote* exports. Such steps include subsidized credit, government assistance with marketing strategies, help with obtaining access to technology, and so on. The U.S. approach, by contrast, emphasizes the removal of impediments, such as overvalued exchange rates, export taxes, and bureaucratic regulations. The assumption is that exports will increase on their own, once these barriers are eliminated. A second difference concerns import liberalization. The U.S. model has put a premium on ending import barriers at a rapid pace, regardless of the impact on domestic productive capacity. Import liberalization itself, both through providing access to low-cost inputs and forcing competition, is portrayed as sufficient to raise the competitiveness of third world products. While the Asian model initially promoted exports in the context of a highly protected

(ed.), *Common Vision, Different Paths.* A similar analysis is found in Fernando Fajnzylber, "The United States and Japan as Models of Industrialization," in Gary Gereffi and Donald L. Wyman (eds.), *Manufacturing Miracles: Paths of Industrialization in Latin America and East Asia* (Princeton, N.J.: Princeton University Press, 1990), pp. 323–52.

domestic market, it too has been affected by the recent trends toward more open economies. But the steps toward liberalization have been slower and more cautious.[28]

With respect to the state, the situation is a bit more complicated. One version of the Asian model (followed in Japan, Korea, and Taiwan) has made extensive use of industrial policy, involving the promotion of certain sectors of the economy. That role is firmly rejected in the U.S./IFI approach, based on the argument that most third world governments do not have the capacity to "pick winners." It has also been rejected more broadly as a result of the Uruguay Round negotiations in the GATT. In addition, and common to all the Asian nations, there is the promotion of capacity for the economy as a whole: both human capital and physical facilities. In the Asian model, support for both types of capital is seen as an essential role for the state to perform, requiring the active design of policies to achieve desired ends. While the U.S./IFI model also claims to approve this function for the state, in practice, budget cuts have undermined such activities. John Williamson, the author of the concept of the Washington Consensus, for example, says that the main way in which Latin American countries have failed to follow the consensus recommendations is in their failure to reassign public expenditure toward social sectors.[29]

If we look at the policies actually followed over the past decade in different parts of the third world, we find that there are indeed strong regional similarities. This clearly does not mean identical sets of policies, nor does it imply there are no "deviant cases." It merely suggests that the variation within regions is less than that across regions.

---

[28] For an analysis of the different views on trade policy, see Williamson (ed.), *Latin American Adjustment;* World Bank, *World Development Report, 1991;* and World Bank, *The East Asian Miracle: Economic Growth and Public Policy* (Washington, D.C.: World Bank, 1993). On the relative openness of Latin American and Asian economies, note that the average tariff in the six largest Latin America countries in 1991 was 15 percent versus 26 percent in five major Asian markets. Maximum tariffs were 65 and 220 percent, respectively, while nontariff barriers in Asia were between two and three times as high as in Latin America. See UNCTAD, *Trade and Development Report, 1993* (New York: United Nations, 1993), pp. 113–17.

[29] John Williamson, presentation at the conference, Sustainable Development with Equity in the 1990s, University of Wisconsin-Madison, May 1993. On variations between Japan, Korea, and Taiwan, on the one hand, and the other Asian economies, on the other, see Danny M. Leipziger and Vinod Thomas, *The Lessons of East Asia: An Overview of Country Experience* (Washington, D.C.: World Bank, 1993).

Analysis of the East and Southeast Asian cases is aided by the recently completed World Bank study of the "East Asian Miracle."[30] Focusing on seven countries in developing Asia (Taiwan, South Korea, Hong Kong, Singapore, Indonesia, Malaysia, and Thailand), plus Japan in the earlier postwar period, the study identifies a set of similar policies followed by the eight. They include two different types of policies. First are policies of the sort that neoclassical economists have traditionally recommended, especially macroeconomic stability and support for the private sector. In addition, however, the governments of most of the eight countries also intervened to promote development. "At least some of these interventions violate the dictum of establishing for the private sector a level playing field, a neutral incentives regime."[31]

For each of a series of intermediate goals, a combination of neoclassical and interventionist approaches was used. For example, in trying to promote exports, stable macroeconomic management was important, but so were import protection and various kinds of export subsidies. With respect to creating the institutional basis for growth, the governments designed extensive mechanisms for coordination with the private sector and sought legitimacy with broader sectors of the population through "shared growth." The accumulation of human and physical capital was achieved by a combination of traditional methods such as the provision of infrastructure, education, and sound financial institutions, but the repression of interest rates, forced savings, and guarantees of private risk were also used. Finally, to bring about efficient allocation and productivity growth, employment generation has been emphasized over wage increases, state intervention in the credits markets has been practiced, foreign technology has been sought, and specific industries have sometimes been promoted.[32]

---

[30] World Bank, *The East Asian Miracle.*

[31] Ibid., p. 6. A slightly different way of looking at the policies is found in one of the background papers for *The East Asian Miracle;* see Peter A. Petri, *The Lessons of East Asia: Common Foundations of East Asian Success* (Washington, D.C.: World Bank, 1993). Petri identifies three functions that all East Asian countries successfully carried out but with differing policies: building a stable macroeconomic environment, guiding resources into efficient activities, and finding a dynamic engine of growth.

[32] It should be added that some experts, in Asia and elsewhere, think that *The East Asian Miracle* underestimates the role of state intervention in creating the very high growth rates in Asia and the complementary equality. See, e.g., Albert Fishlow et al., *Miracle or Design? Lessons from the East Asian Experience* (Washington, D.C.: Overseas Development Council, 1994), and Alice H. Amsden (ed.), "The World Bank's 'The East Asian Miracle: Economic Growth and Public Policy,'" *World Development* (special section) 22, 4 (April 1994), 615–70.

In their discussions of East and Southeast Asia (Chapters 7 and 8), Yun-han Chu and Linda Lim make many similar points. Their emphasis is on the period since the mid-1980s, as both sets of countries adjusted to the new international circumstances. Specifically, greater liberalization occurred, but the governments maintained their role in steering the change. They also took an active role in helping their private firms improve their international competitiveness. Pragmatic attempts to take advantage of new opportunities seems to be the hallmark of the Asian response. For example, state procurement was used to enable Korean and Taiwanese firms to enter technological cooperation agreements. Likewise, their governments, as well as those of the ASEAN countries, have offered help in upgrading worker skills and improving research and development facilities. All have encouraged outward foreign investment as a way to meet competition from lower-wage producers.

In Latin America, with the partial exception of Brazil, policy choice in the 1980s and early 1990s underwent much more dramatic change than in Asia.[33] This change also tended to be more ideological and less pragmatic. Latin America had held onto import-substitution policies for much longer than the Asian countries. In the 1970s, the continuation of this strategy came to rely on increased amounts of foreign debt. With the eruption of the debt crisis in 1982, and the growing realization that the crisis was not just a temporary problem of liquidity, most governments opted for a pendular swing in economic policy. The reasons were many. The need for money to maintain payments on large debts increased the influence of the IFIs. U.S. influence grew during the Reagan administration with its heavy ideological orientation; the election of George Bush in 1988 indicated that no major shifts would take place in U.S. policy stance, despite some change in style. The collapse of socialism moderated the position of many of the leftist parties in the region. Finally, in the late 1980s, high growth rates in Chile, the earliest Latin American country to embrace market-oriented policies, together with some well-publicized failures (e.g., the "heterodox" policies in Peru, Argentina, and Brazil), generated attempts to imitate the Chilean approach.

As a consequence of this panoply of trends, as Augusto Varas points out in Chapter 9, one Latin American country after another opted for what came

---

[33] See World Bank, *Latin America and the Caribbean: A Decade after the Debt Crisis* (Washington, D.C.: World Bank, 1993).

to be labeled "neoliberal" policies. Government budgets were slashed. Greater reliance was placed on the private-sector supply of basic services, ranging from trash collection to education to social security. Public enterprises were auctioned off, frequently to foreign investors. Stock markets were stimulated, based on the newly privatized firms. Tariff structures were dismantled, and new laws were promulgated to encourage foreign investment. In general, reliance on market forces was greatly expanded as the state abruptly withdrew from many of its traditional activities. In contrast with the East and Southeast Asian regions, the Latin American governments paid little attention to institution building, nor did they any longer consider "shared growth" to be a primary aim for governments to pursue; the markets would regulate distribution. Even human capital formation suffered in practice, if not in rhetoric. Faith in the market came to replace faith in government.

Not surprisingly, the new Latin American policies have generated a backlash among those not favored by them. At the national level, Venezuela has retreated from its earlier move in the new policy direction. Elsewhere, political explosions, such as the Chiapas rebellion in Mexico or the Santiago del Estero riots in Argentina, have led to increased stress on social policies. In Chile, even without such intense pressure, the current government has defined the elimination of poverty as its major goal. At the regional level, the Inter-American Development Bank has decided to devote half of its newly expanded lending capacity to social programs. In general, however, the impact of these shifts has not yet had much effect, and equality is seen as a major deficiency of the new Latin American economic policies.[34]

In addition, there are doubts about whether the private sector alone will be able to provide the meso- and microlevel complements to the new macroeconomic policies. For example, private financial markets generally lack the long-term facilities required to finance investment projects. The absence of regulatory agencies may lead to serious financial crises, as recently seen in Venezuela. The widespread withdrawal of foreign investment funds, following the peso devaluation in Mexico, is the most dramatic example of

---

[34] Nathaniel C. Nash, "Latin Economic Speedup Leaves Poor in the Dust," *New York Times,* September 7, 1994. For a more in-depth analysis, see UN Economic Commission for Latin America and the Caribbean (UNECLAC), *Social Panorama in Latin America, 1994* (Santiago: UNECLAC, 1994). A comparison of Latin America and Asia on this dimension is found in Nancy Birdsall and Richard Sabot, "Inequality and Growth," in Inter-American Development Bank (IDB), *The Development Experience in the Latin American/Caribbean Region and East Asian Countries* (Washington, D.C.: IDB, forthcoming).

such problems. The return on infrastructure may be too low to attract adequate private funds. If firms cannot sufficiently internalize the benefits, they may not provide enough training opportunities. In Asia, these problems of market failure continue to be resolved by the public sector or through close public–private collaboration. Latin America has been more reticent to permit state involvement in recent times.[35]

Finally, Sub-Saharan African countries have had trouble in following consistent policies of any sort. Large but weak governments lack the capacity to collect information, formulate strategies, or implement them. Domestic private actors are equally weak, and foreign capital has largely given up on the region, despite its rich natural resources. Dwindling revenues from primary-product exports – caused by lack of demand in industrial countries, deteriorating terms of trade, and lack of money for investment in productive facilities – in conjunction with heavy debt burdens led African countries in desperation to the IFIs. In a number of cases, this resort to the World Bank and the IMF followed the withdrawal of assistance from the Soviet Union as the latter's economy collapsed. As Fred Halliday explains in Chapter 2, Angola, Mozambique, and Ethiopia were major Soviet client states, and about a dozen other Sub-Saharan African nations formed part of the broad Soviet alliance system. For the former group in particular, Soviet economic assistance was important, even if generally not very efficient.

On paper, most African governments adopted structural adjustment policies recommended by the IFIs. Indeed, this began earlier than in Latin America, since Sub-Saharan Africa's crisis became apparent in the 1970s. A frequent situation was that a very thin layer of technocrats, with international training and often work experience in the World Bank or the IMF, convinced their governments that the new policies must be followed. Agreements were signed, but the short-term results were so painful for populations living at the subsistence level, and so dangerous for governments based on patronage, that they were quickly abandoned. Thus, stop–go cycles were the most typical pattern of policy choice in the Sub-Saharan region.

The latest World Bank evaluation of structural reforms in Africa could, at best, be labeled cautiously optimistic.[36] Examining 26 countries that under-

---

[35] UNECLAC, *Latin America and the Caribbean: Policies to Improve Linkages with the Global Economy* (Santiago: UNECLAC, 1994).

[36] World Bank, *Adjustment in Africa: Reforms, Results, and the Road Ahead* (Oxford University Press, 1994).

took adjustment programs in the 1980s, the Bank divides them into three groups: those with large improvements in macroeconomic policies (6 cases), those with small improvements (9 cases), and those with deterioration (11 cases). The positive conclusion is that the strong adjusters performed best on all indicators of growth, the weak adjusters next best, and the nonadjusters worst, often with negative growth. The other side of the picture is that, despite efforts to reform, "most African countries still lack policies that are sound by international standards."[37] At the same time, there remain serious differences of opinion on whether current economic policies are the most appropriate for Sub-Saharan Africa.[38]

These contrasts in policy choice, we would argue, are closely related to the ties that bind the various regions to the international political economy. Although there are obviously global links that span the entire third world, regional hegemons – with different visions of what development is and how it should be pursued – have had a crucial impact on the selection of policies and the speed of their implementation. Acting through the trade, finance, and ideological mechanisms described earlier, the Asian and U.S./IFI clusters of influence had helped create significant differences in regional policy profiles by the early 1990s.

Development outcomes

Beyond policy choice, the new international context has had an impact on development outcomes in more direct ways, skewing the possibilities of success. Discussion here is focused mainly on growth of per capita GDP, but there is increasing evidence linking high growth rates to more equitable

---

[37] Ibid., p. 8.

[38] See, e.g., G. K. Helleiner, "The IMF, the World Bank and Africa's Adjustment and External Debt Problems: An Unofficial View," *World Development* 20, 6 (June 1992), 779–92; Patrick Conway and Joshua Greene, "Is Africa Different?" *World Development* 21 (December 1993), 2017–28. John Williamson, author of the Washington Consensus concept, also suggests that this sort of policy may not be appropriate for Africa; see "Democracy and the 'Washington Consensus,'" *World Development* 21, 8 (August 1993), 1329–36. An interesting alternative is being put forward by the Japanese, who suggest that the Asian development model may be relevant for Africa. See Seiji Naya and Robert McCleery, *Relevance of Asian Development Experiences to African Problems*, Occasional Paper No. 39 (San Francisco: International Center for Economic Growth, 1994); David L. Lindauer and Michael Roemer (eds.), *Asia and Africa: Legacies and Opportunities in Development* (San Francisco: International Center for Economic Growth, 1994).

Table 11.2. *Growth of GDP by third world region, 1980–92*

Region	GDP per capita ($ 1992)		Growth rates, 1980–92 (percent)		Percent Latin American GDP	
	1980	1992	GDP	GDP per capita	1980	1992
East Asia	3,710	8,527	8.0	6.7	1.30	3.17
Southeast Asia	688	1,068	5.9	3.6	0.24	0.40
Latin America	2,857	2,691	1.6	−0.5	1.00	1.00
Sub-Saharan Africa	369	320	1.9	−1.2	0.13	0.12
South Asia	177	252	5.1	2.9	0.06	0.09
Middle East	1,634	1,735	3.6	0.5	0.57	0.64
Eastern Europe	2,232	1,957	−0.4	−1.0	0.78	0.73

Source: Calculated from data in Table 1.1.

distribution of income and wealth.[39] Table 11.2 presents data on per capita GDP for each of the regions in 1980 and 1992 (in 1992 dollars) and on growth rates. It also shows the relative positions of the regions, calculated for convenience as a percentage of Latin American GDP. The table documents several interesting trends.

First, in 1980, East Asia and Latin America were at fairly similar levels. East Asia's per capita GDP exceeded Latin America's by less than one third. This similarity was reflected in the frequent mention of the East Asian and Latin American NICs as an elite group in contrast with the rest of the third world. By the early 1990s, however, East Asia's per capita GDP was more than three times that of Latin America and above several countries in Western Europe. Second, not only was Latin America far outpaced by East Asia, but Southeast Asia was gaining rapidly. Indeed, it is Southeast Asia rather than East Asia with which Latin America is now most frequently compared. The GDP differential still appears large (Southeast Asia only

[39] On the equity dimension, see World Bank, *The East Asian Miracle;* see also the critique on this topic in Dani Rodrik, "King Kong Meets Godzilla: The World Bank and 'The East Asian Miracle,'" in Fishlow et al., *Miracle or Design?* pp. 13–53. For an argument that greater equity promotes growth, see Felipe Larraín and Rodrigo Vergara, "Distribución del ingreso, inversión y crecimiento," *Cuadernos de Economía* 29, 87 (August 1992), 207–28.

Table 11.3. *Variables affecting growth rates in third world regions,*
1981–92 (percent)

Region	Export markets[a]	External finance[b]	Economic capacity Investment[c]	Labor[d]
East Asia[e]	7.8	+0.1	29.6	86
Southeast Asia	7.5	+2.9	30.1	49
Latin America	5.5	−0.5	19.3	47
Sub-Saharan Africa	6.5	+3.3	15.3	18
South Asia	6.0	+1.5	23.1	39
Middle East	5.7	+2.0	23.6	56
Eastern Europe	3.8	−1.9	29.9	81

[a]Growth of imports in region's markets, annual average (1981–91).
[b]Net long-term capital inflows/GDP, annual average (1983–89).
[c]Gross domestic investment/GDP, annual average (1985–92).
[d]Secondary school enrollment/eligible age group (1991).
[e]For a basic list of countries in the regional categories, see Table 1.1.
Sources: IMF, *Direction of Trade Statistics Yearbook* (for export markets); IMF, *Balance of Payments Yearbook* (for external finance); World Bank, *World Tables* (for investment); World Bank, *World Development Report* (for school enrollment).

moved from 24 to 40 percent of Latin America's per capita GDP), but the two wealthiest Southeast Asian countries, Thailand and Malaysia, compare favorably with Brazil and Mexico. Moreover, on social indicators like health and education, the gap has been eliminated (see Table 1.5). Third, the situation in Sub-Saharan Africa deteriorated further, so that the income differential between that region and the others grew; the social gap increased as well. Even compared with South Asia, Africa's situation became worse. The 1980s were a "lost decade" for Latin America and Africa, but a very successful one for virtually all parts of Asia.

How can we account for these trends? As was the case with policy choice, certain domestic factors were clearly very important, as a positive influence in Asia and a definite hindrance in the case of Africa. But international influence can take us a long way in understanding the differing outcomes. The skewed possibilities of success are transmitted through three elements, shown in Table 11.3: access to markets and technology, the availability of financial resources, and the promotion of economic capacity. The Japanese style of capitalism, together with the dynamism of the Asian region, have provided advantages in all three respects to the East Asian and more recently the Southeast Asian nations. Lesser advantage has accrued to Latin America as a result of its proximity to the United States, and Sub-Saharan Africa – increasingly marginalized from all of the world economy – is in an especially disadvantaged position.

First, trade links constitute an important element of any development environment, but they are especially crucial for the new export-oriented development strategies. The particular means for obtaining access to markets varies by type of product. Thus, the large producers of primary goods in third world countries generally have the clout to sell directly on the international market, even when the companies are locally owned. For manufactured goods and other nontraditional exports, intermediaries are more important. The intermediaries can also provide additional advantages. For example, Japanese firms have incorporated other Asian countries into production and trade networks, enabling them to get access to technology and organizational know-how. The large trading companies have been especially important in this respect, but Japanese multinationals in general have been more open than their U.S. counterparts to working with local partners.[40] Through these channels, developing Asian producers have gotten access to the Japanese market for their industrial exports and – ironically – to the U.S. market through Japanese auspices. This use of triangular trade to get around barriers in the United States has become relatively common in Asia (see Chapter 4).

Latin America's greater emphasis on the export of primary goods means that the incorporation of privately owned local companies into trading networks has been less common. Often the main exporters are giant public-sector firms with sophisticated marketing capacity, such as PEMEX (oil) in Mexico, CODELCO (copper) in Chile, or CVRD (iron ore) in Brazil. With the exception of Brazil, manufactured exports are of more recent vintage, although most Latin American countries are trying to increase their exports of these items. Recent analysis indicates that most manufactured exports are

---

[40] On the role of the trading companies, see Kiyoshi Kojima and Terutomo Ozawa, *Japan's General Trading Companies: Merchants of Economic Development* (Paris: OECD, 1984). On differences between U.S. and Japanese multinationals more generally, see Michael Mortimore, "Flying Geese or Sitting Ducks? Transnationals and Industrialization in Developing Countries," *CEPAL Review* 51 (December 1993), 15–34.

sold in the Latin American market itself although sales to the United States increased substantially during the 1980s, often through the intrafirm trade of U.S. multinationals.[41] Latin American industrial goods (as opposed to raw materials) have rarely been able to break into Asian or European markets. Exports from Sub-Saharan Africa are overwhelmingly primary products, generally handled by multinational firms.

The growth rate of markets also has an important impact on trade possibilities. The first column in Table 11.3 shows the average annual growth of imports in the various regions' markets, revealing the advantage accruing to East and Southeast Asia from their strong (and growing) trade links with the dynamic Asian area. Thus, their markets grew by an annual average of 7.8 and 7.5 percent, respectively, in the decade 1981–91. Latin America's closer ties with the Western Hemisphere's market, both the United States and the region itself, provided a lower stimulus (5.5 percent growth), as did Sub-Saharan Africa's trade relations with Europe (6.5 percent).

Moreover, the differences are much greater if we take into account the commodity composition of exports. In all markets, growth of manufactured imports far outpaced primary commodities; fuel imports generally fell in this period. Since East Asian countries specialize heavily in manufactured exports, this – together with sales in the fast-growing Asian markets – gave them a double advantage. Southeast Asia's trade situation was also very positive, as manufactured exports became more significant during the 1980s and the Asian market grew in importance. Latin America's heavier reliance on slow-growing primary product exports meant that trade was less beneficial as a source of growth, while Sub-Saharan Africa was in the worst position of all since about 90 percent of its exports are oil and other raw materials (see Table 1.4).

Second, access to external capital is another important aspect of the development context – although how important depends on the volume of internal savings. Where a large volume of internal savings is available (especially true in East Asia), foreign capital is less relevant. The "external finance" column in Table 11.3 shows access to foreign capital during the 1980s. The most dramatic pattern occurred in Latin America, where capital flows turned negative in the 1980s, with the debt crisis and the withdrawal of private-bank financing. Southeast Asia, by contrast, had access to substantial amounts of external resources, both direct investment and loans

---

[41] UNECLAC, *Latin America and the Caribbean.*

from Japan and the East Asian NICs, to stimulate its rapid growth. The largest inflows relative to GDP were in Sub-Saharan Africa, but the African countries were clearly unable to take advantage of these resources.

For those countries that need to import foreign capital, several characteristics are important to note, as Griffith-Jones and Stallings discuss in Chapter 5. One is the volatility of capital flows. Latin America has been especially prone to boom–bust cycles of capital over the past decades: huge inflows in the 1970s, leading to the debt crisis and capital outflow in the 1980s, a massive return of capital in the early 1990s, and a substantial contraction of funds following the Mexican peso devaluation in 1994–95. Sub-Saharan Africa also suffered a decline in capital in the 1980s, but the cycles were shallower because of the buffering role of official transfers. Flows to Southeast Asia, by contrast, increased on a much steadier basis, while East Asia's reliance on internal savings eliminated much of the volatility problem.

Another important characteristic of foreign capital is its composition. Analysts and governments alike are of the opinion that direct investment (the main type of investment in Southeast Asia in the 1990s) has many advantages over the new portfolio flows (especially important in Latin America in recent years). DFI is more difficult to withdraw if investor preferences shift, exerts less pressure toward exchange rate appreciation (which can undermine exports), and is more closely associated with investment rather than consumption. In all these ways, Southeast Asia was privileged over Latin America. A recent forecasting exercise projects these differences toward the future, showing Latin America far more vulnerable than any other region in the case of a drop in capital flows and/or an increase in interest rates.[42] Sub-Saharan Africa has relied mainly on official transfers (grants and concessional loans), which are available on especially easy terms to the poorest countries. Even with this financial advantage, however, these countries are frequently unable to use the capital effectively.

Third, the growth of economic capacity has disproportionately benefited the Asian developing countries. Recent economic literature has returned to consider the causes of economic growth. Not surprisingly, the accumulation of physical and human capital continues to occupy a central role in the growth process, especially because of the links to technological progress.

---

[42] World Bank, *Global Economic Prospects and the Developing Countries, 1994* (Washington, D.C.: World Bank, 1994), chap. 1.

Increasing the skills of workers, both through more education and vocational training, has payoffs of various kinds, including greater capacity to adapt flexibly to new market conditions. Higher levels of investment in physical capital, whether at the plant level or nationally, will increase the productivity of workers and permit the incorporation of new technology. And, of course, there are positive interaction effects between higher-skilled workers and the ability to take full advantage of new equipment.[43]

A priority on increasing educational opportunities, it should be noted, may also have beneficial effects with respect to equity. By emphasizing education, especially primary education, the East and Southeast Asian countries helped to reduce levels of inequality in comparison with other third world regions. The basic reason for the positive relationship between education and equity is that as the number of educated workers increases, the income premium they can earn falls, and the inequality due to wage differentials declines. There is also evidence that the relationship works in the opposite direction: greater equity leads to greater demand for schooling.[44]

The issue of importance to this discussion is whether (and how) the different models of capitalism have facilitated the accumulation process. Based on comparative data for the United States and Japan, the latter appears to have provided superior incentives in recent years.[45] The Japanese style of capitalism stresses the need for an efficient meritocratic-based bureaucracy to work with the private sector in increasing firms' competitiveness. Two of the most important types of support are education and training to produce a skilled workforce and investment in new equipment

---

[43] The work on endogenous growth theory is especially relevant. See, e.g., Paul Romer, "Increasing Returns and Long-Run Growth," *Journal of Political Economy* 94, 5 (October 1986), 1002–37; Robert E. Lucas, "On the Mechanics of Economic Development," *Journal of Monetary Economics* 80, 2 (June 1988), 3–42; and J. Bradford de Long and Lawrence H. Summers, "Equipment Investment and Economic Growth," *Quarterly Journal of Economics* 106 (May 1991), 1138–54.

[44] The education–equity relationship, of course, is quite complex. The outcome will depend on such questions as the access to education; quality of education; the relationship between public and private education; and expenditure allocation among primary, secondary, and tertiary education. For analysis of the linkage in Asia versus Latin America, see Nancy Birdsall and Richard Sabot, "Growth with Equity in East Asia: The Contribution of Rapid Accumulation and Efficient Utilization of Human Capital," background paper for the East Asian Miracle project, World Bank, 1993; see also Birdsall and Sabot, "Inequality and Growth."

[45] Thus, Japanese investment rates are over twice as high as those of the United States, and students in Japan typically outperform their U.S. counterparts on standardized tests. On comparative investment rates, see IMF, *International Financial Statistics Yearbook;* on test scores, see Birdsall and Sabot, "Growth with Equity in East Asia."

and infrastructure. The United States, by contrast, has placed a greater emphasis on cheap labor and on restricting the role of public investment. The Clinton government recognized both problems but has been unable to make major progress on either.

These differences, in turn, have been reflected in the various third world regions. Table 11.3 shows the Asian advantage over Latin America and especially over Sub-Saharan Africa. Investment rates in East and Southeast Asia were around 30 percent of GDP between 1985 and 1992, while in Latin America they averaged 19 percent and in Sub-Saharan Africa 15 percent. Skill levels for labor (as proxied by secondary school enrollment) highlight both the great advantage of East Asia (86 percent of the eligible age group attending secondary school) and the enormous problems of Sub-Saharan Africa (only 18 percent). Southeast Asia and Latin America are at similar levels, slightly under 50 percent. The decade of the 1980s exacerbated these differences, as can be seen by referring back to Tables 1.3 and 1.5. Asian investment rates increased considerably during this period, while those of Latin America and Africa fell; Southeast Asian enrollment rates also grew more rapidly than in the other regions. The differences in investment and training are further magnified by similar trends with respect to research and development. In part, the trends are explained by the way public-sector deficits were cut in Latin America and Africa, with much of the burden falling on investment and social spending.

These three elements – dynamic markets, adequate financial resources, and increasing economic capacity – are important prerequisites for the development process in all third world countries. Through offering greater availability of all three, the multipolar structure of the new international context of development has provided more favorable conditions to the East and Southeast Asian countries than to Latin America. Sub-Saharan Africa trails all other regions. These conditions, in turn, help to account for the much higher growth rates in the Asian region as well as the greater equality.

Other third world regions

This book concentrates on East Asia, Southeast Asia, Latin America, and Sub-Saharan Africa. The four provide evidence for the propositions that a third world nation's links with the international political economy was an important determinant of success in economic performance and that its geographic location was particularly relevant in defining that environment.

Table 11.4. *Links between industrial countries and third world regions,
1985/86 and 1992 (percent)*

	Trade[a]		Direct foreign investment[b]	
Region	1985	1992	1986	1992
East Asia[c]	58	52	8	9
Southeast Asia	64	61	31	41
Latin America	72	71	31	45
Sub-Saharan Africa	71	66	6	9
South Asia	52	59	4	5
Middle East	61	60	9	14
Eastern Europe	35	64	13[d]	24

[a]Percentage of total exports of region going to industrial countries.
[b]Direct foreign investment from triad countries as the percentage of total net external
finance for the region.
[c]For a basic list of countries in the regional categories, see Table 1.1; East Asia in this
table includes only Korea and Taiwan.
[d]Figure is based on investment and total external finance from Western countries
only.
Sources: IMF, *Direction of Trade Statistics Yearbook, 1992, 1993* (for trade); World
Bank, *World Debt Tables 1993–94* (for investment).

Other "traditional" third world regions, including South Asia and the Middle East, are mentioned occasionally, as are the "new" third world nations of
Central and Eastern Europe. Before concluding, we want to look (albeit
briefly) at these other regions to see if they fit our approach or offer counter-
evidence. We need to examine (1) the nature of the interactions between
these regions and the world economy, (2) the changes (if any) as a result of
the new international context of development, and (3) the impact of these
changes on economic performance.

Despite the vast differences among them, South Asia, the Middle East,
and Eastern Europe share certain historical features in terms of their international relationships. That is, all have had significant interactions with the
nations of Western Europe, and more recently, they were the areas where
the former Soviet Union had the greatest role. Obviously, in the case of
Eastern Europe, the USSR was the dominant factor. It was also important,
but less so, in India and some parts of the Middle East (especially Syria,
Iraq, Libya, South Yemen, and, until 1972, Egypt).[46]

---

[46] Fred Halliday, *From Kabul to Managua: Soviet-American Relations in the 1980s* (New
York: Pantheon Books, 1989); see also Chapter 2, this volume.

At the same time, in part because of the Soviet link, these regions were more isolated from the capitalist industrial economies during the postwar period than the four regions we have emphasized, and they had a more diversified trade and financial base. Table 11.4 provides some data for a comparison. Taking 1985 as a base year, since it was well before the Soviet empire crumbled, the table shows that the largest contrast with respect to trade was between Latin America and Africa, on the one hand, and South Asia and Eastern Europe, on the other. The former sold more than 70 percent of their exports to the industrial countries, while the latter sold around 50 percent or less. The Middle East, with the dominant role of petroleum production, was in between these extremes and near the East and Southeast Asian level, with some 60 percent of exports going to the industrial nations. The main trade partners for Eastern Europe were found in the Soviet bloc itself, while South Asia had a more diversified trade structure, including the Soviet bloc (especially important for India), the Middle East, and other Asian developing countries. By 1992, the picture had changed, especially for Eastern Europe.

Another indicator of links to the industrial world is foreign capital, especially direct investment that gives foreign corporations a strong influence over local economies. Before the end of the cold war, DFI as a share of external finance in all three regions – South Asia, the Middle East, and Eastern Europe – was very low in comparison with Latin America and Southeast Asia. As would be expected, the role of DFI has now increased substantially in Eastern Europe as its ties with the West have grown. Ironically, East Asia also has a low share of DFI in foreign capital flows, precisely because governments in the region are reluctant to allow the foreign control implied by direct investment.

Despite their relative isolation from the triad economies, South Asia, the Middle East, and Eastern Europe were strongly affected by the worldwide changes of the 1980s and early 1990s. Most important, of course, was the end of the cold war and the collapse of communism. This change completely altered the nature of the Eastern European economic and political systems, moving them from state-planned to market-oriented economies and introducing elections, if not all the aspects of democracy found in the industrial West.[47]

---

[47] On political and economic reforms in Central and Eastern Europe, in comparison with those of Latin America, see Adam Przeworski, *Democracy and the Market: Political and Economic Reforms in Eastern Europe and Latin America* (Cambridge University Press, 1991); Joan M. Nelson (ed.), *Intricate Links: Democracy and Market Reform in Latin*

Relations with the institutions of Western capitalism have increased in all three regions, but in differing ways and to differing degrees. Central and Eastern Europe have experienced an overwhelming presence of Western representatives, ranging from IMF and World Bank missions to the European Bank for Reconstruction and Development to private firms and consultants.[48] India has also opened up its economy in some ways in the past decade, first under the Rajiv Gandhi government in the mid-1980s and later, after the Soviet collapse, under P. V. Narasimha Rao. This has meant a reduction of the fiscal deficit, as well as more openness to foreign investment and the abolition of import licenses on many goods. Unlike the situation in Latin America, however, privatization has not been implemented on a large scale.[49] The most dramatic changes in the Middle East have been political. The end of the cold war facilitated the unified attack on Iraq, while the end of Soviet military and economic aid meant that many countries have had to accept reconciliation with old enemies. Nonetheless, even if it has been less visible, economic liberalization has also been occurring.[50]

Ideological trends have been important too, though again in different ways. In Central and Eastern Europe, the new capitalist ideology was embraced in an even purer form than in Latin America. Anything that resembled the old socialist system was rejected, even if the institutions of capitalism (legal system, financial structure, entrepreneurs) were not present. More recently a backlash has emerged, including the election of governments representing the former communist parties, and it is unclear where

America and Eastern Europe (Washington, D.C.: Overseas Development Council, 1994); and Laurence Whitehead (ed.), Economic and Political Liberalization in Latin America and Eastern Europe (Oxford University Press, forthcoming).

[48] See Steve Weber, "EC Conditionality," in Whitehead (ed.), Economic and Political Liberalization.

[49] South Asia as a Dynamic Partner: Prospects for the Future (San Francisco: International Center for Economic Growth, 1993).

[50] On the political economy of the Middle East, see Kiren Aziz Chaudry, "The Price of Wealth: Business and the State in Labor Remittance and Oil Economies," International Organization 43, 1 (Winter 1989), 101–46; Kiren Aziz Chaudry, "Economic Liberalization and the Lineages of the Rentier State," Comparative Politics 27, 1 (October 1994), 1–25; Ilya Harik and Denis J. Sullivan (eds.), Privatization and Liberalization in the Middle East (Bloomington: Indiana University Press, 1992); Daniel Brumberg, "Survival Strategies vs. Democratic Bargains: The Politics of Economic Reform in Contemporary Egypt," in Henri Barkey (ed.), The Politics of Economic Reform in the Middle East (New York: St. Martins, 1992), pp. 73–104; and Steven Heydemann, "Taxation Without Representation and Economic Liberalization in Syria," in Ellia Goldberg, Resat Kasaba, and Joel S. Migdal (eds.), Rules and Rights in the Middle East: Democracy, Law, and Society (Seattle, Wash.: University of Washington Press, 1992), pp. 69–101.

these ideological debates will lead.[51] In South Asia and especially the Middle East, new ideological trends have also appeared, but these are related to the Islamic model that Thomas Biersteker discusses as a possible alternative to the new emphasis on capitalism (see Chapter 6). The economic, as opposed to the social, impact of Islam is unclear since, despite some talk of an "Islamic economic model," there seems to be little behind the phrase.[52]

Table 11.2 and the tables in Chapter 1 provide some evidence for a comparison of the impact of these international changes on economic performance. Growth rates in South Asia and the Middle East during the 1980s and early 1990s were in between those of the fast-growing East Asian economies and the poor performance of Latin America and especially of Sub-Saharan Africa. The gap with respect to East Asia was especially noticeable in per capita growth rates because of the higher population growth in South Asia and the Middle East. This medium-level performance was possible in the Middle East since oil revenues continued to provide a cushion, and the results of earlier oil-financed investments were coming onstream. The oil producers, in turn, were willing to subsidize their neighbors. This assistance was extended to South Asia, first through the employment of immigrant workers and then through aid to replace the remittances when workers were expelled during the Gulf War.

In Central and Eastern Europe, by contrast, growth rates had already declined by the 1980s and fell to catastrophic levels in the early 1990s. These very negative growth rates are clearly linked to decisions to eliminate the old economic structures of the region before anything was ready to replace them. For example, the attempt to privatize state firms very rapidly in Poland (and especially in Russia) meant that production levels collapsed since no one was able to put the new private firms to work again on such short order. Now the situation in Poland seems to be stabilizing.

Not surprisingly, exports also plummeted in Central and Eastern Europe as old markets were abandoned and new ones were not yet consolidated. For South Asia, export growth compared favorably with that of other regions, although increasing from a very low base. In the Middle East, exports

---

[51] "A Return, but Not a Return," *Economist,* April 16, 1994; "Poland: Not as Bad as It Looked – Maybe," *Economist,* September 25, 1993; "Hungary's Elections: Bring Back the Goulash," *Economist,* May 7, 1994.

[52] See Brian Beedham, "A Survey of Islam," *Economist* (special section), August 6, 1994, especially pp. 8–10.

depended on the vagaries of oil prices, once the OPEC cartel ceased to be a major force in the world market. Finally, it should be noted that, in all three regions, the savings/investment picture was much more positive than in Latin America or Sub-Saharan Africa, although less so than in East and Southeast Asia. Likewise, social indicators, especially in Eastern Europe, compare favorably with those of other regions. One of the positive inheritances from the old socialist systems of the postwar period was their emphasis on social policies. South Asia, despite its low per capita GDP, far outstripped Sub-Saharan Africa on social indicators. The Middle East also performed relatively well in this area.

Overall, we can conclude the following: (1) The elements of the new international context of development penetrated even into regions less integrated into the world economy. (2) Some changes in the direction of increased openness and market orientation can be observed in South Asia, the Middle East, and especially in Central and Eastern Europe, although change in the latter was so drastic that a backlash seems inevitable. (3) Economic performance seems at least consistent with the impact of international changes: dramatic falls in output in Central and Eastern Europe, and average performance in South Asia and the Middle East in line with a more protected environment, if not very efficient economies. (4) These three regions reinforce the argument about the importance of region as a mediating variable between the international and national levels. The similarity of their response to the international changes is a notable finding.

Prospects for the future

The principal arguments of this book can be summarized by a set of general and specific points. At the general level, we have shown how the new international context of development constitutes a profoundly important political, economic, and ideological environment that shapes the development prospects of third world nations. This environment does not affect all countries in the same way, however, since it is filtered through a regional prism that refracts the international forces in various ways so as to skew the advantages and disadvantages that the new global structure provides.

At the specific level, we have demonstrated the advantages that East and Southeast Asian countries receive, because of the characteristics of the Japanese development model (especially its emphasis on investment and education and on the supportive public–private relationship), as well as the dynamic trade and capital links within the Asian region. Latin American countries have reaped lesser benefits from their Western Hemisphere location. Trade has been more sluggish, and capital flows more volatile. At the same time, the extremely rapid shift toward the private sector and international openness has led to very fragile economies, as seen in the crisis following the Mexican peso devaluation in 1994–95. Most disadvantaged of all are the African nations, whose vestigial relationships with Western Europe have left them isolated from the assistance that Southern Europe received when it was incorporated into the European Union. Their ailing institutions and truncated economies are so weak that they cannot even take advantage of the large amounts of foreign aid that European governments and the IFIs continue to provide.

The important prospective question is how these differences will play out over the coming years. Projecting toward the twenty-first century based on the trends just summarized leads to some disturbing conclusions. Straight linear projections would have East Asia catching up rapidly with the smaller European countries, and Southeast Asia closing in on a slow-growing Latin America. Sub-Saharan Africa would become ever more mired in poverty. If these trends were to continue, they would imply a strong polarization of the third world in economic and therefore political terms. But linear variation is not always the most likely, and some changes on the horizon need to be factored into the discussion.

The tetrahedron concept used earlier (Figure 11.1) incorporated the four regions highlighted in the book. Trends under way in the late 1980s and early 1990s suggest some likely shifts in that structure. First, several important changes are underway in Asia. The NICs have joined Japan as major actors, and as a result the economic base of the region has been substantially strengthened. As a group, the NICs already exceed Japan's investments in ASEAN, and their combined trade flows are of roughly the same size. Although their role outside the Asian region still lags behind that of Japan, as does their technological capacity, they will be important players in another set of regional changes: the incorporation of China and Indochina into the Asian economic space. Trade and investment links are being expanded with both, although "incorporating" China will undoubtedly involve the transformation of Asia itself in ways that cannot be readily foreseen. Even South Asia may become tied to the rest of Asia, especially if the Indian government continues its reforms.

Second, some parts of Latin America will become more closely linked with the United States. Mexico has already been brought into NAFTA and has recently become a member of the OECD. Through Mexico, many of the Central American and Caribbean nations are also likely to become at least de facto parts of the North American space. South America fears being left to fend for itself and has been showing great enthusiasm for the American Free Trade Area proposed by hemispheric leaders in December 1994. Since adoption of market-oriented policies has been specified as a prerequisite for closer links with the United States, this possibility has reinforced policies already underway. Nonetheless, it is unclear how many of the Latin American countries will be able to transform their economies successfully and whether the U.S. Congress will agree to preferential trade relations with more of its southern neighbors.

Third, there is a strong probability that Central and Eastern Europe will displace Sub-Saharan Africa as the third world area of main concern to the European Union. The United States and Japan have, in effect, delegated to the EU the main task of reconstructing these former communist nations, and many mechanisms are already in place for doing so. Moreover, there has now been agreement, in principle, to incorporate Central and Eastern Europe into the European Union by the end of the century. Insofar as Africa continues to have close relations with Europe, these will probably center on the Maghreb, leaving the Sub-Saharan countries even more isolated than they are at present.

Finally, there will be a large group of marginalized countries (and groups within countries), as changes in economic and security factors make them "dispensable."[53] The question of concern to many nations is which ones will end up in this marginal status – and how best to protect themselves from this fate. The great fear is that marginalization or "delinking" in the 1990s and the next century will not be the basis of growth, as it was in some cases in the earlier postwar period, but of increasing poverty. The strong likelihood is that Sub-Saharan Africa as a region will continue in the trend already underway toward marginalization. In the longer run, a new South Africa might provide an important growth pole for some of the Sub-Saharan countries, but this is not likely to happen for many years. In addition, parts of South Asia, the Middle East, and even Latin America could also end up in this group.

---

[53] An extremely dramatic view of the impact of marginalization in Africa is found in Robert D. Kaplan, "The Coming Anarchy," *Atlantic Monthly* 273, 2 (February 1994), 44–76.

In a more positive vein, two possible trends could spread some of the benefits that Asia has monopolized until now. On the one hand, despite its current political and economic difficulties, Japan seems likely to take a more active role in the international arena in the second half of the 1990s. A first step will probably be in the IFIs. The Japanese government has already begun to criticize IFI policies and to insist that the World Bank pay more attention to the Asian development model. The "East Asian Miracle" study by the World Bank is both the most important result to date and a potential vehicle to spread information on the types of policies followed in Asia. It is interesting to note that the Japanese have even been discussing the relevance of their experience for Africa.[54]

On the other hand, some third world nations themselves are becoming more aggressive in seeking out promising international connections beyond their own regions. A number of Latin American countries, for example, have been reaching out to Europe and Asia for trade and investment opportunities. Several of the developing Asian countries are investing in the United States, Western Europe, and Latin America. South Africa clearly hopes to take advantage of its new legitimacy to establish a diverse set of international connections. These bottom-up approaches may be even more effective than top-down ones in redistributing opportunities for development.

In the short to medium run, these trends are most likely to benefit Latin America. They could also help the development process in Central and Eastern Europe. And, of course, the Asian developing countries will continue to discover ways to strengthen their already impressive economic capacity. Only over a much longer period of time might South Asia, the Middle East, and Sub-Saharan Africa be able to take advantage of the new international context of development. In the meantime, polarization between winners and losers is likely to continue.

---

[54] Although it initially appeared that the Clinton administration's policies would lead to a greater convergence between U.S. and Japanese economic approaches (through an emphasis on greater public–private cooperation to increase productivity plus government support for training and infrastructure), the November 1994 election virtually eliminated this possibility.

Index